APPLICATION DEBUGGING

Prentice-Hall Software Series

Brian W. Kernighan, advisor

APPLICATION DEBUGGING

An MVS Abend Handbook for COBOL, Assembly, PL/I, and FORTRAN Programmers

ROBERT BINDER

PRENTICE-HALL, INC.
Englewood Cliffs, New Jersey 07632

Library of Congress Cataloging in Publication Data

BINDER, ROBERT (date)
Application debugging.

(Prentice-Hall software series)
Bibliography: p.
Includes index.
1. Debugging in computer science. 2. MVS (Computer system) 3. COBOL (Computer program language) 4. Assembler language (Computer program language) 5. PL/I (Computer program language) 6. FORTRAN (Computer program language) I. Title. II. Series.
QA76.6.B56 1985 001.64'2 84-15987
ISBN 0-13-039348-7

Editorial/production supervision: *Kathryn Gollin Marshak and Linda Mihatov*
Interior design: *Linda Mihatov*
Jacket design: *20/20 Services, Inc.*
Manufacturing buyer: *Gordon Osbourne*

Printed in the United States of America

10 9 8 7 6 5 4 3 2 1

ISBN 0-13-039348-7

Prentice-Hall International, Inc., *London*
Prentice-Hall of Australia Pty. Limited, *Sydney*
Editora Prentice-Hall do Brasil, Ltda., *Rio de Janeiro*
Prentice-hall Canada Inc., *Toronto*
Prentice-Hall of India Private Limited, *New Delhi*
Prentice-Hall of Japan, Inc., *Tokyo*
Prentice-Hall of Southeast Asia Pte. Ltd., *Singapore*
Whitehall Books Limited, *Wellington, New Zealand*

CONTENTS

PREFACE

This book contains information and techniques needed to debug application programs that have abended (abnormally ended) under IBM's MVS operating system. It is a reference—a handbook intended to become part of the programmer's, operator's, analyst's, and student's bag of tools and tricks. Faced with an abend, the immediate need is for a solution, not an education in IBM operating system concepts. This book has been organized to address this need. It has four main parts.

First, the why, what, and how of some sixty common abends are given for COBOL, Assembly Language, PL/I, and FORTRAN programs executed via JCL or TSO. A specific, detailed list of possible causes is given for each abend, followed by practical techniques for its solution.

Second, common diagnostic aids are given, including how to use IBM utility programs to list any data set or label, how to find and interpret VSAM and non-VSAM data set control blocks, how to spot JCL or TSO errors, and how to debug program check abends. Abend debugging under MVS/XA is also discussed.

Third, the useful information on a Dump is identified. Each control block and main storage area is explained. The steps to find and interpret the data relevant to your abend are given.

Fourth, the procedure to find source program errors is given for Assembly Language, COBOL, FORTRAN, and PL/I. This part shows how to find the program statement and data fields that caused the abend. It also shows how to find and interpret object code and all S/370 data storage formats. Debugging facilities available in each language are identified and suggestions for their use are given.

This four-part organization parallels the typical steps of abend debugging: analysis of the System Completion Code, data gathering, examination of the dump, and finally, program checkout and correction. Collectively or singly, this is not a simple task. One needs to know where to start, what to look for, and how to interpret compiler listings and dump data. Because of the complexity of MVS and increasingly of application programs, this information (to the extent that it exists) has become scattered across IBM's voluminous documentation and buried in the collective unconscious of the system programming community. This book pulls together the where, what, and how of abend debugging in a comprehensive and quickly accessible format.

This book originally took shape from anonymous debugging crib notes collected from various MVS installations where I worked as a programmer. I found that each set was slightly different, providing a unique trick or insight into a particular abend. After this collection exceeded a half-dozen sets, I realized that by eliminating redundancy, I would have a more useful debugging reference. If such a collection was useful for my purposes, it seemed that it could be for others. The plan for the book then fell into place. First, I would refine and enlarge my collection of notes by using every available source of debugging information. There were three main sources: IBM publications, my associates in system and application programming, and other publications about debugging and programming. Once gathered, I would cross-reference, organize, and present this material in a concise and accessible format. The principle of organization would be to maximize utility for abend debugging.

ACKNOWLEDGMENTS

This proved to be a substantial undertaking. I wish to acknowledge the support and encouragement of my wife, Diane, and Karl Karlstrom of Prentice-Hall. For reading the manuscript and providing detailed commentary, corrections of some overt sins of omission and commission, and not a few fiendishly clever suggestions and insights, I owe gratitude and acknowledgment to Phil Armour, Dave Hicks, Bill Kowalewski, and Dave Loveluck. The unknown authors of the debugging crib notes have also made a contribution. The extensive, if occasionally obtuse, technical publications from IBM about its software have been indispensable. My main contribution has been to organize, cross-check, and research supplemental information to meet the book's objectives. This process yielded a number of original insights which have been passed along.

It is difficult to properly acknowledge the source of the know-how contained in this book. Certainly, a good deal of it is not original. While in progress, I described the contents of the book to nontechnical friends as a "How-to-fix-your-Chevy" for computers. Technical knowledge derives from many places: in the case of Chevrolets, from thousands of engineers, mechanics, tinkers, and teachers who generate it and pass it along numerous channels. Dispersion of computer know-how follows a similar pattern. The aim of this book is to provide yet another channel for this know-how.

I acknowledge the following publishers for permission to reprint material as chapter and section opening quotes: Houghton Mifflin (Raymond Chandler, *The Little Sister*); Little Brown (Tracy Kidder, *The Soul of a New Machine*); IBM Corporation (Technical documents); Southern Illinois University Press (Raymond Chandler, *The Blue Dahlia,* 1976); Tribune Company Syndicate, Inc. (Leonard Hall, *Annie*); McGraw-Hill (Stan Kelly-Bootle, *The Devil's DP Dictionary*).

Robert Binder

APPLICATION DEBUGGING

I do not think at all that I am able to present here any procedure of investigation that was not perceived long ago by all men of talent; and I do not promise at all that you can find here anything quite new of this kind. But I shall take pains to state in clear words the rules and ways of investigation which are followed by all able men, who in most cases are not even conscious of following them.

Bernardo Bolzano
On Heuristics, c. 1800

1 HOW TO USE THIS BOOK

1.1 INTRODUCTION

This book is a reference tool for debugging programs that have abended under MVS.[1] MVS (Multiple Virtual Storage) refers to release 2.0 and subsequent releases of IBM's OS/VS2 operating system. Considerations for abend debugging under MVS/XA are covered in 3.9, Abend Debugging under MVS/XA. The solution strategy is simple: Maximize the likelihood of finding a solution with a minimum of investigative effort. The book is

[1]A general introduction to OS concepts as they relate to abend debugging and some basic diagnostic techniques are provided in: B. H. Boar, *Abend Debugging for COBOL Programmers* (New York: John Wiley & Sons, Inc., 1976); Barbara Burian, *A Simplified Approach to S/370 Assembly Language Programming* (Englewood Cliffs, N.J.: Prentice-Hall, Inc., 1977); Wayne Clary, *OS Debugging for the COBOL Programmer* (Fresno, Calif.: Mike Murach and Associates, Inc., 1981); Daniel H. Rindfleisch, *Debugging System 360/370 Programs Using OS and VS Storage Dumps* (Englewood Cliffs, N.J.: Prentice-Hall, Inc., 1976).

designed to support this strategy. There are four principal chapters. The order of these chapters reflects the general sequence of the debugging process.

As soon as the System Completion Code (SCC) is known, turn to 2.2, SCC Diagnostics, for the SCC in question. For a specific SCC, possible causes are listed from the most general and more likely to the more specific and less likely. Following this, relevant dump components are identified. Suggestions are given where applicable. Not all SCCs are covered and the list of possible causes is not exhaustive. The suggested solutions are not guaranteed, but are commonly used. The solution actually needed is, of course, determined by the specific cause of each abend. Most often, determining the solution is the simplest, even trivial, task of abend debugging. Determining the cause is typically frustrating, difficult, and time consuming.

There are problems and analytical methods which are common to many abends. Several of these are presented in Chapter 3, General Diagnostic Aids. When appropriate, an SCC diagnostic will refer you to one of the sections there.

The meaning and content of an ABEND[2] dump is explained in Chapter 4. Diagrams of the dump format of control blocks, traces, and storage areas are given. Fields in the diagram are labeled, referring to an explanation that covers content, format, function, relationships to other fields, and use in debugging.

Finally, Chapter 5 shows how to find the assembly language, COBOL, FORTRAN, or PL/I source program statement associated with an abend. Relevant object code and data storage formats are presented. Special techniques to locate elements in arrays, tables, and parameter lists are explained. Debugging tools, such as online execution and trace facilities, are discussed for each language.

1.2 CONVENTIONS ON NAMES AND FORMATS

IBM conventions for names, terms, capitalization, and addresses have been followed.[3] The term *problem program* refers to a task that executes in the "problem state" (as opposed to the "supervisor state" or "wait state"). This term seemed descriptive as well, since an abended task is a "problem" program of another sort. In general, it means the program that abended. *Supervisor* is used as a generic name for the multiplicity of functions that MVS provides. Specific subfunctions, such as data management, program management, job scheduling, or task management, are identified when relevant.

The term *nibble* is used to mean 4 bits, or a half byte. It is a convenient term for a unit of storage which is frequently of interest.[4]

[2]The word *abend* is a contraction of "abnormal end." It is pronounced "ăb ĕnd," to rhyme with "crab end." It is capitalized when referring to the ABEND macro (a supervisor routine that formats a dump and terminates execution).

[3]The usage of general terms follows that given in IBM's *Data Processing Glossary*. All other terms and usage follow the style of the primary IBM technical publication for that term.

[4]The etymology of *nibble* is unclear. My impression is that about a third of the computer industry is familiar with it. The earliest published usage of *nibble* that I am aware of is in: Don H. Stabley, *System/360*

Hexadecimal digits are always preceded by a lowercase x. Thus xDCB means a hexadecimal number equal to decimal 3,531, but DCB is the acronym for data control block.

IBM conventions for field names, registers, addresses, displacements, and lengths have been followed. For example, the first flag byte of the IOB (input-output block) is called IOBFLAG1 because that is the name IBM has given it.[5] Field offsets are given in hexadecimal number of bytes, relative to byte zero. So ABC + xFA means the byte at the address of ABC plus hexadecimal FA (decimal 250). ABC + x0 refers to the first byte of field ABC. Field lengths are given in decimal number of bytes. Thus "ABC + xFA for 10" means the 10 bytes from ABC + xFA to ABC + x104.

The convention for registers is followed as well. R0 refers to general register 0, R15 to general register 15. Unless explicitly stated otherwise or implicit by context, the registers referred to are the registers at entry to abend, as listed in the dump. Register contents from other save areas or control blocks are indicated as needed.

References to topics within the book are given as a chapter/section number and title. For example, "See 3.5, Locating VSAM Data Records, for more information" refers you to the VSAM section of Chapter 3, General Diagnostic Aids.

There are references to IBM technical publications throughout the book. It is not within the scope of this book (or the realm of possibility) to supplant the substantial technical reference library provided by IBM. Publications relevant to a particular problem, analytical technique, or solution are cited when further detailed information may be useful. The citation appears in italic type and is given in the text, not as a footnote, to make it easier to find. The citation gives the title. The publication's order number is not given in the citation, following IBM's convention. The order number is given in the Bibliography. Long or frequently cited titles may be condensed: for example, *COBOL Programmer's Guide* instead of *OS/VS COBOL Compiler and Library, Programmer's Guide*. The condensed title is also given in the Bibliography.

1.3 GENERAL DEBUGGING PROCEDURE

Abends are the result of two general problems:

1. The programmer's explicit or implicit assumptions regarding successful execution are incorrect.
2. Unanticipated, coincidental circumstances force an error (I/O device malfunction, main storage failure, operating system bugs, system capacity problems, etc.).

Assembler Language (New York: John Wiley & Sons, Inc., 1967) An alternative term for a 4-bit unit of storage is a *quartet* or *four-bit byte (IBM Data Processing Glossary).*

[5]MVS control blocks and control block fields are defined in the *Debugging Handbook*. The names used here follow these definitions.

The first condition accounts for the majority of problem program abends. The second is difficult to isolate immediately, but since all or most tasks in the system are affected, it tends to be resolved quickly.

Aside from system abends, debugging is generally initiated in response to incorrect output. The causes of incorrect output cannot be listed here as can the causes of abend SCCs. Each application program would require its own list. However, MVS, for most practical purposes, is the same everywhere. There are some common threads in debugging both problems. The techniques for data gathering described in Chapters 3 and 5 also apply to incorrect output debugging. Some causes of system abends listed in the SCC diagnostics can result in incorrect output as well. The general approach has much in common.

Myers, in his excellent book on testing,[6] provides some succinct guidance for debugging incorrect output problems. The strategy emphasizes careful consideration of the symptoms, conscious stimulation of intuitive problem solving, and judicious use of traces and dumps. The goal of the analysis is to form a hypothesis that clearly explains why the problem occurred. The hypothesis is to be derived by either *inductive* analysis or *deductive* analysis, beginning with immediately available evidence. Selective dumping and tracing is justified only when a clear need for more data exists. Collection of data without an analytical purpose is strongly discouraged (the "brute-force method"). Removing code as an experiment to see if the bug goes away is also strongly discouraged. This kind of tinkering usually wastes time and creates problems rather than solving them.

The general process of inductive debugging is shown in Figure 1-1. Myers likens this process to solving a mystery by good detective work. As a starting point, six questions are asked and the answers are recorded in tabular format (the originators of this technique, Brown and Sampson, term this process "The Method"). The questions are:

- What is not functioning correctly?
- What is functioning correctly?
- Where does the incorrect output appear?
- Where does the correct output appear?
- When does the incorrect output appear?
- When does the correct output appear?
- Is there any suspicious pattern or striking contradiction in either the correct or incorrect output?

By answering these questions, either a hypothesis is derived or the need for additional data is determined. The additional data are collected to form a hypothesis—an unambiguous explanation of the bug. The hypothesis is validated by proving that it explains the bug. When validated, the indicated correction is made.

The process of deductive debugging is shown in Figure 1-2. Myers argues that the

[6] Glenford J. Myers, *The Art of Software Testing* (New York: John Wiley & Sons, Inc., 1979). This discussion of incorrect output debugging technique is drawn from the chapter on debugging, pp. 130–146.

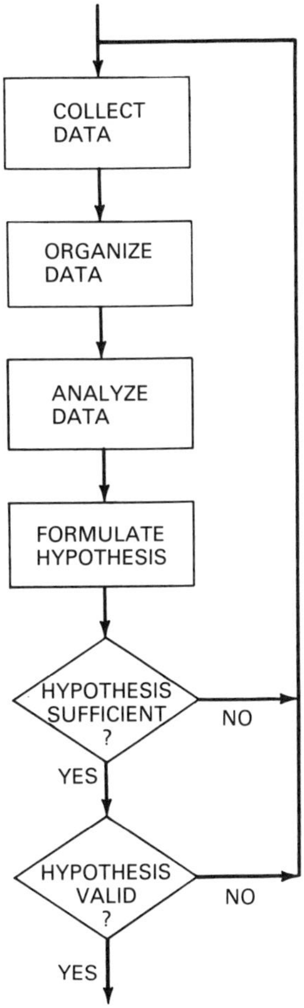

FIGURE 1-1 Inductive Debugging

first step is to prepare a list of possible causes using the symptoms the problem presents. Data are collected as needed to expand or refine the list. Deductive debugging proceeds by eliminating causes from the list as unlikely or impossible. A hypothesis is formed as with inductive debugging, and validated.

Myers points out that both the fix and the program should be retested, regardless of how the analysis was made. This is to validate the fix and to check that no new bugs have been created by the fix.

Both techniques and the recommendation to shun nonmethods apply fully to abend debugging. The debugging procedure described here is a blend of deductive and inductive analysis. The SCC diagnostic lists provide a starting point for deductive analysis. An inductive line of thought will often follow from the initial review of the diagnostic list. Problem solving is an iterative and intuitive process as well as an analytical one. We switch from one mode of analysis to another many times in the course of solving a debugging problem. The important point is that a disciplined, thoughtful approach be

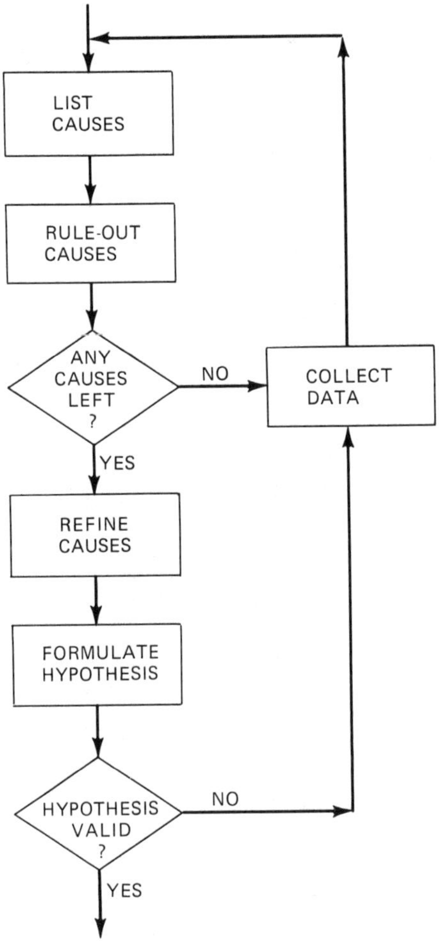

FIGURE 1-2 Deductive Debugging

followed. Doing so allows you to make best use of your problem-solving ability, your time, and available information. One minute of careful reflection typically yields more progress than 10 minutes coding traces and making burnt offerings to propitiate the gods of programming.

The general procedure to determine and correct the cause of an abend has several steps. A list of these steps follows. They may be taken sequentially or selectively. However, information derived from a preceding step is usually required by successive steps. Each step is an escalation of the problem in that more time and effort are required, as well as indicating its increasing difficulty. Relevant sections of the book are indicated in each step. Further explanation and detailed instructions will be found in the section indicated. Clearly, these steps should be followed only until a solution is derived. As soon as the program is corrected, no further diagnostic effort is needed. The last step (11—Verification) should be performed in every case.

1. *Do not assume anything, except that something has gone wrong.*

2. *Obtain the SCC from the JES job log, TSO message, or abend dump.* Look up the SCC in 2.2, SCC Diagnostics. If your SCC is not listed, 3.6, SCC Cross-Reference, may refer you to a similar SCC. Scan the list of general causes, those for JCL and for the source language of the abending program. Try to select several that may apply to the problem at hand. If none seem applicable, try to rule out the least likely. If none of the possible causes seem to apply, use the lists to stimulate your thinking about the problem. They may suggest a theory or an aspect of your problem not seen at first. Several things should be kept in mind:

- The most frequent causes are listed first.
- The lists are not all-inclusive.
- The problem you are working on may be the end result of a chain reaction.
- Correcting the immediate problem may lead to another.

3. *Develop a provisional explanation of the abend using the diagnostics.* Several explanations may suggest themselves. It is just as likely that no plausible explanation will come to mind. In any case, you will need more information. The information required should be suggested by the current status of your investigation: analyze the uncertainty, the hunch, or uncomfortable assumption in your provisional explanation; decide which facts could rule out or prove a theory; identify the missing piece that prevents you from making an explanation.

4. *Collect additional information.* Typical items are:

- Source program compiler listings for the mainline and subroutines in the load module that abended
- Linkage-editor listings for abended load module
- JES job log for the job/step that abended
- Program output or input listings
- Dumps of data sets accessed by the abending load module
- ABEND dump
- Program documentation: flowcharts, narratives, etc.

Be certain that you obtain the *current listings* of any of these items. The relevant version of the program, data set, link, and so on, is the one that abended. Yesterday's listing, even if you "only changed one line of code," is an odds-on favorite to be misleading.

5. *Determine the last source program statement to be executed and the data that were referenced at the time of the abend.* 5.2, Basic Techniques, shows how to find the offset into your load module. Further analysis with this offset depends on the source language used. See 5.5, Assembly Language Analysis; 5.6, COBOL Analysis; 5.7, FORTRAN Analysis; or 5.8, PL/I Analysis. The Relevant Dump Items section under each SCC diagnostic will indicate how to find the last or next instruction. Locate the abending statement and scrutinize the source program for obvious syntax or logic errors.

6. *Carefully examine the items indicated by your tentative explanation.*
    - JCL, JES log
    - Source code
    - Program main storage areas
    - System control blocks
    - Program output
    - Program input

The question to ask at this stage is: What's wrong with this picture? Look for coding or data errors.

7. *Attempt a paper-and-pencil simulation of program execution.* List the data input, control branches, data transformations, and output leading up to the abend. Work backward from the abend if necessary. Look for logic or design errors.

8. *Review the assumptions you have made and your tentative analysis.* What do you know for sure, what is speculation or hunch? What further evidence or information do you need to clarify the problem or prove your explanation? Obtain further data as needed or double-check data you have already gathered.

9. *Trace the execution of the program.* This may be done by using compiler facilities, debugging utilities, or by adding code to create trace messages. Insert trace statements at strategic checkpoints or suspected trouble points. Try to sample the data and control flow leading up to the abend. The cause of an abend may precede the actual point of failure by a significant number of instructions, statements, or iterations. For example, data are inadvertently altered by using a bad index generated under a loop boundary condition in an early iteration. The damaged data are referenced at end of job, resulting in an abend. When in doubt about what to trace, more output is preferable. It is more efficient to code and compile ten traces once than ten traces ten times. Review the program and analyze the output. Look for unexpected patterns or suspicious deviations. Trace facilities in each language are given in Chapter 5, Source Code Debugging.

10. *Review alternative solutions.* If no solution has been found, an indirect course of action may be appropriate.
    - Leave the problem for later. Return to it when you are refreshed. Use the analysis outlined in the following section, 1.4, Backing into a Problem.
    - Scrap the program or module causing the problem. Replace it with new code; use a utility program; deactivate it by commenting it out, removing it, or branching around it.
    - Devise an alternative means to effect the same results. Detune the program, cut back on bells and whistles, use manual intervention, or use a utility program.
    - If a prior working version of the program exists, use it as a stopgap measure until the problem is solved.

11. *Verify the fix.* There are two main items to retest when the bug has been

removed. First, the new code should be exercised under conditions which are the same or similar to those present in the abend. Second, any closely related code should be retested to flush out new bugs inadvertently created by the fix.

1.4 BACKING INTO A PROBLEM

A significant obstacle to the speedy resolution of an abend is often the person doing the debugging. How many times has it been said, "I *know* that (variable, parameter, register, flag, bit, condition code, etc.) was (set, initialized, loaded, incremented, zeroed, cleared, etc.). It *can't* be my (program, JCL, data, etc.)." However, after sufficient time passes, and the fortuitous but necessary stimulus occurs, the sudden, sickening, but sure realization that one has erred comes. The misspelling, the statement deactivated by a comment, the ambiguous or missing logical test suddenly becomes as obvious as a drummer out of step in a marching band.[7] This experience is so common that many seasoned programmers ask "What did I do wrong; what did I omit?" as the first debugging question. In general, the question asked is: "What's wrong with this picture?"

Program logic is abstract. The intended execution is based on a number of explicit and implicit assumptions. They include one's understanding of language syntax, operating system rules, relationships between data items, the sequence of transforms implied by a given set of inputs, and so on. Without this working set of assumptions, programming would be an impossible task. Therefore, one has a vested interest in not questioning these assumptions. Compounding this reluctance is the difficulty of considering multiple abstract relationships simultaneously. It has been demonstrated that the limit on the number of things that can be considered concurrently averages seven ideas, concepts, or facts. This limit provides another motivation to stay with a given interpretation of a problem.[8]

In addition to capacity limitations, we tend toward convenient interpretations of stimuli. We impose patterns on what we see. Given a series of dots, we see a dotted line—not the individual dots. This imposition of patterns is a reflex determined by one's current mental context. In abend debugging, this context is the set of assumptions that we have made about the program, our interpretation of the facts, and the permutations of these which we can consider simultaneously.

In mulling over a difficult debugging problem, often the solution suddenly becomes apparent. What stimulates this insight? It is a shift in our interpretation of the facts, a

[7]This tendency is lampooned by a bit of DP humor. Question: How many programmers does it take to change a light bulb? Answer: None; it's a hardware problem.

[8]George A. Miller, "The Magical Number Seven, Plus or Minus Two: Some Limits on Our Capacity for Processing Information," *Psychological Review,* Vol. 63 (1956), pp. 81–97. According to Michael Franzen, Department of Neuropsychology at the University of Nebraska, the basic premise of the Miller article continues to be valid. For a discussion of how this applies to programming, see Edward Yourdon and Larry L. Constantine, *Structured Design: Fundamentals of a Discipline of Computer Program and Systems Design* (Englewood Cliffs, N.J.: Prentice-Hall, Inc., 1979) pp. 67–83.

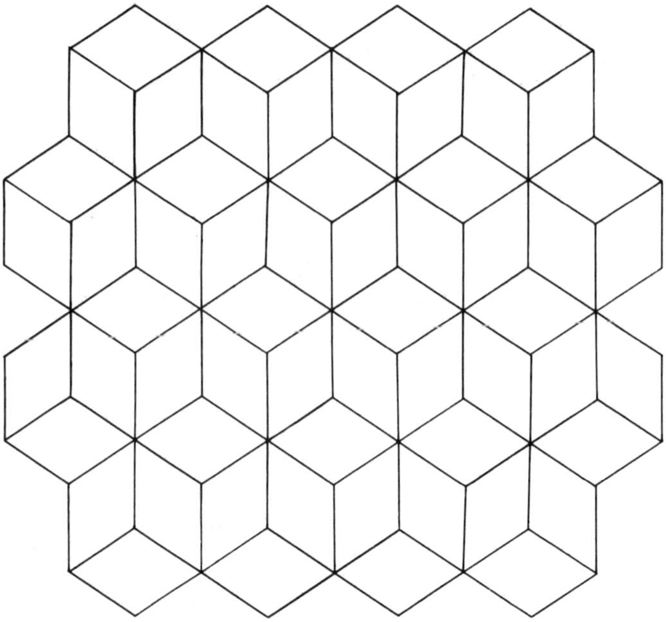

FIGURE 1-3 Illusion of Shifting Cubes

slightly altered set of working assumptions. This shift need not occur as the result of conscious effort. Optical illusions provide an example of this kind of shift in action.

The cubes in Figure 1-3 appear to flip-flop in orientation. Are the tops visible or the bottoms? Are you "looking down" or "looking up"? Perhaps you see only several rows of adjacent diamonds. In the absence of a context to support a particular view, all are plausible. Interpretations shift when viewing an optical illusion because the visual cues for the mind to choose an interpretation are insufficient. This shift happens reflexively.[9]

This innate tendency to shift point of view can prove useful. By harnessing the shift, the task of finding errors is made easier. The technique to put this shift to work is called *backing into a problem*.

Backing into a problem is a means to provide new input to the mental context in which programs are debugged. This new input may lead to a shift in one's mental context, thus leading to a more rapid solution. Backing into a problem is done by asking questions that can cause a flip-flop in one's perception of the problem. Attempt to complete the sentence "The program is acting *as if* it is. . . ." Ask the question: "What would I *have to do* to get the results observed?" Consider the problem: "What kind of logic, data, and so on, would be needed if I *wanted* this abend to occur?"

[9]For an excellent discussion of optical illusions, see M. Luckiesh, *Visual Illusions: Their Causes, Characteristics and Applications* (New York: Dover Publications, Inc., 1965).

These questions may stimulate the insight needed to solve the problem or suggest further investigation. The known facts and desired results of the program's execution logic should be put aside. Try to devise an alternative logic that would explain the observed error. For example, you cannot determine why a subscript exceeded its valid range. Formulate the problem by saying "The program is acting *as if* the subscript were multiplied by 10" or "If I wanted the subscript to go out of bounds, I'd change the end-of-loop test."

The *as if* formulation and its related constructs will probably *not* be the actual problem. However, they can suggest further questions that may lead to a discovery of the abend's actual cause. Clearly, the first question to be asked after a plausible *as if* statement is derived is, then, "Why is the program acting *as if* . . . ?"

The *as if* analysis can be supplemented by two simple techniques which aim at the same mental stimulation. First, walk through your problem with someone who is not familiar with the program at hand. This provides two opportunities to discover errors. Since the other person does not fully share your assumptions, they may see an error that falls in your blind spot. By explaining your program to someone else, you are forced to articulate your reasoning and assumptions. This in itself may be sufficient to cause recognition of an error. Second, put the problem aside for some interval. Take a walk, go to lunch, daydream, sleep on it, do something that focuses your attention away from the problem. This is useful when you feel stuck—not as a first line of attack. You may not consciously be considering the problem, but your mind will be working on it unconsciously. Upon returning to active consideration, you will have shifted your mental context and have the benefit of some background processing. This may be a sufficient catalyst for a solution.

1.5 ESSENTIAL TOOLS

In addition to the techniques and information presented in this book and a multimillion-dollar computing system, there are several items which are very useful in debugging abends.

- Texas Instruments' TI Programmer model or comparable hexadecimal/octal/decimal calculator. This calculator will perform all hexadecimal arithmetic needed in the course of debugging.
- Essential IBM references:
  - (a) *Principles of Operation*
  - (b) *Data Management Services Guide*
  - (c) *Supervisor Services*
  - (d) *MVS JCL*
  - (e) *Debugging Handbook*
  - (f) *System Messages*

(g) *System Codes*
(h) *System/370 Reference Summary*
(i) Programmer's Guide (as needed) for:
  * Assembly language
  * COBOL
  * FORTRAN (G)
  * FORTRAN (H)
  * PL/I

- Miscellaneous items:
  (a) Several colors of highlighting markers, pens, or pencils
  (b) Paper clips or tabs for marking listing or dump pages
  (c) Straightedge for following dump lines

1.6 THE ORIGIN OF DEBUGGING

The term *debugging* was apparently coined in 1945 by Grace Murray Hopper, who was later to be instrumental in the committee which defined the first industry standards for COBOL. The machine involved was the Mark II, the second of four electromechanical machines built by the Harvard Computation Laboratory under the direction of Howard Aiken for the U.S. Navy and Air Force. The Mark series was a conceptual precursor to the vacuum tube machines designed and built by Eckert, Mauchly, and von Neumann. The Mark II was designed toward the end of 1944 and put into use at the Navy's Dahlgren Proving Ground in Virginia for calculating ballistic trajectory tables. It was programmed by punching instruction codes on paper tape. It had storage for 100 ten-digit decimal numbers. It could multiply two such digits in roughly 0.4 seconds.[10] Hopper describes how *debugging* came to be used in this environment:

> In the summer of 1945 we were building Mark II; we had to build it in an awful rush—it was wartime—out of components we could get our hands on. We were working in a World War I temporary building. It was a hot summer and there was no air-conditioning, so all the windows were open. Mark II stopped, and we were trying to get her going. We finally found the relay that had failed. Inside the relay—and these were large relays—was a moth that had been beaten to death by the relay. We got a pair of tweezers. Very carefully we took the moth out of the relay, put it in the logbook, and put scotch tape over it.

[10]Herman H. Goldstine, *The Computer: From Pascal to von Neumann*. (Princeton: Princeton University Press, 1980) pp. 118–19, 137.

Now, Commander Howard Aiken had a habit of coming into the room and saying, "Are you making any numbers?" We had to have an excuse when we weren't making any numbers. From then on if we weren't making any numbers, we told him that we were debugging the computer. To the best of my knowledge that's where it started.[11]

Figure 1-4 is a photograph of the log book page Hopper refers to, showing the "first actual case of bug being found."

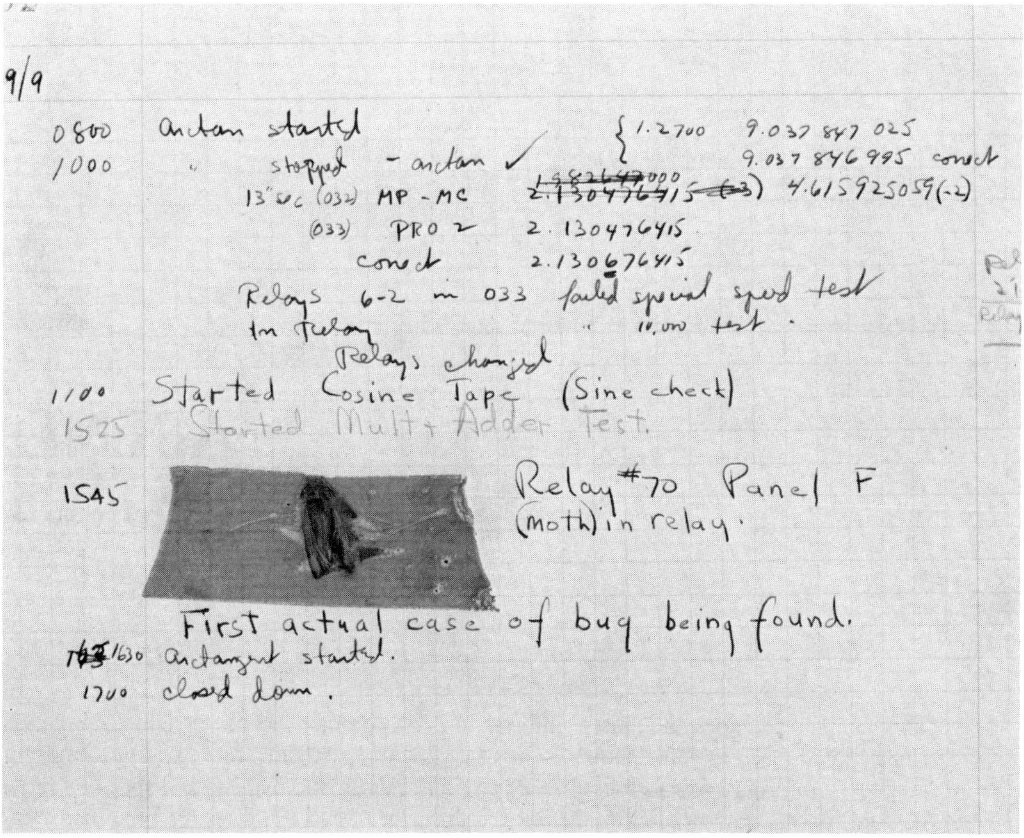

FIGURE 1-4 Hopper's Bug (Photograph courtesy of the Naval Surface Weapons Center, Dahlgren, Virginia)

[11]Transcribed in "Banquet Anecdotes," ACM SIGPLAN History of Programming Languages Conference, Los Angeles, June 1–3, 1978 and published in "Annals of the History of Computing," Volume 3, Number 3, July 1981, 285–86.

She gave it to me. It was right. I won't say the pieces were beginning to fall into place, but at least they were getting to look like parts of the same puzzle. Which is all I ever get or ask.

Raymond Chandler
The Little Sister

2

ABEND DIAGNOSTICS

2.1 INTRODUCTION

This chapter provides diagnostic information for common abend System Completion Codes (SCCs). This information is listed by SCC, from 001 to Fxx. Two kinds of diagnostic information are given: lists of possible causes of the abend and specifics about how to find the data needed to analyze the problem. General causes are presented first, followed by more specific items. Finally, any special solution techniques are suggested.

The same format is used for each SCC. However, not all diagnostic items apply to each SCC. The diagnostic items, in order of presentation, are:

• *System Completion Code/abend description.* The three-digit hexadecimal SCC returned by MVS is printed on the upper corner of each page for easy reference. A brief description is given.

• *Related system message*. The system message number(s) associated with the SCC is given. Not all SCCs result in system messages. Further explanation of some messages is given under "Relevant Dump Items." The prefix of a system message indicates which component of MVS created it. Some common execution-time system message prefixes and their sources are:

IBM	PL/I library routines
IEA	Supervisor
IEC	Data management
IHN	FORTRAN G library routines
IHO	FORTRAN H library routines

• *SVC*. The number of any SVC(s) associated with the SCC is given. Not all SCCs have an associated SVC. The SVC's macro name is also given. An SVC (supervisor call) is a means to invoke an MVS supervisor service: for example, to OPEN a data set (SVC 19) or to LINK an object module (SVC 06). The majority of the abend SCCs presented here result from a problem detected by an SVC.

• *Possible causes*. There are four groups of possible causes. Each group lists conditions, coding errors, data problems, and so on, which may have caused the abend. The groups are:

- General
- JCL related
- Assembly programs
- COBOL programs

General causes apply to all programming languages. If applicable, the first entry will expand on the abend description. The most frequent or likely causes are listed first.

The language-dependent equivalent of the general causes is given for assembly language and COBOL. If the abended program was written in PL/I or FORTRAN, use the diagnostic lists and Appendix C as necessary to derive a PL/I or FORTRAN equivalent. Appendix C is something like a programming Rosetta stone. It shows equivalent data definition, logic, and transformation keywords for the four languages covered here. Debugging of PL/I and FORTRAN source code is also fully covered in 5.7, FORTRAN Analysis, and 5.8, PL/I Analysis.

JCL related causes are given by statement, in the order required (JOB, EXEC, DD). The most frequent or likely errors for a statement are listed first. Keyword parameter names are spelled out (e.g., DSNAME instead of DSN). This does not imply that an acceptable abbreviation is an error or contributing factor to an abend. Possible errors in JCL are presented in two ways. Keyword parameters are explicitly stated, for example:

- DSNAME specification incorrect.

Positional parameters are indicated by a letter in the parameter's position. This letter is referred to in the possible cause description, for example:

- VOLUME=(,,*N*,,SER) specification incorrect:
  - The volume sequence number, *N*, was. . . .

The letter *N* is not actually coded, but serves to indicate which positional parameter is of interest.

Often, a possible cause is stated as "The so-and-so parameter was incorrectly specified or misspelled." The seeming redundancy of this statement has a purpose. It is to suggest two similar but distinct errors. The specification may be correct in spelling or syntax, but substantively incorrect for the purpose intended. For example, the same data set name, correctly spelled, is incorrectly placed on all DD statements in a job. The problem of misspelling is self-explanatory.

Assembly language causes are given in the most frequent first sequence. Assembly operands and mnemonics are capitalized.

COBOL causes are given in division order (identification, environment, data, procedure). The most frequent or likely errors for a division are listed first. COBOL reserved words (e.g., PIC, MOVE, PERFORM) are capitalized.

- *Relevant dump items*. The portions of an abend dump that may provide data useful for analysis of the SCC are identified. They are listed in the order in which they appear on the dump. Only relevant control blocks, pointers, and so on, are discussed. For a complete and more detailed explanation of the dump, see Chapter 4, The Anatomy of a Dump. If a system message requires further explanation, it is given here.

- *What to do*. This section gives suggestions about how the problem may be analyzed and corrected, above and beyond the normal debugging procedures. Any special programming techniques or analytical tools that may help to solve the problem are presented. Possible uses for the techniques given in Chapter 3 are identified.

2.2 SYSTEM COMPLETION CODE DIAGNOSTICS

> Some problems are easy to find and hard to fix; some are hard to find and easy to fix; some go both ways. They have seen and will continue to encounter permutations of all three.
>
> *Tracy Kidder*
> *The Soul of a New Machine*

---

001 Conflict in data set DCB parameters, incorrect usage, or I/O error for sequential, partitioned, indexed sequential, or direct data set. No special error handling (SYNAD) was specified.

Related System Messages: IEC020I, IEA000I

POSSIBLE CAUSES:

General:

- Record or block size specified by problem program, JCL or data set label conflicts with actual record or block size.
- Attempt to read:
  - From a data set opened for output.
  - After end of file.
  - After close of a data set.
- Attempt to write to a data set opened as input.
- Secondary space allocation for an output DASD data set is insufficient. Problem program is writing a greater than anticipated quantity of output because:
  - It is in a write loop.
  - It is processing substantially increased quantity of input.
  - Output estimates or allocation too low.
  - See SCC B37.
- No end-of-file marker for a DASD data set.
- I/O device problem:
  - Power fluctuation.
  - Physical damage to recording medium.
  - Incorrect switch setting (e.g., read only).
  - I/O error in channel or device:
    - Parity check.
    - Bad block.

JCL Related:

DD statement:

- DCB subparameters specified conflict with actual data set characteristics:
  - LRECL or BLKSIZE.
  - RECFM.
  - DEN (for an input tape data set) not the same as actual recording density.
  - EROPT=ABE specified for a QSAM data set.
  - TRTCH=ET incompatible with RECFM=V.
- DISP specified SHR for update of a PDS in this step or a previous step. Simultaneous updates occurred. The PDS was partially or totally damaged.
- Passing DCB parameters by backward reference failed.
- LABEL IN or OUT keyword conflicts with usage specified by problem program's open.
- Secondary allocation subparameter *S* of the SPACE parameter, SPACE=(*U*, (*P*,*S*)), specifies insufficient allocation for an output data set. See SCC B37.
- Data set with largest block size is not the first in a group concatenated for input.
- See 3.3, Common JCL Errors.

Assembly Programs:

- DCB or OPEN macro parameters, or DCB fields were incorrectly specified, omitted, or overlaid—check BLKSIZE, DDNAME, DSORG, KEYLEN, LRECL, and RECFM.
- A DCB abend EXLST was specified, but is ignored for ISAM or partitioned data sets.
- An incorrect relative track address TTR was specified for the POINT macro.
- RECFM = U was specified for the DCB macro and no logical record length was given for a BSAM data set.

COBOL Programs:

- SELECT file-name ASSIGN TO device-organization-DDname specification is in error, resulting in mismatched DCB information:
  - File-name misspelled or incorrect.
  - DDname misspelled or incorrect.
- Attempt to override the FD RECORDING MODE or BLOCK CONTAINS via DD statement parameters failed (problem program specifications take precedence).
- One or more FD specifications conflict with the actual data set characteristics:
  - RECORD CONTAINS.
  - BLOCK CONTAINS.
  - RECORDING MODE.
  - LABEL RECORDS.
- USE AFTER STANDARD ERROR declarative (SYNAD exit) not specified.
- Attempt to execute a READ:
  - After AT END condition has been sensed.
  - From a file OPENed as OUTPUT.
  - From a CLOSEd file.
- Attempt to write to a sequential (QSAM) file after the supervisor indicated an out-of-space condition (see SCC B37). The out-of-space condition was flagged by either:
  - An INVALID KEY imperative statement.
  - A FILE STATUS code of 34.

RELEVANT DUMP ITEMS:

- There are several possible locations of the offending data set's DCB address:
  - R1 or R2 in the third SVRB from the bottom of the RB list.
  - R2 in the second SVRB from the bottom of RB list.
  - R2 in REGS AT ENTRY TO ABEND.
  - R2 in REGS AT TIME OF ERROR under the RTM2WA SUMMARY.
  - If the DCB was open, it will be formatted in the control block section of the dump and have a DEB and IOBs associated with it.
    - The 2-byte TIOT offset is at x28 into the DCB.
    - The DDname of this DCB is given in the TIOT at this offset.

  - If the DCB was not opened or has been closed, it will not be formatted in the control block section, but will be found in the main storage dump. The DEB will contain the DCB's address. The 8-byte DDNAME will be at x28 into the DCB.
- The IOB prefix pointer should be at x1C into the DCB. IOB fields may indicate if a hardware-related I/O error has occurred. The IOB prefix is 16 bytes long, so the IOB proper begins at the prefix address plus x10. Fields of interest are:
  - IOB + 0, IOBFLAG1: If bit 5 is on (x04), a permanent I/O error has occurred. System message IEA000I will probably have been printed.
  - IOB + 4, ECBCC: ECB completion code. First byte of the 4-byte ECB. If this byte is not x00 or x7F, a channel error has occurred.
  - IOB + xC, second word of the CSW: Contains the channel status bits. Bits 36 and 37 should be on if an I/O operation has completed successfully. Further explanation of the ECB and the CSW is given in 4.2, Dump Components, Input-Output Block.
  - If the 2 low-order bytes of the ECB (IOB + 6) contain x0C40, a wrong-length record has been encountered.
- The DEB associated with offending DCB is usually printed immediately before this data set's DCB on the dump. The DEB is also pointed to from the DCB.
  - DCB for the offending data set + x2C points to its associated DEB (DCBDEBAD).
- An output data set may have used all its allocated space. Evidence of a write loop may be found by scanning the data set's buffer. The DEB will have 16 full extents if the allocation has been exhausted.
- Examine the buffer preceding and following the last record processed for evidence of an output loop (the same record is repeated).
- The last record written to an output QSAM data set is at the address for the next record less LRECL (last = next − LRECL). Both fields are found in the DCB:
  - + x4C 4-byte address of the next record to be written or the last record read (DCBRECAD).
  - + x52 2-byte LRECL (DCBLRECL).

  If the last record read or written was also the last in a block, the buffer may have been overlaid with a new data block. In this case, the last record cannot be located by the method outlined above. You may be able to find evidence of it in other program work areas, counters, saved keys, and so on. See *Data Management Services* for more information about non-VSAM buffering.
- The DEB describes the extents allocated to a DASD device. Since up to 16 extents may be allocated, up to 16 DEB extent descriptors may be present. Each descriptor is 16 bytes long.
  - DEB + x10: 1-byte extent count.
  - DEB + x20: First extent descriptor field (for primary allocation).
  - DEB + x30: Second extent descriptor field (for secondary allocation).
  - DEB + x40: Third extent descriptor; and so on.
  - The format of each extent descriptor is as follows:
    - •• Bytes 0,3 UCB address.
    - •• Bytes 4,5 Cylinder start address for this extent.

  - •• Bytes 8,9 Track start address for this extent.
  - •• Bytes 10,11 Cylinder end address for this extent.
  - •• Bytes 12,13 Track end address for this extent.
  - •• Bytes 14,15 Number of tracks in this extent.
- • The total of the track count fields equals the total tracks used. Storage per track varies with the capacity of the device in use.

– At DCB + x5 is the 8-byte DCBFDAD (full disk address) field. This field contains the full DASD address of the last seek (read or write). Compare this address to the DEB extents to verify that the last address was within an allocated extent. DCBFDAD is of the form MBBCCHHR, where each letter represents 1 byte containing the following address components (as binary numbers):
  - • M 1-byte relative extent number (first extent is zero).
  - • BB Halfword cell number. Relevant for MSS devices only—zero for DASD devices.
  - • CC Halfword cylinder address.
  - • HH Halfword track address.
  - • R 1-byte relative block number (first block is zero).

– R4 points to the OPEN/CLOSE/EOV work area for the offending data set. It contains:
  - • The data set label at R4 + 0.
  - • The JFCB (DD statement parameters) at R4 + x64.

Examination of the work area will indicate conflicting or incorrectly specified data set parameters. 3.4, Analysis of the O/C/EOV Work Area, provides a detailed description of fields in this work area.

– Message IEC020I may indicate the offending DDname, device address, volume serial, and data set name. R15 contains a return code documented in *System Messages,* under this message. Briefly:
  - • 01 I/O error or improper data set usage.
  - • 02 Error occurred during close.
  - • 03 QSAM I/O error.
  - • 04 Improper DCB error option for QSAM data set.
  - • 05 Attempt to read after end of file.

– Message IEA000I may display portions of the CSW and CCW if an I/O error has occurred.

WHAT TO DO:

– Follow the steps outlined in 1.3, General Debugging Procedure, and 5.2, Basic Techniques.

– Specify a SYNAD routine and analyze the error further.

– If an I/O error has occurred, specify a different device, volume, or both and rerun the job.

– For information on how to dump data set labels, DASD labels, and DASD tracks, see 3.8, Dumping and Printing Data.

- The IEHATLAS utility may be used to diagnose and list data about a bad DASD track. See *MVS Utilities* for more information.

---

002 Conflict in data set record or block size parameters, incorrect usage, or I/O error for sequential, indexed sequential, or direct data set.

Related System Messages: IEC036I, IEC129I

POSSIBLE CAUSES:

General:

- Typically occurs for an output data set during open.
- A conflict has occurred in record, block, or track size:
  - Under QSAM (sequential organization) fixed-length record processing, a write was attempted and:
    - LRECL was greater than block size.
  - Under QSAM variable-length record processing:
    - A read was attempted and the RDW was:
      - Less than 4.
      - Greater than the LRECL specified by open.
    - A write was attempted and the RDW was:
      - Less than 4.
      - Less than 5 and DD statement parameter RECFM specified ASA control characters.
      - Greater than the device track capacity and no track overflow specified.
      - Greater than 32,752 and track overflow was specified.
      - Greater than 32,767.
- The RDW may be invalid due to the following chain of events: An input DASD data set was allocated [via JCL, DISP=(NEW,CATLG)] but never opened in a previous job or step. The problem program opened and read this data set, but all records are garbage (i.e., whatever happened to have been written previously on the first track of the new allocation).
- An attempt to create a sequential or direct data set was made but:
  - LRECL was greater than device track capacity and track overflow was not specified.
  - Block size was greater than the:
    - Secondary extent allocation.
    - Primary extent allocation.
    - Largest fragment of a split primary extent allocation and all secondary extents.
  - Under BSAM, a write was attempted and LRECL was greater than:
    - 32,767 bytes.
    - Device track capacity.

- Under QISAM (sequential access of indexed data set), block size was:
  - Not an integral multiple of LRECL.
  - Greater than device track capacity.
- Under spanned record processing (QSAM, BSAM, BDAM):
  - The accumulated length of an output spanned record being built is greater than the DCB LRECL.
  - An attempt was made to read a variable spanned record segment out of sequence.

– Attempt to move, copy, reload, or recreate a DASD data set on a device which has a smaller track capacity than the original device.
– I/O error due to physical damage to recording medium or device malfunction.
– The destination data set name specified to the IEHMOVE utility via the RENAME parameter already exists.

JCL Related:

DD statement:

– DCB subparameters specified conflict with actual data set characteristics:
- LRECL or BLKSIZE incorrect.
- RECFM specification incorrect:
  - VBA or FBA not appropriate for the offending data set.
  - VT was not specified for a track overflow data set.
- EROPT = ABE was specified for a QSAM data set.
- For an ISAM data set, CYLOFL specification is equal to the total number of tracks specified by CYL, leaving no room for the PRIME area.

– SPACE parameter:
- Primary extent allocation too small:
  - DCB BLKSIZE is larger than the block size of SPACE.
  - Attempt was made to output a block larger than any allocated extent for a direct data set under BDAM or BSAM.
- Did not specify CONTIG.
- Specified insufficient or incorrect CYL for an ISAM data set. May be related to CYLOFL problem noted above.

– UNIT parameter specifies generic DASD device (e.g., SYSDA). Device assigned has smaller track size than BLKSIZE or LRECL specification.
– See 3.3, Common JCL Errors.

Assembly Programs:

– A DCB abend EXLST was specified, but is ignored for ISAM or partitioned data sets.

COBOL Programs:

– SELECT file-name ASSIGN TO device-organization-DDname specification is in error, resulting in mismatched DCB information:

  - File-name misspelled or incorrect.
  - DDname misspelled or incorrect.
- Conflict between FD specification, DD statement, or actual data set attributes:
  - RECORD CONTAINS.
  - BLOCK CONTAINS.
  - RECORDING MODE.
  - LABEL RECORDS.
- USE AFTER STANDARD ERROR declarative (SYNAD Exit) was not specified.
- The RDW of a variable-length record was inadvertently overlaid due to a runaway subscript or index.

RELEVANT DUMP ITEMS:

- R2, R1 of SA or R2 of the second SVRB will point to the problem DCB.
- DCB address plus:
  - x28 contains the 2-byte TIOT offset. The DDname of this DCB is given in the TIOT at this offset.
  - x52 contains DCBLRECL (2 bytes).
  - x3E contains DCBBLKSI (2 bytes).
- The last record written to an output QSAM data set is at the address for the next record less LRECL (last = next − LRECL). Both fields are found in the DCB:
  - \+ x4C 4-byte address of the next record to be written or the last read (DCBRECAD).
  - \+ x52 2-byte LRECL (DCBLRECL).

  If the last record read or written was also the last in a block, the buffer may have been overlaid with a new data block. In this case, the last record cannot be located by the method outlined above. You may be able to find evidence of it in other program work areas, counters, saved keys, and so on. See *Data Management Services* for more information about nonVSAM buffering.
- Message IEC036I may indicate the offending device, DDname, volume serial number, and data set name. R15 contains a return code documented in *System Messages* under this message. Briefly:
  - 04 Invalid RDW in QSAM read.
  - 08 Record or block size greater than 32,767 (QSAM or BSAM write).
  - 0C Record or block size greater than track for QSAM/BSAM write.
  - 10 RDW greater than 32,752 for track overflow QSAM.
  - 14 Record greater than block for QSAM write.
  - 18 Invalid RDW for QSAM write.
  - 1C Record greater than track or DCB parameter missing for Direct Data Set (BDAM or BSAM) creation.
  - 20 Block greater than secondary extent for BDAM or BSAM write.
  - 24 Block greater than primary extent BDAM or BSAM write.
  - 28 Block greater than primary extent for BDAM or BSAM open.

- If the problem occurred for a BDAM (direct) data set, message IEC129I may indicate the offending device, DDname, volume serial number, and data set name. R15 contains a return code documented in *System Messages* under this message. Briefly:
  - 04 DCB MACRF does not specify A, K, or I.
  - 08 Zero extents in DSCB.
  - 1C Record size greater than track size.
  - 20 Block greater than secondary extent on write.
  - 24 Block greater than primary extent on write.
  - 28 Block greater than primary extent on OPEN.

WHAT TO DO:

- Follow the steps outlined in 1.3, General Debugging Procedure, and 5.2, Basic Techniques.
- Supply a SYNAD routine to analyze or correct the source of the error.
- Specify a DASD device with a larger track capacity, if needed.
- If an I/O error has occurred, specify a different device, volume, or both and rerun the job.
- For information on how to dump data set labels, see 3.8, Dumping and Printing Data.
- The IEHATLAS utility may be used to diagnose and list data about a bad DASD track. See *MVS Utilities* for more information.

---

013 OPEN error: Conflicting or insufficient DCB parameters.

Related System Messages: IEC141I
SVC 19 OPEN

POSSIBLE CAUSES:

General:

- Block size not integral multiple or record length.
- Problem program DCB parameters incorrectly specified or modified.
- SYSIN or SYSOUT data sets incorrectly used:
  - Attempt to open SYSIN for output.
  - Attempt to open SYSOUT for input.
  - Problem program block size not 80 bytes for SYSIN.
  - I/O error on open.
- PDS open failed because:
  - Member was not found.
  - I/O error during directory search.
  - Incorrect DD statement (see JCL related causes).

- Track overflow attempted on a device that does not support it, possibly due to attempt to move, copy, or recreate a data set on different device.
- the DCB of a data set shared by several tasks has been opened or closed several times. This DCB was incorrectly modified or the accessing modules specified conflicting DCB parameters.
- Attempt to open a nonpartitioned data set as a PDS.

JCL Related:

DD statement:

- SYSIN DD statement missing.
- DSNAME or PDS member name specification incorrect or misspelled.
- VOLUME specification incorrect or missing.
- DCB subparameter:
  - BLKSIZE:
    - Cannot be zero (DD *, DD DATA, DD DUMMY).
    - Omitted or conflicts with problem program DCB specification.
    - Not specified for a DUMMY data set.
    - Not an integral multiple of LRECL.
    - Must be at least 4 bytes greater than LRECL for variable-length data sets.
    - Is greater than 32,760 bytes.
  - RECFM:
    - Incorrectly specifies track overflow (=xT, . . .).
    - Specifies V, VS, or VBS for SYSIN or SYSOUT.
    - Specifies FBS or FS for a PDS.
    - Omitted for a direct (BDAM) data set.
  - DSORG:
    - Does not specify PS for SYSIN or SYSOUT.
    - Specifies PS, PO, or POU (partitioned organization), but data set is not a PDS.
    - Was specified for 9-track tape.
- The type subparameter, *T*, of the LABEL=(,*T*) parameter was incorrect.
  - *T* specified AL or ALU) and:
    - UNIT specified 7-track device (9-track required).
    - System does not support ANS labels (ASCII).
  - *T* specified NL or BLP, and no DCB parameters were supplied by the DD statement or problem program.
  - *T* conflicts with format indicated by tape header label.
- Directory allocation subparameter *D* of SPACE=(*U(P,S,D)*) was omitted for an output PDS.
- DD DUMMY or DSNAME=NULLFILE specified for an ISAM (indexed sequential) or BDAM (direct) data set.
- See 3.3, Common JCL Errors.

Assembly Programs:

- READ or WRITE macro requests dynamic buffering via an 'S' for the area address, but buffer length parameter was zero.
- Options specified via the OPEN or DCB macros are incorrect, missing, or inconsistent:
  - BLKSIZE.
  - MACRF.
  - BUFCB.
  - BUFL.
  - RECFM.
- A DCB ABEND EXLST was specified but is ignored for ISAM or partitioned data sets.

COBOL Programs:

- SELECT file-name ASSIGN TO device-organization-DDname specification is in error, resulting in mismatched DCB information:
  - File-name misspelled or incorrect.
  - DDname misspelled or incorrect.
- FD specifications incorrect, missing, or inconsistent:
  - BLOCK CONTAINS 0 RECORDS given, but BLKSIZE omitted in DD statement for an output data set.
  - BLOCK CONTAINS specification too small for an input variable-length record.
- OPEN specifications inconsistent with DD statement LABEL IN, INPUT, or OUT keyword.

RELEVANT DUMP ITEMS:

- The address of the next problem program instruction may be found in the PSW field of the problem programs's PRB under ACTIVE RBS. This RB is usually the first printed. The FL-CDE of this PRB will point to a CDE entry which has the problem program's name printed in NM. To verify that this address points to the next instruction, check the 2 bytes immediately preceding it. They should contain x0A13—the object code for the OPEN SVC.
- R2 points to the offending DCB.
  - If the DCB was open, it will be formatted in the control block section of the dump and have a DEB and IOBs associated with it.
    - The 2-byte TIOT offset is at x28 into the DCB.
    - The DDname of the DCB is given in the TIOT at this offset.
    - DCB + x1C points to the IOB prefix. IOB fields will indicate an I/O error if it has occurred.
  - If the DCB was not opened or has been closed, it will not be formatted in the control

block section, but will be found in the main storage dump and the O/C/EOV work area. The 8-byte DDNAME will be at x28 into the DCB.

- The last record written to an output QSAM data set is at the address for the next record less LRECL (last = next − LRECL). Both fields are found in the DCB:
  - + x4C 4-byte address of the next record to be written or the last read (DCBRECAD).
  - + x52 2-byte LRECL (DCBLRECL).

  The last record read is at DCBRECAD.

  If the last record read or written was also the last in a block, the buffer may have been overlaid with a new data block. In this case, the last record cannot be located by the method outlined above. You may be able to find evidence of it in other program work areas, counters, saved keys, and so on. See *Data Management Services* for more information about non-VSAM buffering.
- R4 points to the OPEN/CLOSE/EOV work areas for the offending data set. It contains:
  - The data set label at R4 + 0.
  - The JFCB (DD statement parameters) at R4 + x64.

  Examination of this work area will indicate conflicting or incorrectly specified data set parameters. 3.4, Analysis of the O/C/EOV Work Area, provides a detailed description of fields in this work area.
- Message IEC141I may indicate the offending DDname, device address, volume serial number, and data set name. R15 contains a return code documented in *System Messages* under this message. Briefly:

  - 04, 08 ANS tape label conflict.
  - 0C BDAM buffer length is zero.
  - 10 BLKSIZE and BUFL are zero for a DUMMY or NULLFILE data set.
  - 14 Conflict in DSORG and DSCB.
  - 18 PDS member not found.
  - 1C I/O error searching PDS directory.
  - 20 BLKSIZE not an integral multiple of LRECL.
  - 24, 28 Incorrect MACRF specification.
  - 2C/48 DCB buffer control block address (DCBBUFCA +x15) is zero.
  - 34 Incorrect LRECL, RECFM, or BLKSIZE.
  - 4C Buffer length incorrect.
  - 50 Output not specified to open a printer.
  - 54 1419 device error.
  - 58 Paper tape concatenation incorrect.
  - 5C Spanned variable-length data set open failed or buffer specification conflicts with MACRF.
  - 60 Block size not equal to LRECL (RECFM F).
  - 64 Attempt to DUMMY non-QSAM or BSAM data set.
  - 68 Block size greater than 32,760.
  - 6C Track overflow not supported.

- 70 Tape label or QSAM/ISAM conflict.
- 74/84 3890 OCR device errors.
- 8C RECFM not specified for a BDAM data set.
- 88 TSO device error.
- 90/A0 3890 OCR device errors.
- A4 SYSIN or SYSOUT DSORG is not PS.
- A8 SYSIN or SYSOUT RECFM invalid.
- AC AMP DD statement parameter coded for a non-VSAM data set.
- B0 Attempted backward read of variable spanned data set.
- B4 Incorrect MACRF specification.
- B8 3890 OCR open error.
- BC Open specified unallowed access to SYSIN or SYSOUT.
- C0 Open failed for SYSIN or SYSOUT.
- C4 Open MACRF does not specify WL for direct data set create.
- C8 Supervisor error.
- CC 3800 printer open error.
- D0 RECFM FBS or FB specified for PDS.

WHAT TO DO:

– Follow the steps outlined in 1.3, General Debugging Procedure, and 5.2, Basic Techniques.
– Recall that to open a data set, DCB parameters are drawn from three sources: the problem program, the DD statement, and the data set label. The parameters supplied by the problem program supersede those in the DD statement and the data set label. Similarly, the DD statement's parameters supersede the label's. However, if the actual data set's characteristics differ from the DCB parameters, an abend will result. Common practice is to define as many parameters as possible via the DD statement to allow for flexibility.
– For information on how to dump data set labels, see 3.8, Dumping and Printing Data.

---

031 I/O error during sequential processing of an indexed sequential data set. No SYNAD exit specified.

Related System Messages: IEC203I, IEC011I

POSSIBLE CAUSES:

General:

– For an ISAM data set:

- Key out of sequence for load.
- The problem program did not issue a close for the abending data set. An I/O error was detected and abend occurred when the supervisor attempted a close at task termination.
- Incorrect record length or block.
- Invalid key specified for SETL macro.
- Device malfunction or physical damage to recording medium.
- For ISAM/VSAM interface:
  - VSAM physical or logical I/O error.
  - RDW greater than LRECL for variable-length record.

JCL Related:

DD statement:

- AMP parameter did not specify SYNAD mode for the ISAM/VSAM interface.
- DCB parameter specified EROPT=ABE.

Assembly Programs:

- A DCB ABEND EXLST was specified, but is ignored for ISAM data sets.
- The DCB SYNAD address (DCBSYNAD, DCB + x38) was invalid:
  - A SYNAD routine was not specified.
  - The address was incorrectly built or overlaid.

COBOL Programs:

- USE AFTER STANDARD ERROR declarative (SYNAD) was not specified.
- INVALID KEY imperative statement not specified.
- Input SORT for an ISAM load failed or SORT KEY was inconsistent with key specified for an ISAM data set.

RELEVANT DUMP ITEMS:

- The offending ISAM DCB is found as follows:
  - Locate the module in the load list that contains the PSW interrupt address. Under SAVE AREA TRACE, find where this module was ENTERED VIA CALL.
  - RET in this area gives the return address of the program calling this module. This should point to the address after the last macro (or statement) which issued the abended SVC.
  - R1 in the SAVE AREA TRACE for this module contains the offending DCB address. R1 plus:
    - x28 contains the 2-byte TIOT offset. The DDname of this DCB is given in the TIOT at this offset.
    - x50 points to DCBEXCD1 and DCBEXCD2.
    - When on, the bits of these fields indicate the type of error (for QISAM):

Bit	DCBEXCD1	DCBEXCD2
0	Lower limit reached, record not found	Sequence check
1	Invalid device address	Duplicate records
2	Space not found	DCB closed when ERR RTN entered
3	Invalid request	Overflow records
4	Uncorrectable input error	Invalid LRECL
5	Uncorrectable output error	Reserved
6	Unreachable block (input)	Reserved
7	Unreachable block (output) (overflow area)	Reserved

- If the error occurred for an ISAM/VSAM data set, see 3.5, Locating VSAM Data Records, for a description of VSAM control blocks.
- Messages IEC203I and IEC011I may indicate the offending DDname, device address, volume serial number, and data set name. R15 contains a return code documented in *System Messages,* under these messages. Briefly:
  - 04, 08 I/O error during ISAM close.

WHAT TO DO:

- Follow the steps outlined in 1.3, General Debugging Procedure, and 5.2, Basic Techniques.
- For ISAM/VSAM interface, VSAM return codes are translated to their equivalent in the table above. See *VSAM Programmer's Guide* for the VSAM codes.
- The SYNAD exit will be taken if a close is issued after the I/O error is detected. It is poor programming practice to rely on the default system close invoked by task termination.
- This abend indicates that the integrity of the data set is damaged. Records probably have been lost or scrambled. Delete the data set and reload it if possible.
- Specify a SYNAD module and analyze the error codes.
- If an I/O error has occurred, specify a different device, volume, or both and rerun the job.
- For information on how to dump an ISAM or VSAM data set, see 3.8, Dumping Printing Data.

03B OPEN error for sequential processing of an indexed sequential data set.

Related System Messages: IEC161I (VSAM-related only)

POSSIBLE CAUSES:

General:

- Error occurred during open.
- Attempt to access an ISAM data set before it has been loaded and closed.
- A conflict exists in the parameters of the DSCB, DCB, or DD statement (see JCL related causes).
- Data set specified does not exist because:
  - It was never created.
  - A previous step failed to create it.
  - It was inadvertently deleted.
  - It was deleted because its retention period expired.
- Data set specified cannot be opened because:
  - It must be closed first (i.e., it is already open).
  - Previous close failed.
  - Load not allowed under QISAM.
- For ISAM/VSAM interface:
  - Conflict between ISAM DCB and AMS values for LRECL, KEYLEN, or RKP.
  - Attempt to reload (data set was opened for output with DISP=OLD).
  - VSAM open failed due to previous improper close or because data set is in use by another task.
- The data set label (DSCB) for this data set was incorrectly created or altered. This situation is indicated if both the problem program and DD statement DCB parameters are correct and in agreement. The DSCB could be damaged on disk or may have been inadvertently overlaid when placed into main storage for OPEN, CLOSE, or EOV processing.

JCL Related:

DD statement:

- JOBCAT or STEPCAT statement incorrect or missing.
- DSNAME misspelled or incorrect.
- DCB subparameters incorrect:
  - RKP invalid or less than 4 for variable-length record data sets.
  - KEYLEN invalid or zero.
  - BLKSIZE not an even multiple of LRECL.
  - BLKSIZE is less than LRECL.
  - LRECL is zero.
  - RKP plus KEYLEN greater than LRECL.
  - RECFM incorrect (e.g., VB instead of FB).
- UNIT=TAPE specified for ISAM data set.

Assembly Programs:

- DCB subparameter MACRF did not specify an ISAM data set.
- DCB was opened for a PUT:
  - OPEN did not specify OUTPUT as option 1.
  - DISP=SHR was specified in DD statement.
- A DCB ABEND EXLST was specified, but is ignored for ISAM.

COBOL Programs:

- SELECT statement did not specify DA-I-DDname for an ISAM data set.
- Data set was OPENed as OUTPUT or I/O and DISP=SHR was specified in DD statement.

RELEVANT DUMP ITEMS:

- The address of the next problem program instruction may be found at the RET field of the last SA under SAVE AREA TRACE.
- R2 points to the offending DCB:
  - The 2-byte TIOT offset is at x28 into this DCB.
  - The DDname of the DCB is given in the TIOT at this offset.
  - DCB + xA0 points to the ISAM status byte. If bit 2 is on (x20), the data set has been created (the error is probably a DCB conflict).
- R4 points to the OPEN/CLOSE/EOV work area for the offending data set. It contains:
  - The data set label at R4 + 0.
  - The JFCB (DD statement parameters) at R4 + x64. Examination of this work area will indicate conflicting or incorrectly specified data set parameters. 3.4, Analysis of the O/C/EOV Work Area, provides a detailed description of fields in this work area.
- Presence of a format 2 DSCB indicates that the data set has been created.
- If the error occurred for an ISAM/VSAM data set, see 3.5, Locating VSAM Data Records, for a description of the VSAM control blocks.
- Message IEC161I is issued for this abend under the ISAM/VSAM interface only.

WHAT TO DO:

- Follow the steps outlined in 1.3, General Debugging Procedure, and 5.2, Basic Techniques.
- For information on how to dump an ISAM or VSAM data set, see 3.8, Dumping and Printing Data. In particular, comparison of the DSCB (data set label) DCB parameters to those from the DD statement and the problem program will often reveal the cause of an 03B.

03D OPEN error for direct or indexed sequential data set.

Related System Messages: IEC156I

POSSIBLE CAUSES:

General:

- BDAM (direct) or BSAM (basic sequential) open issued for an ISAM data set.
- Not all volumes of a multivolume data set were mounted.

JCL Related:

DD statement:

- DSNAME is incorrect or misspelled.
- DSNAME=dsname(INDEX) is not specified first for an ISAM data set with a separate index data set.
- DSORG subparameter of DCB:
  - Was omitted.
  - Does not specify IS or ISU for an ISAM data set (required).
  - Specified DA for an ISAM data set.
- SER subparameter of VOLUME:
  - Does not specify all volumes of a multivolume data set.
  - Sequence specified is incorrect. Serial numbers must be given in the same order used to create the data set.
- The volume quantity subparameter, *N* of UNIT=(*device, N*) was not equal to the number of volumes specified in SER.
- See 3.3, Common JCL Errors.

Assembly Programs:

- A DCB ABEND EXLST was specified, but is ignored for ISAM data sets.

RELEVANT DUMP ITEMS:

- The address of the next problem program instruction may be found at the RET field of the last SA under SAVE AREA TRACE.
- R2 points to the offending DCB:
  - The 2-byte TIOT offset is at x28 into this DCB.
  - The DDname of this DCB is given in the TIOT at this offset.
- R4 points to the OPEN/CLOSE/EOV work area for the offending data set. It contains:
  - The data set label at R4 + 0.
  - The JFCB (DD statement parameters) at R4 + x64. Examination of this work area will indicate conflicting or incorrectly specified data set parameters. 3.4, Analysis

of the O/C/EOV Work Area, provides a detailed description of fields in this work area.

– Message IEC156I may indicate the offending DDname, device address, volume serial number, and data set name. R15 contains a return code documented under this message in *System Messages*. Briefly:
  - 04 Incorrect volume serial number sequence.
  - 08 Format 2 DSCB not found on first volume of an ISAM data set. Incorrect DSORG specification.
  - 0C BDAM or BSAM OPEN issued for ISAM data set.

WHAT TO DO:

– Follow the steps outlined in 1.3, General Debugging Procedure, and 5.2, Basic Techniques.
– For information on how to dump an ISAM data set, see 3.8, Dumping and Printing Data.

0C1 Operation exception: Attempt to execute an invalid instruction.

Related System Messages: IBM531I, IHO210I

POSSIBLE CAUSES:

General:

– Invalid branch resulted in an attempt to execute data.
– Valid instructions were overlaid by:
  - A runaway program loop.
  - Incorrect address calculation.
  - Incorrect index or subscript usage.
– Missing, misspelled, or incorrect entry point or module name specified in subroutine call.
– Attempt to execute a module with unresolved link-edit references. The NCAL or LET parameter was specified when the abending program was linked, allowing an executable but incomplete load module to be created in a previous job or step. The linkage editor could not find an input module(s) because:
  - SYSLIB DD, INCLUDE, or LIBRARY omits or specifies an incorrect data set name or member.
  - It was never created.
  - It was deleted.
  - It was renamed.
  - See also SCC 806.

- The most recent version of a called module(s) was not linked into the abending load module. The linkage editor obtains a new copy of an external reference (called module) only when (1) the reference does not exist in the input load module, or (2) when specifically directed to replace existing references by the linkage editor REPLACE statement.
- Attempt to access an unopened data set.
- Failure to reinitialize a field(s). Common examples are application programs run under IMS DC or CICS and dynamically called subroutines. In each of these situations the module is reloaded frequently, possibly every time it is invoked. Upon entry into the module, the content of main storage data fields are unpredictable unless explicitly initialized or refreshed.
- Instruction requires hardware feature not installed on this CPU.
- See also 3.2, 0Cx Abend Diagnostics.

JCL Related:

EXEC statement:

- Entire statement duplicated.

DD statement:

- Entire statement omitted:
  - SYSIN or SYSOUT omitted and problem program attempted I/O to either default data set.
  - Statement "commented-out" (//* statement).
  - Procedure overrides incorrect or omitted.
- DDname misspelled or incorrect.
- DCB subparameter errors:
  - BLKSIZE specified for random access processing of an ISAM data set (BISAM mode).
  - DEN parameter omitted or incorrect for an input tape data set processed with LABEL=NL, AL, or BLP.
- Load library specified or selected as a default is incorrect:
  - STEPLIB or JOBLIB DD statement missing.
  - DSNAME misspelled or incorrect.
  - Order of concatenation incorrect. Modules are selected from the first library they are found in.
- See 3.3, Common JCL Errors.

Assembly Programs:

- CSECT name misspelled.
- Misplaced constant interpreted as an instruction.
- Incorrectly formed branch address.
- Instruction overlaid or incorrectly modified.

– B R10 was coded instead of BR R10 to return from a subroutine entered via a BALR.
– Branching to an assembler-generated slack byte resulted in violation of instruction alignment requirements. For example, branching to LABEL results in a next instruction address which is a slack byte:

```
         B     LOOP
SSN      DS    CL9
LABEL    EQU   *
         MVC   A,B
```

– See the following under 3.2, 0Cx Abend Diagnostics:
  • Table 3-2 for instructions that can cause an 0C1.
  • Diagnosing an Invalid Branch.

COBOL Programs:

– PROGRAM-ID name for a subroutine is not the same as the entry point name defined to the linkage editor.
– OBJECT-COMPUTER specifies a processor model which has instructions not installed on your CPU.
– SELECT file-name ASSIGN TO device-organization-DDname specification is in error:
  • DA-I-DDname not specified for an ISAM data set.
  • File-name misspelled or incorrect.
  • DDname misspelled or incorrect.
– RECORDING MODE specifies record format different from actual data set.
– Entry specified entry point name is the same as PROGRAM-ID name in a called program.
– ACCEPT verb executed, but SYSIN DD statement missing.
– DISPLAY, EXHIBIT, or TRACE verb executed but SYSOUT DD statement missing.
– Attempt to OPEN a data set:
  • Twice (no intervening CLOSE executed).
  • That was CLOSEd WITH LOCK.
– The problem program OPENs a sort input data set before or after execution of the SORT . . . USING verb. SORT USING automatically issues an open for the sort input data set. Either situation results in an attempt to open this data set twice.
– Program logic error:
  • PERFORM section name, paragraph name, or exit name is incorrect or misspelled.
  • Section name, paragraph name, or exit name missing, misspelled, or misplaced. The entry/exit point of a block(s) of code is incorrect.
  • GO TO branches out of a performed section or paragraph and never returns.
  • STOP RUN or GOBACK omitted. Program "falls through" to next statement when it should have terminated. This error is frequently the cause of a double OPEN, a READ after end, or a double CLOSE.
  • Invalid logic in SORT INPUT PROCEDURE or OUTPUT PROCEDURE section:

  - STOP RUN or GOBACK.
  - CALL.
  - GO TO or PERFORM references a paragraph name outside the section.
- Invalid usage of the ALTER verb:
  - GO TO missing in the paragraph specified by ALTER.
  - GO TO in paragraph specified by ALTER does not specify a paragraph name. This GO TO was initialized by executing its associated ALTER prior to its own execution and points to an invalid address.
  - The ALTER construct is so prone to error that many installations prohibit its use. Recoding this construct is recommended.

RELEVANT DUMP ITEMS:

– See Table 3-2 for operation disposition and ILC value.
– Determine the next instruction address in the problem program:
  - If the PSW gives an address within the problem program load module, the abending instruction is near the PSW address. It is not always possible to determine the exact address by subtracting the ILC, since it may not be meaningful in this interrupt. An invalid branch or overlaid code are good suspects in this case.
  - If the PSW is not within the load module, R14 may point the next instruction to be executed in the problem program. An I/O related problem is likely in this case.

– Many 0C1 abends result from I/O or JCL related problems. If the PSW has either a very high or low instruction address, such a problem may be indicated. Specific values of the PSW instruction address may indicate the problem as follows:

PSW	*Possible Problem*
x00 00 40	Attempt to access an unopened data set.
x00 00 48	Missing DD statement or attempt to write to an unopened data set.
x00 00 4A	Missing DD statement.
x00 00 4F	Conflict in DCB parameters supplied by problem and DD statement.
x00 00 50	Missing DD statement or misspelled DDname.
x00 40 02	Attempt to access unopened data set.
x00 48 00	Attempt to write an unopened data set or missing DD statement.
xC0 00 42	Attempt to open same file twice.
xC0 40 02	Attempt to open same file twice.

– If an I/O related problem has occurred, R1 or R2 may point to the offending DCB:
  - If the DCB is open, the 2-byte TIOT offset is at x28 into the DCB. This offset into the TIOT will give the DD statement's DDname.
  - If the DCB is not open, it will not be formatted in the control block section but will be found in the main storage dump. x28 into the closed DCB will give the DDname supplied by the problem program.

– The last record written to an output QSAM data set is at the address for the next record less LRECL (last = next − LRECL). Both fields are found in the DCB:
  - + x4C 4-byte address of the next record to be written or last read (DCBRECAD).
  - + x52 2-byte LRECL (DCBLRECL).

  If the last record read or written was also the last in a block, the buffer may have been overlaid with a new data block. In this case, the last record cannot be located by the method outlined above. You may be able to find evidence of it in other program work areas, counters, saved keys, and so on. See *Data Management Services* for more information about non-VSAM buffering.

– The last record read or written to a VSAM cluster may be found by the method outlined in 3.5, Locating VSAM Data Records.

WHAT TO DO:

– Follow the steps outlined in 1.3, General Debugging Procedure, and 5.2, Basic Techniques.

– If an uninstalled extended floating-point instruction is the cause, certain SVCs are available which simulate the extended floating-point feature. See *Supervisor Services* for details of their use.

– The actual contents of a suspect data set may be dumped or printed to check for invalid data. The actual modules used in a load module may be listed. The utility programs to do this are described in 3.8, Dumping and Printing Data.

0C2 Attempt to execute a privileged instruction in the problem state.

Related System Messages: IBM532I

POSSIBLE CAUSES:

General:

– Certain instructions are executable only when the task is executing in the supervisor state. Bit 15 of the PSW must be set to 1 to indicate this state.

– The instruction code fetched was interpreted as a privileged operation. This may have resulted from:
  - An invalid branch address.
  - An attempt to execute data.
  - Valid instructions overlaid by:
    - Runaway program loop.
    - Incorrect address calculation.
    - Incorrect index or subscript usage.
  - An attempt to execute an instruction reserved for the supervisor [e.g., set storage

key (SSK)].
- Misspelled or incorrect privileged subroutine name in call.
- See SCC 0C1.
- See 3.2, 0Cx Abend Diagnostics.

JCL Related:

DD statement:

- Missing, misspelled, or incorrect DD statement.
- Load library specified or selected as a default is incorrect:
  - STEPLIB or JOBLIB DD statement missing.
  - DSNAME specification incorrect or misspelled.
  - Order of concatenation incorrect. Modules are selected from the first library they are found in.

Assembly Programs:

- See the following under 3.2, 0Cx Abend Diagnostics:
  - Table 3-2 for instructions that can cause an 0C2.
  - Diagnosing an Invalid Branch.

COBOL Programs:

- See SCC 0C1, COBOL causes.

RELEVANT DUMP ITEMS:

- See Table 3-2 for operation disposition and ILC value.
- PSW instruction address less the ILC is the abending instruction address.
- R1 or R2 plus x28 may point to the DCB for the offending DD statement. R2 is more likely to point to it if R1 and R2 contain different addresses. The DCB plus x28 contains the 2-byte TIOT offset. The DDname of this DCB is given in the TIOT at this offset.
- If R15 contains hex zeros, R14 may point to the address of the instruction that attempted to call an unloadable routine.

WHAT TO DO:

- Follow the steps outlined in 1.3, General Debugging Procedure, and 5.2, Basic Techniques.

0C3 Execute exception: The object of an execute instruction is another execute instruction.

Related System Messages: IBM532I

POSSIBLE CAUSES:

Assembly Programs:

- Incorrect coding or usage of the execute (EX) instruction.
- Invalid branch or instruction modification.
- See 3.2, 0Cx Abend Diagnostics.

WHAT TO DO:

- Follow the steps outlined in 1.3, General Debugging Procedure, and 5.2, Basic Techniques.

0C4 Protection exception: An invalid main storage address was generated.

Related System Messages: IBM534I, IHN210I, IH0210I

POSSIBLE CAUSES:

General:

- An attempt to use an invalid virtual address was made. Data items used to create an address are incorrectly loaded or initialized. The virtual address could not be translated into a real address.
- Uninitialized or runaway subscript or index due to program loop.
- Attempt to:
  - Read an unopened data set.
  - Close a data set twice (no intervening open).
  - Move data to or from the buffer of an unopened data set.
- Missing, misspelled, or incorrect entry point or module name specified in subroutine call.
- Attempt to execute a module with unresolved link-edit references. The NCAL or LET parameter was specified when the abending program was linked, allowing an executable but incomplete load module to be created in a previous job or step. The linkage editor could not find an input module(s) because:
  - SYSLIB DD, INCLUDE, or LIBRARY omits or specifies an incorrect data set name or member.
  - It was never created.
  - It was deleted.
  - It was renamed.
  - See also SCC 806.

- The most recent version of a called module(s) was not linked into the abending load module. The linkage editor obtains a new copy of an external reference (called module) only when (1) the reference does not exist in the input load module, or (2) when specifically directed to replace existing references by the linkage editor REPLACE statement.
- Failure to reinitialize a field(s). Common examples are application programs run under IMS DC or CICS and dynamically called subroutines. In each of these situations the module is reloaded frequently, possibly every time it is invoked. Upon entry into the module, the content of main storage data fields is unpredictable unless explicitly initialized or refreshed.
- I/O error occurred while reading an ISAM data set.
- The storage or PSW protection key of an instruction, operand, or data item does not match the problem program's key.
- Main storage page or segment table entry not found.
- The supervisor was unable to translate a page address.
- See 3.2, 0Cx Abend Diagnostics.

JCL Related:

DD statement:

- Entire statement missing.
- DDname misspelled or incorrect.
- DCB subparameters:
  - BLKSIZE not an integral multiple of LRECL.
  - BLKSIZE must be at least 4 bytes greater than LRECL for a variable-length record data set.
- Load library specified or selected as a default is incorrect:
  - STEPLIB or JOBLIB DD statement missing.
  - DSNAME misspelled or incorrect.
  - Order of concatenation incorrect. Modules are selected from the first library they are found in.
- Incorrect SORTLIB DD parameters:
  - DSNAME specification incorrect or misspelled.
  - VOLUME specification incorrect.

Assembly Programs:

- Failure to establish addressability.
- CSECT statement missing.
- See the following under 3.2, 0Cx Abend Diagnostics:
  - Table 3-2 for instructions that can cause an 0C4.
  - Diagnosing an Invalid Branch.

COBOL Programs:

- SELECT file-name ASSIGN TO device-organization-DDname is inconsistent with DD statement:
  - File-name misspelled or incorrect.
  - DDname misspelled or incorrect.
  - Specifies wrong device or organization.
  - File-name and DDname are mismatched.
- LINKAGE SECTION header is incorrectly placed, inadvertently specified, or omitted.
  - If omitted in a called program, the program may be invoked but no data can be passed in or back.
  - If incorrectly placed or inadvertently specified in a calling program, addressability cannot be established for any data item following the LINKAGE SECTION header. Reference to such an item may result in a protection exception. This problem may result from:
    - Copying a subroutine parameter list (with the LINKAGE SECTION header) into a calling program.
    - Converting a subroutine into a calling or mainline program.
    - Converting a mainline program into a subroutine.
- Invalid parameter list specified for:
  - PROCEDURE DIVISION USING.
  - ENTRY . . . USING.
  - CALL . . . USING.
  - See SCC 0C7, COBOL causes.
  - The items specified in the USING lists of the calling and called programs are assumed, by the compiler, to be identical in order, data type, and field length. Any discrepancy in this correspondance may result in an 0C4. See 5.6, COBOL Analysis, Finding Parameter Lists, for further details.
- Attempt to MOVE data to or from:
  - An unOPENed FD area.
  - An OPEN FD area for which no READ has been executed.
  - An SD area prior to the execution of the SORT verb.
- Attempt to READ after AT END condition.
- Attempt to READ or WRITE an unOPENed file.
- Attempt to reOPEN a file that has been CLOSEd WITH LOCK.
- Report writer specifies a SOURCE that is CLOSEd or AT END.
- Program logic error:
  - PERFORM section name, paragraph name, or exit name is incorrect or misspelled.
  - Section name, paragraph name, or exit name missing, misspelled, or misplaced. The entry/exit point of a block(s) of code is incorrect.
  - GO TO branches out of a performed section or paragraph and never returns.
  - STOP RUN or GOBACK omitted. Program "falls through" to next statement when it should have terminated. This error is frequently the cause of a double OPEN, a READ after end, or a double CLOSE.

- Invalid logic in sort INPUT PROCEDURE or OUTPUT PROCEDURE section:
  - STOP RUN or GOBACK.
  - CALL.
  - GO TO or PERFORM references a paragraph name outside the section.
- Invalid usage of the ALTER verb:
  - GO TO missing in the paragraph specified by ALTER.
  - GO TO in paragraph specified by ALTER does not specify a paragraph name. This GO TO was initialized by executing its associated ALTER prior to its own execution and points to an invalid address.
  - The ALTER construct is so prone to error that many installations prohibit its use. Recoding this construct is recommended.

RELEVANT DUMP ITEMS:

- See Table 3-2 for operation disposition and ILC value.
- The INTC (interrupt code) listed on the first page of the dump is useful in diagnosing the cause of an 0C4 abend:
  - 0004 Conflict between problem program instruction or operand protection key and PSW protection key. PSW points to next instruction.
  - 0010 Virtual segment or page not allocated to this task was specified. The PSW points to the abending instruction, not the next instruction.
  - 0011 Same as INTC 0010 or may be due to page request made by routine disabled for I/O interrupts. The PSW points to abending instruction, not the next instruction.
- If the PSW points to low address (e.g.., x004814), an attempt to access an unopened data set or to open a data set without a DD statement may have been made.
- If the PSW instruction address is not within the problem program, R14 may point to the instruction within the problem program following an I/O macro call that invoked ABEND.
- R1 or R2 may point to the offending data set's DCB if the abend is I/O related. At the DCB + x28 is the 2-byte TIOT offset. This offset will yield the data set's DDname from the TIOT.
- The last record written to an output QSAM data set is at the address for the next record less LRECL (last = next − LRECL). Both fields are found in the DCB:
  - + x4C 4-byte address of the next record to be written or the last read (DCBRECAD).
  - + x52 2-byte LRECL (DCBLRECL).

  If the last record read or written was also the last in a block, the buffer may have been overlaid with a new data block. In this case, the last record cannot be located by the method outlined above. You may be able to find evidence of it in other program work areas, counters, saved keys, and so on. See *Data Management Services* for more information about non-VSAM buffering.
- The last record read or written to a VSAM cluster may be found by the method outlined in 3.5, Locating VSAM Data Records.

WHAT TO DO:

- Follow the steps outlined in 1.3, General Debugging Procedure, and 5.2, Basic Techniques.
- The actual contents of a suspect data set may be dumped or printed to check for invalid data. The actual modules in the load module may be listed. The utility programs to do this are described in 3.8, Dumping and Printing Data.

0C5 Addressing exception: An address specified is outside available main storage.

Related System Messages: IBM535I, IHN210I, IHO210I

POSSIBLE CAUSES:

General:

- Data items used to create an address are incorrectly loaded or initialized.
- Uninitialized or runaway subscript or index due to program loop.
- Attempt to:
  - Read after end of file.
  - Read or write before an open.
  - Access the buffer of an unopened file.
  - Close a file twice (with no intervening open).
- An open failed to complete a DCB, causing a subsequent I/O operation failure.
- Invalid length or order of items passed in a linkage area.
- Incorrect RDW for a variable-length record.
- Calling a module name instead of its entry point.
- Entering a module via an entry point and falling into a new entry point or a data section.
- Executing a program written for a machine with more main storage.
- Attempt to access a main storage address that resided in a storage unit that was powered down.
- See SCC 0C4.
- See 3.2, 0Cx Abend Diagnostics.

JCL Related:

JOB or EXEC statement:

- ADDRSPC=REAL was specified and the REGION specification or its default was too small. The problem program generated an address outside the real storage boundary.

DD statement:

- DCB subparameters BLKSIZE and LRECL are equal for a variable-length record data set.
- SORTLIB DD parameters incorrect:
  - DSNAME incorrect or misspelled.
  - VOLUME specification incorrect.
- See 3.3, Common JCL Errors.

Assembly Programs:

- See the following under 3.2, 0Cx Abend Diagnostics:
  - Table 3-2 for operation instructions that can cause an 0C5.
  - Diagnosing an Invalid Branch.

COBOL Programs:

- LINKAGE SECTION header is incorrectly placed, inadvertently specified, or omitted:
  - If omitted in a called program, the program may be invoked but no data can be passed in or back.
  - If incorrectly placed or inadvertently specified in a calling program, addressability cannot be established for any data item following the LINKAGE SECTION header. Reference to such an item may result in an addressing exception. This problem may result from:
    - Copying a subroutine parameter list (with the LINKAGE SECTION header) into a calling program.
    - Converting a subroutine into a calling or mainline program.
    - Converting a mainline program into a subroutine.
- Incorrect alignment of COMP (binary) data items for blocked records with no inter-record slack bytes.
- Attempt to reference via MOVE, IF, or arithmetic verb a data item in an:
  - Unopen FD area (buffer).
  - Open FD area for which no READ has been issued.
- No records have been RELEASEd by a sort INPUT PROCEDURE before the OUTPUT PROCEDURE is executed.
- WRITE used for variable-length data set for which APPLY WRITE-ONLY was specified. WRITE FROM must be used with APPLY WRITE-ONLY.
- N of GO TO DEPENDING ON N is defined as COMP and contains a negative number, which is interpreted as a very large address.
- Program logic error:
  - PERFORM section name, paragraph name, or exit name is incorrect or misspelled.
  - Section name, paragraph name, or exit name missing, misspelled, or misplaced. The entry/exit point of a block(s) of code is incorrect.
  - GO TO branches out of a performed section or paragraph and never returns.

- STOP RUN or GOBACK omitted. Program "falls through" to next statement when it should have terminated. This error is frequently the cause of a double OPEN, a READ after end, or a double CLOSE.

– Invalid logic in SORT INPUT PROCEDURE or OUTPUT PROCEDURE section:
  - •• STOP RUN or GOBACK.
  - •• CALL.
  - •• GO TO or PERFORM references a paragraph name outside the section.
- Invalid usage of the ALTER verb:
  - •• GO TO missing in the paragraph specified by ALTER.
  - •• GO TO in paragraph specified by ALTER does not specify a paragraph name. This GO TO was initialized by executing its associated ALTER prior to its own execution and points to an invalid address.
  - •• The ALTER construct is so prone to error that many installations prohibit its use. Recoding this construct is recommended.

– Attempt to re-OPEN a file that has been CLOSEd with LOCK.
– Report writer specifies a SOURCE that is CLOSEd or AT END.

RELEVANT DUMP ITEMS:

– See Table 3-2 for operation disposition and ILC value.
– PSW contains the next instruction address. If this address is not within the problem program, R14 may point to the instruction within the problem program following an I/O macro call that invoked ABEND.
– R1 or R2 may point to the offending data set's DCB if the abend is I/O related. At the DCB + x28 is the 2-byte TIOT offset. This offset will yield the data set's DDname from the TIOT.
– The last record written to an output QSAM data set is at the address for the next record less LRECL (last = next − LRECL). Both fields are found in the DCB:
  - + x4C 4-byte address of the next record to be written or the last read (DCBRECAD).
  - + x52 2-byte LRECL (DCBLRECL).

  If the last record read or written was also the last in a block, the buffer may have been overlaid with a new data block. In this case, the last record cannot be located by the method outlined above. You may be able to find evidence of it in other program work areas, counters, saved keys, and so on. See *Data Management Services* for more information about non-VSAM buffering.
– The last record read or written to a VSAM cluster may be found by the method outlined in 3.5, Locating VSAM Data Records.

WHAT TO DO:

– Follow the steps outlined in 1.3, General Debugging Procedure, and 5.2, Basic Techniques.
– The actual contents of a suspect data set may be dumped or printed to check for invalid

data. The utility programs to do this are described in 3.8, Dumping and Printing Data.

0C6 Specification exception: Incorrect instruction specification.

Related System Messages: IBM536I, IHN210I, IHO210I

POSSIBLE CAUSES:

General:

- An instruction was incorrectly coded or its usage for certain data was invalid.
- Uninitialized or runaway subscript or index due to program loop.
- Attempt to:
  - Read after end of file.
  - Close a data set twice with no intervening open.
  - Write to a closed data set.
  - Write to an input only file.
- An address does not specify required boundary—incorrect alignment.
- The result of a packed decimal multiplication would have overflowed the product field.
- See 3.2, 0Cx Abend Diagnostics.

JCL Related:

- Missing, misspelled, or incorrect DD statement parameters.
- See 3.3, Common JCL Errors.

Assembly Programs:

- An odd-numbered registered address was specified in the R1 field of an instruction using a pair of general registers containing a 64-bit operand. An even-numbered register must be the first specified.
- Register 0, 2, 4, or 6 is not specified for a floating-point instruction.
- The specification of a packed decimal multiplier exceeds 15 digits and a sign (8 bytes).
- Length operand is used incorrectly in definition of a floating-point constant, causing incorrect halfword, fullword, or doubleword boundary alignment.
- The second operand length in packed decimal multiply or divide is greater than or is equal to the first operand length.
- The 4 low-order bits of a block address in a SET STORAGE KEY (SSK) or INSERT STORAGE KEY (ISK) instruction are nonzero.
- PSW protection is on when protection not installed for your CPU.
- Branching to an assembler-generated slack byte resulted in violation of instruction

alignment requirements. For example, branching to LABEL results in a next instruction address that is a slack byte:

```
              B      LOOP
        SSN   DS     CL9
        LABEL EQU    *
              MVC    A,B
```

- See the following under 3.2, 0Cx Abend Diagnostics:
  - Table 3-2 for instructions that can cause an 0C6.
  - Diagnosing an Invalid Branch.

COBOL Programs:

- Alignment of COMP data is incorrect. Interrecord slack bytes were not inserted when a record was blocked.
- REPORT WRITER specifies a SOURCE that is AT END or CLOSEd.
- Program logic error:
  - PERFORM section name, paragraph name, or exit name is incorrect or misspelled.
  - Section name, paragraph name, or exit name missing, misspelled, or misplaced. The entry/exit point of a block(s) of code is incorrect.
  - GO TO branches out of a performed section or paragraph and never returns.
  - STOP RUN or GOBACK omitted. Program "falls through" to next statement when it should have terminated. This error is frequently the cause of a double OPEN, a READ after end, or a double CLOSE.
  - Invalid logic in SORT INPUT PROCEDURE or OUTPUT PROCEDURE section:
    - STOP RUN or GOBACK.
    - CALL.
    - GO TO or PERFORM references a paragraph name outside the section.
  - Invalid usage of the ALTER verb:
    - GO TO missing in the paragraph specified by ALTER.
    - GO TO in paragraph specified by ALTER does not specify a paragraph name. This GO TO was initialized by executing its associated ALTER prior to its own execution and points to an invalid address.
    - The ALTER construct is so prone to error that many installations prohibit its use. Recoding this construct is recommended.

RELEVANT DUMP ITEMS:

- See 3.2, 0Cx Abend Diagnostics, for operation disposition and ILC value.
- See Table 3-2 for operation disposition and ILC value.
- PSW contains the next instruction address. If this address is not within the problem program, R14 may point to the instruction within the problem program following an

I/O macro call that invoked the abend.

- R1 or R2 may point to the offending data set's DCB if the abend is I/O related. At the DCB + x28 is the 2-byte TIOT offset. This offset will yield the DDname from the TIOT.
- The last record written to an output QSAM data set is at the address for the next record less LRECL (last = next − LRECL). Both fields are found in the DCB:
  - + x4C 4-byte address of the next record to be written or the last read (DCBRECAD).
  - + x52 2-byte LRECL (DCBLRECL).

  If the last record read or written was also the last in a block, the buffer may have been overlaid with a new data block. In this case, the last record cannot be located by the method outlined above. You may be able to find evidence of it in other program work areas, counters, saved keys, and so on. See *Data Management Services* for more information about non-VSAM buffering.
- The last record read or written to a VSAM cluster may be found by the method outlined in 3.5, Locating VSAM Data Records.

WHAT TO DO:

- Follow the steps outlined in 1.3, General Debugging Procedure, and 5.2, Basic Techniques.
- If the abend has resulted from a packed decimal multiply overflow:
  - Define the product field size such that it is large enough to contain the result of the maximum possible values of the multiplier and multiplicand fields.
  - Restructure the calculation:
    - Work with the smallest numbers first.
    - Rewrite expressions so that intermediate results do not get too large; for example:
      - a * (b + c) as (a * b) + (a * c).
      - a * (b − c) as (a * b) − (a * c).
  - See Table 2-1 for a comparison of relative field sizes.
  - If the offending calculation is embedded in a loop, the maximum number of iterations must be considered in determining the result field size.
- The actual contents of a suspect data set may be dumped or printed to check for invalid data. The utility programs to do this are described in 3.8, Dumping and Printing Data.
- Internal decimal (packed) format is explained in 5.4, Data Storage Formats.

0C7 Data exception: Data in a field are incompatible with the instruction referencing them.

Related System Messages: IBM537I, IHN210I, IHO210I

POSSIBLE CAUSES:

General:

- Packed (internal) decimal field contains invalid data:
  - Alphanumeric (EBCDIC) format.
  - Binary format.
  - Invalid sign nibble.
  - Garbage.
  - Instructions.
- Packed decimal fields in an arithmetic operation not aligned on rightmost byte.
- Too many significant (nonzero) high-order digits in a packed decimal multiplicand field due to:
  - Runaway loop containing add or multiply arithmetic, causing field to become too large.
  - Incorrect initialization.
  - Failure to clear after completion of computation.
  - Field size insufficient for calculation required.
- Invalid index or subscript due to incorrect initialization or runaway program loop:
  - Value is outside intended range, causing packed decimal or CVB instruction to reference nonpacked data.
  - Literal pool literal written over.
- Attempt to access a buffer while the data set is not open:
  - Before it is opened.
  - After it is closed.
- Attempt to close a file twice in succession (no intervening open).
- Attempt to write to a closed file.
- Data structure (DELCARE, DS, DC, FD, 01, Format, DS, copy member, etc.) is incorrect or does not correspond to the physical record it defines:
  - Field definition is wrong format (e.g., zoned instead of packed).
  - Wrong data structure used:
    - Name misspelled.
    - Incorrect version.
    - Structure changed, but program was not recompiled or relinked.
  - Filler or slack bytes missing.
- Invalid data were obtained:
  - An input DASD data set was allocated [via JCL, DISP=(NEW,CATLG)] but never opened in a previous job or step. The problem program opened and read this data set, but all records are garbage (i.e., whatever was previously written on the first track of the new allocation).
  - The problem program or a previous job or step incorrectly created a field.
  - Operator, data entry, or keypunch error:
    - Improper or missing initialization (spaces instead of zeros).
    - Numeric field padded with leading spaces instead of zeros.

- Failure to reinitialize a field(s). Common examples are application programs run under IMS DC or CICS and dynamically called subroutines. In each of these situations the module is reloaded frequently, possibly every time it is invoked. Upon entry into the module, the contents of main storage data fields are unpredictable unless explicitly initialized or refreshed.
- See 3.2, 0Cx Abend Diagnostics.

JCL Related:

DD statement:

- Wrong data set selected for input:
  - DSNAME or VOLUME specification misspelled or incorrect.
  - Generation number of a GDG incorrect.
- DCB subparameter OPTCD=Q was not specified for an ASCII input tape data set. Conversion to EBCDIC was not performed.
- See 3.3, Common JCL Errors.

Assembly Programs:

- The sign or digit code of an operand in a decimal, edit, or CVB instruction is incorrect.
- Base register contains an incorrect address.
- Packed operands not aligned on rightmost byte.
- An invalid zoned constant or data item was packed, resulting in an invalid packed field. A subsequent reference to this field failed.
- Insufficient high-order zeros in multiplicand field (first operand) of an MD instruction.
- See the following under 3.2, 0Cx Abend Diagnostics:
  - Table 3-2 for instructions that can cause an 0C7.
  - Diagnosing an Invalid Branch.

COBOL Programs:

- SELECT file-name ASSIGN TO device-organization-DDname specification is in error. The wrong data records have been read into the problem program due to a mismatch:
  - File-name misspelled or incorrect.
  - DDname misspelled or incorrect.
- Problem with definition of a data item(s):
  - Numeric PICTURE used for alphanumeric data.
  - USAGE clause or its default incorrect or omitted.
  - PICTURE of COMP data item too small.
  - An alphanumeric field is REDEFINEd as numeric, but the alignment or length of the numeric field is incorrect.
  - Incorrect initialization due to:
    - Missing VALUE clause.
    - Data given via VALUE are incorrect.
    - Wrong literal or field MOVEd.

  - Part or all of data structure (e.g., 01 level record description) does not agree with the actual record content:
    - REDEFINES object is incorrect or misspelled.
    - COPY member specified is incorrect or misspelled; or selects an out-of-date version of the record layout.
  - Subscript VALUE given as 0. A subscript of 0 is invalid.
- LINKAGE SECTION coding errors:
  - Parameters in wrong order.
  - Parameter added or omitted.
  - Invalid data definition (USAGE, PICTURE).
  - Inconsistent data definition between calling and called module.
  - Wrong parameter list name specified in COPY.
- LINKAGE SECTION header is incorrectly placed, inadvertently specified, or omitted:
  - If omitted in a called program, the program may be invoked but no data can be passed in or back.
  - If incorrectly placed or inadvertently specified in a calling program, addressability cannot be established for any data item following the LINKAGE SECTION header. Reference to such an item may result in a data exception. This problem may result from:
    - Copying a subroutine parameter list (with the LINKAGE SECTION header) into a calling program.
    - Converting a subroutine into a calling or mainline program.
    - Converting a mainline program into a subroutine.
- MOVE at group level was executed to a COMP or COMP-3 field. No data conversion was performed on the element level, resulting in invalid data.
- MOVE to group level item was executed using figurative constants ZERO(S) or LOW-VALUE(S). No data conversion was performed on the element level.
- A single-level occurs index was set to a multiple-level occurs index. No conversion was done.
- A numeric display data item contains nonnumeric data and is referenced by arithmetic or IF statement:
  - Runaway subscript or index caused by PERFORM loop.
  - Alpha data input incorrectly.
- Argument N used in GO TO DEPENDING ON N is not numeric.
- A packed decimal field is REDEFINEd as an alphanumeric field, allowing nonnumeric data to be moved in to it. Subsequent reference by a packed decimal operation results in an abend.

RELEVANT DUMP ITEMS:

- See Table 3-2 for operation disposition and ILC value.
- PSW contains the next instruction address. The PSW minus the ILC points to the abending instruction address.

- The fields referenced by the abending instruction may give a clue to the source of the invalid data. If the program performs arithmetic using zoned decimal fields (e.g., COBOL usage of display numeric), a PACK instruction must be used to convert the zoned decimal fields into packed decimal format before the arithmetic can be done. The PACK instruction will not cause an 0C7 even if the sending field is not in valid zoned decimal format. The PACK instruction simply rearranges the nibbles from the sending zoned decimal field. The following example shows how the digits and sign of a sending zoned decimal field containing −9876 would be PACKed into a receiving field.

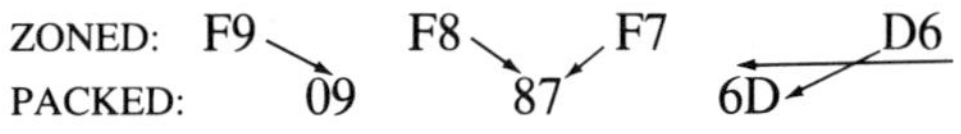

  Notice that the sign nibble switches position. Suppose, however, that the sending zoned decimal field contained all x40 (the "space" character).

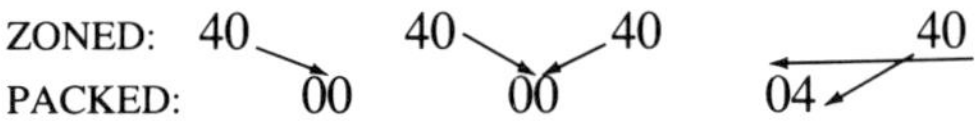

  The rearrangement follows the same rules. The last byte of the receiving packed field contains the last 2 nibbles of the sending field, switched in position.

  The switched rightmost byte and digit nibbles of the abending fields may then give a clue to the contents of the invalid sending field. Some common before and after patterns are:

After PACK	*Before PACK*
x04	x40 " " (space)
x06	x60 "—" (dash)
x18	x81 lowercase "a"
x1C	xC1 "A"
x2C	xC2 "B"
⋮	⋮
x9E	xE9 "Z"
x99	x99 lowercase "r"
xB5	x5B "$"

  The reversal of the rightmost alphanumeric nibbles does not always yield an invalid rightmost internal decimal byte. x2C (an unpacked "B") is interpreted as +2. All EBCDIC uppercase-letter codes may be packed into a valid rightmost internal decimal byte.

- The following registers may point to the I/O control blocks of the last accessed data set if the interrupt occurred shortly after an I/O operation completed.
  - R1 or R2 may point to the DCB. The DCB plus x28 contains the 2-byte TIOT offset. The DDname of this DCB is given in the TIOT at this offset.

- R4 may point to the O/C/EOV work area. See 3.4, Analysis of the O/C/EOV Work Area.

– The last record written to an output QSAM data set is at the address for the next record less LRECL (last = next – LRECL). Both fields are found in the DCB:
  - + x4C 4-byte address of the next record to be written or the last read (DCBRECAD).
  - + x52 2-byte LRECL (DCBLRECL).

  If the last record read or written was also the last in a block, the buffer may have been overlaid with a new data block. In this case, the last record cannot be located by the method outlined above. You may be able to find evidence of it in other program work areas, counters, saved keys, and so on. See *Data Management Services* for more information about non-VSAM buffering.

– The last record read or written to a VSAM cluster may be found by the method outlined in 3.5, Locating VSAM Data Records.

WHAT TO DO:

– Follow the steps outlined in 1.3, General Debugging Procedure, and 5.2, Basic Techniques.

– The actual contents of a suspect data set may be dumped or printed to check for invalid data. The utility programs to do this are described in 3.8, Dumping and Printing Data.

– Internal (packed) decimal and binary formats are explained in 5.4, Data Storage Formats.

0C8 Fixed-point overflow exception: The receiving field of a signed binary integer arithmetic operation was too small.

Related System Messages: IBM482I

POSSIBLE CAUSES:

General:

– The high-order (leftmost) bit of a fullword or halfword binary field has been lost. This may be due to:
  - A signed fullword arithmetic operation whose result was greater than 2^{31} (2,147,483,648).
  - A signed halfword arithmetic operation whose result was greater than 2^{15} (32,767):
    - •• A halfword field may have been inadvertently specified.
  - A sign change or bit shift operation without sufficient preediting.

– Addend or multiplier has become very large due to:

- Runaway program loop.
- Incorrect initialization.
- Incorrect numeric analytic design.
- Invalid input data.

– See 3.2, 0Cx Abend Diagnostics.

COBOL Programs:

– The assumed decimal point symbol "V" is misplaced or omitted. The actual value of a data item is too large or too small.
– ON SIZE ERROR not specified for arithmetic statement using COMP fields.
– COMP specification results in halfword—PIC 9(1) to PIC 9(4)—when fullword is needed—PIC 9(5) to PIC 9(9).

Assembly Programs:

– Attempt to mix unsigned and signed binary operations (e.g., AL and A).
– Logic for radix-point scaling of arithmetic operations on FS or HS type constant is incorrect, allowing an addend or multiplier to become too large.
– See Table 3-2 for instructions that can cause an 0C8 abend.

RELEVANT DUMP ITEMS:

– See Table 3-2 for operation disposition and ILC value.
– PSW instruction address less ILC points to the abending instruction.
– The result field is obtained by completing the operation and ignoring the overflow.

WHAT TO DO:

– Follow the steps outlined in 1.3, General Debugging Procedure, and 5.2, Basic Techniques.
– This interrupt may be disabled. See 3.2, 0Cx Abend Diagnostics, Controlling Interrupts.
– Substitute decimal or floating-point fields for computations with large results.
– The actual contents of a suspect data set may be dumped or printed to check for invalid data. The utility programs to do this are described in 3.8, Dumping and Printing Data.
– Binary format is explained in 5.4, Data Storage Formats.

0C9 Fixed-point divide exception: Division by zero, quotient, or conversion overflow has occurred in binary integer instruction.

Related System Messages: IBM500I, IHN210I

POSSIBLE CAUSES:

General:

- Division of a binary integer by zero was attempted.
- The quotient of a division of signed binary integers exceeds 2^{31} (2,147,483,648).
- Divisor has become zero or is very small relative to dividend due to:
  - Runaway program loop.
  - Incorrect initialization.
  - Incorrect numeric analytic design.
  - Invalid input data.
- An integer divisor field is loaded from fields with fractional parts. The absolute value of the sending field is less than 1.0 (i.e., it contains only a fractional value). When moved to the divisor, the fractional part of the field is truncated, resulting in a zero divisor.
- The divisor field contained an absolute value less than 0.5 and was rounded to zero prior to division.
- See 3.2, 0Cx Abend Diagnostics.

Assembly Programs:

- Attempt to mix usage of unsigned and signed binary fields.
- Logic for radix-point scaling of arithmetic operations of FS or HS type fields is incorrect, causing divisor to become too small or dividend too large.
- The result of a CVB (CONVERT TO BINARY, x4F) instruction is greater than 2^{31} (2,147,483,648).
- See Table 3-2 for a list of instructions that can cause an 0C9.

COBOL Programs:

- An assumed decimal point symbol "V" is misplaced or omitted. The actual value of a data item is too large or too small.
- Attempt to MOVE a COMP-3 field containing a number greater than 2^{31} to a COMP field.
- ON SIZE ERROR not specified for arithmetic statements using COMP fields.

RELEVANT DUMP ITEMS:

- See Table 3-2 for operation disposition and ILC value.
- PSW instruction address less ILC points to abending instruction.
- If a divide instruction caused the exception, the operation is suppressed.
- If a CONVERT TO BINARY (CVB) instruction caused the exception, the operation is completed and the overflow bits are lost.

WHAT TO DO:

- Follow the steps outlined in 1.3, General Debugging Procedure, and 5.2, Basic Techniques.
- Substitute decimal or floating-point fields for computations with very large results.
- Attempt prescaling. Divide the dividend by a constant before the division, then multiply the quotient afterward by this constant.
- The actual contents of a suspect data set may be dumped or printed to check for invalid data. The utility programs to do this are described in 3.8, Dumping and Printing Data.
- Binary format is explained in 5.4, Data Storage Formats.

0CA Decimal overflow exception: The result of a decimal instruction is too large for the receiving field.

Related System Messages: IBM482I

POSSIBLE CAUSES:

General:

- Packed decimal addend, multiplier, divisor, or subtrahend too large or too small due to:
  - Runaway program loop.
  - Incorrect initialization.
  - Incorrect numeric analytic design.
  - Invalid input data.
- Result field specified is too small.
- See 3.2, 0Cx Abend Diagnostics.

Assembly Programs:

- Logic for decimal-point scaling of arithmetic operations on P- or PL-type fields is incorrect.
- P or PL field length definition is incorrect.
- See Table 3-2 for a list of instructions that can cause an 0CA.

COBOL Programs:

- ON SIZE ERROR not specified for arithmetic statement using COMP-3 data items.
- PICTURE specification for COMP-3 data item is:

- Too large or too small.
- Omits or contains a misplaced assumed decimal point symbol "V." The actual value of a data item is too large or too small.

RELEVANT DUMP ITEMS:

- See Table 3-2 for operation disposition and ILC value.
- PSW instruction address less ILC points to abending instruction.
- The operation is completed with the overflow digit nibbles being lost.

WHAT TO DO:

- Follow the steps outlined in 1.3, General Debugging Procedure, and 5.2, Basic Techniques.
- This interrupt may be disabled. See 3.2, 0Cx Abend Diagnostics, Controlling Interrupts.
- Increase the field size to accommodate the magnitude of the data items to be processed. The maximum representable value of an internal (packed) decimal field varies considerably depending on the length of the field and the implicit decimal point (decimal scaling). Integer values from 1 to 15 decimal digits long may be represented. Specifying a decimal point will increase precision and decrease maximum magnitude by an equal number of digits. Table 2-1 gives some examples of this relationship for COBOL, assembly language, and PL/I. Typically, an 0CA abend may be corrected by increasing the size of the fields involved, or restructuring the calculation. For example, a column total for a report is accumulated in a packed field that has the same definition (number of integer and fraction digits) as the detail item to be totaled. After adding two or more large-valued detail items, the accumulator overflows. A larger accumulator would solve this problem. Similar situations may occur with subtraction. The following rules of thumb may be used to estimate the field size need:

Table 2-1
Internal (Packed) Decimal Field Sizes

		Field Definition		
Maximum Representable Value	*Length (bytes)*	*COBOL (COMP-3)*	*Assembly*	*PL/I*
± 9.0	1	S9(1)	PL1	FIXED (1,0)
± 0.9	1	SV9(1)	PL1	FIXED (1,1)
±999.0	2	S9(3)	PL2	FIXED (3,0)
± 9.99	2	S9(1)V99	PL2	FIXED (3,2)
±999,999,999,999,999.0	8	S9(15)	PL16	FIXED (15,0)
±999,999,999.999999	8	S9(9)V9(5)	PL16	FIXED (15,6)

- For addition or subtraction, define the sum or difference field such that it is large enough to contain at least:
  - Ten times the maximum possible value of a detail item (minuend, subtrahend, or addend) to be processed.
  - The average value of the detail items (minuend, subtrahend, or addend) times the maximum possible number of detail items to be processed. If the offending calculation is embedded in a loop, the maximum number of iterations must also be considered in determining the result field size.
- The actual contents of a suspect data set may be dumped or printed to check for invalid data. The utility programs to do this are described in 3.8, Dumping and Printing Data.
- Internal decimal (packed) format is explained in 5.4, Data Storage Formats.

0CB Decimal divide exception: Division by zero or quotient overflow has occurred in decimal divide instruction.

Related System Messages: IBM500I

POSSIBLE CAUSES:

General:

- Division of internal (packed) decimal field by zero was attempted.
- Divisor has become zero or is very small relative to dividend due to:
  - Runaway program loop.
  - Incorrect initialization.
  - Incorrect numeric analytic design.
  - Invalid input data.
- An integer divisor field is loaded from fields with fractional parts. The absolute value of the sending field is less than 1.0 (i.e., it contains only a fractional value). When moved to the divisor, the fractional part of the field is truncated, resulting in a zero divisor.
- The divisor field contained an absolute value less than 0.5 and was rounded to zero prior to division.
- See 3.2, 0Cx Abend Diagnostics.

Assembly Programs:

- Logic for decimal point scaling is incorrect.
- P or PL definition is too large or too small.
- See Table 3-2 for instructions that can cause an 0CB.

COBOL Programs:

- PICTURE specification for a COMP-3 data item:
  - Is too large or too small.
  - Omits or contains a misplaced assumed decimal point symbol "V." The actual value of a data item is too large or too small.
- ON SIZE ERROR not specified for arithmetic statement using COMP-3 data items.
- A very large number was multiplied by or added to another very large number.

RELEVANT DUMP ITEMS:

- PSW instruction address less ILC points to the abending instruction.
- The operation is suppressed. See Table 3-2.

WHAT TO DO:

- Follow the steps outlined in 1.3, General Debugging Procedure, and 5.2, Basic Techniques.
- If the abend has resulted from a division overflow:
  - Define the quotient field such that it is large enough to contain at least the maximum possible dividend value divided by the minimum possible divisor value. See Table 2-1 for a comparison of relative field sizes.
  - Restructure the calculation:
    - Work with the smallest numbers first.
    - Rewrite the expressions so that intermediate results do not get too large or too small; for example:
      - (a + b)/c as (a/c) + (b/c).
      - (a − b)/d as (a/c) − (b/c).
- The actual contents of a suspect data set may be dumped or printed to check for invalid data. The utility programs to do this are described in 3.8, Dumping and Printing Data.
- Internal decimal (packed) format is explained in 5.4, Data Storage Formats.

0CC Exponent overflow exception: A floating-point arithmetic operation has resulted in an exponent that is too large.

Related System Messages: IBM451I, IHN210I, IHO210I

POSSIBLE CAUSES:

General:

- A floating-point arithmetic operation has resulted in (1) a nonzero fraction and (2) an exponent too large for representation by the excess-64 convention. The maximum allowable is 1.0×16^{63} (roughly 7.2×10^{75}). This may be due to:

  - Runaway program loop.
  - Incorrect initialization.
  - Incorrect numeric analytic design.
  - Invalid input data.
- A very large number was multiplied by or added to another very large number.
- A floating-point constant or input value incorrectly specifies a decimal point or exponent value; for example, +1234E+50 instead of +0.1234E+5.
- A very large number was divided by a very small number.
- A negative number greater than the difference of a very large number and the upper limit of the excess-64 convention was subtracted from the very large number.
- See 3.2, 0Cx Abend Diagnostics.

Assembly Programs:

- D, E, or L type constant incorrectly defined.
- See Table 3-2 for instructions that can cause an 0CC.

COBOL Programs:

- ON SIZE ERROR not specified for statements using COMP-1 or COMP-2 data items.
- COMP-1 or COMP-2 usage specified when COMP or COMP-3 intended.
- PICTURE or VALUE specification for COMP-1 or COMP-2 items incorrect.

RELEVANT DUMP ITEMS:

- See Table 3-2 for operation disposition and ILC value.
- PSW less ILC points to abending instruction.
- The operation is completed by subtracting 128 from the overflow exponent. For example:

$$1.0 \times 16^{63} * 1.0 \times 16^{20} = 1.0 \times 16^{83}$$

  16^{83} cannot be represented, so an 0CC exception occurs. 128 is subtracted from the overflow exponent, (83) making the result 1.0×16^{-45}. The sign and fraction of the result are not altered.

WHAT TO DO:

- Follow the steps outlined in 1.3, General Debugging Procedure, and 5.2, Basic Techniques.
- Implement some form of downward scaling. For example, predivide by some large constant prior to the abending calculation and then scale up afterward by multiplying by the same constant.

- The actual contents of a suspect data set may be dumped or printed to check for invalid data. The utility programs to do this are described in 3.8, Dumping and Printing Data.
- Floating-point format is explained in 5.4, Data Storage Formats.

0CD Exponent underflow exception: A floating-point point arithmetic operation has resulted in an exponent that is too small.

Related System Messages: IBM321I, IHN210I, IHO210I

POSSIBLE CAUSES:

General:

- A floating-point arithmetic operation has resulted in (1) a nonzero fraction and (2) an exponent too small to be represented by the excess-64 convention. The minimum allowable is 1.0×16^{-64} (roughly 5.4×10^{-79}). This may be due to:
  - Runaway program loop.
  - Incorrect initialization.
  - Incorrect numeric analytic design.
  - Invalid input data.
- A very small number was divided by a very large number.
- A very small number was multiplied by a very small number.
- A number greater than the difference of a very small number and the lower floating-point limit was subtracted from this very small number.
- A negative number greater than the difference of a very small number and the lower limit was added to this very small number.
- A floating-point constant or input value incorrectly specifies a decimal point or exponent value; for example, +.1234E-50 instead of +12.34E-5.
- See 3.2, 0Cx Abend Diagnostics.

Assembly Programs:

- D, E, or L type constant incorrectly defined.
- See Table 3-2 for instructions that can cause an 0CD.

COBOL Programs:

- Inadvertent specification of COMP-1, COMP-2.
- ON SIZE ERROR not specified for arithmetic statements using COMP-1 or COMP-2 data items.
- PICTURE or VALUE specification for COMP-1 or COMP-2 is incorrect.

RELEVANT DUMP ITEMS:

- See Table 3-2 for operation disposition and ILC value.
- PSW less ILC points to the abending instruction.
- The operation is completed. The disposition of the operand contents depend on the PSW program mask bit for exponent underflow (EC mode PSW bit 22)
  - If the interrupt is enabled (PSW bit 22 = 1), the operation is completed by adding 128 to the underflow exponent; for example:

    $$1.0 \times 16^{-64} * 1.0 \times 16.^{-10} = 1.0 \times 16^{-74}$$

    Since 16^{-74} cannot be represented, an 0CD exception occurs. 128 is added to the underflow exponent $[128 + (-74) = 54]$, making the result 1.0×16^{54}. The sign and the fraction are not altered.
  - If the interrupt is disabled (PSW bit 22 is 0), the operation is completed by setting both the exponent and the fraction to zero.

WHAT TO DO:

- Follow the steps outlined in 1.3, General Debugging Procedure, and 5.2, Basic Techniques.
- This interrupt may be disabled. See 3.2, 0Cx Abend Diagnostics, Controlling Interrupts.
- Implement some form of upward scaling. For example, premultiply by some large constant prior to the abending calculation and scale down afterward.
- Consider restructuring calculations:
  - Work with the smallest numbers first.
  - Do not subtract nearly equal numbers.
  - Rewrite expressions, so that intermediate results do not get too large; for example:
    - a*(b − c) as (a*b) − (a*c).
    - (a − b)/c as (a/c) − (b/c).
- The actual contents of a suspect data set may be dumped or printed to check for invalid data. The utility programs to do this are described in 3.8, Dumping and Printing Data.
- Floating-point format is explained in 5.4, Data Storage Formats.

0CE Significance exception: A floating-point arithmetic operation has resulted in a meaningless number—a fractional base of zero raised to some nonzero exponent.

Related System Messages: None

POSSIBLE CAUSES:

General:

- A floating-point add, subtract, multiply, or divide operation has yielded a number that has binary zeros in the fractional field and a value greater or less than zero (x64) in the exponent field. This may be due to:
  - Incorrect initialization.
  - Invalid input data.
  - Incorrect numeric analytic design.
  - Runaway program loop.
- A number was added to or subtracted from itself. Since the resultant fraction is computed in an intermediate step, a zero fraction resulted while the exponent was still nonzero.
- See 3.2, 0Cx Abend Diagnostics.

Assembly Programs:

- D, E, or L type constant incorrectly specified.
- See Table 3-2 for instructions that can cause an 0CE.

COBOL Programs:

- Inadvertent specification of COMP-1, COMP-2.
- ON SIZE ERROR not specified for arithmetic statements using COMP-1 or COMP-2 data items.
- PICTURE or value specification for COMP-1 or COMP-2 data items is incorrect.

RELEVANT DUMP ITEMS:

- See Table 3-2 for operation disposition and ILC value.
- PSW instruction address less ILC points to abending instruction.
- The operation is completed with no alteration of the exponent or sign unless the EC mode PSW mask bit 23 is on. In this case the result is made a "true zero."

WHAT TO DO:

- Follow the steps outlined in 1.3, General Debugging Procedure, and 5.2, Basic Techniques.
- The actual contents of a suspect data set may be dumped or printed to check for invalid data. The utility programs to do this are described in 3.8, Dumping and Printing Data.
- Floating-point format is explained in 5.4, Data Storage Formats.

0CF Floating-point divide exception: Division by zero attempted in a floating-point instruction.

Related System Messages: IHN210I, IHO210I

POSSIBLE CAUSES:

General:

- A floating-point divisor had a zero fraction. This may be due to:
  - Runaway program loop.
  - Incorrect initialization.
  - Incorrect numeric analytic design.
  - Invalid input data.
- A divisor field defined as integer is loaded from fields with fractional parts. The absolute value of the sending field is less than 1.0 (i.e., it contains only a fractional value). When moved to the divisor, the fractional part of the field is truncated, resulting in a zero divisor.
- The divisor field contained an absolute value less than 0.5 and was rounded to zero prior to division.
- See 3.2, 0Cx Abend Diagnostics.

Assembly Programs:

- D, E, or L type constant incorrectly specified.
- See Table 3-2 for instructions that can cause a 0CF.

COBOL Programs:

- Inadvertent specification of COMP-1, COMP-2.
- ON SIZE ERROR not specified for arithmetic statements using COMP-1 or COMP-2 data items.
- PICTURE or VALUE specification for COMP-1 or COMP-2 data items is incorrect.

RELEVANT DUMP ITEMS:

- See Table 3-2 for operation disposition and ILC value.
- PSW instruction address less ILC points to abending instruction.
- Operation is always suppressed.

WHAT TO DO:

- Follow the steps outlined in 1.3, General Debugging Procedure, and 5.2, Basic Techniques.

- The actual contents of a suspect data set may be dumped or printed to check for invalid data. The utility programs to do this are described in 3.8, Dumping and Printing Data.
- Floating-point format is explained in 5.4, Data Storage Formats.

---

102 Invalid ECB address found during execution of POST macro.

Related System Messages: None
SVC 2 POST.

POSSIBLE CAUSES:

General:

- Invalid ECB (Event Control Block) address:
  - Address incorrectly specified.
  - Address overlaid or incorrectly computed.
- Program issuing POST does not have storage protection key required to update the ECB.
- Incorrect usage of ECB given intended data set access.

RELEVANT DUMP ITEMS:

- The address of the next problem program instruction may be found at:
  - The PSW field of the problem program's PRB under ACTIVE RBS. This RB is usually the first printed. The FL-CDE of the problem program's PRB will point to a CDE entry that has the problem program's name printed in NM.
  - The RET field of the last SA under SAVE AREA TRACE.
- If the problem program issued the POST, the ECB address will be in R1 of ABEND's SVRB (ABEND's SVRB can be identified by an x0D in the low-order byte of the WC-L-IC field of the RBs in the ACTIVE RB list).
- If the I/O interrupt handler issued the POST, the ECB is in the IOB associated with the event. R2 may point to the associated DCB.

WHAT TO DO:

- Follow the steps outlined in 1.3, General Debugging Procedure, and 5.2, Basic Techniques.

---

106 Noncorrectable I/O error occurred while placing a module in virtual storage for execution.

Related System Messages: IEA703I, IEA000I

SVC 6 LINK
7 XCTL
8 LOAD
42 ATTACH

POSSIBLE CAUSES:

General:

- I/O error or program check occurred in program management routines while attempting to begin execution of a problem program. Message IEA000I may accompany an I/O error.
- Incorrect LINK or LOAD parameters:
  - SIZE specifies insufficient virtual storage. Storage for LOAD's buffer and tables and the problem program load module is given by this parameter.
  - NAME misspelled or incorrect.
- SYSLMOD data set (loader input/output) was unusable:
  - Simultaneous updates resulted in the loss or alteration of a member of the directory.
  - A bad track has developed.

JCL Related:

JOB or EXEC statement:

- REGION parameter:
  - Specifies incorrect or insufficient quantity of virtual storage.
  - Overrides larger REGION request for a step, specified via an EXEC statement.

DD statement:

- JOBLIB or STEPLIB DSNAME specification incorrect or misspelled.

RELEVANT DUMP ITEMS:

- The offending module's member name and its DASD address may be located as follows:
  - Locate the ABEND SVRB. It can be identified by an x0D in the low-order byte of the WC-L-IC field of the RBs on the ACTIVE RB list.
  - The ABEND SVRB + x74 points to the fetch work area (FWA) used by program management routines. R6 of REGS AT ENTRY TO ABEND may also point to the FWA. The FWA is contained in subpool 253. However, depending on when the abend was issued by program management, the FWA may have been FREEMAINed. If so, it will not be listed in the dump.

  - FWA + x400 points to the ECB for the offending load library data set. If the first byte of the ECB is not x00 or x7F, a channel error has occurred. A detailed explanation of ECB bit settings is given in 4.2, Dump Components, under the IOB.
  - FWA + x528 points to the offending data set's IOSB. IOSB bit flags may provide more data about a hardware I/O error.
- R12 may point to the BLDL area. Each BLDL entry will contain the member name and extent address for the offending load library. The entries are formatted as follows:
  - Member name, 8 bytes.
  - Starting track address, 3 bytes, binary format as TTR where:

TT = relative track address (halfword)
R = relative block address (1 byte, binary format)

- If a JOBLIB DD statement was specified, the address of its DCB is in the TCB field labeled JLB (TCBJLB, TCB + x28). If not specified, this field will contain zeros. If the JES log is not available, the data set name may be found by examining the O/C/EOV work area. See 3.4, Analysis of the O/C/EOV Work Area.
- See also SCC 806.
- Message IEA703I may indicate the offending module name. R15 contains a return code documented in *System Messages* under this message. Briefly:
  - 0B Program check or loop in FETCH.
  - 0C GETMAIN failed; insufficient virtual storage available for load module plus buffers and table.
  - 0D Invalid record type in load module.
  - 0E Invalid relocation address in load module.
  - 0F "Hard" I/O error. See above to locate bad track address.

  This return code is also contained in R15 of the ABEND SVRB.
- If an I/O error has occurred, message IEA000I may have been issued. It may give the device address and I/O status flags pertinent to the error. Further explanation may be found in *System Messages* under this message.

WHAT TO DO:

- Follow the steps outlined in 1.3, General Debugging Procedure, and 5.2, Basic Techniques.
- Recompile and link the problem program. If an I/O error has occurred, specify a different device, volume, or load library. Resubmit the job for execution.
- Recreate the entire load library PDS. Resubmit the job for execution.
- See 3.8, Dumping and Printing Data, Listing Load Module Data.

113 Type J OPEN error.

Related System Messages: IEC142I
SVC 19 OPEN

POSSIBLE CAUSES:

General:

- Uncorrectable I/O error on read or write of JFCB (DD statement parameters) during OPEN.
- Incorrect or missing JFCB exit specified in DCBEXLST.
- JFCB extension block could not be found.

RELEVANT DUMP ITEMS:

- The address of the next problem program instruction may be found in the PSW field of the problem program's PRB under ACTIVE RBS. This RB is usually the first printed. The FL-CDE of this PRB will point to a CDE entry that has the problem program's name printed in NM. To verify that this address points to the next instruction, check the 2 bytes immediately preceding it. They should contain x0A13—the object code for the OPEN SVC.
- R2 points to the offending DCB.
  - If the DCB was open, it will be formatted in the control block section of the dump and have a DEB and IOBs associated with it.
    - The 2-byte TIOT offset is at x28 into the DCB.
    - The DDname of this DCB is given in the TIOT at this offset.
- DCB + x1C points to the IOB prefix. IOB fields will indicate an I/O error if it has occurred. The IOB prefix is 16 bytes long, so the IOB proper begins at prefix address plus x10. Fields of interest are:
  - IOB + 0, IOBFLAG1: If bit 5 is on (x04), a permanent I/O error has occurred. System message IEA000I will probably have been issued.
  - IOB + 4, ECBCC: ECB completion code. First byte of the 4-byte ECB. If this byte is not x00 or x7F, a channel error has occurred.
  - IOB + xC, second word of the CSW: Contains the channel status bits. Bits 36 and 37 should be on if an I/O operation has been completed successfully.
  - Further explanation of the ECB and CSW is given in 4.2, Dump Components, Input-Output Block.
- If the DCB was not opened or has been closed, it will not be formatted in the control block section, but will be found in the main storage dump. The DEB will contain the DCB address. The 8-byte DDname will be at x28 into the DCB.
- R4 points to the OPEN/CLOSE/EOV work area for the offending data set. It contains:
  - The data set label at R4 + 0.

  - The JFCB (DD statement parameters) at R4 + x64. Examination of this work area will indicate conflicting or incorrectly specified data set parameters. 3.4, Analysis of the O/C/EOV Work Area, provides a detailed description of its fields.
- Message IEC142I may indicate the offending DDname, device, volume serial number, and data set name. R15 contains a return code documented in *System Messages* under this message. Briefly:
  - 08 JF=CB extension block missing (QSAM data set).
  - 0C JF=CB exit not specified for TYPE-J OPEN.
  - 18 JF=CB extension block missing (ISAM or BDAM data set).

WHAT TO DO:

- Follow the steps outlined in 1.3, General Debugging Procedure, and 5.2, Basic Techniques.
- If an I/O error has occurred, specify a different device, volume, or both and rerun the job.
- For information on how to dump data set labels, see 3.8, Dumping and Printing Data.

---

122 Job canceled and dump requested by operator.

Related System Messages: None
SVC 34 MGCR/QEDIT

POSSIBLE CAUSES:

General:

- The problem program:
  - Was in a loop, evidenced by an abnormal quantity or content of output.
  - Was deadlocked or in a wait state.
  - Requested unavailable or unauthorized resources.
  - Violated installation procedures.
  - "Owned" resources required by a higher-priority job and was canceled to make them available.
- The operator erred.
- See also SCC 322.

JCL Related:

DD statement:

- DISP=OLD or MOD was specified instead of DISP=SHR:
  - By another job for a data set needed by the problem program.
  - By the problem program for a data set needed by another job(s).

- Too many devices were requested to mount sequentially processed data sets. Specifying UNIT parameters AFF or DEFER may correct this problem.

RELEVANT DUMP ITEMS:

- If the PSW points to an instruction within the problem program, check for a possible loop.
- If the PSW is outside the problem program, a system routine was active when the cancel command was processed. This is highly likely for an I/O bound application.
- Evidence of a loop or the progress of the program may be found by examining data set buffers. For QSAM data sets, R2 may point to the DCB of the last data set accessed. The last record written to an output QSAM data set is at the address for the next record less LRECL (last = next − LRECL). Both fields are found in the DCB:
  - + x4C 4-byte address of the next record to be written or the last read (DCBRECAD).
  - + X52 2-byte LRECL (DCBLRECL).

  If the last record read or written was also the last in a block, the buffer may have been overlaid with a new data block. In this case, the last record cannot be located by the method outlined above. You may be able to find evidence of it in other program work areas, counters, saved keys, and so on. See *Data Management Services* for more information about non-VSAM buffering.
- See 3.5, Locating VSAM Data Records, to conduct a similar analysis for VSAM data sets.
- Determine the address of problem program counters, switches, or other items that would indicate the progress of the program. Find these fields in the dump and try to interpret their meaning. The techniques to locate and interpret problem program data fields in main storage are given in Chapter 5, Source Code Debugging.

WHAT TO DO:

- Follow the steps outlined in 1.3, General Debugging Procedure, and 5.2, Basic Techniques.
- Check SYSMSG or the JES log for operator comments. Ask the operator why the job was canceled. Usually, a resubmit will correct this abend.

---

137 I/O error for a tape data set while positioning to process a standard header or trailer label.

Related System Messages: IEC022I

SVC 55 EOV

POSSIBLE CAUSES:

General:

- A tape device I/O error occurred while:
  - Reading a standard header or trailer label.
  - Writing an EOV label or tapemark.
  - Positioning the volume for processing:
    - End of volume.
    - Standard labels.
    - First data record.
- Device malfunction or physical damage to tape (e.g., a crimp).
- Wrong tape mounted.
- No tape marks on this volume.
- Incorrect label format.
- No trailer labels for an input data set.
- The *n*th volume of a multivolume output data set has inconsistent label data or has unexpired data sets.
- Attempt to use a volume not initialized by IEHINITT utility.

JCL Related:

DD statement:

- DSNAME specification error:
  - Data set name incorrect or misspelled.
  - Wrong generation of a GDG specified.
- VOLUME specifies incorrect serial number.
- Label type subparameter, *T* of LABEL=(,*T*) does not match actual label format.

RELEVANT DUMP ITEMS:

- The address of the next problem program instruction may be found at the RET field of the last SA under SAVE AREA TRACE.
- R2 points to the offending DCB:
  - The 2-byte TIOT offset is located at + x28 into the DCB.
  - The DDname of the DCB is given in the TIOT at this offset.
  - If this DCB has been CLOSEd, it will not be formatted in the control block section of the dump, but should be the main storage listing. The DEB will contain the DCB address.
- The IOB prefix pointer should be at x1C into the DCB. IOB fields may indicate if a hardware-related I/O error has occurred. The IOB prefix is 16 bytes long, so the IOB proper begins at the prefix address plus x10. Fields of interest are:

- IOB + 0, IOBFLAG1: If bit 5 is on (x04), a permanent I/O error has occurred. System message IEA0001 will probably have been issued.
- IOB + 4, ECBCC: ECB completion code. First byte of the 4-byte ECB. If this byte is not x00 or x7F, a channel error has occurred.
- IOB + xC, second word of the CSW: Contains the channel status bits. Bits 36 and 37 should be on if an I/O operation has completed successfully.

– Further explanation of the ECB and CSW is given in 4.2, Dump Components, Input-Output Block.

- If the ECB completion code is x4B, an unexpected load point was encountered.

– Message IEC022I may indicate the offending DDname, device, volume serial number, and data set name. R15 contains a return code documented in *System Messages* under this message. Briefly:

- 04 I/O error writing EOV or tapemark.
- 08 I/O error positioning tape.
- 0C I/O error reading trailer label.
- 10 I/O error positioning tape to end of data set.
- 14 I/O error reading header label.
- 18 I/O error while positioning to first record.
- 1C Invalid trailer label at EOV.
- 20 Invalid header label at EOV.
- 24 Attempt to write on a volume with an unexpired data set.
- 28 Operator rejected rewrite of a volume label.
- 2C Invalid ASCII label.
- 30 Invalid label format.

WHAT TO DO:

– Follow the steps outlined in 1.3, General Debugging Procedure, and 5.2, Basic Techniques.

– If an I/O error has occurred, specify a different device, volume, or both and rerun the job.

– By using IEBPTPCH and BLP as explained in 3.8 under dumping labels, the data portion of a reel with an invalid label may be copied to another data set.

– For information on how to dump tape labels, see 3.8, Dumping and Printing Data.

---

213 DASD open error: Data set not found.

Related System Messages: IEC143I

SVC 19 OPEN

POSSIBLE CAUSES:

General:

- Attempted to open a data set for input, but the data set cannot be found.
- Data set does not exist because it:
  - Was never created.
  - Was inadvertently deleted.
  - Expired and was deleted.
  - Was incorrectly created.
- Space not allocated for an output data set.
- Data set to be passed from a previous job step was not created.
- The data set label (DSCB):
  - Was not found.
  - Could not be read for OLD, MOD, or SHR data set.
  - Was unavailable due to uncorrectable I/O error during read or write of DSCB.
- A non-VSAM open for input was issued against a VSAM data set.
- In a multi-CPU installation, the data set may not be accessible to all CPUs.
- SYSRES password data set could not be found during open of password protection data set.

JCL Related:

DD statement:

- DDname misspelled.
- DSNAME specification misspelled or incorrect:
  - A temporary (&&dsname) or refer-back data set was not created because a previous job or step failed or did not execute due to condition codes.
  - DD DUMMY or DSNAME=NULLFILE specified in a previous job or step. No data set was created.
  - Generation data group (GDG) data set was specified by its fully qualified name (e.g., A.B.G000V0012), instead of relative generation. The data set specified no longer exists or has not been created.
  - Specifies a data set that was inadvertently deleted or has expired.
  - Specifies a data set that was cataloged but never created (a null data set).
  - Specifies a data set that was scratched but not uncataloged. DISP=DELETE, UNIT, and VOL=SER were specified in a previous job or step for this data set, causing it to be deleted but not uncataloged.
  - A data set was inadvertently created as temporary and automatically deleted when the creating job or step ended:
    - &&dsname was incorrectly specified.
    - DSNAME parameter was omitted and the default of a temporary data set was taken.

- DISP parameter specification was incorrect in a previous job or step. The data set does not exist:
  - DISP was omitted for an output data set. The normal termination default of delete was taken at end of step.
  - DISP=(NEW,PASS) was specified for an output data set. KEEP was not specified in a subsequent step. The normal termination default of delete was taken at end of job.
  - The status subparameter specified:
    - OLD or SHR for an output data set.
    - MOD instead of NEW, when no data set existed, so no space was allocated.
    - NEW in conjunction with unit affinity (e.g., UNIT=AFF=DDname). Deferred mount was assumed and no space was allocated.
  - The normal or abnormal termination subparameters incorrectly specified DELETE or UNCATLG.
- VOLUME specifies incorrect volume via SER.
- JOBCAT or STEPCAT incorrect or omitted.

COBOL Programs:

- SELECT file-name ASSIGN TO device-organization-DDname specification is in error:
  - File-name misspelled or incorrect.
  - DDname misspelled or incorrect.
  - Organization omitted or incorrect:
    - Must be AS-DDname for VSAM ESDS.
    - Must be IS-DDname for ISAM.

RELEVANT DUMP ITEMS:

- The address of the next problem program instruction may be found in the PSW field of the problem program's PRB under ACTIVE RBS. This RB is usually the first printed. The FL-CDE of this PRB will point to a CDE entry that has the problem program's name printed in NM. To verify that this address points to the next instruction, check the 2 bytes immediately preceding it. They should contain x0A13—the object code for the OPEN SVC.
- R2 points to the offending DCB.
  - If the DCB was open, it will be formatted in the control block section of the dump and have a DEB and IOBs associated with it.
    - The 2-byte TIOT offset is at x28 into the DCB.
    - The DDname of the DCB is given in the TIOT at this offset.
  - If the DCB was not opened or has been closed, it will not be formatted in the control block section, but will be found in the main storage dump. The DEB will contain the DCB address. The 8-byte DDname will be at x28 into the DCB.

- The IOB prefix pointer should be at x1C into the DCB. IOB fields may indicate if a hardware-related I/O error has occurred. The IOB prefix is 16 bytes long, so the IOB proper begins at the prefix address plus x10. Fields of interest are:
  - IOB + 0, IOBFLAG1: If bit 5 is on (x04), a permanent I/O error has occurred. System message IEA000I will probably have been issued.
  - IOB + 4, ECBCC: ECB completion code. First byte of the 4-byte ECB. If this byte is not x00 or x7F, a channel error has occurred.
  - IOB + xC, second word of the CSW: Contains the channel status bits. Bits 36 and 37 should be on if an I/O operation has completed successfully.
- Further explanation of the ECB and CSW is given in 4.2, Dump Components, Input-Output Block.
- Message IEC143I may indicate the offending DDname, device, volume serial number, and data set name. R15 contains a hexadecimal return code documented in *System Messages* under this message. Briefly:
  - 04 A format 1 DSCB was not found or an I/O error occurred while reading it during OPEN. Attempt to open a VSAM data set with a non-VSAM open.
  - 08 Password data set not found during password check by OPEN.
  - 0C Same as 04, but for ISAM or BDAM data sets.
  - 18 I/O error occurred while rewriting format 1 DSCB.
  - 20 More than 16 extents exist.
  - 24 Split cylinder allocation not supported.
  - 28 127 users already active on SYSDA.
  - 2C Format 1 DSCB was not found and an error occurred in default error exit.

WHAT TO DO:

- Follow the steps outlined in 1.3, General Debugging Procedure, and 5.2, Basic Techniques.
- The IEFBR14 utility may be used to rectify catalog inconsistencies, by specifying appropriate DD statement parameters. IEFBR14 does nothing itself. It takes its name from the fact that its only action is to branch to register 14 (i.e., to terminate the step). However, all standard allocation/unallocation processing invoked via JCL is performed. The example below shows how to delete a data set "SOON.TOBE.GONE" and to catalog "NEW.DSNAME" using IEFBR14.

```
//CATSTEP  EXEC PGM=IEFBR14
//DELETEDD DD DSN=SOON.TOBE.GONE,DISP=(OLD,DELETE)
//CATLGDD  DD DSN=NEW.DSNAME,DISP=(NEW,CATLG)
```

- Recovery from a missing DSCB (R15=04) may be attempted, preventing the abend termination. The address of a recovery routine may be specified via the EXLST parameter of the DCB macro or placed in DCBEXLSA (DCB + x25). *Data Management Services* gives a detailed explanation of this feature.
- For information on how to dump DASD labels, see 3.8, Dumping and Printing Data.

214 I/O error on close of a tape data set.

Related System Messages: IEC210I
SVC 20 CLOSE

POSSIBLE CAUSES:

General:

- An I/O error occurred while:
  - Reading a user label.
  - Positioning the volume for close processing.
- Since the data set has been opened and processed successfully, a hardware or recording media problem is more likely than a problem program or supervisor error.
- Device malfunction.
- Physical damage to tape (e.g., crimp).
- No tapemark—the volume may have not been initialized by IEHINITT.

RELEVANT DUMP ITEMS:

- The address of the next problem program instruction may be found at:
  - The PSW for the problem program's PRB under ACTIVE RBS. This RB is usually the first printed. The FL-CDE of the problem program's PRB will point to a CDE entry that has the problem program's name printed in NM.
  - The RET field of the last SA under SAVE AREA TRACE.
- R2 points to the offending DCB.
  - If the DCB was open, it will be formatted in the control block section of the dump and have a DEB and IOBs associated with it.
    - The 2-byte TIOT offset is at x28 into the DCB.
    - The DDname of this DCB is given in the TIOT at this offset.
  - If the DCB was not opened or has been closed, it will not be formatted in the control block section, but will be found in the main storage dump. The DEB will contain the DCB address. The 8-byte DDname will be at x28 into the DCB.
- The IOB prefix pointer should be at x1C into the DCB. IOB fields may indicate if a hardware-related I/O error has occurred. The IOB prefix is 16 bytes long, so the IOB proper begins at the prefix address plus x10. Fields of interest are:
  - IOB + 0, IOBFLAG1: If bit 5 is on (x04), a permanent I/O error has occurred. System message IEA000I will probably have been issued.
  - IOB + 4, ECBCC: ECB completion code. First byte of the 4-byte ECB. If this byte is not x00 or x7F, a channel error has occurred.
  - IOB + xC, second word of the CSW: Contains the channel status bits. Bits 36 and 37 should be on if an I/O operation has completed successfully.

- Further explanation of the ECB and CSW is given in 4.2, Dump Components, Input-Output Block.
- R4 points to the OPEN/CLOSE/EOV work area for the offending data set. It contains:
  - The data set label at R4 + 0.
  - The JFCB (DD statement parameters) at R4 + x64. Examination of this work area will indicate conflicting or incorrectly specified data set parameters. 3.4, Analysis of O/C/EOV Work Area, provides a detailed description of its fields.
- Message IEC210I may indicate the offending DDname, device, volume serial number, and data set name. R15 contains a return code documented in *System Messages* under this message. Briefly:
  - 04 I/O error while reading user label.
  - 08 I/O error while positioning for CLOSE.

WHAT TO DO:

- Follow the steps outlined in 1.3, General Debugging Procedure, and 5.2, Basic Techniques.
- Specify a different device, volume, or both and rerun the job.
- For information on how to dump tape labels, see 3.8, Dumping and Printing Data.

---

222 Job canceled and no dump was requested by operator.

Related System Messages: None
SVC34 MGCR/QEDIT

POSSIBLE CAUSES:

General:

- Although no dump is requested, one may be produced depending on which supervisor routine was active when the cancel was processed.
- See also SCCs 122 and 322.

WHAT TO DO:

- Follow the debugging steps outlined in 1.3, General Debugging Procedure, and 5.2, Basic Techniques.
- Ask the operator or operations department why the job was canceled. Jobs are often canceled because they violate an installation standard or to release a resource for higher-priority jobs. Usually, a resubmit will run to completion.

---

237 EOV or positioning error for tape data set.

Related System Messages: IEC0231
SVC 55 EOV

POSSIBLE CAUSES:

General:

- For an input tape data set, the EOV1 or EOF1 trailer label block count was not equal to the DCB block count. The DCB's block count reflects blocks actually processed. A block(s) may have been skipped due to an I/O error.
- Wrong volume mounted for the second or subsequent volume of a multivolume data set.
- Invalid tape label format or content encountered by EOV.

JCL Related:

DD statement:

- For the *n*th volume of a multivolume input data set:
  - SER subparameter specification is incorrect.
  - DSNAME specification is incorrect or misspelled.
- DCB subparameter EROPT specifies SKP causing bad block(s) to be skipped.
- BLKSIZE incorrectly specified as 18 or less.

RELEVANT DUMP ITEMS:

- The address of the next problem program instruction may be found at the RET field of the last SA under SAVE AREA TRACE.
- R0 may contain the tape label block count.
- R1 or R2 will point to the offending DCB.
  - The 2-byte TIOT offset is at x28 into the DCB.
  - The DDname for this DCB is given in the TIOT at this offset.
  - The DCB block count (DCBBLKCT) is at xC into the DCB. If R11 contains zeros, DCBBLKCT contains the label's block count.
- R4 points to the OPEN/CLOSE/EOV work area for the offending data set. It contains:
  - The data set label at R4 + 0.
  - The JFCB (DD statement parameters) at R4 + x64. Examination of this work area will indicate conflicting or incorrectly specified data set parameters. 3.4, Analysis of the O/C/EOV Work Area, provides a detailed description of its fields.
- Message IEC023I may indicate the offending DDname, device address, volume serial number, and data set name. R15 contains a return code documented in *System Messages* under this message. Briefly:

- 04 Trailer block count not equal DCB block count.
- 08 Nth header label data set name not the same as DD statement data set name.

WHAT TO DO:

- Follow the steps outlined in 1.3, General Debugging Procedure, and 5.2, Basic Techniques.
- For information on how to dump tape labels, see 3.8, Dumping and Printing Data.
- If appropriate, use FEOV instead of EOV. FEOV does not do block count checking.
- If an I/O error has occurred, specify a different device, volume, or both and rerun the job.
- Recovery from unequal block counts (R15 = x04) may be specified via the EXLST operand of the DCB macro or placed in DCBEXLSA (DCB + x25). *Data Management Services* gives a detailed explanation of this feature.
- If blocks less than 18 bytes are being used, increase the block size. When a data check occurs on a tape read, records shorter than 18 bytes are treated as noise (dropped). When a data check occurs on a tape write, records shorter than 12 bytes are treated as noise (dropped). In either case, a larger block or record size will correct the problem.

---

301 WAIT macro specified an ECB whose WAIT was already on.

Related System Messages: None
SVC 1 WAIT

POSSIBLE CAUSES:

General:

- A WAIT macro was issued, specifying an ECB (Event Control Block) that was not POSTed from a previous event.
- The ECB has been reinitialized by the problem program prior to a second WAIT for this ECB.
- The high-order ECB bit has been incorrectly turned on.

RELEVANT DUMP ITEMS:

- If the problem program issued the WAIT, R1 of ABEND's SVRB will contain either the ECB address or, if negative, the address of an ECB list. The ABEND SVRB can be identified by an x0D in the low-order bytes of the WC-L-IC field of the RBs on the ACTIVE RB list.

WHAT TO DO:

- Follow the steps outlined in 1.3, General Debugging Procedure, and 5.2, Basic Techniques.

---

322 A job, job step, or cataloged procedure exceeded the specified or default CPU time limit.

Related System Messages: None
SVC 34 MGCR/QEDIT

POSSIBLE CAUSES:

General:

- CPU time estimate specified or default limit is insufficient for this application.
- Input or output quantity increased by a significant amount (see SCC B37).
- Inefficient problem program or application design; for example:
  - High volume of additions are processed randomly for an ISAM or VSAM data set.
  - Inefficient programming techniques. For example, in COBOL, using DISPLAY NUMERIC fields instead of COMP or COMP-3 for repetitive calculations. See the source language Programmer's Guide for a good discussion of efficient coding techniques.
  - High-volume table or file searches are processed by an inefficient algorithm (e.g., serial instead of binary or hashing search).
- Endless loop in problem program.
- Outstanding volume mount or device request.
- Job was run on a slower CPU.
- Data set(s) was transferred to a device with slower access time.

JCL Related:

JOB statement:

- TIME parameter incorrect or omitted.
- CLASS parameter incorrect or omitted. Job was run in a CLASS (SYSIN reader) whose default time limit was too low for this application.

EXEC statement:

- TIME parameter incorrect or omitted.
- A step was added to the problem program's job stream which caused the previously sufficient time specification or default to be exceeded.

DD statement:

- A substantially increased quantity of input has been processed because:
  - The DSNAME specification for an input data set(s) is incorrect or misspelled:
    - The generation number for a GDG data set was omitted. All existing generations of this data set were automatically concatenated.
    - A large production data set was specified in a test environment.
  - DISP specified MOD instead of OLD in a previous job(s) or step(s). The offending input data set(s) was extended every time it was used, instead of being written over.
  - DDname was omitted on a DD statement(s) following an input DD statement, causing concatenation of two or more data sets.

RELEVANT DUMP ITEMS:

- The only thing certain about the PSW is that it points to the instruction being executed when the time limit was exceeded. If the PSW is:
  - Within the problem program, a "compute" loop is a possibility. Examine loop counters, and the loop or branch logic controlling execution of this instruction.
  - Outside the problem program, a supervisor I/O routine was probably active when the time limit was exceeded. An examination of the buffers may indicate an I/O loop.
- Evidence of a loop or the progress of the program may be found by examining data set buffers. For QSAM data sets, R2 may point to the DCB of the last data set accessed. The last record written to an output QSAM data set is at the address for the next record less LRECL (last = next − LRECL). Both fields are found in the DCB:
  - + x4C 4-byte address of the next record to be written or the last read (DCBRE-CAD).
  - + x52 2-byte LRECL (DCBLRECL).

  If the last record read or written was also the last in a block, the buffer may have been overlaid with a new data block. In this case, the last record cannot be located by the method outlined above. You may be able to find evidence of it in other program work areas, counters, saved keys, and so on. See *Data Management Services* for more information about non-VSAM buffering.
- The last record read or written to a VSAM cluster may be found by the method outlined in 3.5, Locating VSAM Data Records.
- The ASCB contains several time-related fields. These fields are fullword unsigned binary integers and represent time in TOD (time of day) clock units. (See *Principles of Operation* for a detailed discussion of the TOD clock.) TOD clock units in the ASCB timing fields may be approximately (±1 second) converted to seconds by multiplying TOD units by 1.05 and rounding to the nearest second. The ASCB timing fields are listed here by their dump label. The actual name and offset into the ASCB are also given.

- EJST and XJST (ASCBEJST, + x40) elapsed job time. Although printed separately, these fields are treated as a single 8-byte TOD field. To obtain the job's elapsed running time in seconds, treat the 2 low-order bytes of EJST and the 2 high-order bytes of XJST as a single binary integer. Convert to seconds as explained above.
- JSTL (ASCBJSTL, + x50) job step CPU time limit. Convert to seconds as explained above.
- SWTL (ASCBSWTL, + xC4) job step wait time limit. Convert to seconds as explained above.
- SRBT (ASCBSRBT, + xC8) accumulated SRB (service request block) time. Convert to seconds as explained above.

WHAT TO DO:

- Follow the steps outlined in 1.3, General Debugging Procedure, and 5.2, Basic Techniques.
- Specify a job class (SYSIN reader) that has a higher default time limit.
- If a high volume of random updates are at fault, process the updates on a sequential copy and then reload the data set from sorted input instead of doing random updates. This will usually reduce processing time.
- Specify an increased TIME value on the JOB or EXEC statement. Specifying TIME = 1440 will cause CPU time checking to be bypassed entirely.
- Examine the I/O counts given by the JES listing for each step. This may indicate:
  - The presence of an I/O loop.
  - How much processing has been completed and therefore how much to increase the JOB or EXEC statement TIME parameter. For example, if 50 percent of the input was processed, double the TIME specification. In general, if x percent was processed, then $1/x$ is the minimum factor to increase TIME (x being the decimal fraction equivalent of percent, e.g., 0.50 in the case cited).

---

400 Conflict in data management control block parameters during EXCP I/O.

Related System Messages: None
SVC 0 EXCP

POSSIBLE CAUSES:

General:

- The problem program incorrectly modified or initialized a data management control block(s) passed to EXCP:
  - The DEB's DCB address is not the same as the IOB's DCB address.
  - The DEB's protection key (DEBPROTE) is different from the TCB protection key

(TCBPKF) or from the IOB protection key. When the user is not in the supervisor state, these keys must be the same.
- The UCBID field of the UCB referenced by DEBUCBAD (in a DEB extent entry) does not contain xFF.
- The DEB address in IOBECBPT is not aligned on a fullword boundary.
- IOBSEEK address is invalid:
  - For an ISAM data set:
    - An incorrect index address is stored in the data set.
    - Insufficient main storage allocated for high-level index.
    - High-level index overlaid and rewritten.
  - Invalid "M" value in first byte of MBBCCHHR field. IOBSEEK's "M" is greater than DEBENT's total extent count for DEB extents.

- A compiler input PDS member could not be accessed.
- A data set was not properly opened.
- Data management control blocks were inadvertently freed or overlaid.

JCL Related:

DD statement:

- DCB parameter is missing or incorrect:
  - KEYLEN incorrect for ISAM data set.
- Attempt to access a multivolume DASD data set without specifying parallel mounting via UNIT=(,P).
- Generation data group data set is overridden to DD DUMMY.

Assembly Programs:

- EXCP processing incorrectly loaded an IOB or ECB address.
- Data management control blocks overlaid due to bad address or runaway loop.
- DCBKEYLE incorrectly specified for an ISAM data set via OPEN macro.

RELEVANT DUMP ITEMS:

- The address of the next problem program instruction may be found in the RET field of the last SA under SAVE AREA TRACE.
- R0 may contain the tape label block count.
- R1 or R2 will point to the offending DCB.
- The TCBEXCPD (TCB + xC0, labeled XCPD in the formatted TCB), points to the EXCP problem determination area (PDA):
  - At PDA + x10 is a register save area taken when EXCP discovered a problem:
    - R2 points to the IOB.
    - R3 points to the DEB.
    - R4 points to the DCB.

- •• R6 may point to the seek address.
- •• R7 points to the UCB.
- • PDA + x54 contains the RQE for this EXCP (if allocated).

WHAT TO DO:

- Follow the steps outlined in 1.3, General Debugging Procedure, and 5.2, Basic Techniques.
- For more information about the EXCP problem determination area (PDA), see *OS/VS2 I/O Supervisor Logic*.

---

406 Attempt to execute an only loadable module by LINK, XCTL, or ATTACH.

Related System Messages: IEA703I
SVC 6 LINK
7 XCTL
42 ATTACH

POSSIBLE CAUSES:

General:

- Attempt to execute a module via LINK, XCTL, OR ATTACH which was marked only loadable by the linkage editor.
- Attempt to execute a module whose entry point was established via the IDENTIFY macro.
- Misspelled or incorrect module name specified to LINK, XCTL, or ATTACH.

RELEVANT DUMP ITEMS:

- The address of the next problem program instruction may be found at:
  - • The PSW field of the problem program's PRB under ACTIVE RBS. This RB is usually the first printed. The FL-CDE of the problem program's PRB will point to a CDE entry that has the problem program's name printed in NM.
  - • The RET field of the last SA under SAVE AREA TRACE.
    - •• If the problem program has not been loaded, no PRB will be listed. The problem program's name will not appear in the CDE. In this case, the abend was issued by the program manager function of the supervisor.
- The 8-byte name of the offending module may be found as follows:
  - • Check message IEA703I first.
  - • Locate ABEND's SVRB. It will likely be the first or second RB listed under ACTIVE RBS and will contain x0D in the low-order byte of the WC-L-IC field. The module

name is in the first 8 bytes of the field labeled EXTSA in ABEND's SVRB (this is the RBEXSAVE field located at x60 into the SVRB). The EBCDIC characters are shown in hexadecimal. Convert them to their alphanumeric equivalent to obtain the module name.

- Alternatively, the offending module name may be obtained from the SVC parameter list.
- If the LINK, XCTL, or ATTACH was issued by the problem program, its parameter list will be pointed to by R15 of the problem program's PRB register save area. The problem program's PRB is usually the first RB under ACTIVE RBs and its FL-CDE points to a CDE entry that names the problem program in its EPA. The SVC issued may be determined from the low-order byte of this PRB's WC-L-IC field (RBINTCOD). If RBINTCOD is:
  - x06, a LINK was issued.
  - x07, an XCTL was issued.
  - x42, an ATTACH was issued.
- The first byte of the parameter list pointed to by R15 indicates whether an entry point (x00) or directory (x80) request was made. The second, third, and fourth bytes of the parameter list either point to an entry point name (x00) or directory area created by BLDL (x80).
- If a JOBLIB DD statement was specified, the address of its DCB is in the TCB field labeled JLB (TCBJLB, TCB + x28). If not specified, this field will contain zeros. If the JES log is not available, the data set name may be found by examining the O/C/EOV work area. See 3.4, Analysis of the O/C/EOV Work Area.

WHAT TO DO:

- Follow the steps outlined in 1.3, General Debugging Procedure, and 5.2, Basic Techniques.
- An only loadable module must be placed in main storage by the LOAD macro and entered via a CALL or branch instruction.
- The only loadable attribute may be removed by relinking the module and omitting the OL linkage editor parameter.
- For information on how to list load module data, see 3.8, Dumping and Printing Data.

---

413 Open error for tape or DASD data set related to label or mount problems.

Related System Messages: IEC145I
SVC 19 OPEN

POSSIBLE CAUSES:

General:

- A request to mount a particular volume on a specific device could not be processed. Another volume is mounted on this device and could not be demounted because:
  - It is permanently resident.
  - It is enqueued by another task.
  - It is reserved.
  - It contains data sets OPEN for another task.
- An uncorrectable I/O error occurred while:
  - Positioning a tape volume.
  - Reading a tape or DASD volume label.
  - Writing a tapemark.
- A tape volume mounted for output did not contain standard labels or had not been initialized by IEHINITT.
- An input-only data set was opened for output, or vice versa.
- Mass storage system problem:
  - I/O error—see message IEC166I.
  - Incorrect virtual volume.

JCL Related:

DD statement:

- Incorrect specification or omission of the volume parameter, VOLUME=(,,*S*,*N*,SER=(v_1, . . . ,v_m)).
  - SER missing for an uncataloged input tape data set.
  - SER specifies a volume that is already mounted or permanently allocated to another device.
  - Sequence subparameter *S* is greater than:
    - The explicit volume allocation *N*.
    - The default or existing allocation for number of volumes.
    - *m*, the number of explicit volumes requested via SER.
    - 1 for a VIO data set.
  - For a multivolume ISAM or BDAM data set, *m*, the number of explicit volumes requested via SER, is less than *C*, the unit count subparameter of UNIT=(,*C*). More volumes were expected but were not specified.
- Unit parameter, UNIT=(*type*,*C*), specifies:
  - Fewer units via the unit count subparameter *C* than volumes given via SER (see the volume parameter errors above).
  - A device type or address that does not support the recording density requested via the DEN subparameter of DCB.
  - A device with a permanently resident volume.

  - DEFER not specified and the problem program supplies the volume serial number(s) by modifying the JFCB.
- A DCB subparameter specification is not supported by the requested or allocated device:
  - DEN (for tape data sets).
  - DSORG (e.g., PO for tape device).
- Incorrect specification of the label parameter, LABEL=(*D*,*T*):
  - The label type subparameter, *T* is not NL or BLP for a nonstandard label tape.
  - The data set sequence subparameter, *D*, is greater than 1 and the volume parameter is omitted.
- Fewer volumes were specified via SER than UNIT subparameters were specified for a multivolume ISAM of BDAM data set.

Assembly Programs:

- INPUT, INOUT, or RDBACK specified for OPEN macro, but VOLUME parameter was omitted in DD statement.

COBOL Programs:

SORTLIB DD statement omitted for program using SORT verb.

RELEVANT DUMP ITEMS:

- The address of the next problem program instruction may be found in the PSW field of the problem program's PRB under ACTIVE RBS. This RB is usually the first printed. The FL-CDE of this PRB will point to a CDE entry that has the problem program's name printed in NM. To verify that this address points to the next instruction, check the 2 bytes immediately preceding it. They should contain x0A13—the object code for the OPEN SVC.
- R2 points to the offending DCB.
  - If the DCB was open, it will be formatted in the control block section of the dump and have a DEB and IOBs associated with it.
    - The 2-byte TIOT offset is at x28 into the DCB.
    - The DDname of this DCB is given in the TIOT at this offset.
  - If the DCB was not opened or has been closed, it will not be formatted in the control block section, but will be found in the main storage dump. The DEB will contain the DCB's address. The 8-byte DDname will be at x28 into the DCB.
- The IOB prefix pointer should be at x1C into the DCB. IOB fields may indicate if a hardware related I/O error has occurred. The IOB prefix is 16 bytes long, so the IOB proper begins at the prefix address plus x10. Fields of interest are:
  - IOB + 0, IOBFLAG1: If bit 5 is on (x04), a permanent I/O error has occurred. System message IEA000I will probably have been issued.
  - IOB + 4, ECBCC: ECB completion code. First byte of the 4-byte ECB. If this byte is not x00 or x7F, a channel error has occurred.

- IOB + xC, second word of the CSW: Contains the channel status bits. Bits 36 and 37 should be on if an I/O operation has completed successfully.

– Further explanation of the ECB and CSW is given in 4.2, Dump Components, Input-Output Block.
– Message IEC145I may indicate the offending DDname, device address, volume serial number, and data set name. R15 contains a return code documented in *System Messages* under this message. Briefly:
  - 04 No device available to mount requested volume.
  - 08 I/O error positioning tape.
  - 0C I/O error reading tape volume label.
  - 10 I/O error writing a tapemark.
  - 18 VOL = SER omitted for an input data set.
  - 1C Volume sequence count incorrect.
  - 20 I/O error reading DASD volume label.
  - 24 Tape density incorrect.
  - 28 Supervisor error.
  - 2C MSS error.
  - 30 MSS wrong virtual volume.
  - 34 LABEL parameter incorrect or VOL = SER omitted.

WHAT TO DO:

– Follow the steps outlined in 1.3, General Debugging Procedure, and 5.2, Basic Techniques.
– If an I/O error has occurred, specify a different device, volume, or both and rerun the job.
– Recovery from a missing volume serial number for an input data set (R15 = x04) may be attempted, preventing an abend termination. The address of a recovery routine may be specified via the EXLST operand of the DCB macro or placed in DCBEXLSA (DCB + x25). *Data Management Services* gives a detailed explanation of this feature.
– For information on how to dump data set labels, see 3.8, Dumping and Printing Data.

---

506 Module requested by an overlay program could not be loaded.

Related System Messages: IEA703I

SVC 6 LINK
7 XCTL
8 LOAD
42 ATTACH

POSSIBLE CAUSES:

General:

- An overlay structure program issued a LINK, XCTL, ATTACH, or LOAD macro and the module requested could not be processed.
- Insufficient storage to load both the module and the overlay supervisor.

JCL Related:

JOB statement:

- REGION parameter specifies incorrect or insufficient quantity of virtual storage.

EXEC statement:

- See "JOB statement" above.
- JOB statement REGION parameter overrides all EXEC statement REGION parameters.

RELEVANT DUMP ITEMS:

- The address of the next problem program instruction may be found at:
  - The PSW field of the problem program's PRB under ACTIVE RBS. This RB is usually the first printed. The FL-CDE of the problem program's PRB will point to a CDE entry that has the problem program's name printed in NM.
  - The RET field of the last SA under SAVE AREA TRACE.
- If the problem program has not been loaded, no PRB will be listed. The problem program's name will not appear in the CDE. In this case, the abend was issued by the program manager function of the supervisor.
- The 8-byte name of the offending module may be found as follows:
  - Check message IEA703I first.
  - Locate ABEND's SVRB. It will probably be the first or second RB listed under ACTIVE RBS and will contain x0D in the low-order byte of the WC-L-IC field.
  - The module name is in the first 8 bytes of the field labeled EXTSA in ABEND's SVRB (this is the RBEXSAVE field located at x60 into the SVRB). The EBCDIC characters are shown in hexadecimal. Convert them to their alphanumeric equivalent to obtain the module name.
- Alternatively, the offending module name may be obtained from the SVC parameter list, pointed to from R1.
- If the LINK, XCTL, or ATTACH was issued by the problem program, their parameter list will be pointed to by R15 of the problem program's PRB register save area. The problem program's PRB is usually the first RB under ACTIVE RBs and its FL-CDE points to a CDE entry that names the problem program in its EPA. The SVC issued may be determined from the low-order byte of this PRB's WC-L-IC field (RBINTCOD). If RBINTCOD is:

  - x06, a LINK was issued.
  - x07, an XCTL was issued.
  - x42, an ATTACH was issued.
- The first byte of the parameter list pointed to by R15 indicates whether an entry point (x00) or directory (x80) request was made. The second, third, and fourth bytes of the parameter list point to name or directory area created by BLDL (program management SVCs use R15 for parameter lists). R1 is used by optional "user" parameter lists.
- If a LOAD was issued by the problem program, a similar analysis may be used to find the offending module name. LOAD does not use a parameter list. Locate the PRB's register save area as explained above. RBINTCOD for a LOAD will be x08. In the register save area:
  - R0 contains the entry point name address in its low-order 3 bytes if the first byte is x00; the address of the BLDL-created directory entry if the first byte is x80.
  - R1 contains the DCB address of the load library or zeros if the default library is to be used.
- If a JOBLIB DD statement was specified, the address of its DCB is in the TCB field labeled JLB (TCBJLB, TCB + x28). If not specified, this field will contain zeros. If the JES log is not available, the data set name may be found by examining the O/C/EOV work area. See 3.4, Analysis of the O/C/EOV Work Area.

WHAT TO DO:

- Follow the steps outlined in 1.3, General Debugging Procedure, and 5.2, Basic Techniques.
- Load the module dynamically instead of with an overlay. Overlays are not generally needed in a virtual storage system.
- Decrease the module or segment size.
- If the program resides in the SVC library, it must be moved since overlays cannot be loaded from this library.
- For information on how to list load module data, see 3.8, Dumping and Printing Data.

---

513 OPEN error for tape data set.

Related System Messages: IEC146I, IEC512I
SVC 19 OPEN

POSSIBLE CAUSES:

General:

- Attempt to open more than one data set on a single tape volume or device:
  - The device specified by a DD statement UNIT parameter already had an open data set on it.

  - The data sets reside on the same volume.
  - Concurrent open is allowed for SYSOUT data sets only.
- Two or more data sets assigned to the same tape device.
- DASD data sets have been transferred to tape. Opening them concurrently is supported when they are DASD resident but not when they are tape resident.
- A data set whose DD statement specifies DEFER was opened prior to closing its precedent data set.
- Invalid tape label format.
- Attempt to access a volume not initialized by IEHINITT.

JCL Related:

DD statement:

- UNIT parameters for tape data sets that are accessed concurrently specified:
  - AFF.
  - Same unit address.
- SYSOUT was omitted or incorrectly overridden.
- DSNAME was specified instead of SYSOUT.
- The label parameter did not specify NL or BLP for a tape with nonstandard labels.
- The volume parameter specifies an incorrect serial via SER.
- See 3.3, Common JCL Errors.

COBOL Programs:

- SORT USING is specified. The input data set (the USING data set) resides on tape and has been OPENed but not CLOSEd prior to the execution of the SORT verb.

RELEVANT DUMP ITEMS:

- The address of the next problem program instruction may be found in the PSW field of the problem program's PRB under ACTIVE RBS. This RB is usually the first printed. The FL-CDE of this PRB will point to a CDE entry that has the problem program's name printed in NM. To verify that this address points to the next instruction, check the 2 bytes immediately preceding it. They should contain x0A13—the object code for the OPEN SVC.
- R2 points to the offending DCB.
  - The 2-byte TIOT offset is at x28 into the DCB.
  - The DDname of the DCB is given in the TIOT at this offset.
- R4 points to the OPEN/CLOSE/EOV work area for the offending data set. It contains:
  - The data set label at R4 + 0.
  - The JFCB (DD statement parameters) at R4 + x64. Examination of this work area will indicate conflicting or incorrectly specified data set parameters. 3.4, Analysis of the O/C/EOV Work Area provides a detailed description of its fields.

- Message IEC146I may indicate the offending DDname, device address, volume serial number, and data set name. R15 contains a return code documented *System Messages* under this message. Briefly:
  - 04 Attempt to open more than one data set on the same tape.
  - 08 Invalid tape label. Message IEC512I indicates the specific error.
  - 0C Invalid tape volume label.

WHAT TO DO:

- Follow the steps outlined in 1.3, General Debugging Procedure, and 5.2, Basic Techniques.
- If a unit address is specified in the unit parameter of the DD statement, change it to a generic device type (e.g., 3400) or user-assigned group name (e.g., TAPE or the equivalent for your installation).
- If data sets residing on the same tape volume are needed simultaneously, transfer at least one to another tape volume or DASD prior to the abending step's execution. The IEBGENER or IEHMOVE utilities provide an easy means to do this. *MVS Utilities* describes how to do the transfer.

---

522 Wait-time limit exceeded by all tasks in a job step.

Related System Messages: None
SVC 34 MGCR/QEDIT

POSSIBLE CAUSES:

General:

- Job step was in a wait state:
  - For 30 minutes.
  - For the duration specified by JWT parameters, when the SMF (systems management facility) is active.
- The problem program is dependent on an external event(s) that has not occurred in the time frame required:
  - Outstanding operator reply (WTOR).
  - Outstanding mount or other operator action request.
  - Required device or data set not released by another job(s).
  - Higher-priority task(s) in a tight loop has not released control of the CPU, preventing execution of the abending task.
  - No messages have arrived for processing in a telecommunications application (often a legitimate situation).

- A deadlock condition has occurred (also known as "interlock" or "deadly embrace"). The problem program is waiting for a second task to free a needed system resource, but the second task is waiting for the problem program to free another system resource. Neither can proceed.
- See also SCCs 122 and 322.

JCL Related:

JOB statement:

- TIME parameter incorrect or omitted.
- CLASS parameter incorrect or omitted. The job was run in a CLASS whose default time limit was too low for this application.

EXEC statement:

- TIME parameter incorrect or omitted.

DD statement:

- Another task specifies DISP=OLD or MOD instead of SHR for a data set required by the problem program.

ASSEMBLY PROGRAMS:

- Problem with ECB usage:
  - WAIT issued for wrong ECB.
  - ECB was not POSTed upon event completion.
  - ECB's address referenced instead of its content.
  - EXCP appendage incorrectly coded.
- Deadlock condition has resulted from:
  - Incorrect, misspelled, or omitted resource name in ENQUE or DEQUE request.
  - ENQUE/DEQUE usage prone to deadlock (see What to Do below).
  - STATUS macro that specifies both START and SYNCH parameters.

RELEVANT DUMP ITEMS:

- PSW instruction address points to the instruction after the WAIT.
- The presence of three or more SVRBs may indicate an unavailable device or data set.
- TCBTCT points to SMF TCT table.
- The ASCB contains several time-related fields. These fields are fullword unsigned binary integers and represent time in TOD (time of day) clock units. (See *Principles of Operation* for a detailed discussion of the TOD clock.) TOD clock units in the ASCB timing fields may be approximately (±1 second) converted to seconds by multiplying TOD units by 1.05 and rounding to the nearest second. The ASCB timing fields are listed here by their dump label. The actual name and offset into the ASCB are also given.

- EJST and XJST (ASCBEJST + x40) elapsed job time. Although printed separately, these fields are treated as a single 8-byte TOD field. To obtain the job's elapsed running time in seconds, treat the 2 low-order bytes of EJST and the 2 high-order bytes of XJST as a single binary integer. Convert to seconds as explained above.
- JSTL (ASCBJSTL, + x50) job step CPU time limit: Convert to seconds as explained above.
- SWTL (ASCBSWTL, + xC4) job step wait time limit: Convert to seconds as explained above.
- SRBT (ASCBSRBT, + xC8) accumulated SRB (service request block) time: Convert to seconds as explained above.

WHAT TO DO:

- Follow the steps outlined in 1.3, General Debugging Procedure, and 5.2, Basic Techniques.
- Specifying TIME=1440 on the JOB or EXEC statement causes the wait check (and all other time checks) to be bypassed. Any TIME specification other than 1440 will cause the wait test to be applied.
- Under SMF, a user-written exit can control the disposition of 522 abends. This exit is selective by job and step.
- If a deadlock has occurred, there are several design strategies that can be followed to minimize its probability of occurrence:
  - ENQUE resources singly and not before they are required.
  - DEQUE resources as soon as they are not needed.
  - Share resources that do not require exclusive control.
  - ENQUE resources that are jointly required with a single request.
  - Have all users ENQUE resources in the same sequence.
  - Establish a timer exit with the STIMER macro when using STATUS with STOP SYNCH.

---

604 GETMAIN macro error: Unable to allocate main storage.

Related System Messages: IEA700I
SVC 4 GETMAIN

POSSIBLE CAUSES:

General:

- An invalid request to allocate virtual storage was made.
- A free area exceeds the area assigned to the task, possibly due to a modified FQE.
- The A or LA GETMAIN operand:

  - Specified an address outside the private area assigned to the task.
  - Specified an address that was not aligned on a fullword boundary.
- Invalid parameter list:
  - List address was invalid.
  - User's key does not allow read access of list specified.
- Program inadvertently modified parameter list or list pointer.

RELEVANT DUMP ITEMS:

- R1 contains the parameter list address.
- See SCC 804.

WHAT TO DO:

- Follow the steps outlined in 1.3, General Debugging Procedure, and 5.2, Basic Techniques.

---

613 I/O error on a tape data set.

Related System Messages: IEC147I
SVC 19 OPEN

POSSIBLE CAUSES:

General:

- Device malfunction or physical damage to tape.
- An uncorrectable I/O error occurred while:
  - Positioning the tape.
  - Reading or writing a tape label.
  - Writing a tapemark.
- Standard header label one (HDR1) missing for an input data set.
- Scratch tape was incorrectly labeled or not initialized via IEHINITT.

JCL Related:

DD statement:

- UNIT does not specify tape device.
- DEN or TRTCH DCB subparameter conflicts with actual tape characteristics or device capabilities.
- Label type subparameter *T* of LABEL=(,*T*), specifies incorrect label type.

- NL or BLP not specified for a tape with nonstandard labels.
- NL coded instead of BLP.

RELEVANT DUMP ITEMS:

- The address of the next problem program instruction may be found in the PSW field of the problem program's PRB under ACTIVE RBS. This RB is usually the first printed. The FL-CDE of this PRB will point to a CDE entry that has the problem program's name printed in NM. To verify that this address points to the next instruction, check the 2 bytes immediately preceding it. They should contain x0A13—the object code for the OPEN SVC.
- R2 points to the offending DCB.
  - If the DCB was open, it will be formatted in the control block section of the dump and have a DEB and IOBs associated with it:
    - The 2-byte TIOT offset is at x28 into the DCB.
    - The DDname of this DCB is given in the TIOT at this offset.
  - If the DCB was not opened or has been closed, it will not be formatted in the control block section, but will be found in the main storage dump. The DEB will contain the DCB address. The 8-byte DDname will be at x28 into the DCB.
- The IOB prefix pointer should be at x1C into the DCB. IOB fields may indicate if a hardware-related I/O error has occurred. The IOB prefix is 16 bytes long, so the IOB proper begins at the prefix address plus x10. Fields of interest are:
  - IOB + 0 IOBFLAG1: If bit 5 is on (x04), a permanent I/O error has occurred. System message IEA000I will probably have been issued.
  - IOB + 4, ECBCC: ECB completion code. First byte of the 4-byte ECB. If this byte is not x00 or x7F, a channel error has occurred.
  - IOB + xC, second word of the CSW: Contains the channel status bits. Bits 36 and 37 should be on if an I/O operation has completed successfully.
- Further explanation of the ECB and CSW is given in 4.2, Dump Components, Input-Output Block.
- R4 points to the OPEN/CLOSE/EOV work area for the offending data set. It contains:
  - The data set label at R4 + 0.
  - The JFCB (DD statement parameters) at R4 + x64. Examination of this work area will indicate conflicting or incorrectly specified data set parameters. 3.4, Analysis of the O/C/EOV Work Area, provides a detailed description of its fields.
- Message IEC147I may indicate the offending DDname, device address, volume serial number, and data set name. R15 contains a return code documented in *System Messages* under this message. Briefly:
  - 04 I/O error positioning a tape.
  - 08 I/O error reading a tape label.
  - 0C Invalid label.
  - 10 I/O error occurred writing a tape label.
  - 14 I/O error occurred writing a tapemark after a header.

WHAT TO DO:

- Follow the steps outlined in 1.3, General Debugging Procedure, and 5.2, Basic Techniques.
- If an I/O error has occurred, specify a different device, volume, or both and rerun the job.
- Recovery from:
  - Tape label I/O error (R15 = x08)
  - Invalid tape label (R15 = x0C)
  - Tape label I/O write error (R15 = x10)
  - Tapemark I/O write error (R15 = x14)

  may be attempted, preventing an abend termination. The address of a recovery routine may be specified via the EXLST operand of the DCB macro or placed in DCBEXLSA (DCB + x25). *Data Management Services* gives a detailed explanation of this feature.
- For information on how to dump tape labels, see 3.8, Dumping and Printing Data.

---

637 I/O error at end of volume for tape data set.

Related System Messages: IEC026I
SVC 55 EOV

POSSIBLE CAUSES:

General:

- Error occurred during EOV processing for a volume just read or when a subsequent volume of the same data set is mounted.
- An uncorrectable I/O error occurred while:
  - Positioning the tape.
  - Writing a tapemark.
  - Reading a tape label.
  - Rewinding.
  - Sensing for file protect ring.
- Attempt to concatenate data sets with unlike attributes (e.g., record length, record format, block size, or data sets resident on different device types). Concatenation of unlike attributes may be done only if the problem program sets the correct DCB bit switches.
- Device malfunction or physical damage to tape.

JCL Related:

DD statement:

- DSNAME incorrect or misspelled.
- DDname was omitted on a DD statement(s) following an input DD statement, causing an inadvertent concatenation of two or more data sets.
- DCB parameters were incorrectly specified when one or more of the data sets in the concatenation list was created:
  - LRECL.
  - BLKSIZE.
  - RECFM.

Assembly Programs:

- DCBOFLGS (DCB + x2C) was not properly flagged (bit 4 set to zero) to process unlike concatenation attributes:
  - Wrong DCB modified.
  - Wrong mask or offset used.
  - Logic error—flags not set prior to EOV.

RELEVANT DUMP ITEMS:

- The address of the next problem program instruction may be found at the RET field of the last SA under SAVE AREA TRACE.
- R2 points to the offending DCB:
  - The 2-byte TIOT offset is located at + x28 into the DCB.
  - The DDname of the DCB is given in the TIOT at this offset.
  - If this DCB has been CLOSEd, it will not be formatted in the control block section of the dump, but should be the main storage listing. The DEB will contain the DCB's address.
- DCB + x2C points to the DCBOFLGS field (1 byte). For concatenation of unlike attributes, bit 4 must be set to zero.
- DCB + x1C points to the IOB prefix. IOB fields may indicate if a hardware-related I/O error has occurred. The IOB prefix is 16 bytes long, so the IOB proper begins at prefix address plus x10. Fields of interest are:
  - IOB + 0, IOBFLAG1: If bit 5 is on (x04), a permanent I/O error has occurred. System message IEA000I will probably have been issued.
  - IOB + 4, ECBCC: ECB completion code. First byte of the 4-byte ECB. If this byte is not x00 or x7F, a channel error has occurred.
  - IOB + xC, second word of the CSW: Contains the channel status bits. Bits 36 and 37 should be on if an I/O operation has been completed successfully.

  - Further explanation of the ECB and CSW is given in 4.2, Dump Components, Input-Output Block.
- R4 points to the OPEN/CLOSE/EOV work area for the offending data set. It contains:
  - The data set label at R4 + 0.
  - The JFCB (DD statement parameters) at R4 + x64. Examination of this work area will indicate conflicting or incorrectly specified data set parameters. 3.4, Analysis of the O/C/EOV Work Area, provides a detailed description of its fields.
- Message IEC026I may indicate the offending DDname, device address, volume serial number, and data set name. R15 contains a return code documented in *System Messages* under this message. Briefly:
  - 04 I/O error while reading tape label, writing tapemark, or positioning.
  - 08 I/O error while positioning tape with user trailer labels.
  - 0C Concatenation of unlike attributes.
  - 10 I/O error on backward read.
  - 14 I/O error in conjunction with OPEN option LEAVE.
  - 18 I/O error in conjunction with OPEN option REREAD.
  - 1C I/O error for FEOV under DISP=PASS.
  - 24,2C I/O error rewinding.
  - 34 I/O error at EOV while reading VOL label.
  - 38 I/O error while positioning with nonstandard labels.
  - 3C I/O error for concatenated data set.
  - 40 I/O error while positioning.
  - 44 I/O error sensing for file protect.
  - 4C I/O error positioning after header label processing.

WHAT TO DO:

- Follow the steps outlined in 1.3, General Debugging Procedure, and 5.2, Basic Techniques.
- If an I/O error has occurred, specify a different device, volume, or both and rerun the job.
- See *Data Management Services* for more information on how to concatenate data sets with unlike attributes.
- Recovery from a 637 abend may be attempted via a user exit specified in the DCB. See *Data Management Services* for more information.
- For information about how to dump tape labels, see 3.8, Dumping and Printing Data.

---

706 Attempt to execute a module marked not executable by the linkage editor.

Related System Messages: IEA703I
SVC 6 LINK

7 XCTL
8 LOAD
42 ATTACH

POSSIBLE CAUSES:

General:

- A module marked as "nonexecutable" by the linkage editor was requested for execution.
- The linkage editor marked this module as nonexecutable because the LET or NCAL options were not specified and a severity level 2 error occurred or a severity level 3 or 4 error occurred. Some common level 2 errors are:
  - Unresolved external reference. The linkage editor could not find an input module(s) because:
    - A data set name or member specified in SYSLIB DD, INCLUDE, or LIBRARY statement is incorrect or omitted.
    - It was never created.
    - It was deleted.
    - It was renamed.
  - Invalid control cards.
  - Invalid overlay specified.
  - Input or output data set problem:
    - I/O error.
    - DCB parameters incorrect.
- Module name specified to LINK, XCTL, LOAD, or ATTACH is misspelled or incorrect or was inadvertently modified.

JCL Related:

JOB statement:

- COND test incorrectly coded. Linkage editor severity level 2 errors generate a return code of 8. Severity level 3 and 4 errors generate return codes of 12 and 16, respectively.

EXEC statement:

- See COND problem above.
- PARM specifies incorrect or missing attribute to linkage editor program.
- PGM module name specification incorrect or misspelled.
  - Invalid procedure default or override name.

DD statement:

- See the general causes listed above.

RELEVANT DUMP ITEMS:

- The address of the next problem program instruction may be found at:
  - The PSW field of the problem program's PRB under ACTIVE RBS. This RB is usually the first printed. The FL-CDE of the problem program's PRB will point to a CDE entry that has the problem program's name printed in NM.
  - The RET field of the last SA under SAVE AREA TRACE.
  - If the problem program has not been loaded, no PRB will be listed. The problem program's name will not appear in the CDE. In this case, the abend was issued by the program manager function of the supervisor.
- The 8-byte name of the offending module may be found as follows:
  - Check message IEA703I first.
  - Locate ABEND's SVRB. It will probably be the first or second RB listed under ACTIVE RBS and will contain x0D in the low-order byte of the WC-L-IC field. The module name is in the first 8 bytes of the field labeled EXTSA in ABEND's SVRB (this is the RBEXSAVE field located at x60 into the SVRB). The EBCDIC characters are shown in hexadecimal. Convert them to their alphanumeric equivalent to obtain the module name.
- Alternatively, the offending module name may be obtained from the SVC parameter list:
  - If the LINK, XCTL, or ATTACH was issued by the problem program, their parameter list will be pointed to by R15 of the problem program's PRB register save area. The problem program's PRB is usually the first RB under ACTIVE RBs and its FL-CDE points to a CDE entry that names the problem program in its EPA. The SVC issued may be determined from the low-order byte of this PRB's WC-L-IC field (RBINT-COD). If RBINTCOD is:
    - x06, a LINK was issued.
    - x07, an XCTL was issued.
    - x42, an ATTACH was issued.

    The first byte of the parameter list pointed to by R15 indicates whether an entry point (x00) or directory (x80) request was made. The second, third, and fourth bytes of the parameter list either point to an entry point name (x00) or a directory area created by BLDL (x80).
  - If a LOAD was issued by the problem program, a similar analysis may be used to find the offending module name. LOAD does not use a parameter list. Locate the PRB's register save area as explained above. RBINTCOD for a LOAD will be x08. In the register save area:
    - R0 contains the entry point name address in its low-order 3 bytes if the first byte is x00; the address of the BLDL-created directory entry if the first byte is x80.
    - R1 contains the DCB address of the load library or zeros if the default library is to be used.
  - If a JOBLIB DD statement was specified, the address of its DCB is in the TCB field labeled JLB (TCBJLB, TCB + x28). If not specified, this field will contain zeros.

If the JES log is not available, the data set name may be found by examining the O/C/EOV work area. See 3.4, Analysis of the O/C/EOV Work Area.

WHAT TO DO:

- Follow the debugging steps outlined in 1.3, General Debugging Procedure, and 5.2, Basic Techniques.
- Correct the linkage editor errors, or specify LET as a parameter, if the omission of an input module(s) or other errors are acceptable. However, subsequent attempts to execute an incomplete load module may result in 0C1, 0C4, or 0C5 abends.
- For information on how to list load module data, see 3.8, Dumping and Printing Data.

---

713 Attempt to OPEN an unexpired tape or DASD data set for output.

Related System Messages: IEC148I, IEC507D
SVC 19 OPEN

POSSIBLE CAUSES:

General:

- Problem program attempted to open for output a data set whose expiration date had not yet passed. Operator was notified of this condition via message IEC507D and:
  - Canceled the job.
  - Replied "M," causing open to issue an abend.
- Error in scheduling update or retention of a data set.
- Problem program incorrectly specifies OUTPUT or INOUT for open processing.

JCL Related:

DD statement:

- Incorrect or misspelled DSNAME specification.
- Incorrect VOLUME specification.
- DISP specified OLD for output DASD data set instead of NEW or MOD.
- LABEL=(,,,OUT,,,) specified instead of LABEL=(,,,IN,,,).
- RETPD or EXPDT specified when this data set was created were incorrect or of inappropriate duration.

RELEVANT DUMP ITEMS:

- The address of the next problem program instruction may be found in the PSW field of the problem program's PRB under ACTIVE RBS. This RB is usually the first printed. The FL-CDE of this PRB will point to a CDE entry that has the problem program's name printed in NM. To verify that this address points to the next instruction, check the 2 bytes immediately preceding it. They should contain x0A13—the object code for the OPEN SVC.

- R2 points to the offending DCB:
  - If the DCB was open, it will be formatted in the control block section of the dump and have a DEB and IOBs associated with it:
    - The 2-byte TIOT offset is at x28 into the DCB.
    - The DDname of this DCB is given in the TIOT at this offset.
  - If the DCB was not opened or has been closed, it will not be formatted in the control block section, but will be found in the main storage dump. The DEB will contain the DCB address.
    - The 8-byte DDname will be at x28 into the DCB.
- R4 points to the OPEN/CLOSE/EOV work area for the offending data set. It contains:
  - The data set label at R4 + 0.
  - The JFCB (DD statement parameters) at R4 + x64. Examination of this work area will indicate conflicting or incorrectly specified data set parameters. 3.4, Analysis of the O/C/EOV Work Area, provides a detailed description of its fields.
- If the UCB volume serial (UCBVOLI, UCB + x1C) for a DASD device is zero (EBCDIC), a supervisor error is indicated.
- Message IEC148I may indicate the offending device, DDname, volume serial number, and data set name. R15 contains a return code documented in *System Messages* under this message: Briefly:
  - 04 Tape data set problem.
  - 08 DASD data set problem.
  - 0C Operator disallowed VOL1 rewrite.

WHAT TO DO:

- Follow the steps outlined in 1.3, General Debugging Procedure, and 5.2, Basic Techniques.
- Have the operator reply "U" to message IEC507D. This will cause the date check to be bypassed.
- Recovery from unexpired retention date on an output tape volume (R15 = x04) may be attempted, preventing an abend termination. The address of a recovery routine may be specified via the EXLST operand of the DCB macro or placed in DCBEXLSA (DCB + x25). *Data Management Services* gives a detailed explanation of this feature.
- The IEFBR14 utility may be used to rectify catalog inconsistencies by specifying appropriate DD statement parameters. IEFBR14 does nothing itself. It takes its name from the fact that its only action is to branch register 14 (i.e., to terminate the step). However, all standard allocation/unallocation processing invoked via JCL is performed. This example below shows how to delete a data set "SOON.TOBE.GONE" and to catalog "NEW.DSNAME" using IEFBR14.

```
//CATSTEP  EXEC PGM=IEFBR14
//DELETEDD DD DSN=SOON.TOBE.GONE,DISP=(OLD,DELETE)
//CATLGDD  DD DSN=NEW.DSNAME,DISP=(NEW,CATLG)
```

- For information on how to dump data set labels, see 3.8, Dumping and Printing Data.
- A data set with an expiration or retention data can be deleted prior to this date. For data sets in a VSAM catalog, use the IDCAMS DELETE command. For more information, see *Access Method Services*. To delete uncataloged data sets, use the IEHPROGM utility. For more information about IEHPROGM, see *MVS Utilities*.

---

714 I/O error during close of an output tape data set.

Related System Messages: IEC215I
SVC 20 CLOSE

POSSIBLE CAUSES:

General:

- Device malfunction or physical damage to tape (e.g., a crimp).
- Attempt to output invalid tape trailer label.
- I/O error in close processing while writing:
  - Trailer label 1 (EOF1).
  - Trailer label 2 (EOF2).
  - Tapemark.

RELEVANT DUMP ITEMS:

- The address of the next problem program instruction may be found at:
  - The PSW field of the problem program's PRB under ACTIVE RBS. This RB is usually the first printed. The FL-CDE of the problem program's PRB will point to a CDE entry that has the problem program's name printed in NM.
  - The RET field of the last SA under SAVE AREA TRACE.
- R2 points to the offending DCB:
  - If the DCB was open, it will be formatted in the control block section of the dump and have a DEB and IOBs associated with it.
    - The 2-byte TIOT offset is at x28 into the DCB.
    - The DDname of this DCB is given in the TIOT at this offset.
  - If the DCB was not opened or has been closed, it will not be formatted in the control block section but will be found in the main storage dump. The DEB will contain the DCB address. The 8-byte DDname will be at x28 into the DCB.

- The IOB prefix pointer is at x1C into the DCB. IOB fields may indicate if a hardware-related I/O error has occurred. The IOB prefix is 16 bytes long, so the IOB proper begins at the prefix address plus x10. Fields of interest are:
  - IOB + 0, IOBFLAG1: If bit 5 is on (x04), a permanent I/O error has occurred. System message IEA000I will probably have been issued.
  - IOB + 4, ECBCC: ECB completion code. First byte of the 4-byte ECB. If this byte is not x00 or x7F, a channel error has occurred.
  - IOB + xC, second word of the CSW: Contains the channel status bits. Bits 36 and 37 should be on if an I/O operation has completed successfully.
- Further explanation of the ECB and CSW is given in 4.2, Dump Components, Input-Output Block.
- R4 points to the OPEN/CLOSE/EOV work area for the offending data set. It contains:
  - The data set label at R4 + 0.
  - The JFCB (DD statement parameters) at R4 + x64. Examination of this work area will indicate conflicting or incorrectly specified data set parameters. 3.4, Analysis of the O/C/EOV Work Area, provides a detailed description of its fields.
- Message IEC215I may indicate the offending device, DDname, volume serial number, and data set name. R15 contains a return code documented in *System Messages* under this message. Briefly:
  - 04 I/O error writing trailer label 1.
  - 08 I/O error writing trailer label 2.
  - 0C I/O error writing tapemark.

WHAT TO DO:

- Follow the steps outlined in 1.3, General Debugging Procedure, and 5.2, Basic Techniques.
- If an I/O error has occurred, specify a different device, volume, or both and rerun the job.
- For information on how to dump tape labels, see 3.8, Dumping and Printing Data.

---

737 I/O error for DASD data set during EOV processing or while allocating secondary quantity of storage.

Related System Messages: IEC027I
SVC 55 CLOSE

POSSIBLE CAUSES:

General:

- Device malfunction or physical damage to recording medium.
- A DSCB (data set label) of a multivolume or concatenated data set could not be processed:
  - An uncorrectable I/O error occurred while:
    - Reading a format 1 DSCB.
    - Reading a format 3 DSCB.
    - Reading a DSCB for a concatenated PDS.
  - The DSCB was not found.
- And uncorrectable I/O error occurred while:
  - Reading the DASD volume label.
  - Writing a DSAD file mark.
- Mass storage system error:
  - I/O error occurred; see message IEC066I.
  - Wrong virtual volume mounted.

JCL Related:

DD statement:

- DSNAME specification is misspelled or incorrect.
- VOLUME specification is incorrect.

Assembly Programs:

- FEOV was issued but the DCB seek address (DCBFDAD, DCB + x5) was inadvertently modified or overlaid. The seek address points to an extent outside of the DEB's extent range.

RELEVANT DUMP ITEMS:

- The address of the next problem program instruction may be found at the RET field of the last SA under SAVE AREA TRACE.
- R2 points to the offending DCB.
  - The 2-byte TIOT offset is located at + x28 into the DCB.
  - The DDname of the DCB is given in the TIOT at this offset.
  - If this DCB has been CLOSEd, it will not be formatted in the control block section of the dump but should be the main storage listing. The DEB will contain the DCB address.

- DCB + x1C points to the IOB prefix. IOB fields may indicate if a hardware-related I/O error has occurred. The IOB prefix is 16 bytes long, so the IOB proper begins at prefix address plus x10. Fields of interest are:
  - IOB + 0, IOBFLAG1: If bit 5 is on (x04), a permanent I/O error has occurred. System message IEA000I will probably have been issued.
  - IOB + 4, ECBCC: ECB completion code. First byte of the 4-byte ECB. If this byte is not x00 or x7F, a channel error has occurred.
  - IOB + xC, second word of the CSW: Contains the channel status bits. Bits 36 and 37 should be on if an I/O operation has been completed successfully.
  - Further explanation of the ECB and CSW is given in 4.2, Dump Components, Input-Output Block.
- R4 points to the OPEN/CLOSE/EOV work area for the offending data set. It contains:
  - The data set label at R4 + 0.
  - The JFCB (DD statement parameters) at R4 + x64. Examination of this work area will indicate conflicting or incorrectly specified data set parameters. 3.4, Analysis of the O/C/EOV Work Area, provides a detailed description of its fields.
- Message IEC027I may indicate the offending device, DDname, volume serial, and data set name. R15 contains a return code documented in *System Messages* under this message. Briefly:
  - 04 I/O error or DSCB not found on read.
  - 08 I/O error reading a DASD volume label.
  - 0C I/O error reading DCSB for a concatenated PDS.
  - 10 I/O error writing DASD file mark.
  - 14 I/O error reading a DSCB for trailer processing.
  - 1C I/O error reading a format 3 DSCB.
  - 24 PDS member not found.
  - 28 Supervisor error.
  - 2C FEOV could not determine where to write a tapemark.
  - 34 MSS I/O error (see message IEC066I).
  - 38 MSS mounted wrong virtual volume.
  - 3C Format 1 DSCB not found.

WHAT TO DO:

- Follow the steps outlined in 1.3, General Debugging Procedure, and 5.2, Basic Techniques.
- If an I/O error has occurred, specify a different device, volume, or both and rerun the job.
- For information about how to dump DASD labels, see 3.8, Dumping and Printing Data. DASD labels are described in *Data Management Services*.

804 Unable to satisfy GETMAIN request for main storage.

Related System Messages: IEA700I
SVC 4 GETMAIN

POSSIBLE CAUSES:

General:

- Region size too small for task's requirements:
  - Default limit exceeded.
  - Limit defined via JOB or EXEC insufficient or incorrect.
- Task storage requirements increased but allocation was not:
  - Additional buffers (increased block size).
  - Additional load modules.
- Problem program formatted storage request incorrectly.

JCL Related:

JOB statement:

- REGION parameter specifies incorrect or insufficient quantity of virtual storage.

EXEC statement:

- See "JOB statement" above.
- JOB statement REGION parameter overrides all EXEC statement REGION parameters.
- PARM-supplied SIZE parameter for compiler, linkage editor, sort, or other utility exceeds available storage or is too large.
- DD statement:
  - A change to or incorrect specification of buffer-related parameters has increased main storage requirements:
    - •• DCB subparameters:
      - BUFL.
      - BUFNO.
      - BLKSIZE.
    - •• AMP subparameters:
      - BUFND.
      - BUFNI.
      - BUFSP.
      - STRNO.

COBOL Programs:

- A COBOL module is frequently invoked by a non-COBOL caller (e.g., IMS), but the ENDJOB compiler option was not specified at compile time. The ENDJOB option causes storage allocated to a COBOL module to be freed upon termination or upon return to the system component that invoked the program (ENDJOB is not allowed for CICS/VS COBOL, however).

Assembly Programs:

- FREEMAIN not issued frequently enough in a dynamic task environment.
- GETMAIN's parameter list incorrectly specified or overlaid:
  - Negative length specified for EU or VU type GETMAIN.
  - Request was incorrectly specified or calculated.

RELEVANT DUMP ITEMS:

- The address of the next problem program instruction may be found at:
  - The PSW field of the problem program's PRB under ACTIVE RBS. This RB is usually the first printed. The FL-CDE of the problem program's PRB will point to a CDE entry that has the problem program's name printed in NM.
  - The RET field of the last SA under SAVE AREA TRACE.
- R1 points to GETMAIN's parameter list. The format of this list depends on the type of request: single, variable, or list. The type is indicated by a flag byte at R1 + 8. The types are:

Type	*Request Offset*	*Length*	*Flag*
Single	R1 + 0	3	x00,x20
Variable			
Min.	R1 + 1	3	xC0,xE0
Max.	R1 + 5	3	
List	Varies, list starts at R1 + 0	3	x80,xA0

- Actual virtual storage available is equal to the sum of fullword SZ fields to the right of the FBQE fields under D-PQE. Comparing the requested to available storage should indicate how much to increase the REGION parameter.
- R2 may point to the DCB of a data set whose increased buffer requirements caused the abend.
  - The 2-byte TIOT offset is at x28 into the DCB.
  - The DDname of this DCB is given in the TIOT at this offset.
  - At x14, the DCBBUFNO byte gives the buffer count.
  - At x3E, the 2-byte DCBBLKSI gives the block size.
  - Buffer count times block size equals total buffer requirement.
- See 3.5, Locating VSAM Data Records, for the steps to find VSAM buffer-size parameters.

WHAT TO DO:

- Follow the steps outlined in 1.3, General Debugging Procedure, and 5.2, Basic Techniques.
- Increase the REGION specification and rerun the job.

---

806 A requested program load module could not be found.

Related System Messages: IEA703I

SVC 6 LINK
7 XCTL
8 LOAD
42 ATTACH

POSSIBLE CAUSES:

General:

- An attempt to bring a module into execution failed because the requested load module could not be found:
  - Module name incorrect or misspelled.
  - The member or data set containing the module was:
    - Deleted.
    - Expired and deleted.
    - Renamed.
    - Moved.
  - Module was never created:
    - Compile or assemble error prevented link-edit step from executing.
    - Link-edit job or step was not run.
  - Module was not moved to a production library from a test or development library.
  - In a multi-CPU installation, the load module's data set may not be accessible from the CPU running the task.
  - A load library PDS was opened for output simultaneously by several jobs (e.g., a compress and a link-edit) and was partially or totally destroyed.
- An error occurred during link-edit processing in a previous step or job. The requested load module was not created:
  - A severity level 4 error occurred. No output load module was created.
  - A control card was omitted or specified an incorrect or misspelled member name:
    - ALIAS.
    - ENTRY duplicates are skipped. A statement has been duplicated with the intent

of changing it (e.g., PGM01, PGM01 to PGM01, PGM02), but the change was not made.
  - NAME. NAME's member name overrides SYSLMOD's member name.
  - REPLACE. The member(s) to be deleted and replaced was not found, so no update occurred.
- Uncorrectable I/O error occurred while searching a load library directory.
- An invalid DEB was encountered.

JCL Related:

JOB statement:

- See COND parameter under "EXEC statement" below.

EXEC statement:

- COND parameter omitted or incorrectly specified. Compile, assemble, or link-edit step gave a nonzero return code, but further processing was attempted. For the linkage editor:
  - Severity level 2 error gives a return code of 4.
  - Severity level 3 error gives a return code of 8.
  - Severity level 4 error gives a return code of 16.
- PGM specifies incorrect or misspelled program name.

DD statement:

- SYSLMOD DD (in link-edit step):
  - DSNAME or member name incorrect, misspelled, or uses invalid refer-back.
  - BLKSIZE was incorrectly specified or overridden.
  - Member was overridden by NAME control card given to linkage editor.
- DISP specified SHR during previous update of load library PDS. Simultaneous updates occurred and the data set was partially or totally destroyed.
- JOBLIB or STEPLIB DD:
  - Was omitted—load module not in SYS1.LINKLIB.
  - DSNAME specification is misspelled or incorrect.
  - Is incorrectly overridden.
  - Concatenation is in wrong sequence or omits a load library.
- See 3.3, Common JCL Errors.

Assembly Programs:

- Parameters specified to a LINK, XCTL, LOAD, or ATTACH are incorrect:
  - Module name misspelled.
  - Entry point or list entry address incorrectly calculated or overlaid.
- CSECT name misspelled.

COBOL Programs:

- The DYNAM compiler option or dynamic CALL is used. The module name supplied to a CALL is misspelled or incorrect.

RELEVANT DUMP ITEMS:

- The address of the next problem program instruction may be found at:
  - The PSW field of the problem program's PRB under ACTIVE RBS. This RB is usually the first printed. The FL-CDE of the problem program's PRB will point to a CDE entry that has the problem program's name printed in NM.
  - The RET field of the last SA under SAVE AREA TRACE.
  - If the problem program has not been loaded, no PRB will be listed. The problem program's name will not appear in the CDE. In this case, the abend was issued by the program manager function of the supervisor.
- The 8-byte name of the offending module may be found as follows:
  - Check message IEA703I first.
  - Locate ABEND's SVRB. It will probably be the first or second RB listed under ACTIVE RBS and will contain x0D in the low-order byte of the WC-L-IC field.
  - The module name is in the first 8 bytes of the field labeled EXTSA in the ABEND's SVRB (this is the RBEXSAVE field located at x60 into the SVRB). The EBCDIC characters are shown in hexadecimal. Convert them to their alphanumeric equivalent to obtain the module name.
- Alternatively, the offending module name may be obtained from SVC's parameter list:
  - If the LINK, XCTL, or ATTACH was issued by the problem program, its parameter list will be pointed to by R15 of the problem program's PRB register save area. The problem program's PRB is usually the first RB under ACTIVE RBs and its FL-CDE points to a CDE entry that names the problem program in its EPA. The SVC issued may be determined from the low-order byte of this PRB's WC-L-IC field (RBINT-COD). If RBINTCOD is:
    - x06, a LINK was issued.
    - x07, an XCTL was issued.
    - x42, an ATTACH was issued.

    The first byte of the parameter list pointed to by R15 indicates whether an entry point (x00) or directory (x80) request was made. The second, third, and fourth bytes of the parameter list point either to an entry point name (x00) or a directory area created by BLDL (x80).
  - If a LOAD was issued by the problem program, a similar analysis may be used to find the offending module name. LOAD does not use a parameter list. Locate the PRB's register save area as explained above. RBINTCOD for a LOAD will be x08. In the register save area:
    - R0 contains the entry point name address in its low-order 3 bytes if the first byte is x00, the address of the BLDL created directory entry if the first byte is x80.

  - •• R1 contains the DCB address of the load library or zeros if the default library is to be used.
- If a JOBLIB DD statement was specified, the address of its DCB is in the TCB field labeled JLB (TCBJLB, TCB + x28). If not specified, this field will contain zeros. If the JES log is not available, the data set name may be found by examining the O/C/EOV work area. See 3.4, Analysis of the O/C/EOV Work Area.
- Message IEA703I may indicate the missing module name. R15 contains a return code documented in *System Messages* under this message. Briefly:
  - 04 Requested module could not be found in SYS1.LINKLIB, JOBLIB, or STEPLIB data set.
  - 08 An uncorrectable I/O error occurred during FETCH.
  - 0C Requested SVC not found in the link pack area.
  - 10 DCB of requested module's library was not open or otherwise invalid.

WHAT TO DO:

- Follow the steps outlined in 1.3, General Debugging Procedure, and 5.2, Basic Techniques.
- For information on how to list load module data, see 3.8, Dumping and Printing Data.

80A Unable to satisfy R-form GETMAIN request for main storage.

Related System Messages: IEA700I
SVC 10 GETMAIN

POSSIBLE CAUSES:

General:

- Region size too small for task's requirements:
  - Default limit exceeded.
  - Limit defined via JOB or EXEC insufficient or incorrect.
- Task storage requirements increased but allocation was not:
  - Additional buffers (increased block size).
  - Additional load modules.
- Problem program formatted storage request incorrectly.

JCL Related:

JOB statement:

- REGION parameter specifies incorrect or insufficient quantity of virtual storage.

EXEC statement:

- See "JOB statement" above.
- JOB statement REGION parameter overrides all EXEC statement REGION parameters.
- PARM-supplied SIZE parameter for compiler, linkage editor, sort, or other utility exceeds available storage.

DD statement:

- A change to or incorrect specification of buffer-related parameters has increased main storage requirements:
  - DCB subparameters:
    - BUFL.
    - BUFNO.
    - BLKSIZE.
  - AMP subparameters:
    - BUFND.
    - BUFNI.
    - BUFSP.
    - STRNO.

COBOL Programs:

- A COBOL module is frequently invoked by a non-COBOL caller (e.g., IMS), but the ENDJOB compiler option was not specified at compile time. The ENDJOB option causes storage allocated to a COBOL module to be freed upon termination or upon return to the system component that invoked the program (ENDJOB is not allowed for CICS/VS COBOL, however).

Assembly Programs:

- FREEMAIN not issued frequently enough in a dynamic task environment.
- GETMAIN parameter list incorrectly built.

RELEVANT DUMP ITEMS:

- The address of the next problem program instruction may be found at:
  - The PSW field of the problem program's PRB under ACTIVE RBS. This RB is usually the first printed. The FL-CDE of the problem program's PRB will point to a CDE entry that has the problem program's name printed in NM.
  - The RET field of the last SA under SAVE AREA TRACE.
- R0 Contains:
  - The subpool ID requested in the high-order byte.
  - The length of the area requested in bytes 1 through 3.

- Actual virtual storage available is equal to the sum of fullword SZ fields to the right of FBQE fields under D-PQE.
- Comparing the requested to available storage should indicate how much to increase the REGION parameter.
- R2 may point to the DCB of a data set whose increased buffer requirements caused the abend.
  - The 2-byte TIOT offset is at x28 into the DCB.
  - The DDname of this DCB is given in the TIOT at this offset.
  - At x14, the DCBBUFNO byte gives the buffer count.
  - At x3E, the 2-byte DCBBLKSI gives the block size.
  - Buffer count times block size equals total buffer requirement.
- See 3.5, Locating VSAM Data Records, for the steps to find VSAM buffer parameters.

WHAT TO DO:

- Follow the steps outlined in 1.3, General Debugging Procedure, and 5.2, Basic Techniques.
- Increase the REGION specification and rerun the job.

---

813 OPEN error for tape data set.

Related System Messages: IEC149I
SVC 19 OPEN

POSSIBLE CAUSES:

General:

- Data set contained in tape header label conflicts with that specified in the DD statement.
- Wrong volume mounted.
- Another data set has been written over the requested volume or data set.
- Incorrect volume serial number contained in the catalog.
- DD statement specifies a data set name longer than 17 characters. A standard tape label contains the rightmost 17 characters of the data set name, so the tape name and the requested name were not identical. This may be due to transferring a DASD data set to tape.
- The desired data set does not exist:
  - It was never created.
  - It was inadvertently deleted.
  - It has expired and was written over.

JCL Related:

DD statement:

- DDname misspelled.
- DSNAME specification misspelled or incorrect:
  - A temporary (&&dsname) or refer-back data set was not created because a previous job or step failed or did not execute due to condition codes.
  - DD DUMMY or DSNAME = NULLFILE specified in a previous job or step. No data set was created.
  - Generation Data Group (GDG) data set specified by its fully qualified name (e.g., A.B.G000V0012) instead of relative generation. This data set no longer exists or has not been created.
  - A data set name longer than 17 characters was specified. Tape labels contain only the rightmost 17 characters of the data set name.
- DISP parameter specification was incorrect in a previous job or step. The data set does not exist:
  - DISP was omitted for an output data set. The default normal termination of delete was taken at the end of the step.
  - DISP = (NEW,PASS) was specified for an output data set. KEEP was not specified in a subsequent step. The default normal termination of delete was taken at the end of the job.
  - The status subparameter NEW was specified for an output Generation Data Group (GDG) data set which was allocated but not opened in a previous job or step. A catalog entry with a null volser was created. Subsequent requests for this data set cause a scratch tape to be mounted.
  - MOD was specified for a new output data set or an existing input data set.
  - The normal termination subparameter did not specify DELETE for an output data set processed under NL or BLP in a previous job or step (DELETE causes a physical demount of a tape reel—the data set is intact). Since nonstandard label processing was specified, the system assumed the volume was a scratch tape. It was subsequently written over or relabeled.
  - The abnormal termination subparameter incorrectly specified DELETE or UNCATLG in a previous job or step. The previous step abended, causing the data set to be deleted.
- Subparameters of the volume parameter, VOLUME = (,,*S*,,SER =) were incorrectly specified:
  - The volume sequence number, *S*, selected a reel of a multireel volume which was greater than the reel number containing the desired data set.
  - The volume serial numbers specified by SER or obtained via REF are incorrect or omit the reel containing the desired data set.
- Subparameters of the label parameter, LABEL = (*D*,*T*), were incorrectly specified:
  - The data set sequence number, *D*, pointed to a data set that was not the same as specified by the DSNAME:

- - *D* was incorrect.
  - *D* was omitted. A default of 1 was used or was obtained from the system catalog.
  - For a multireel volume:
    - Processed under standard labels, *D* was specified relative to a particular reel instead of the entire volume.
    - Processed under BLP or NL, *D* was specified relative to the entire volume instead of a particular reel.
  - The correct value of *D* depends on the label type, *T*. The *D* used for SL (standard label) processing will not give the same results for nonstandard label processing. If an SL tape is processed under BLP or NL, the correct *D* is given by the formula: $D_{blp} = (3(D_{sl} - 1)) + 2$. This formula reflects the fact that tapemarks are equated to end-of-file marks under nonstandard label processing. A tapemark is placed (on SL tapes) after every:
    - Header label (VOL1, HDR1, HDR2).
    - Data set.
    - End-of-file label (EOF1, EOF2).
    - End-of-volume label (EOV1).
- The label type subparameter, *T,* specified BLP or NL:
  - When SL was needed.
  - For a generation data group (GDG). The data set sequence number was obtained from the system catalog. Since tapemarks are counted as data sets under nonstandard label processing (see above), the tape could not be positioned to the requested data set.

Assembly Programs:

- JFCB parameters incorrectly modified or overlaid.

RELEVANT DUMP ITEMS:

- The address of the next problem program instruction may be found in the PSW field of the problem program's PRB under ACTIVE RBS. This RB is usually the first printed. The FL-CDE of this PRB will point to a CDE entry that has the problem program's name printed in NM. To verify that this address points to the next instruction, check the 2 bytes immediately preceding it. They should contain x0A13—the object code for the OPEN SVC.
- R2 points to the offending DCB:
  - If the DCB was open, it will be formatted in the control block section of the dump and have a DEB and IOBs associated with it.
    - The 2-byte TIOT offset is at x28 into the DCB.
    - The DDname of this DCB is given in the TIOT at this offset.
  - If the DCB was not opened or has been closed, it will not be formatted in the control block section but will be found in the main storage dump. The DEB will contain the DCB address. The 8-byte DDname will be at x28 into the DCB.

- R4 points to the OPEN/CLOSE/EOV work area for the offending data set. It contains:
  - The data set label at R4 + 0.
  - The JFCB (DD statement parameters) at R4 + x64. Examination of this work area may indicate conflicting or incorrectly specified data set parameters. 3.4, Analysis of the O/C/EOV Work Area, provides a detailed description of its fields.
- Message IEC149I may indicate the offending DDname, device address, volume serial number, and data set name.

WHAT TO DO:

- Follow the steps outlined in 1.3, General Debugging Procedure, and 5.2, Basic Techniques.
- Recovery from header label/DD statement data set name mismatch may be attempted, preventing an abend termination. The address of a recovery routine may be specified via the EXLST operand of the DCB macro or placed in DCBEXLSA (DCB + x25). *Data Management Services* gives a detailed explanation of this feature.
- The IEFBR14 utility may be used to rectify catalog inconsistencies by specifying appropriate DD statement parameters. IEFBR14 does nothing itself. It takes its name from the fact that its only action is to branch to register 14 (i.e., to terminate the step). However, all standard allocation/unallocation processing invoked via JCL is performed. The example below shows how to delete a data set "SOON.TOBE.GONE" and to catalog "NEW.DSNAME" using IEFBR14.

```
//CATSTEP EXEC PGM=IEFBR14
//DELETED DD DSN=SOON.TOBE.GONE,DISP=(OLD,DELETE)
//CATLGDD DD DSN=NEW.DSNAME,DISP=(NEW,CATLG)
```

- For information on how to dump tape labels, see 3.8, Dumping and Printing Data.

---

913 OPEN failed for password protected, checkpoint, or ISAM data set.

Related System Messages: IEC150I, IEC301A
SVC 19 OPEN

POSSIBLE CAUSES:

General:

- An attempt to open a password protected data set failed because:
  - Incorrect password supplied.
  - Access specified via JCL or open parameters conflicts with password-defined access (e.g., OPEN OUTPUT), but password allows read only.

- Attempted access violates RACF or ACF rules.
- An operator responded twice with an incorrect password to message IEC301A because:
  - The job or step was not authorized to access the data set.
  - The operator did not know the password.
  - The operator erred.
- The system password data set:
  - Does not have a record for the data set being accessed, but password checking was invoked.
  - Has a record for this data set, but the protection mode field (third byte, which indicates read, write, or delete access) was invalid.
  - Has incorrectly specified data set name or password.

– The password record for a tape data set whose name was longer than 17 characters could not be found. The data set name used to look up the password record of a tape data set is taken from the HDR1 tape label data set name field that contains the rightmost 17 bytes of the name. Tape data sets with a longer name may be not found or may point to an incorrect record. This may be due to:
  - Transferring a password-protected DASD data set to tape.
  - Specifying a name of 18 or more characters for a tape data set.

– Invalid ANS tape label found.

– IEHPROGM was incorrectly used to create a password record.

– Password protection was specified for at least one data set used in conjunction with other data sets, forcing password checking for all associated data sets. Previous use of the unprotected data sets did not require a password, so none was supplied in the new context. The password-protected data set was in:
  - A tape volume containing two or more data sets.
  - A list of concatenated data sets.

– TYPE=J OPEN for a DASD data set failed:
  - For ISAM data sets defined by multiple DD statements, the data set name specified to OPEN conflicted with the DD statement or the JFCB.
  - The data set was already exclusively ENQUED (in use) by:
    - Another task's OPEN.
    - Another job stream.

– Unauthorized job or step attempt to open a VTOC data set.

JCL Related:

JOB statement:

– RACF parameters incorrect, missing, or misspelled:
  - PASSWORD omitted or incorrect.
  - GROUP omitted, default used.
  - USER omitted, default used.

DD statement:

- DDname misspelled or incorrect.
- DSNAME specification:
  - Misspelled or incorrect.
  - Is not identical for an ISAM data set defined by several DD statements.
  - A checkpoint data set is not BPAM or BSAM organization.
- DISP of OLD or MOD specified by another job instead of SHR for the requested data set.
- A concatenation list:
  - Contains incorrect or misspelled data set name(s).
  - For a checkpoint data set specifies non-BPAM or non-BSAM data set(s).
  - Contains both password-protected and nonprotected data sets.
- Label subparameters or keywords of LABEL=(*T*, . . .) parameter were omitted or incorrect:
  - Label type *T* (tape data sets):
    - Must be SL, SUL, AL, or AUL to support password protection.
    - Specified BLP or NL for password-protected data set.
    - BLP or NL not specified for a tape wtih nonstandard labels.
  - No entry for the data set existed or was found on the system password data set and:
    - PASSWORD keyword was specified.
    - NOPWREAD keyword was specified for a data set opened for output.
- See 3.3, Common JCL Errors.

Assembly Programs:

- Parameters for OPEN or CHKPT macros incorrectly specified, omitted, or overlaid.
- Parameters for PROTECT macro invalid:
  - Protection code indicator was not x00, x01, x02, or x03.
  - Either the wrong password, data set name, or both were added, replaced, or deleted.
  - An error occurred, but R15 return code was not tested, so successful execution was incorrectly assumed.
- Inadvertent or incorrect modification of the JFCB:
  - R4 + x64 points to the user's JFCB.
  - TIOT JFCB entry (TIOEJFCB, DD entry + x24) points to the system's JFCB.

COBOL Programs:

- SELECT file-name ASSIGN TO device-organization-DDname specification is in error:
  - DA-I-DDname not specified for an ISAM data set.
  - File-name misspelled or incorrect.
  - DDname misspelled or incorrect.

- RERUN statement for a checkpoint data set specifies a system name that is not the same as the DDname.
- OPEN access (INPUT, OUTPUT) conflicts with password processing specified via JCL.

RELEVANT DUMP ITEMS:

- The address of the next problem program instruction may be found in the PSW field of the problem program's PRB under ACTIVE RBS. This RB is usually the first printed. The FL-CDE of this PRB will point to a CDE entry that has the problem program's name printed in NM. To verify that this address points to the next instruction, check the 2 bytes immediately preceding it. They should contain x0A13—the object code for the OPEN SVC.
- R2 points to the offending DCB.
  - If the DCB was open, it will be formatted in the control block section of the dump and have a DEB and IOBs associated wtih it.
    - The 2-byte TIOT offset is at x28 into the DCB.
    - The DDname of this DCB is given in the TIOT at this offset.
    - DCB + x1C points to the IOB prefix. IOB fields will indicate an I/O error if it has occurred.
  - If the DCB was not opened or has been closed, it will not be formatted in the control block section but will be found in the main storage dump. The DEB will contain the DCB address. The 8-byte DDname will be at x28 into the DCB.
- R4 points to the OPEN/CLOSE/EOV work area for the offending data set. It contains:
  - The data set label at R4 + 0.
  - The JFCB (DD statement parameters) at R4 + x64. Examination of this work area will indicate conflicting or incorrectly specified data set parameters. 3.4, Analysis of the O/C/EOV Work Area, provides a detailed description of its fields.
- Message IEC150I may indicate the offending DDname, device, volume serial number, and data set name. R15 contains a return code documented in *System Messages* under this message. Briefly:
  - 04 Nonstandard ANS tape label.
  - 0C Incorrect password specified.
  - 10 Unauthorized VTOC access.
  - 14 Attempt to concatenate checkpoint and noncheckpoint data set.
  - 18 Problem program attempt to specify BLP via the JFCB.
  - 1C Bad JFCB or a data set not available.
  - 20 EXCP appendages not found.
  - 28 Checkpoint data set is not BSAM or BPAM.
  - 2C DSNAME conflict for ISAM data set.
  - 30 Inconsistent tape data set protection mode.
  - 38 Unauthorized access under RACF.

- 3C Data set unrecognized by RACF.
- 40 VSAM data set is RACF defined.
- 44/5C RACF PROTECT incorrectly specified.

WHAT TO DO:

- Follow the steps outlined in 1.3, General Debugging Procedure, and 5.2, Basic Techniques.
- To remove password protection on a DASD data set, scratch the existing data using the IEHPROGM utility and then recreate it. (The password must be supplied to scratch the data set.)

A13 OPEN error on multidata set tape volume.

Related System Messages: IEC151I
SVC 19 OPEN

POSSIBLE CAUSES:

General:

- The data set specified via the DD statement's data set sequence number could not be found on the specified volume.
- The end of a data set could not be found for DISP=MOD processing on the volume specified.
- A previous job or step failed to create the data set or incorrectly deleted it.

JCL Related:

DD statement:

- DDname misspelled.
- DSNAME specification misspelled or incorrect:
  - A temporary (&&dsname) or refer-back data set was not created because a previous step failed or did not execute due to condition codes.
  - DD DUMMY or DSNAME=NULLFILE specified in a previous job or step. No data set created.
  - Generation data group (GDG) data set specified by fully qualified name (e.g., A.B.G000V0012), instead of relative generation. The specific data set no longer exists or has not been created.

- A data set name longer than 17 characters was specified. Tape labels contain only the rightmost 17 characters of the data set name.

– DISP parameter specification was incorrect in a previous job or step. The data set does not exist:

- The status subparameter NEW was specified for an output generation data group (GDG) data set that was allocated but not opened in a previous job or step. A catalog entry with a null volser was created. Subsequent requests for this data set cause a scratch tape to be mounted.
- MOD was specified for a new output data set or an existing input data set.
- The normal termination subparameter did not specify DELETE for an output data set processed under NL or BLP in a previous job or step (DELETE causes a physical demount of a tape reel—the data set is intact). Since nonstandard label processing was specified, the system assumed the volume was a scratch tape. It was subsequently written over or relabeled.
- The abnormal termination subparameter incorrectly specified DELETE or UNCATLG in a previous job or step.

– Subparameters of the volume parameter, VOLUME=(,,*S*,,SER=), were incorrectly specified:

- The volume sequence number, *S*, selected a reel of a multireel volume that was greater than the reel number containing the data set desired.
- The volume serial numbers specified by SER are incorrect or omit the reel containing the desired data set.

– Subparameters of the label parameter, LABEL=(*D*,*T*) were incorrectly specified:

- The data set sequence number, *D*, pointed to a data set that was not the same as specified by DSNAME:
  - *D* was incorrect.
  - *D* was omitted and a default of 1 was used or a value was obtained from the system catalog.
  - For a multireel volume:
    - Processed under standard labels, *D* was specified relative to a particular reel instead of the entire volume.
    - Processed under BLP or NL, *D* was specified relative to the entire volume instead of a particular reel.
  - The correct value of *D* depends on the label type, *T*. The *D* used for SL (standard label) processing will not give the same results for nonstandard label processing. If an SL tape is processed under BLP or NL, the correct *D* is given by the formula: $D_{\text{blp}} = (3(D_{\text{sl}} - 1)) + 2$. This formula reflects the fact that tapemarks are equated to end-of-file marks under nonstandard label processing. A tapemark is placed (on SL tapes) after every:
    - Header label (HDR1, HDR2).
    - Data set.
    - End-of-file label (EOF1, EOF2).
    - End-of-volume label (EOV1).
- The label type subparameter, *T*, specified BLP or NL:

- •• When SL was needed.
- •• For a generation data group (GDG). The data set sequence number was obtained from the system catalog. Since tapemarks are counted as data sets under non-standard label processing (see above), the tape could not be positioned to the data set requested.

RELEVANT DUMP ITEMS:

- The address of the next problem program instruction may be found in the PSW instruction field of the problem program's PRB under ACTIVE RBS. This RB is usually the first printed. The FL-CDE of this PRB will point to a CDE entry that has the problem program's name printed in NM. To verify that this address points to the next instruction, check the 2 bytes immediately preceding it. They should contain x0A13—the object code for the OPEN SVC.
- R2 points to the offending DCB.
  - If the DCB was open, it will be formatted in the control block section of the dump and have a DEB and IOBs associated with it.
    - •• The 2-byte TIOT offset is at x28 into the DCB.
    - •• The DDname of this DCB is given in the TIOT at this offset.
  - If the DCB was not opened or has been closed, it will not be formatted in the control block section, but will be found in the main storage dump. The DEB will contain the DCB address. The 8-byte DDname will be at x28 into the DCB.
- R4 points to the OPEN/CLOSE/EOV work area for the offending data set. It contains:
  - The data set label at R4 + 0.
  - The JFCB (DD statement parameters) at R4 + x64. Examination of this work area will indicate conflicting or incorrectly specified data set parameters. 3.4, Analysis of the O/C/EOV Work Area, provides a detailed description of its fields.
- Message IEC151I may indicate the offending DDname, device, volume serial number, and data set name. R15 contains a return code documented in *System Messages* under this message. Briefly:
  - 04 Unexpected load point.
  - 08 Data set sequence number less than data set sequence number of first file.
  - 0C Same as x08 for DISP=MOD.
  - 10 Data set not found on this volume.
  - 14 Volume ends just before specified data set.
  - 18 For DISP=MOD processing, end of data set not on this volume.

WHAT TO DO:

- Follow the steps outlined in 1.3, General Debugging Procedure, and 5.2, Basic Techniques.
- For information on how to dump tape labels, see 3.8, Dumping and Printing Data.

B14 CLOSE error for a PDS, opened for output to a member.

Related System Messages: IEC217I
SVC 20 STOW

POSSIBLE CAUSES:

General:

- The STOW SVC could not place the output member name in the directory because:
  - An uncorrectable I/O error occurred.
  - The directory was full.
  - The name already exists in the directory.
- Simultaneous updates to a PDS resulted in a loss or alteration of a member or directory.
- Insufficient main storage available for work areas to process a PDS update.
- Attempt to allocate a PDS and add a member from an invalid COBOL compilation.
- I/O error during directory update.

JCL Related:

JOB statement:

- REGION parameter specifies incorrect or insufficient quantity of virtual storage.

EXEC statement:

- See "JOB statement" above.
- JOB statement REGION parameter overrides all EXEC statement REGION parameters.

DD statement:

- DSNAME specifies incorrect data set or member name.
- DISP specification incorrect:
  - NEW specified for replace processing instead of OLD.
  - MOD was specified in an attempt to extend an existing member. MOD is valid only for adding members to an existing PDS. OLD must be used to update existing members.
  - SHR specified for update. Simultaneous updates occurred and the data set was partially or totally destroyed.
- The directory block allocation subparameter, *D*, of the space parameter SPACE=(*U*,(*P*,*S*,*D*)) specifies an insufficient quantity. See What to Do for a space estimate formula.

Assembly Programs:

- A DCB abend EXLST was specified but is ignored for partitioned data sets.

RELEVANT DUMP ITEMS:

- The address of the next problem program instruction may be found at:
  - The PSW field of the problem program's PRB under ACTIVE RBS. This RB is usually the first printed. The FL-CDE of the problem program's PRB will point to a CDE entry that has the problem program's name printed in NM.
  - The RET field of the last SA under SAVE AREA TRACE.
- R2 points to the offending DCB.
  - If the DCB was open, it will be formatted in the control block section of the dump and have a DEB and IOBs associated with it.
    - The 2-byte TIOT offset is at x28 into the DCB.
    - The DDname of this DCB is given in the TIOT at this offset.
  - If the DCB was not opened or has been closed, it will not be formatted in the control block section but will be found in the main storage dump. The DEB will contain the DCB address. The 8-byte DDname will be at x28 into the DCB.
- If the PDS was opened for output, the DEB will contain the offending member name. The DEB associated with the offending data set is usually printed immediately before this data set's DCB on the dump. The DEB is also pointed to from this DCB.
  - DCB for the offending data set + x2C points to its associated DEB.
  - DEB address + x24 points to the start of the 8-byte DEBDSNM field containing the member name.
- DCB + x1C points to the IOB prefix. IOB fields may indicate if a hardware-related I/O error has occurred. The IOB prefix is 16 bytes long, so the IOB proper begins at prefix address plus x10. Fields of interest are:
  - IOB + 0, IOBFLAG1: If bit 5 is on (x04), a permanent I/O error has occurred. System message IEA000I will probably have been issued.
  - IOB + 4, ECBCC: ECB completion code. First byte of the 4-byte ECB. If this byte is not x00 or x7F, a channel error has occurred.
  - IOB + xC, second word of the CSW: Contains the channel status bits. Bits 36 and 37 should be on if an I/O operation has been completed successfully.
  - Further explanation of the ECB and CSW is given in 4.2, Dump Components, Input-Output Block.
- Message IEC217I may indicate the DDname, data set name, and volume of the offending PDS. R15 contains a return code documented in *System Messages* under this message. Briefly:
  - 04 Member already exists in directory.
  - 08 Member not found for replace or delete.
  - 0C Directory is full.
  - 10 I/O error while updating directory.
  - 14 Invalid DCB encountered—already closed.
  - 18 Insufficient virtual storage available for update work areas.
- The contents of R0 provide information if an I/O error has occurred (R15 = x10):
  - 01 A permanent I/O error occurred while reading or writing directory blocks.

• 02 For an add or replace of a member, a permanent I/O error occurred while writing the member EOF marker.

WHAT TO DO:

- Follow the steps outlined in 1.3, General Debugging Procedure, and 5.2, Basic Techniques.
- The IEBCOPY utility may be used to compress the PDS if it is full. The PDS is copied to a temporary data set and then back to the original data set.
- IEHPROGM utility may be used to delete or rename members.
- Do not specify DISP=SHR for a critical PDS when doing updates.
- The quantity of PDS directory blocks needed may be estimated by dividing the number of anticipated members by 5 and rounding up to the nearest whole number. On average, five directory entries can fit in one 256-byte block. As few as 3 or as many as 20 can fit in a single block. The directory allocation is taken from the primary space allocation in tracks. Therefore, the primary allocation should also allow for directory space.

  If the PDS is to be used in conjunction with the SPF facility of TSO, the directory allocation should be increased from the estimate above by a factor of 4. The statistics maintained by SPF require the additional space.

B37 Insufficient space for output DASD or tape data set.

Related System Messages: IEC030I
SVC 55 EOV

POSSIBLE CAUSES:

General:

- Primary allocation filled and secondary allocation could not be met—no more space is available on the last volume used:
  - Insufficient space specified for an output data set.
  - All or most of the temporary workspace has been allocated to other jobs or consumed by other data sets.
- Problem program is writing a greater than anticipated quantity of output because:
  - It is in a write loop.
  - It is processing a substantially increased quantity of input.
- A DASD data set requires more than 16 extents.
- A DASD volume needed to meet space requirements could not be mounted (or dismounted) because:

  - It was permanently resident.
  - It contained data sets allocated to other jobs.
  - Problem program had other data sets open on this volume.
- The VTOC (volume table of contents) was full—no more entries could be made.
- An inefficient block size was specified. An inordinate amount of the allocation has been used by interblock gaps or wasted track space.
- No devices were available for mounting another volume.
- See SCC 001.

JCL Related:

DD statement:

- Volume parameter, VOLUME=(,,,*N*,SER=. . .):
  - Specifies insufficient number of SERs or obtained an incorrect list via REF.
  - Specifies insufficient number of volumes via the volume count subparameter *N*.
  - Omits the volume count subparameter *N* and the default volume count is too low.
- Unit parameter, UNIT=(*type*,,DEFER):
  - *Type* subparameter specifies device address instead of generic device, causing mount or demount conflict (e.g., UNIT=FB0 instead of UNIT=SYSDA).
  - Does not specify DEFER.
  - Specifies generic device, but device assigned by the supervisor has a smaller track or cylinder capacity than assumed for space estimates.
- Space parameter, SPACE=(*U*,(*P*,*S*)):
  - The primary allocation subparameter, *P*, specifies insufficient quantity of space.
  - The secondary allocation subparameter, *S*:
    - Was omitted.
    - Was defined in a previous job or step but was overridden to an insufficient allocation when the offending data set was opened for update (DISP of MOD or OLD).
    - Could not be filled because CONTIG was also specified. The primary allocation consumed all the available contiguous space, leaving none for the secondary.
  - The unit of allocation subparameter, *U*, is incorrect relative to the primary or secondary allocation:
    - Number of blocks was specified when TRK or CYL was intended or required.
    - TRK was specified when CYL was intended or required.
  - See SCC B14 if the offending data set is a PDS.
- A substantially increased quantity of input has been processed because:
  - The DSNAME specification for an input data set(s) is incorrect or misspelled:
    - The generation number for a GDG data set was omitted. All generations of this data set were automatically concatenated.
    - A large production data set was specified in a test environment.
  - DISP specified MOD instead of OLD in a previous job(s) or step(s). The offending input data set(s) was extended every time it was used, instead of being written over.

- DDname was omitted on a DD statement(s) following an input DD statement, causing concatenation of two or more data sets.

RELEVANT DUMP ITEMS:

- The address of the next problem program instruction may be found in the RET field of the last SA under SAVE AREA TRACE.
- R2 may point to the offending DCB:
  - The 2-byte TIOT offset is located at x28 into the DCB.
  - The DDname of the DCB is given in the TIOT at this offset.
  - For QSAM data sets, the current record address is at x4C into this DCB. Examine this buffer preceding and following this record for evidence of an output loop (same record is repeated).
- The DEB associated with offending DCB is usually printed immediately before this data set's DCB on the dump. The DEB is also pointed to from this DCB.
  - DCB for the offending data set + x2C points to its associated DEB (DCBDEBAD).
- The DEB describes the extents allocated to a DASD device. Since up to 16 extents may be allocated, up to 16 DEB extent descriptor fields may appear in a DEB. Each extent descriptor is 16 bytes long.
  - DEB + x10, 1-byte extent count.
  - DEB + x20, first extent descriptor field (for primary allocation).
  - DEB + x30, second extent descriptor field (for secondary allocation).
  - DEB + x40, third extent descriptor; and so on.
  - Up to 16 extent descriptors may be present. The format of each is:
    - Bytes 0,3 UCB address.
    - Bytes 4,5 Cylinder start address for this extent.
    - Bytes 8,9 Track start address for this extent.
    - Bytes 10,11 Cylinder end address for this extent.
    - Bytes 12,13 Track end address for this extent.
    - Bytes 14,15 Number of tracks in this extent.
  - The total of the track count fields equals the total tracks used. Storage per track varies with the capacity of the device in use.
- At DCB + x5 is the 8-byte DCBFDAD (full disk address) field. This field contains the full DASD address of the last seek (read or write). Compare this address to the DEB extents to verify that the last address was within an allocated extent. DCBFDAD is of the form MBBCCHHR, where each letter represents 1 byte containing the following address components (as binary numbers):
  - M 1-byte relative extent number (first extent is zero).
  - BB Halfword cell number; zero for DASD devices.
  - CC Halfword cylinder address.
  - HH Halfword track address.
  - R 1-byte relative block number (first block is zero).

- Message IEC030I many indicate the offending data set, DDname, and volume serial number. R15 contains a return code documented in *System Messages* under this message. Briefly:
  - 04 Insufficient space or volumes specified.
  - 08 Could not continue processing of a DOS or DIRF data set.
  - 0C 127 users (maximum) already active on specified DASD volume.

WHAT TO DO:

- Follow the steps outlined in 1.3, General Debugging Procedure, and 5.2, Basic Techniques.
- A B37 abend may be intercepted in COBOL programs writing to sequential (QSAM) data sets. By specifying the INVALID KEY clause with the WRITE verb, the INVALID KEY imperative statements will be executed if conditions for a B37 abend arise.
- If an output loop is suspected, code tests to limit output of identical records.
- Specify a DASD volume or device type that has:
  - Larger track or cylinder capacity.
  - Fewer data sets (more available space).
- Increase available space by:
  - Deleting unused or "work" data sets.
  - PDS compression.
  - Offloading infrequently accessed data sets to tape.
  - Reorganize fragmented keyed data sets.
- Change block size to make more efficient use of a given DASD device's track capacity.
- Reestimate the space requirement and increase the allocation accordingly. Accurate calculation of output DASD data set space requires a number of device specific variables (track capacity, tracks per cylinder, cylinders per volume, and device overhead). The data set's block size, key length, and expected number of blocks must also be known. Additional variables must be considered for ISAM (indexed sequential) and BPAM (partitioned) data sets. *Data Management Services* details the calculations, device characteristics, and data set organization parameters for estimation. Space may be automatically allocated if the data set's block size, key length, and expected quantity of output is known. The supervisor handles the device-dependent calculations. The DD statement parameter, SPACE = (Blocksize,(primary quantity, secondary quantity)) and the DCB subparameter KEYLEN (if appropriate) are all that is needed. For example, to allocate space for 5000 blocks of 800 bytes each, code SPACE=(800,(5000,500)). If the data set has keys [i.e., direct (BDAM) organization], KEYLEN must be specified to give the number of bytes in the key.

  The primary quantity is allocated when the data set is created; the secondary quantity specifies the allocation when additional space is needed. In the example above, 5000 blocks would be allocated when the data set was opened. When these 5000 blocks were used, additional space would be made available 500 blocks at a time, up to 15 times. The total space available would be 12,500 blocks (5000 primary + 15 × 500 secondary). Two caveats apply to automatic allocation. Space allocated via a block request usually results in slower access and less efficient usage of DASD space than track or cylinder allocation. The SPACE subparameter RLSE should be specified in the DD statement to free unused space unless there is a good reason to retain it.

C03 One or more open data sets could not be closed when task termination was attempted.

Related System Messages: IEC999I

POSSIBLE CAUSES:

General:

- The problem program opened but did not close a data set before terminating (e.g., executing a STOP RUN in COBOL). The supervisor's TASK CLOSE routine was not able to close this data set because its DCB was unavailable or invalid.
- The close processing in the problem program is in error because:
  - Program design assumes the supervisor will close data sets not closed by the problem program. Relying on the supervisor to handle close processing instead of handling it within the problem program is poor programming practice.
  - Program design or coding is incorrect, causing existing close processing to be bypassed due to a logic or data error.
  - Module intended to handle close processing was not linked, loaded, or called correctly; or was inadvertently modified.
- The open data set's DCB was not in main storage at termination time because:
  - It was located in a module that:
    - Was DELETEd.
    - Issued an XCTL macro (deleted itself).
    - Was in an overlay structure segment not available at task termination.
    - It was in storage freed by a FREEMAIN.
- The open data set's DCB was invalid and could not be closed because it was:
  - Damaged by an inadvertent data move due to an:
    - Uninitialized or runaway subscript or index.
    - Incorrectly loaded or initialized based register.
    - Program coding error.
  - Damaged during execution and the resulting error was handled by a DCB ABEND or STAE exit which allowed execution to continue with the invalid DCB.
  - Incorrectly modified by a supervisor routine.
- An IMS batch program did not close a data set.

COBOL Programs:

- A dynamically loaded subroutine OPENed a data set and was CANCELed before it CLOSEd the data set. The data set's DCB was contained in the CANCELed module's storage, which was deleted (as was the remainder of its storage and instructions) when the CANCEL was executed. Recompile and link the mainline program specifying NODYNAM as a compiler option, or make sure that a CLOSE is issued before the CANCEL.

Assembly Programs:

- The result of an OPEN or CLOSE is not tested and either operation was not successful. However, OPEN or CLOSE did not issue an ABEND. Task termination attempted to close, received a nonzero return code, and issued a C03 ABEND.
  - R15 contains the OPEN or CLOSE return code.
  - If the OPEN is unsuccessful, DCBOFLGS (DCB + x30) will be set to x10.
- Base address incorrectly loaded, causing overlay of DCB fields.
- Incorrect usage of DELETE, XCTL, PGRLSE, or FREEMAIN resulted in loss of storage containing an open DCB.

RELEVANT DUMP ITEMS:

- R2 of the second SVRB following the PRB or R1 or R2 of REGS AT ENTRY TO ABEND may contain the address of the invalid or missing DCB.
- If an invalid DCB is at fault, it should be listed on the dump. DCBs that have been successfully closed are restored to the preopen state. A closed DCB will contain the 8-byte DDname beginning at offset x28. Closed DCBs can be eliminated as sources of this abend. An open DCB will contain the 2-byte TIOT offset at +x28. The DDname of the DCB can be found in the TIOT.
- Task termination was following the DEB chain when C03 was issued, so it is likely that the missing DCB will be pointed to from a DEB listed in the dump. The address of this DEB may be found in two ways:
  - It may be given in message IEC999I.
  - From the DEB chain, which ends with the DEB pointed to from the TCBDEB field (TCB + 8). The next DEB on the chain is pointed by DEBDEBB (DEB + 5). Attempt to find the DCB pointed to from DEBDEBAD (DEB + x18) in each DEB on the chain. DEBs are listed on the dump in reverse order of open (the DEB for the first data set opened is listed last). There will be one DEB for each non-VSAM data set that has been opened. There will be two DEBs for each open ESDS or RRDS VSAM cluster, three DEBs for each KSDS VSAM cluster, and two additional DEBs for each alternate index associated with a base cluster. VSAM DEBs are not of interest since they do not have associated DCBs. A VSAM DEB can be identified by a x01 in the AMTYP field of the formatted DEB (DEBAMTYP, DEB − 3).

- If a DCB is not formatted on the dump, it probably has been released. A scan of the SPQE/DQE list will confirm the virtual storage assigned to the task (DQE blocks begin at the address in the field labeled BLK and extend by the amount indicated in the adjacent LN field). The next step is to determine why the DCB's storage was released. Storage is released by:
  - DELETE or XCTL for a load module (implicit release).
  - FREEMAIN or PGRLSE for main storage (explicit release).
- If the module containing the DCB has been DELETEd or XCTLed, the module may not be present on the CDE. Scan the CDE to see what modules were present. Modules that are known to have been brought into execution and which open data sets but are not present in the CDE list are good candidates for further examination.
- R4 in the second SVRB following the problem program PRB may point to the OPEN/CLOSE/EOV work area for the offending data set. It contains:
  - The data set label at R4 + 0.
  - The JFCB (DD statement parameters) at R4 + x64. Examination of this work area will indicate conflicting or incorrectly specified data set parameters. 3.4, Analysis of the O/C/EOV Work Area, provides a detailed description of its fields.
- If an incorrect FREEMAIN caused the DCB to be deallocated, it is likely that other portions of problem program main storage may be missing. Save areas, buffers, tables, and control blocks are good candidates. Also, the particular pieces missing may suggest a pattern leading to the offending FREEMAIN.

WHAT TO DO:

- Follow the steps outlined in 1.3, General Debugging Procedure, and 5.2, Basic Techniques.

C13 OPEN error for concatenated PDS or graphic device.

Related System Messages: IEC153I, IEC157I
SVC 19 OPEN

POSSIBLE CAUSES:

General:

- Attempt to open a concatenated PDS for output.
- Uncorrectable I/O error occurred while reading the:
  - DASD volume label for a volume containing a concatenated PDS.
  - JFCB from a DASD data set.
  - Format 1 or 3 DSCB from a VTOC.
- Format 1 DSCB not found in VTOC.

- Attempt to concatenate PDS with non-DASD data set.
- Graphic device already opened (in use) by another task.

JCL Related

DD statement:

- DDname omitted. The interpreter assumed that a concatention list was specified. The offending DD statement is for:
  - A PDS immediately preceded by a DD statement for another PDS intended for output.
  - A PDS immediately preceded by a DD statement for a nonpartioned data set. Mixed organization is not allowed in a concatenation list.
  - A nonpartioned data set immediately preceded by a DD statement for a PDS. Mixed organization is not allowed in a concatention list.
- DDname misspelled or incorrectly exchanged between input and output data sets.
- DSNAME specification misspelled or incorrect.
- VOLUME specification incorrect or omitted.
- JOBLIB or STEPLIB DD statement missing or incorrect.

Assembly Programs:

- OPEN macro specification incorrect:
  - DCB address incorrectly modified or loaded; misspelled in parameter list.
  - Processing method specifies OUTPUT, INOUT, or OUTIN for a concatenated PDS.

COBOL Programs:

- SELECT file-name ASSIGN TO device-organization-DDname specification is in error:
  - File-name misspelled or incorrect.
  - DDname misspelled or incorrect.
- OPEN specifies OUTPUT for a concatenated PDS.

RELEVANT DUMP ITEMS:

- The address of the next problem program instruction may be found in the PSW field of the problem program's PRB under ACTIVE RBS. This RB is usually the first printed. The FL-CDE of this PRB will point to a CDE entry that has the problem program's name printed in NM. To verify that this address points to the next instruction, check the 2 bytes immediately preceding it. They should contain x0A13—the object code for the OPEN SVC.
- R2 points to the offending DCB.
  - If the DCB was open, it will be formatted in the control block section of the dump and have a DEB and IOBs associated with it.
    - The 2-byte TIOT offset is at x28 into the DCB.
    - The DDname of this DCB is given in the TIOT at this offset.
  - If the DCB was not opened or has been closed, it will not be formatted in the control

block section but will be found in the main storage dump. The DEB will contain the DCB address.

  •• The 8-byte DDname will be at x28 into the DCB.

– DCB + x1C points to the IOB prefix. 1OB fields may indicate an I/O error if it has occurred. The IOB prefix is 16 bytes long, so the IOB proper begins at the prefix address plus x10. Fields of interest are:
  - IOB + 0, IOBFLAG1: If bit 5 is on (x04), a permanent I/O error has occurred. System message IEA000I will probably have been issued.
  - IOB + 4, ECBCC: ECB completion code. First byte of the 4-byte ECB. If this byte is not x00 or x7F, a channel error has occurred.
  - IOB + xC, second word of the CSW: Contains the channel status bits. Bits 36 and 37 should be on if an I/O operation has completed successfully.

– Further explanation of the ECB and CSW is given in 4.2, Dump Components, Input-Output Block.

– If the PDS was opened for output, the DEB will contain the offending member name. The DEB associated with the offending data set is usually printed immediately before this data set's DCB on the dump. The DEB is also pointed to from this DCB.
  - DCB for the offending data set + x2C points to its associated DEB.
  - DEB address + x24 points to the start of the 8-byte DEBDSNM field containing the member name.

– R4 points to the OPEN/CLOSE/EOV work area for the offending data set. It contains:
  - The data set label at R4 + 0.
  - The JFCB (DD statement parameters) at R4 + x64. Examination of this work area will indicate conflicting or incorrectly specified data set parameters. 3.4, Analysis of the O/C/EOV Work Area, provides a detailed description of its fields. The contents of the O/C/EOV work area may indicate an I/O error. R4 + x64 points to the JFCB data set name field.
    •• If a valid data set name is not present, an uncorrectable I/O error may have occurred while the initiator was attempting to do allocation for the abended job step.
    •• If a valid data set name is present, an uncorrectable I/O error may have occurred while attempting to read the DSCB.

– Message IEC153I may indicate the offending data set name, DDname, and volume serial number. R15 contains a return code documented in *System Messages* under this message. Briefly:
  - 10 Attempt to concatenate output PDSs.
  - 18 Attempt to concatenate PDS with non-PDS data set.

WHAT TO DO:

– Follow the steps outlined in 1.3, General Debugging Procedure, and 5.2, Basic Techniques.

– If an I/O error has occurred, specify a different device, volume, or both and rerun the job.

- If a graphic device error has occurred, a system IPL may be necessary to correct the problem.

D37 Insufficient primary space for an output DASD data set. No secondary allocation available.

Related System Messages: IEC031I
SVC55 EOV

POSSIBLE CAUSES

General:

- Primary or directory allocation for a PDS exhausted:
  - Directory full.
  - Data set has become fragmented by frequent updates.
- Problem program is writing a greater than anticipated quantity of output because it is:
  - In a write loop.
  - Processing a substantially increased quantity of input.
- See SCC B37.

JCL Related:

DD statement:

- Space parameter, SPACE=(*U*,(*P*,*S*,*D*)) specifies:
  - Insufficient quantity of primary space via the *P* subparameter:
    - For a PDS, the directory allocation *D* is taken from the primary allocation. *P* may not be sufficient for both the directory and data requirement. See SCC B14.
  - No secondary allocation—the *S* subparameter was omitted.
- UNIT parameter specifies generic device type (e.g., SYSDA). Track or cylinder capacity of device assigned by the supervisor is less than assumed for space estimates.

RELEVANT DUMP ITEMS:

- See SCC B37.
- Message IEC031I may indicate the offending data set name, DDname, and volume serial number.

WHAT TO DO:

- Follow the steps outlined in 1.3, General Debugging Procedure, and 5.2, Basic Techniques.
- See SCC B37.

E37 Insufficient space or number of volumes allocated for an output data set.

Related System Messages: IEC032I
SVC 55 EOV

POSSIBLE CAUSES:

General:

- For an output tape or DASD data set an additional volume was needed, but the volume allocation was already used.
- The problem program is writing a greater than anticipated quantity of output because it is:
  - In a write loop.
  - Processing a substantially increased quantity of input.
- A PDS has become fragmented due to frequent updates.
- A data set exists on two or more DASD volumes. During output, the allocation for this data set was exhausted on the first volume. The next volume specified for output already contained this data set.
- A DASD data set was moved, copied to, or recreated on a device with smaller track or cylinder capacity than a previous device, but the space allocation was not increased.
- For an output PDS or VIO data set:
  - All 16 extents were used. No more could be allocated.
  - Less than 16 extents were used, but no more space was available on the primary volume (a PDS or VIO data set must reside on a single volume).
- Also see SCC B37.

JCL Related:

DD statement:

- Incorrect or insufficient volume allocation specified via the volume parameter, VOLUME=(PRIVATE,,,*N*,SER=(S_1,S_2, . . . , S_m)), or the specification conflicts with the unit count subparameter *C* of the UNIT=(*type*,*C*) parameter. Table 2-2 shows

Table 2-2
Volume Allocation Factors

Device Type	*Usage*	*Request Type*	*Limiting Parameter*
DASD	Private	Specific SER	Maximum of N, S_m
		Nonspecific	N
	Nonprivate	Specific SER	Maximum of N, S_m
		Nonspecific	C
Tape			Maximum of N, S_m

the factors that determine volume allocation. The error may be due to a VOLUME parameter for another DD statement if REF is coded.

- The volume count subparameter N is insufficient or omitted. The maximum number of volumes allocated via N is derived from a rather bizarre calculation. The allocation is a step function which follows the rule

$$\text{volume allocation} = 5 + 15x$$

where x is a function of N such that

$$x = \begin{cases} 0 & 1 \leq N \leq 5 \\ 1 & 6 \leq N \leq 20 \\ \dfrac{N}{15} + 1 & 21 \leq N \leq 255 \end{cases}$$

Thus a volume allocation is always the same for a given range of N. The function gives allocations of 5, 20, 35, 50, 65, 80, 95, . . . ,255. If N is insufficient, it must be increased to the next "step" to increase volume allocation. The required increase in N may be calculated, or as a shortcut, must be at least 15 more than abending value of N.

- The volume count subparameter N is greater than the unit count subparameter C, UNIT=(,C), and the usage keyword PRIVATE is omitted from the VOLUME parameter for a DASD data set. In this case, the value of C determines the volume allocation.
- The quantity of volumes, m, specified via SER is insufficient, and the volume count subparameter N was omitted or insufficient.
- The volume(s) specified via SER already contains the offending data set.

– The primary, secondary, or unit of allocation specified via the SPACE parameter is incorrect or insufficient.

– See SCC B37, JCL diagnostics.

– A substantially increased quantity of input has been processed because:

- The DSNAME specification for an input data set(s) is incorrect or misspelled:
  - The generation number for a GDG data set was omitted. All generations of this data set were automatically concatenated.
  - A large production data set was specified in a test environment.
- DISP specified MOD instead of OLD in a previous job(s) or step(s). The offending input data set(s) was extended every time it was used, instead of being written over or recreated.
- DDname was omitted on a DD statement(s) following an input DD statement, causing concatenation of two or more data sets.

RELEVANT DUMP ITEMS:

- See SCC B37.
- Message IEC032I may indicate the offending DDname, device, volume serial number, and data set name. R15 contains a return code documented in *System Messages* under this message. Briefly:
  - 04 Insufficient volume count or space allocation.
  - 08 Data set already exists on a second volume.
  - 0C Installation defined volume limit reached.

WHAT TO DO:

- Follow the steps outlined in 1.3, General Debugging Procedure, and 5.2, Basic Techniques.
- See SCC B37.
- A simple solution to an E37 abend due to insufficient tape allocation is to increase the volume allocation (number of reels) to some arbitrarily large value (e.g., 100, 200). However, so doing may not be feasible or wise. Many installations prohibit or frown on such practices. If your program enters an unwanted output loop, the normal check for a reasonable number of volumes would be circumvented, resulting in wasted resources. Specifying a reasonable allocation would prevent this problem.

  The number of output tape reels required may be a useful estimate for other reasons. It can serve as an estimate of CPU or elapsed job time, the need for operators (tapes are manually mounted), number of drives, total reels needed over the life of a data set, and so on.

  To estimate the number of tape reels (volumes) a data set will need, the following facts must be known:
  - LRECL, BLKSIZE, and RECFM.
  - The recording density (BPI—bits per inch) of the tape drives used.
  - The length of the reels to be used (a standard 12-inch reel contains 2400 feet of tape when new).
  - The actual or estimated number of records to be output.

  If variable-length record processing will be used (RECFM V or U), additional data are needed:
  - The actual or estimated number of records of a given length to be output.
  - The actual or estimated length of each different length record to be output.

  The accuracy of your estimate will depend on the accuracy of the output record quantity estimates.

  Once the relevant data have been obtained, use the formula corresponding to RECFM to calculate feet required, F. Feet are converted into reels by dividing feet by reel length and rounding up. The formula for reels is

$$V = \left\{ \frac{F}{L(S)} \right\}$$

where V = number reels (volumes required)

F = feet of tape required, as determined by the formula for the RECFM to be used

$L(S)$ = length (in feet) of a standard reel as a function of diameter (see Table 2-3)

Alternatively, if your tape is supplied in metric dimensions:

$$V = \left\{ \frac{0.3048F}{L(M)} \right\}$$

where V,F = as above

$L(M)$ = length (in meters) of a standard reel of tape as a function of metric diameter (see Table 2-3)

Braces { } and brackets [ ] have special meaning in the following formulas. Braces indicate that a quantity is to be increased to the next greatest integer. For example, {5.09} becomes 6; {23.68} becomes 24; and so on. Brackets indicate that a quantity is to be truncated to the next lower integer. For example, [42.81] becomes 42; [103.25] becomes 103; and so on. The general formula to calculate F is

$$\begin{array}{c}\text{total}\\ \text{feet}\\ \text{required}\end{array} = \begin{array}{c}\text{total data}\\ \text{foot/bytes}\end{array} + \left(\begin{array}{c}\text{number}\\ \text{of}\\ \text{blocks}\end{array} \times \begin{array}{c}\text{interblock}\\ \text{gap}\end{array} \right)$$

F (length in feet) depends on the record format (RECFM) of the data set. Formulas for RECFM F (fixed length, unblocked), RECFM FB (fixed length, blocked), RECFM V (variable-length, unblocked), RECFM VB (variable-length, blocked), and RECFM U (undefined length, unblocked) are given, followed by examples.

Table 2-3
Tape Reel Lengths

Approximate Reel Diameter, S (inches)	*Approximate Reel Length, L(S) (feet)*	*Approximate Reel Diameter, M (centimeters)*	*Approximate Reel Length, L(M) (meters)*
6	600	16	183
9	1200	23	366
12	2400	30	732

Table 2-4
Tape Recording Density Factors

Tape Density (bits per inch)	*Equivalent DEN Parameter*	*K (D) (bytes/foot)*	*Interblock Gap Factor, G (D)*
200	0	2,400	0.0625
556	1	6,672	0.0625
800	2	9,600	0.0500
1,600	3	19,200	0.0500
6,250	4	75,000	0.0250

- Feet of tape required for RECFM F or RECFM FB data sets:

$$F = \frac{NR}{K(D)} + \left(\frac{NR}{B}\right) G(D)$$

where F = feet of tape required

N = actual or estimated number of records

R = record length in bytes (LRECL)

B = block size in bytes (BLKSIZE)

$K(D)$ = bytes per foot as a function of recording density (see Table 2-4)

$G(D)$ = interblock gap factor as a function of recording density (see Table 2-4)

- Feet of tape required for RECFM V (variable length, unblocked) data sets:

$$F = \left(\frac{\sum_{i=1}^{T} N_i(R_i + 4)}{K(D)}\right) + \sum_{i=1}^{T} N_i G(D)$$

where F = feet of tape required

i = index of the ith length record; $i = 1, \ldots, T$

T = number of different record lengths

N_i = actual or estimated quantity of records of length R_i

R_i = actual or estimated length in bytes of the ith length record

$K(D)$ = bytes per foot as a function of density (see Table 2-4)

$G(D)$ = interblock gap factor as a function of recording density (see Table 2-4)

- Feet of tape required for RECFM VB (variable length, blocked) data sets:

$$F = \left\{ \frac{4\text{NB} + \sum_{i=1}^{T} N_i(R_i + 4)}{K(D)} \right\} + \text{NB} \cdot G(D)$$

where F = feet of tape required

i = index of the ith length record; $i = 1, \ldots, T$

T = number of different record lengths

R_i = actual or estimated length in bytes of the ith length record.

N_i = actual or estimated quantity of records of length R_i

$K(D)$ = bytes per foot as a function of density (see Table 2-4)

$G(D)$ = interblock gap factor as a function of recording density (see Table 2-4)

NB = estimated number of blocks:

$$\text{NB} = \left\{ \frac{\sum_{i=1}^{T} N_i(R_i + 4)}{B^*} \right\}$$

where N_i, R_i, i, T = as above

B^* = weighted average block size:

$$B^* = \left[\frac{B - 4}{R^*}\right] \cdot R^*$$

where B = block size in bytes

R^* = weighted average record length:

$$R^* = \left\{\frac{\sum_{i=1}^{T} N_i(R_i + 4)}{\sum_{i=1}^{T} N_i}\right\}$$

The order of computation is R^*, B^*, NB, and finally F.

The formula for RECFM VB assumes that there is no significant pattern in output records. If a nonrandom grouping of output record lengths is present, the estimate for number of blocks will be less accurate. Weighted average bytes per block, R^*, assumes a random sequence. Certain sequences of output lengths in combination with a given block size may result in higher or lower actual bytes per block. This will affect the number of blocks and, in turn, the tape needed for interblock gaps. For example, let $B = 100$, $R_1 = 75$, $N_1 = 1000$, $R_2 = 35$, $N_2 = 10{,}000$, and $D = 6250$. Using the calculation given above (assuming a random mix of two record lengths), 5449 blocks are estimated. Suppose, however, that each R_1 is always followed by 10 R_2s (a typical header/detail pattern). Since B is 100, 6 blocks will be needed for each group of R_1 and 10 R_2s (75; 35,35; 35,35; 35,35; 35,35; 35,35). Since there are 1000 R_1s, 6000 blocks will be used. 501 more interblock gaps will occur than estimated by weighted average block size.

- Feet of tape required for RECFM U (undefined length, unblocked) data sets:

$$F = \left(\frac{\sum_{i=1}^{T} N_i R_i}{K(D)}\right) + \sum_{i=1}^{T} N_i G(D)$$

where F = feet of tape required

i = index of the ith length record; $i = 1, \ldots, T$

T = number of different record lengths

N_i = actual or estimated quantity of records of length R_i

R_i = actual or estimated length in bytes of the ith length record

$K(D)$ = bytes per foot as a function of density (see Table 2-4)

$G(D)$ = interblock gap factor as a function of density (see Table 2-4)

Note: If N_iR_i cannot be estimated, use the next best approximation of average record length and total quantity:

- R_i^* Weighted average record length (see RECFM VB).
- R_i^{**} Approximate record length. This may be estimated by

$$R_i^{**} = \frac{(minimum\ length + maximum\ length)}{2}$$

or

$$R_i^{**} = \text{maximum record length}$$

or

$$R_i^{**} = \text{your best guess}$$

Two examples of these calculations follow. Example 1 is for a fixed block data set (RECFM F). Example 2 is for a variable block data set (RECFM VB).

Example 1

For a RECFM F data set and given

$$N = 10{,}000{,}000$$

$$R = 80$$

$$B = 16{,}000$$

$$D = 6250$$

How many 12-inch reels are needed?

$$F = \frac{10{,}000{,}000\ (80)}{75{,}000} + \frac{10{,}000{,}000\ (80)}{16{,}000} \times 0.025$$

$$= 11{,}917$$

$$V = \left\{\frac{11{,}917}{2{,}400}\right\}$$

$$= 5$$

Five reels would be required.

Example 2

Given RECFM VB with record lengths and frequency estimates per Table 2-5, and

$$B = 16{,}000$$

$$D = 6250$$

How many reels are required?

$$R^* = \frac{12{,}077{,}212{,}000}{3{,}183{,}000}$$

$$= 3795$$

$$B^* = \frac{16{,}000 - 4}{3795} \times 3795$$

$$= 15{,}180$$

$$\text{NB} = \frac{12{,}077{,}212{,}000}{15{,}180}$$

$$= 795{,}601$$

$$F = \frac{4(795{,}601) + 12{,}077{,}212{,}000}{75{,}000} + 795{,}601 \times 0.025$$

$$= 180{,}692$$

$$V = \left\{\frac{180{,}692}{2400}\right\}$$

$$= 75$$

Thus 75 reels of tape are required.

Table 2-5
Variable-Length Record Example

i	N_i	$R_i + 4$	N_iR_i
1	33,000	564	18,612,000
2	150,000	10,004	1,500,600,000
3	1,000,000	5,604	5,604,000,000
4	2,000,000	2,477	4,954,000,000
Total	3,183,000		12,077,212,000

Fxx Invalid call to SVC xx.

Related System Messages: IEC900I

POSSIBLE CAUSES:

General:

- This SCC is issued when an SVC call cannot be processed. 'xx' is the hexadecimal number of the SVC that failed (e.g., 13—OPEN, 19—CLOSE, 37—EOV, etc.). The call may have failed because:
  - SVC xx is not a valid SVC.
    - It was not defined in system generation (sysgen).
    - It is nonexistent.
    - The call instruction was incorrectly coded or inadvertently modified.
  - An invalid parameter list was passed to SVC xx:
    - Conflicting or missing DCB fields.
    - The list was incorrectly formatted or inadvertently modified.
- An I/O error occurred in SVC 37 (EOV) which was not handled by other abend logic (e.g., SCCs 137 and 237). This occurred while:
  - Reading or writing a first volume format 1 DSCB.
  - Reading or writing a second volume format 1 DSCB.
  - Reading a first volume format 3 DSCB.
  - Reading a second volume tape volume label.
  - DSCB for a data set in a concatenation list not found.
- Certain SVCs are called to issue an abend for other SVCs. Such a call was made, but the abend code passed was invalid.

JCL Related:

DD statement:

- SYSOUT DCB parameters missing.
- DSNAME specification for a PDS gives incorrect data set name or member name.
- DD DUMMY or DSN=NULLFILE was specified and no DCB parameters were given. Problem program also did not specify DCB parameters.

Assembly Programs:

- SVC call incorrect due to:
  - Coding error.
  - Inadvertent modification of parameter list or call instruction by:
    - Invalid base address or operand length.

•• Runaway loop or index.

– DCB macro specification omits block size parameter for DD DUMMY data set.

COBOL Programs:

– DCB parameters not specified for a DD DUMMY data set:
  - BLOCK CONTAINS ZERO RECORDS was coded for this data set's FD.
  - SELECT statement DDname or file name specification incorrect or misspelled.

RELEVANT DUMP ITEMS:

– The address of the next problem program instruction may be found at:
  - The PSW field of the problem program's PRB under ACTIVE RBS. This RB is usually the first printed. The FL-CDE of the problem program's PRB will point to a CDE entry that has the problem program's name printed in NM.
  - The RET field of the last SA under SAVE AREA TRACE.

– R2 points to the offending DCB.
  - The 2-byte TIOT offset is located at + x28 into the DCB.
  - The DDname of the DCB is given in the TIOT at this offset.
  - If this DCB has been CLOSEd, it will not be formatted in the control block section of the dump, but should be the main storage listing. The DEB will contain the DCB address.

– R4 points to the OPEN/CLOSE/EOV work area for the offending data set. It contains:
  - The data set label at R4 + 0.
  - The JFCB (DD statement parameters) at R4 + x64.

  Examination of this work area will indicate conflicting or incorrectly specified data set parameters. 3.4, Analysis of the O/C/EOV Work Area, provides a detailed description of its fields.

– R12 will contain the invalid ABEND code if one was passed.

– Message IEC900I may indicate that module name that issued the Fxx ABEND. This module name is an entry point within the SVC itself.

WHAT TO DO:

– Follow the steps outlined in 1.3, General Debugging Procedure, and 5.2, Basic Techniques.

–Who's on first.
–Who's on first?
–Yes.
–Well, go ahead and tell me.
–Who.
–The first baseman.
–Who.
–The guy playing first.
–Who's on first.
–Why do you keep asking me!!?
–I'm not asking you, I'm telling you.
–I'm asking you—who's on first?
–That's right.
–Go ahead and tell me.
–Who.
–The guy on first!
–Who.

Bud Abbott and Lou Costello
Who's on First

3

GENERAL DIAGNOSTIC AIDS

3.1 INTRODUCTION

This chapter presents techniques and information useful for solving a wide variety of abends and program bugs. The topics are as follows.

- *0Cx abend diagnostics.* An extensive list of possible causes common to program check (0Cx) abends is given. Specific, detailed diagnostic procedures are described. For each S/370 instruction that can cause a program check, the disposition of the interrupt is given. Techniques to enable and disable interrupts are given.
- *Common JCL errors.* JCL coding and specification errors that can result in many different abends or incorrect output are listed.
- *Analysis of the O/C/EOV work area.* The location and interpretation of critical data management control blocks is described. Techniques to locate fields from DD

statements, the program, and data set labels are described. Tracing O/C/EOV logic is explained.

- *Locating VSAM data records*. The pointer chain to the VSAM record buffer is described. Techniques to locate the current VSAM record and relevant VSAM control blocks are given.
- *System completion code cross-reference*. For SCCs not covered in 2.2, SCC Diagnostics, this cross-reference will show which SCC diagnostic may provide some useful debugging information.
- *Debugging abends under TSO*. The information needed to use 2.2, SCC Diagnostics, for programs executed via TSO instead of JCL is given here.
- *Dumping and printing data*. The IBM utility programs that will print or dump data sets, data set labels, catalog entries, and other useful items are identified. Sample JCL for each utility is given together with an outline of available output options. This section shows how to:

  (a) Print or dump sequential, direct, or ISAM data sets.
  (b) Print or dump VSAM components.
  (c) Print or dump partitioned data set directories and members.
  (d) List load module data.
  (e) List catalog entries.
  (f) Print DASD and tape data set labels.
  (g) Dump DASD tracks.
- *Abend debugging under MVS/XA*. The major differences for debugging under XA are identified.

These general diagnostic techniques, together with the data-gathering techniques outlined in the sections under each source language in Chapter 5, Source Code Debugging, and Relevant Dump Items in each SCC diagnostic, should provide a means to find and list any data germane to your debugging problem.

3.2 0Cx ABEND DIAGNOSTICS

System completion codes 0Cl through 0CF result from an error detected by the CPU in the execution of a single instruction. The CPU monitors program execution for certain types of critical error conditions. The subset of these conditions that causes 0Cx abends are generically called "program interrupts." An interrupt is analogous to a subroutine call in that the instruction pointer (PSW) and registers of the abending program are saved and a program to handle the error is then executed. Although some interrupts may be disabled, an abend or a language-specific error handler is usually invoked.

Program exceptions are frequently the end result of a series of logical errors. The instruction in which the exception was detected may be, in and of itself, correct. However, assumptions about the instruction or the source statement that generated the instruction are violated in some way, or the necessary conditions for correct execution have not been fulfilled.

Since the CPU will detect certain interrupts before others, it is possible to fix one problem only to have another occur at the same instruction. For example, an addressing exception is caused by an invalid index in a decimal arithmetic instruction. Upon correcting the index error, a decimal-divide exception from the same instruction results on attempt to divide by zero.

Two other events are associated with the detection of a program exception. They are (1) the disposition of further execution of the instruction once the exception is recognized, and (2) setting the ILC (instruction length code). A single instruction is comprised of a series of suboperations. The disposition of suboperations prior to and following the exception are dependent on the nature of the instruction, the type of exception, and the point at which the exception is detected. The disposition of an operation can range from suppression (where all suboperations are nullified) to completion (where all suboperations are fully executed and adjustments are made to compensate for the error). The ILC designates the length in halfwords (2 bytes) of the current instruction. For most program exceptions this will reflect the length of the abending instruction. However, for certain types of exceptions, the ILC will indicate only the extent to which the suboperation had been completed. The ILC is important in determining the address of the abending instruction. Table 3-2 indicates how the ILC is set by instruction and abend SCC.

Possible Causes

1. Problems in program design or logic.
   - (a) Insufficient editing of input data for valid format or content. Storage areas not initialized correctly or reset after use.
   - (b) Insufficient tests for control of iterative logic.
   - (c) Do until structure instead of do while structure results in at least one iteration of a loop. See Figure 3-1.
   - (d) Overly complex data structures.
   - (e) Error-handling routines not present or insufficient.
   - (f) Naming conventions for data items, program labels, or modules are confusing, unclear, or susceptible to inversions or other spelling errors, for example:
     * TOTAL, T0TAL, TOTALS, T0TALS
     * A, AA, AAA
     * WS-1234567-MWMQPFD-YTD-AA-01
   - (g) Excessive module coupling or insufficient module strength.[1]
   - (h) Failure to reinitialize a field(s). Common examples are application programs run under IMS DC and dynamically called subroutines. In each of these situations the module is reloaded frequently, possibly every time it is invoked.

[1]See Edward Yourdon and Larry L. Constantine, *Structured Design: Fundamentals of a Discipline of Computer Program and Systems Design* (Englewood Cliffs, N.J.: Prentice-Hall, Inc., 1979) pp. 84–140.

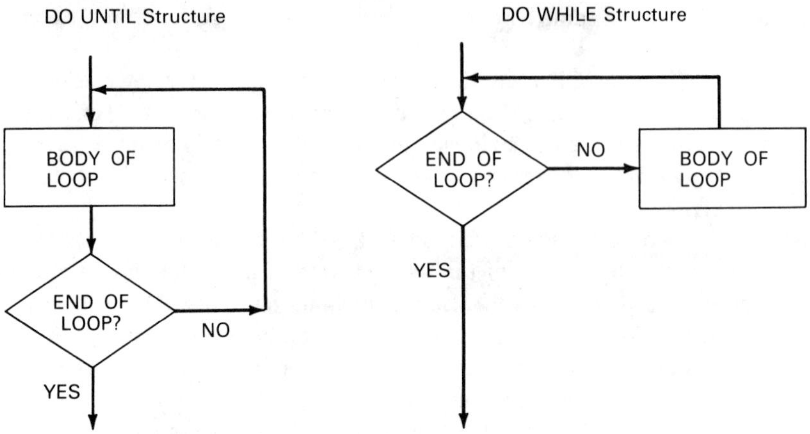

FIGURE 3-1 Do Until versus Do While

Upon entry into the module, the contents of main storage data fields are unpredictable unless explicitly initialized or refreshed.

2. Program coding or compilation errors due to typographical mistakes that are not found by the compiler or assembler:
   (a) Wrong copy member, macro, and so on.
   (b) Spelling, syntax, or punctuation.
   (c) Failure to use correct subroutine:
      * Relink overlooked.
      * Recompile overlooked.
   (d) Copied code, but did not change names.
3. An incorrect sequence of events occurred in an I/O operation. An attempt was made to:
   (a) Read from or write to an unopened or closed data set.
   (b) Move data to or from the buffer of an unopened or closed data set.
   (c) Read from a data set after end of file had been reached.
   (d) Close a data set before it was opened or after it was previously closed.
4. An invalid subscript or index was used in the abending instruction or prior to it. The value of the subscript or index may have been invalid due to:
   (a) A value outside the minimum or maximum range of its associated data structure.
   (b) A program loop that increments or decrements the value iterates too many or too few times. The test for exit from the loop:
      * Is incorrectly coded or misspelled, specifies wrong data item or range.
      * Is logically incorrect (e.g., "less than" is specified instead of "less than or equal," etc.). For example, the intended exit condition for a loop is when a counter is equal to 10. The counter is initialized to 1 and incremented by 2.

The counter will never equal 10 (1, 3, 5, 7, 9, 11, . . .). The result is a runaway loop. If the loop counter is used to set an index or subscript, an invalid address is highly likely.

  * Tests for a switch or flag that is never set, incorrectly set, or initialized.
  * Tests the wrong switch or flag.

(c) A loop is entered at the wrong point in the logical sequence of execution.
(d) Attempting to use the same index or subscript for data structures of different dimensions. For example, the physical displacement of I in the structures A(I) and B(I, J, K) is not the same, even though its logical displacement is.
(e) Incorrect initialization or failure to initialize.
(f) Faulty conversion of some data attribute into an index (e.g., a calendar date into a single integer).

5. An invalid address was generated. This may have been due to an invalid subscript or index. The invalid address was:
   (a) An address outside the valid range for the problem program.
   (b) A protected high or low address.
   (c) An address within the valid range for the problem program which:
      * Causes data that are incorrect in content or format to be used.
      * Causes an index, subscript, flag, or switch to be set incorrectly but does not result in an immediate abend.
      * Causes data or instructions to be overlaid or altered with incorrect values, which later results in an abend.
6. A branch was made to an address that was:
   (a) Logically invalid (i.e., to a section of code not intended to be executed, or at point in execution where it would be logically incorrect).
   (b) Physically invalid (i.e., to a protected part of storage, or to a section of storage containing data instead of instructions).
7. See the section Diagnosing an Invalid Branch below.

JCL Related Causes

1. EXEC statement:
   (a) Specifies wrong program name.
   (b) Incorrect data supplied via PARM.
2. DD statement parameters, especially DDname or DCB are missing, misspelled, or otherwise incorrect.
3. Incorrect load library concatenation list resulted in the use of the wrong version of a load module or called routine. The concatenation list:
   (a) Specified an incorrect or mispelled DSNAME or member name.
   (b) Gave load library data sets in wrong order. Modules are loaded or linked from the first library they are found in. Libraries are searched in the order given in the concatenation list.

The incorrect list may have been given in a:

(a) SYSLIN DD.
(b) JOBLIB DD.
(c) STEPLIB DD.

4. See 3.3, Common JCL Errors.

Assembly Programs

1. Branch, base, or index register incorrectly loaded, specified, or modified.
2. LA specified instead of L, or vice versa.
3. ADCON incorrectly specified.
4. BAL destination address can be composed from two registers. Either or both may be incorrect.
5. Linkage between called and calling modules is incorrect.
   (a) Length, content, or order of items passed is incorrect.
   (b) Usage of items passed is not consistent (e.g., an item is passed as fixed-point binary but subroutine expects floating-point).
   (c) Language-dependent register usage, save area, and return address conventions not adhered to for calls between programs written in same or different languages.
6. Invalid save area address used in STM instruction, overlaying code, or data. The save area contents or address may indicate what the problem program was doing when the overlay occurred.

Relevant Dump Items

In most cases, the address of the abending instruction is found by subtracting the ILC from the PSW AT ENTRY TO ABEND. However, there are two situations in which the value of the ILC is unpredictable: (1) on a specification exception, or (2) on an access (0C4, 0C5) or specification exception due to an odd address (0C6) on an instruction fetch. If the PSW points to a high or low storage address (e.g., xC00000 or x004000), the ILC will not be of much use in locating the cause of the abend.

For all other 0Cx abends the ILC depends on the instruction format and will indicate 2, 4, or 6 bytes. The address of the next instruction to be executed in the problem program is contained in the low-order 3 bytes of the PSW. This PSW address minus the ILC should point to the address of the abending instruction. Mapping this instruction back into the problem program is described in Chapter 5, Source Code Debugging. If the address does not map back into the problem program or subroutines, the abend may have occurred in a supervisor module. This is often the result of an invalid branch and less frequently of a supervisor software problem.

Once the abending instruction has been located, Table 3-2 may be used to isolate the immediate cause. Further investigation will probably be needed to determine why the instruction was used improperly.

Diagnosing an Invalid Branch

Many 0Cx abends can be caused by an invalid branch address. This problem is most likely to occur in assembly language programs. The invalid address may have been loaded and branched to, resulting in a subsequent exception interrupt, or it may have been loaded and, when the branch was attempted, an exception interrupt resulted. The steps to identify an invalid branch are:

1. Determine if the next instruction (PSW AT ENTRY TO ABEND) is within a load module in the CDE/EPA and XL/LN addresses.
2. If the address falls within a problem program load module, the address of the abending instruction is usually given by subtracting the ILC from the PSW instruction address.
3. If the operation code at this address is invalid, an 0C1 has probably resulted. If it is a valid operation code, referencing invalid data has probably been the immediate cause of the interrupt. An invalid branch is a good suspect when execution of a portion of code is peculiar given the program's intended logic.
4. Scan the REGS AT ENTRY TO ABEND for an address close to the last instruction executed. Note the register number containing such an address. Find a BAL or BALR instruction in the problem program which uses this register as its second operand. The logic immediately preceding the address contained in the first operand's register may have generated the invalid branch address. The branch address of a BAL may be composed of a base, index, and displacement. A BALR branch address is composed in the register as its second operand. Frequently, invalid branch addresses are the result of an improperly formed ADCON or incorrectly loaded register.

Controlling Interrupts

There are two primary means to control the hardware-initiated interrupts resulting from program check exceptions (SCCs 0C1 through 0CF). First, the SPIE macro may be used to specify a user-written exit to service any of the 15 program check interrupts. This user exit routine will be executed in place of the normal 0Cx abend processing. See Figure 5-9, section 5.5, Assembly Language Analysis, and *Supervisor Services* for more detailed information. The second method is to disable an interrupt from within the problem program.

The SPM (Set Program Mask) instruction may be used to disable or enable the interrupt processing associated with four program exceptions. There are 4 bits in the PSW that control these interrupts. If the bit is 1, the interrupt associated with the exception is enabled (i.e., when detected, the exception will be processed by an interrupt). When the bit is 0, the interrupt associated with the exception is disabled (i.e., when detected, the exception will not be processed by an interrupt). However, even if the interrupt is disabled, the standard exception handling (truncation, exponent reset, etc.) for the instruction is performed. Table 3-1 shows the relationships of the interrupt control bits.

Table 3-1
Program Interrupt Masks

Exception	ABEND SCC	PSW Bit Controlling	SPM Operand Register Bit[a]
Fixed-point overflow	0C8	20	4
Decimal overflow	0CA	21	5
Exponent underflow	0CD	22	6
Significance	0CE	23	7

[a]Bit is set to 1 to enable the interrupt, to 0 to disable the interrupt.

Disabling interrupts is a practice that should be used with caution. Interrupts provide a useful function in that the conditions which normally cause them are almost always indicative of a logic or data error. If interrupts are disabled, it is good practice to (1) provide some compensating form of error detection and handling (e.g., checking the condition code of arithmetic instructions, data validation) and (2) to test programs with interrupts enabled.

The following code would cause the fixed-point overflow interrupt bit to be set on (i.e., when detected, the interrupt would occur). The other masks correspond to the remaining interrupts.

```
          BALR    10,0           *GET CURRENT PSW
          O       10,FPOVFMSK    *SET FLOATING POINT BIT
          SPM     10             *RESET PSW
FPOVFMSK  DC X'08000000'
DCOVFMSK  DC X'07000000'
EXUNFMSK  DC X'06000000'
SIGNFMSK  DC X'05000000'
```

Interrupt Table

Table 3-2 shows, by instruction:

- Which program check abends can be caused by an instruction
- The disposition of the instruction and its operands once the exception is detected
- An indication of the immediate cause of the abend, where appropriate

The instructions are listed in order of their hexadecimal operation code, which is how they will appear in the dump. The format, name, and mnemonic are also given. Instructions that cannot result in program check interrupts are not listed. To match an instruction to an abend SCC, find the instruction and then look under the column for the SCC in question. The numbers and letters are explained in the table footnotes. If the column is blank for an instruction, it means that the instruction cannot create that interrupt. For more information about how each interrupt is handled, see *Principles of Operation*.

Table 3-2

Program Interrupts by Instruction[a]

Instruction				*Interrupt Code*													
Type	*Mnemonic*	*Op. Code*	*Name*	*0C1*[b]	*0C2*	*0C4*[c]----	*0C5*[d]	*0C6*[e]	*0C7*[f]	*0C8*[g]	*0C9*[h]	*0CA*[i]	*0CB*[j]	*0CC*[k]	*0CD*[l]	*0CE*[m]	*0CF*[n]
RR	SSK	08	Set Storage Key		S		T	6									
RR	ISK	09	Insert Storage Key		S		T	6									
RR	MVCL	0E	Move Characters Long			P s f	P	1									
RR	CLCL	0F	Compare Characters Long			P s f	P	1									
RR	LPR	10	Load Positive							C							
RR	LCR	13	Load Complement							C							
RR	AR	1A	Add Register							C							
RR	SR	1B	Subtract Register							C							
RR	MR	1C	Multiply Register					1									
RR	DR	1D	Divide Register					1			S						
RR	LPDR	20	Load Positive Long	1				3									
RR	LNDR	21	Load Negative Long	1				3									
RR	LTDR	22	Loan and Test Long	1				3									
RR	LCDR	23	Load Complement Long	1				3									
RR	HDR	24	Halve Long	1				3							C		
RR	LRDR	25	Load Rounded (XL)	2				3						T			
RR	MXR	26	Multiply Extended	2				3						T	C		
RR	MXDR	27	Multiply Long to Extended	2				3						T	C		
RR	LDR	28	Load Long	1				3									
RR	CDR	29	Compare Long	1				3									
RR	ADR	2A	Add Normalized Long	1				3						T	C	C	
RR	SDR	2B	Subtract Normalized Long	1				3						T	C	C	
RR	MDR	2C	Multiply Normalized Long	1				3						T	C		
RR	DDR	2D	Divide Long	1				3						T	C		S
RR	AWR	2E	Add Unnormalized Long	1				3						T		C	
RR	SWR	2F	Subtract Unnormalized Long	1				3						T		C	
RR	LPER	30	Load Positive Short	1				3									
RR	LNER	31	Load Negative Short	1				3									
RR	LTER	32	Load and Test Short	1				3									
RR	LCER	33	Load Complement Short	1				3									

Table 3-2 (continued)

Instruction				Interrupt Code													
Type	*Mnemonic*	*Op. Code*	*Name*	*0C1*[b]	*0C2*	*0C4*[c]----	*0C5*[d]	*0C6*[e]	*0C7*[f]	*0C8*[g]	*0C9*[h]	*0CA*[i]	*0CB*[j]	*0CC*[k]	*0CD*[l]	*0CE*[m]	*0CF*[n]
RR	HER	34	Halve Short	1				3							C		
RR	LRER	35	Load Rounded	2				3						T			
RR	AXR	36	Add Normalized Extended	2				3						T	C	C	
RR	SXR	37	Subtract Normalized Extended	2				3						T	C	C	
RR	LER	38	Load Short	1				3									
RR	CER	39	Compare Short	1				3									
RR	AER	3A	Add Normalized Short	1				3						T	C	C	
RR	SER	3B	Subtract Normalized Short	1				3						T	C	C	
RR	MER	3C	Multiply Normalized Short	1				3						T	C		
RR	DER	3D	Divide Short	1				3						T	C		S
RR	AUR	3E	Add Unnormalized Short	1				3						T		C	
RR	SUR	3F	Subtract Unnormalized Short	1				3						T		C	
RX	STH	40	Store Halfword			X s	X										
RX	STC	42	Store Character			X	X										
RX	IC	43	Insert Character			X f	X										
RX	EX	44	Execute			X	X	2									
RX	LH	48	Load Halfword			X	X										
RX	CH	49	Compare Halfword			X	X										
RX	AH	4A	Add Halfword			X	X			C							
RX	SH	4B	Subtract Halfword			X	X			C							
RX	MH	4C	Multiply Halfword			X	X										
RX	CVD	4E	Convert to Decimal			X	X										
RX	CVB	4F	Convert to Binary			X	X		T								
RX	ST	50	Store			X	X										
RX	N	54	And			X	X										
RX	CL	55	Compare Logical			X	X										
RX	O	56	Or			X	X										
RX	X	57	Exclusive Or			X	X										
RX	L	58	Load			X f	X										
RX	C	59	Compare			X f	X										
RX	A	5A	Add			X f	X										

Table 3-2 (continued)

Instruction				*Interrupt Code*													
Type	*Mnemonic*	*Op. Code*	*Name*	*0C1*[b]	*0C2*	*0C4*[c]----	*0C5*[d]	*0C6*[e]	*0C7*[f]	*0C8*[g]	*0C9*[h]	*0CA*[i]	*0CB*[j]	*0CC*[k]	*0CD*[l]	*0CE*[m]	*0CF*[n]
RX	S	5B	Subtract			X f	X										
RX	M	5C	Multiply			X f	X										
RX	D	5D	Divide			X f	X	1,4			S						
RX	AL	5E	Add Logical			X f	X										
RX	SL	5F	Subtract Logical			X f	X										
RX	STD	60	Store Long	1		X s	X	3,8									
RX	MXD	67	Multiply Long to Extended	2		X	X	3,8						T	C		
RX	LD	68	Load Long	1		X f	X	3,8									
RX	CD	69	Compare Long	1		X f	X	3,8									
RX	AD	6A	Add Normalized Long	1		X f	X	3,8						T	C	C	
RX	SD	6B	Subtract Normalized Long	1		X f	X	3,8						T	C	C	
RX	MD	6C	Multiply Long	1		X f	X	3,8						T	C		
RX	DD	6D	Divide Long	1		X f	X	3,8						T	C		S
RX	AW	6E	Add Unnormalized Long	1		X f	X	3,8						T		C	
RX	SW	6F	Subtract Unnormalized Long	1		X f	X	3,8						T		C	
RX	STE	70	Store Short	1		X s	X	3,4									
RX	LE	78	Load Short	1		X f	X	3,4									
RX	CE	79	Compare Short	1		X f	X	3,4									
RX	AE	7A	Add Normalized Short	1		X f	X	3,4						T	C	C	
RX	SE	7B	Subtract Normalized Short	1		X f	X	3,4						T	C	C	
RX	ME	7C	Multiply Short	1		X f	X	3,4						T	C		
RX	DE	7D	Divide Short	1		X f	X	3,4						T	C		S
RX	AU	7E	Add Unnormalized Short	1		X f	X	3,4						T		C	
RX	SU	7F	Subtract Unnormalized Short	1		X f	X	3,4						T		C	
S	SSM	80	Set System Mask		S	Y	S	9									
S	LPSW	82	Load PSW		S	Y	S	8									
SI	—	83	Diagnose		S	f,s,b	S										
SI	WRD	84	Write Direct	3	S	X f	X										
SI	RDD	85	Read Direct	3	S	X s	X										
RS	SLA	8B	Shift Left Single							C							

Table 3-2 (continued)

Instruction				Interrupt Code													
Type	*Mnemonic*	*Op. Code*	*Name*	*0C1*[b]	*0C2*	*0C4*[c]----	*0C5*[d]	*0C6*[e]	*0C7*[f]	*0C8*[g]	*0C9*[h]	*0CA*[i]	*0CB*[j]	*0CC*[k]	*0CD*[l]	*0CE*[m]	*0CF*[n]
RS	SRDL	8C	Shift Right Double Logical					1									
RS	SLDL	8D	Shift Left Double Logical					1									
RS	SRDA	8E	Shift Right Double					1									
RS	SLDA	8F	Shift Left Double					1		C							
RS	STM	90	Store Multiple			X s	X										
SI	TM	91	Test Under Mask			X f	X										
SI	MVI	92	Move Immediate			X s	X										
S	TS	93	Test and Set			X	X										
SI	NI	94	And Immediate			X	X										
SI	CLI	95	Compare Logical Immediate			X f	X										
SI	OI	96	Or Immediate			X s	X										
RS	LM	98	Load Multiple			X f	X										
S	SIO	9C00	Start I/O		S												
S	SIOF	9C01	Start I/O Fast Release		S												
S	TIO	9D00	Test I/O		S												
S	CLRIO	9D01	Clear I/O		S												
S	HIO	9E00	Halt I/O		S												
S	HDV	9E01	Halt Device		S												
S	TCH	9F00	Test Channel		S												
S	CLRCH	9501	Clear Channel	11	S												
SI	STNSM	AC	Store Then And System Mask	4	S	S	S										
SI	STOSM	AD	Store Then Or System Mask	4	S	S	S	9									
RS	SIGP	AE	Signal Processor	8	S												
SI	MC	AF	Monitor Call					7									
RX	LRA	B1	Load Real Address	4	S	X	X										
S	CONCS	B200	Connect Channel Set	10	S												
S	DISCS	B201	Disconnect Channel Set	10	S												
S	STIDP	B202	Store CPU ID		S	X s	X	8									
S	STIDC	B203	Store Channel ID		S												
S	SCK	B204	Set Clock		S	X s,f	X	8									
S	STCK	B205	Store Clock			X	X										

Table 3-2 (continued)

Instruction				*Interrupt Code*													
Type	*Mnemonic*	*Op. Code*	*Name*	*0C1*[b]	*0C2*	*0C4*[c]----	*0C5*[d]	*0C6*[e]	*0C7*[f]	*0C8*[g]	*0C9*[h]	*0CA*[i]	*0CB*[j]	*0CC*[k]	*0CD*[l]	*0CE*[m]	*0CF*[n]
S	SCKC	B206	Set Clock Comparator	5	S	Y	S	8									
S	STCKC	B207	Store Clock Comparator	5	S	X	X	8									
S	SPT	B208	Set CPU Timer	5	S	Y	S	8									
S	STPT	B209	Store CPU Timer	5	S	X	X	8									
S	SPKA	B20A	Set PSW Key From Address	6	S												
S	IPK	B20B	Insert PSW Key From Adress	6	S												
S	PTLB	B20D	Purge TLB	4	S												
S	SPX	B210	Set Prefix	8	S	Y	S	8									
S	STPX	B211	Store Prefix	8	S	X	X	8									
S	STAP	B212	Store CPU Address	2	S	X	X	8									
S	RRB	B213	Reset Reference Bit	4	S	X	X										
RRE	IPTE	B221	Invalidate Page Table Entry	9	S	X	X										
RS	STCTL	B6	Store Control		S	X	X	4									
RS	LCTL	B7	Load Control		S	X f	X	4									
RS	CS	BA	Compare and Swap	12		X	X	1,4									
RS	CDS	BB	Compare Double and Swap	12		X	X	1,8									
RS	CLM	BD	Compare Logical Characters Under Mask			X	X										
RS	STCM	BE	Store Characters Under Mask			X	X										
RS	ICM	BF	Insert Characters Under Mask			X	X										
SS	MVN	D1	Move Numerics			X	X										
SS	MVC	D2	Move Characters			X	X										
SS	MVZ	D3	Move Zones			X	X										
SS	NC	D4	And			X	X										
SS	CLC	D5	Compare Logical Characters			X	X										
SS	OC	D6	Or			X	X										
SS	XC	D7	Exclusive Or			X	X										
SS	TR	DC	Translate			X	X										
SS	ED	DE	Edit			X	X		2								
SS	EDMK	DF	Edit and Mark			X	X		2								
SSE	TPROT	E501	Test Protection	9	S	X	S										
SS	MVCIN	E8	Move Inverse	7		X	X										

Table 3-2 (continued)

SS	SRP	F0	Shift and Round Decimal	X	X				
SS	MVO	F1	Move with Offset	X	X				
SS	PACK	F2	Pack	X	X				
SS	UNPK	F3	Unpack	X	X				
SS	ZAP	F8	Zero and Add Packed	X	X		1,3	C	
SS	CP	F9	Compare Decimal	X	X		1,3		
SS	AP	FA	Add Decimal	X	X		1,3	C	
SS	SP	FB	Subtract Decimal	X	X		1,3	C	
SS	MP	FC	Multiply Decimal	X	X	5	1,3,4		
SS	DP	FD	Divide Decimal	X	X	5	1,2		S

[a]Symbols

Blank This instruction not a cause of this abend.

C Operation completed. The instruction is fully executed with any alteration of the operand contents necessary for completion. The alteration is not likely to provide the intended results. The interrupt occurs after completion.

P Operation partially completed. Certain instructions requiring iterative execution are interruptible during iteration. The contents of the operands will reflect changes made up to the point where the exception was detected.

S Operation suppressed. The instruction is executed as if it were a NOP (no operation). The contents of the operands are not changed.

T Operation terminated: The operation was interrupted at the point the exception was detected. Contents of the operands may or may not have been altered.

X Operation terminated if some but not all of the address operands cause an access exception (key protection, low address protection, or invalid address). If all address operands are invalid, the operation is suppressed. Operand contents follow rules for termination or suppression.

Y See note c.

[b]0C1, operation exception. The operation is always suppressed. This interrupt can result from attempting to execute an instruction not installed on a particular CPU. The ILC depends on the format of the instruction attempted. The codes in the 0C1 column represent the S/370 hardware feature required to support the instruction as follows:

Code	Hardware Feature Required
1	Floating point
2	Extended precision floating point

3	Direct control
4	Translation
5	CPU timer and clock comparator
6	PSW key handling
7	Move inverse
8	Multiprocessing
9	Extended facility
10	Channel set switching
11	Recovery extension
12	Conditional swapping

See also SCC 0C1.

[c]0C4, protection exception. For the interpretation of P, S, and X codes, see note a. An "f" in this column indicates that this instruction is subject to protection exceptions from fetch operations. An "s" in this column indicates that this instruction is subject to protection exceptions from store operations. Where a "Y" appears in the 0C4 column, the disposition of the operation depends on the type of access exception. If the exception results from an attempt to access key-protected storage, the operation is suppressed. If the exception results from an attempt to access a protected low storage address, the operation is terminated. However, if all address operands are invalid, the operation is suppressed. Alteration of operand contents (for a store operation) follows the action for termination or suppression given above. The value of the ILC depends on whether the exception resulted from a data access or instruction fetch. The ILC of a data access exception depends on the instruction format. The ILC of an instruction fetch depends on how many halfwords were fetched before the protection exception was recognized. See also SCC 0C4.

[d]0C5, addressing exception. For interpretation of P, S, T, and X codes, see note a. The value of the ILC depends on whether the exception resulted from a data access or instruction fetch. The ILC of a data access exception depends on how many halfwords were fetched before the addressing exception was recognized. However, if the fetch exception was the result of an execute instruction, the ILC will be 2 (2 halfwords, 4 bytes).

[e]0C6, specification exception. The operation is always suppressed. Digits in this column indicate the immediate cause as follows:

1 An odd-numbered register is specified in the R field when an even-numbered register is required.
2 An operand address is not aligned on a halfword (2-byte) boundary.
3 A floating-point register other than 0, 2, 4, or 6 was specified in a floating-point instruction or other than 0 or 4 for an extended floating-point instruction.
4 An operand address is not aligned on a fullword (4-byte) boundary.
5 Decimal instruction specifies a multiplier or divisor greater than 15 digits and a sign, or the multiplicand or dividend fields are not large enough to contain the result.

Table 3-2 (continued)

6 Storage key instruction specifies an operand address that does not contain zeros in the four low-order bits (28–31).
7 Monitor call instruction does not specify zeros in bits 8 through 11.
8 An address is not aligned on a doubleword (8-byte) boundary.
9 Invalid load of PSW in EC mode. A 1 has been placed in the unassigned PSW bit positions (0, 2–4, 16, 17, 24–39). If an LPDW (x82) has caused this to occur, the ILC is set to zero. If a SSM (x80) or STOSM (xAD) has caused this to occur, the ILC is set to 2 (4 bytes).

See also SCC 0C6.

[f]0C7, data exception. Operation is terminated if the digit portion of an operand field is invalid, or suppressed if the sign field is invalid. The sign field test does not apply to ED (Edit) or EDMK (Edit and Mark), which are always terminated on invalid digits. Codes in the columns refer to the following causes:

1 Invalid sign or digit code.
2 Invalid digit codes.
3 Invalid alignment. Overlapping fields do not share the same rightmost byte.
4 The multiplicand field contains fewer high-order zeros than the number of significant digits in the multiplier. ILC depends on instruction format.

See also SCC 0C7 and 5.4, Data Storage Formats.

[g]0C8, fixed-point overflow exception. Operation always completed. ILC depends on instruction format. See also SCC 0C8.

[h]0C9, fixed-point divide exception. Operation suppressed on division by zero, completed otherwise. ILC depends on instruction format. See also SCC 0C9.

[i]0CA, decimal overflow exception. Operation completed. ILC depends on instruction format. See also SCC 0CA.

[j]0CB, decimal divide exception. Operation suppressed. ILC depends on instruction format. See also SCC 0CB.

[k]0CC, exponent underflow exception. Operation completed. ILC depends on instruction format. See also SCC 0CC and 5.4, Data Storage Formats.

[l]0CD, exponent underflow exception. Operation completed. ILC depends on instruction format. See also SCC 0CD.

[m]0CE, significance exception. Operation completed. ILC depends on instruction format. See also SCC 0CE and 5.4, Data Storage Formats.

[n]0CF, floating-point divide exception. Operation is suppressed. ILC depends on instruction format. See also 0CF and 5.4, Data Storage Formats.

3.3 COMMON JCL ERRORS

In addition to the specific JCL errors listed for each System Completion Code, there are coding errors common to many abends. Some of the more frequent are listed here.

1. A data set name, volume serial number, control card value, or other parameter is incorrect or misspelled:
   (a) Letters or numbers transposed.
   (b) Alpha/numeric substitutions:
      * 0, O, Q
      * 1, I, L
      * 2, Z
      * 7, I, T
   (c) Similar fields or statements were replicated to speed coding. Intended changes to copies were not made or made incorrectly. For example, the DD statement

```
//DD01 DSN=A.B.01,DISP=SHR
```

   was copied, intending to change it to

```
//DD02 DSN=A.B.02,DISP=SHR
```

   However, it ended up as

```
//DD02 DSN=A.B.01,DISP=SHR
```

2. A space(s) was inadvertently inserted before the end of a statement. The operands after the space were interpreted as a comment. For example, the following DISP specification would be ignored:

```
//SYSUT1 DD DSN=MYFILE  ,DISP=NEW
```

3. A comma was omitted or inserted in a positional parameter; for example,

```
VOL=(,,,15)
```

   specifies a volume count of 15, but

```
VOL=(,,15)
```

   specifies the fifteenth volume of a set.
4. Invalid specifications were obtained by a backward reference. The reference is incorrect, misspelled, or omitted. It points to:

(a) The wrong:
  * DDname.
  * STEPname.
  * PROCSTEPname.
(b) A data set that was never created or has been deleted.
(c) A DD DUMMY statement.
(d) A DD statement where parameters have been altered via procedure override.
(e) A DD statement or data set where DCB parameters conflict with these of the referring data set.

5. Invalid usage of a default library. Incorrect, omitted, or overridden specification for:
   (a) JOBCAT or STEPCAT DD.
   (b) JOBLIB or STEPLIB DD.
     * If a concatenation list was given, order of DSNAMEs determines order of access. The concatenation list may be out of sequence for the purpose intended.
6. Specifications for an in-stream or cataloged procedure are incorrect:
   (a) A symbolic parameter is incorrectly specified or allowed to default.
   (b) An override specification is incorrect or applied to the wrong stepname or DDname.
7. An incorrect or omitted COND parameter has caused a step or steps to be executed or skipped. The opposite result of whatever was supposed to happen or not happen has been produced. The oblique syntax of this parameter contributes to the frequency of such errors. The COND parameter causes its associated step(s) to be skipped when it is true. Thus COND=(8,LT) means "skip this step if any previous step's return code is greater than or equal to 8" (equivalently, if 8 is less than any previous step's return code). Common coding errors are:
   (a) Omitting the test: Previous steps have failed but not abended. Further execution is not appropriate. However, no COND test is made, so a step begins execution and abends due to the absence of a data set, incorrect data, and so on.
   (b) Logical reversals: Incorrectly coding or interpreting the test. For example, assuming "Do if true" instead of "Skip if true."
   (c) Checking the condition code of the wrong step, a misspelled stepname, or incorrectly defaulting to all previous steps.
   (d) Confusing the usage of EVEN and ONLY:
     * EVEN will allow a step to execute regardless of normal or abnormal termination of previous steps.
     * ONLY will allow a step to execute only when a previous step abends.
   (e) Inconsistent coding of multiple COND tests for a single step. For example, COND=((8,LT),(8,GE)) will always cause the step to be skipped, since one condition will always be true.
8. The DD statement or end of data delimiter for in-stream data was omitted or incorrectly specified. The JCL statements for a subsequent step or steps have been

interpreted as problem program input instead of operating system commands. Instream data begin following a DD * or DD DATA statement. The default end-of-data delimiter is //, followed by any characters (i.e., a JCL statement).

(a) The standard delimiter statement /* was not placed at the end of the data.
(b) The delimiter specified by the DLM parameter was not placed at the end of the data.
(c) The DLM parameter specification is incorrect, misspelled, or incorrectly overridden. Under JES2, if one character is given (instead of two), the default of /* is assumed.

3.4 ANALYSIS OF THE O/C/EOV WORK AREA

The SVCs called by the OPEN, CLOSE, and EOV (end of volume) macros issue the x13, x19, and x37 SCCs. The particular causes are detailed under each SCC diagnostic. All of these data management routines use the O/C/EOV (OPEN/CLOSE/EOV) work area. This work area frequently contains data useful for debugging x13, x19, and x37 abends. It can also provide useful data for debugging other data-related abends.

The O/C/EOV work area is constructed and used exclusively by Data Management routines. These include OPEN, CLOSE, EOV, TYPE J OPEN, TCLOSE, and RDJFCB. One work area is created by OPEN for each DCB. It is updated at end of volume (e.g., mounting a second tape reel) and when a CLOSE is issued.

The O/C/EOV work area is allocated from main storage subpool 230. A SYSABEND DD statement must be specified to print this area on a dump. When an OPEN is issued, main storage is allocated for the work area. The data set label is placed in the work area, followed by a copy of the JFCB from the SWA (Scheduler Work Area). The JFCB contains the DD statement parameters. The problem program's DCB is "completed" and partially copied into the work area. This copy (not the problem program's) is used for most O/C/EOV processing. Copies of the DEB and IOB are also placed in the work area.

Before a data set can be processed, parameters from the DCB (supplied from the problem program), the JFCB (supplied from the DD statement in most cases), and the data set label (the DSCB for DASD data sets or standard tape labels) must be merged by the OPEN macro. The parameters to be merged are placed in the O/C/EOV work area. Parameters supplied by the problem program (DCB) override those from the DD statement and the data set label. Parameters supplied by the DD statement (JFCB) override those from the data set label. The DCB serves as the repository for the merged information. When the DCB is completed, the JFCB is updated.

Depending on the processing requirements, the data set label(s) is updated by OPEN, CLOSE, or EOV. Conflicting or missing data in these parameters frequently results in an abend.

The O/C/EOV work area is especially useful because it contains the data set label. Unless a utility program or a trace is used to list labels, their actual content can usually be known only by inference. This can make debugging data management abends difficult. For example, an 001 abend occurs due to a conflict between the DD statement and data set label specification for block size. Suppose further that you must change the JCL, the data set cannot be recreated, and its block size is unknown. The O/C/EOV work area could provide the correct block size in this case.

Finding the O/C/EOV Work Area

The O/C/EOV work area relevant to your abend may be found by (1) the address in register 4, or by (2) inspection of subpool 230. Recall that a SYSABEND Dump is required to list subpool 230. If you have the more common SYSUDUMP, the O/C/EOV work area will not be listed.

Locating the O/C/EOV work area by registers is fairly straightforward. The O/C/EOV base registers in use when abend was issued are found in the EXSTA of the SVRB for the abending SVC (usually, the second from the top of ACTIVE RB list formatted on the dump). The SVRB for the abending SVC will contain that SVC's number, in hex, in the rightmost two bytes of the WC-L-IC field of the SVRB. For example, in x37 or some 001 abend dumps, this would be the SVRB with 00020037 in the WC-L-IC field. The O/C/EOV work area, the DCB, and other fields are pointed to from the registers in that SVRB's EXSTA. If these addresses do not point to an O/C/EOV work area, try REGS AT ENTRY TO ABEND or REGS AT TIME OF ERROR listed under the RTM2WA summary. O/C/EOV processing uses the following register assignments:

- R1 Address of O/C/EOV parameter list. Each entry is one full word. The last entry is ORed with x80000000 since multiple DCBs may be processed by a single call.
- R2 Points to the DCB for the data set being processed.
- R3 Base register for O/C/EOV routines.
- R4 Points to O/C/EOV work area for the data set being processed.
- R6 Points to the O/C/EOV where-to-go table. The current entry in this table is the address of the next routine (within data management) to receive control.

If you are unable to locate the work area by register 4, a visual inspection of subpool 230 may suffice. All O/C/EOV work areas are constructed in subpool 230. The dump index on the last page of the dump will give the first page for subpool 230. Data other than O/C/EOV work areas are placed in subpool 230 since they are used by other supervisor routines. Scan the character column for the DDname or data set name of the suspect or offending DCB. The data set name is usually the second field of the data set label, which is the first section of the O/C/EOV work area.

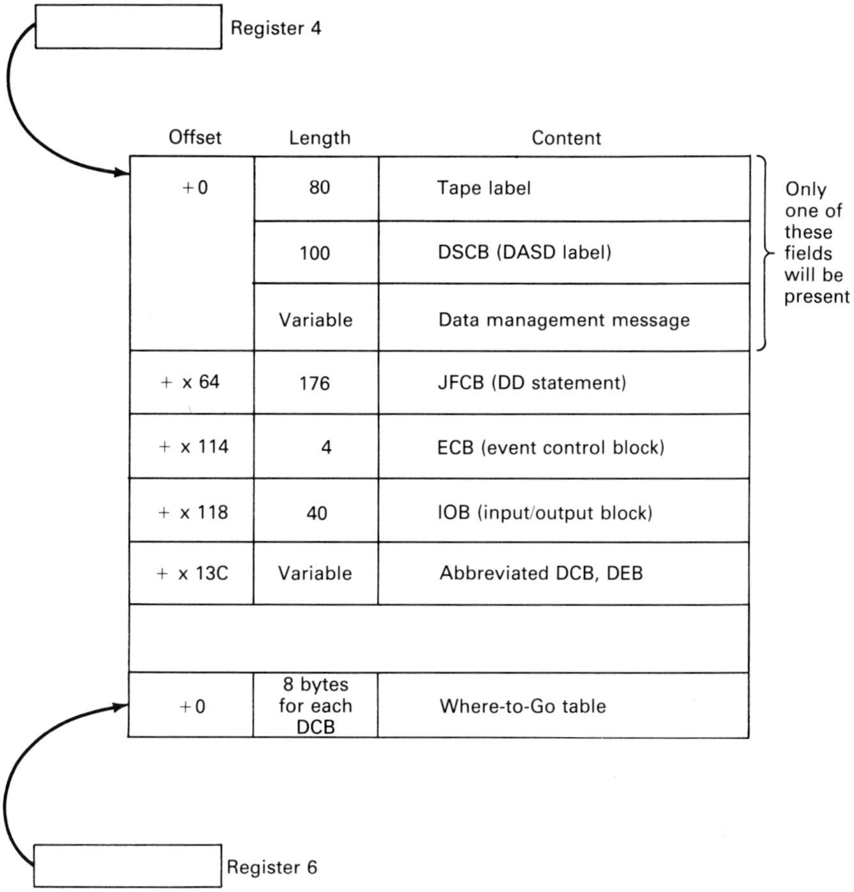

FIGURE 3-2 O/C/EOV Work Area Layout

O/C/EOV Work Area Format

Figure 3-2 shows the general layout of each O/C/EOV work area. The data set label is followed by the JFCB (data supplied from the DD statement) and then by data management control blocks. All data set parameters in the O/C/EOV work area are copied from control blocks.

Data-set-related fields are followed by internally used O/C/EOV fields. The last item in the work area is the where-to-go table. It indicates which O/C/EOV module is to receive control next. There is one 8-byte entry in this table for each DCB passed in the data management macro parameter list (if three data sets were opened with a single call, there would be three entries). The format of the table (offset, length, name) is:

+0, 8	Current module name
+8, 2	Last 2 bytes of the name of next module to receive control
+xA, 3	Disk (TTR) or virtual (EPA) address of next module
+xD, 3	Address of the O/C/EOV work area for this data set

Once the address of the work area has been determined, the next step is to identify what kind of data set label is present. The first few bytes (in character format) of the work area suffice:

- 'F1' in bytes 1 and 2 indicate a format 1 DSCB (DASD label); 'F2', a format 2 DSCB; and so on.
- 'VOL1' in bytes 1 through 4 indicate a standard volume tape label.
- 'HDR1', 'EOV1', 'EOF1' in bytes 1 through 4 indicate a standard type 1 tape label.
- 'HDR2', 'EOV2', 'EOF2' in bytes 1 through 4 indicate a standard type tape 2 label.
- If none of the above are found, a nonstandard label may be present. If the text for system message IEC999I is present, a serious supervisor software error has occurred.

The data set name will usually follow the label identifier field.

Together, the problem program's data management control blocks and the O/C/EOV work area present nearly every piece of data that is needed to debug I/O-related abends. If the JES log or JCL listing is not available, it can supply the DDname, data set name, volume serial number, and so on. Table 3-3 gives a list of these fields. Since most O/C/EOV abends result from missing or conflicting data set parameters, Table 3-3 is arranged to facilitate field-by-field comparison. For example, you suspect that an abend has been caused by conflicting block size specifications. You would look up block size and find that the problem program block size is in DCB at R2 + x3E. The JCL block size (via the JFCB) is in the work area at R4 + xCA. Inspection of the contents of these two fields will indicate if a conflict exists.

The contents of tape and DASD labels may be listed by utility programs, as well as their associated data records. These utilities are described in 3.8, Dumping and Printing Data.

O/C/EOV Traces

Under certain circumstances, it may be useful to trace the contents of the O/C/EOV work area as a data set is opened, closed, and at end of volume. A trace of the O/C/EOV work area as these data management functions are invoked may be obtained by coding the DD statement DCB subparameter DIAGNS=TRACE for the data set of interest. This will activate built-in trace logic in the OPEN, CLOSE, and EOV SVCs.

GTF (generalized trace facility) must be running for trace records to be written. A utility program is then needed to select, format, and print these trace records. The format

Table 3-3

OPEN/CLOSE/EOV Work Area Fields

Location:	*Problem Program*				*OPEN/CLOSE/EOV Work Area*										
Source:	*Problem Program*				*DD Statement*			*Data Set Labels*							
								DASD		*Tape*					
Control Block:	*DCB*		*DEB*			*JFCB*		*Format 1 DSCB*		*VOL*		*Type 1 HDR EOF, EOV*		*Type 2 HDR EOF, EOV*	
Base Register or Pointer:	*R2*		*DCB*		*Parameter/*	*R4*		*R4*		*R4*		*R4*		*R4*	
Generic Field Name:	*Disp.*	*Len.*	*Disp.*	*Len.*	*Subparameter*	*Disp.*	*Len.*	*Disp.*	*Len.*	*Disp.*	*Len.*	*Disp.*	*Len.*	*Disp.*	*Len.*
Block size	3E	2	C[a]	2	DCB BLKSIZE	CA	2	56	2	—	—	—	—	5	5
Block count	C	4	—	—	[c]	—	—	—	—	—	—	36	6	—	—
Buffer, number of	14	1	—	—	DCB BUFNO	BC	1	—	—	—	—	—	—	—	—
Buffer length	18	2	—	—	DCB BUFL	BE	2	—	—	—	—	—	—	—	—
Data set access	—	—	C	1	LABEL IN, OUT	B2	1	—	—	—	—	—	—	—	—
Data set creation date	—	—	—	—	[c]	B4	3	35	3	—	—	29	6	—	—
Data set expiration date	—	—	—	—	LABEL EXPDT, RETPD	B7	3	38	3	—	—	2F	6	—	—
Data set name	—	—	—	—	DSNAME	64	44	0	44	—	—	4	17	—	—
Data set organization	10	2	1A	2	DCB DSORG	C6	2	52	2	—	—	—	—	—	—
Data set sequence number	—	—	—	—	LABLE[b]	A8	2			—	—	1F	4	—	—
Data set status	—	—	8	1	DISP	BB	1	—	—	—	—	—	—	—	—
DDname	28	8	—	—	DDNAME	—	—	—	—	—	—	—	—	—	—
Extent, first descriptor	—	—	20	14	[c]	—	—	69	10	—	—	—	—	—	—
Extents, number of	—	—	10	1	[c]	—	—	3B	1	—	—	—	—	—	—
Key length	10	1	—	—	DCB KEYLEN	C1	1	5A	1	—	—	—	—	—	—
Key relative position	3C	2	—	—	DCB RKP	D0	2	5B	2	—	—	—	—	—	—
Label type	—	—	—	—	LABLE[b]	A6	1	2C	1	0	4	0	4	0	4
Option code	34	1	—	—	DCB OPTCD	C9	1	55	1	—	—	—	—	—	—
Password flags	—	—	E	1	LABLE[b]	BB	1	5D	1	—	—	35	1	—	—
Record format	24	1	—	—	DCB RECFM	C8	1	54	1	—	—	—	—	4	1
Record length	52	2	E	2	DCB LRECL	CC	2	58	2	—	—	—	—	A	5
Space allocation, directory	—	—	—	—	SPACE[b]	104	3	—	—	—	—	—	—	—	—

Table 3-3 (continued)

Location:	*Problem Program*				*OPEN/CLOSE/EOV Work Area*										
Source:	*Problem Program*				*DD Statement*			*Data Set Labels*							
								DASD		*Tape*					
Control Block:	*DCB*		*DEB*			*JFCB*		*Format 1 DSCB*		*VOL*		*Type 1 HDR EOF, EOV*		*Type 2 HDR EOF, EOV*	
Base Register or Pointer:	*R2*		*DCB*		*Parameter/*	*R4*		*R4*		*R4*		*R4*		*R4*	
Generic Field Name:	*Disp.*	*Len.*	*Disp.*	*Len.*	*Subparameter*	*Disp.*	*Len.*	*Disp.*	*Len.*	*Disp.*	*Len.*	*Disp.*	*Len.*	*Disp.*	*Len.*
Space allocation, primary	—	—	—	—	SPACE[b]	FC	3	—	—	—	—	—	—	—	—
Space allocation, secondary	—	—	—	—	SPACE[b]	100	3	5E	4	—	—	—	—	—	—
Tape density	12	1	—	—	DCB DEN	C2	1	—	—	—	—	—	—	10	1
Tape recording technique	10	1	—	—	DCB TRTCH	C1	1	—	—	—	—	—	—	22	2
Volumes, number of	—	—	2[a]	2	VOLUME[b]	D9	1	—	—	—	—	—	—	—	—
Volume serial number	—	—	—	—	VOLUME SER	DA	(6 × 5)	2D	6	4	6	—	—	—	—
Volume sequence number	—	—	D[a]	2	VOLUME[b]	AA	2	33	2	—	—	—	—	—	—

[a]Relative to start of access method-dependent section.
[b]Positional parameter.
[c]No corresponding DD statement parameter.

```
USRFF     FFF      ASCB xxxxxxxx  JOBN tttttttt
DCB       xxxxxxxxxxxxxxx
WKAREA1   xxxxxxxxxxxxxxxxxxx
WKAREA2   xxxxxxxxxxxxxxxxx
WKAREA3   xxxxxxxxxxxxxxxxxxxxxx
WKAREA4   xxxxxxxxxxxxxxxx
WKAREA5   xxxxxxxxxxxxxxxxxxx
WTG TBL   xxxxxxxxxxxxxxxxxxxxx
```

FIGURE 3-3 O/C/EOV Trace Output

of the trace output is shown in Figure 3-3. Each "WKAREA" line corresponds to a major portion of the O/C/EOV work area (see Figure 3-2). The meaning of the fields in Figure 3-3 is:

USRFF	Identifies the trace as coming from O/C/EOV
ASCB	The address of the ASCB for the task issuing the trace
JOBN	The JOBNAME of the task issuing the trace
DCB	Horizontal hex dump of the problem program DCB for the data set traced
WKAREA1	Horizontal hex dump of data set label area from the O/C/EOV work area for the data set traced
WKAREA2	Horizontal hex dump of the JFCB area (DD statement parameters) from the O/C/EOV work area for the data set traced
WKAREA3	Horizontal hex dump of O/C/EOV copy of the DCB, DEB, and IOB for the data set traced
WKAREA4	O/C/EOV save area for registers and CCW
WKAREA5	O/C/EOV work items
WTG TBL	Horizontal hex dump of the where-to-go table

Interpretation of an O/C/EOV Trace

The trace records represent the contents of the control blocks and work area when the issuing module completed its function. A trace record from OPEN will show the trace items immediately upon completion of OPEN processing.

To determine which function issued the trace record, the WTG TBL line is used. The first 8 bytes of the WTG TBL contain the name of the issuing module. The function of the module is determined from the numeric portion of its name:

IFG019xx	OPEN
IFG020xx	CLOSE
IFG055xx	EOV

The data in the remaining work areas may be analyzed for inconsistencies as described above. The trace gives additional information in that the sequence of events leading up to an abend is shown.

Obtaining an O/C/EOV Trace

The trace is invoked by simply coding DIAGNS=TRACE on the DCB of the DD statements of interest, and executing the problem program when GTF is running. AMDPRDMP, an IBM utility program, is required to select, format, and print the trace records.

A JCL example to invoke and print an O/C/EOV trace follows. The first step will cause trace records to be written as PROBPROG opens, closes, or reaches ends of volume on data set AN.EXAMPLE. The second step runs the AMDPRDMP utility program to select and print the trace records. The input data set is specified by the SYSUT1 DD statement. SYS1.TRACE is a commonly used data set name for GTF trace output. SYSPRINT will receive any AMDPRDMP messages. The trace output will be directed to the PRINTER DD. The control statements are supplied via the SYSIN DD.

The EDIT control statement supplies the selection criterion. GTF is a system-wide tracing facility. When it is running, trace data from many jobs for many types of events are typically collected. The JOBNAME parameter specifies that only trace records for the job name given are to be selected. The USR parameter further limits selection to trace records written by O/C/EOV. Although the example creates and prints trace data in the same job, the trace and print steps could be separate.

```
//TRACEOCE JOB(.....)
//GENTRACE EXEC PGM=PROBPROG
//TRACEDD  DD
//   DSN=AN.EXAMPLE,
//   DISP=OLD,
//   DCB=DIAGNS=TRACE
//LISTGTF   EXEC PGM=AMDPRDMP
//SYSPRINT DD SYSOUT=A
//PRINTER   DD SYSOUT=A
//SYSUT1    DD
//   DSN=SYS1.TRACE,
//   DISP=SHR
//SYSIN     DD *
  EDIT JOBNAME=TRACEOCE,USR=(IMDMA)
  END
/*
```

JCL requirements for your installation should be verified with your systems programmer. For more information about AMDPRDMP and GTF, see *Service Aids, Debugging Handbook,* and *MVS Overview*.

3.5 FINDING VSAM DATA RECORDS

VSAM (virtual storage access method) is a data management facility of MVS which supports random and sequential access to VSAM-defined data sets. It provides many features not found in other access methods. The most significant for debugging purposes is that VSAM does not issue abends. The multitude of data management abends (e.g., SCCs x13, x14, and x37) have no direct VSAM counterpart. If an error occurs during VSAM I/O, OPEN, CLOSE, or EOV, a status code and other relevant data are returned to the problem program. No abend is issued. JCL related errors are treated in the same way. In addition to the error indicators returned, a system message is output. The return codes given with these system messages are extensively documented in *System Messages*. The most common messages and associated functions are:

IEC161I	Open
IEC251I	Close
IEC252I	Temporary close
IEC070I	End of volume

For more general information about VSAM, see *VSAM Programmer's Guide*. However, abends still occur in programs using VSAM data sets. Data needed to diagnose and correct these abends may be contained in VSAM data records or control blocks. The method to locate these data is presented in this section. The main topics are:

- How to find a current VSAM record and buffers
- Structure and function of VSAM control blocks

How to Find VSAM Records and Buffers

Since it is highly likely that VSAM will not be in control when an abend occurs, starting with register addresses (the common technique for non-VSAM data management abends) is not usually effective. Locating VSAM data records in an ABEND dump is a two-step process. First, find the DEBs for the cluster of interest (a VSAM cluster has several DEBs). These DEBs will point to control blocks for the cluster. Second, follow the chain of VSAM control blocks to the current record (the last record read or written). The specifics of this analysis are as follows:

1. Locate the DEBs for the cluster of interest. There are two ways to do this: (a) by counting DEBs and (b) by checking the TIOT DDname entry associated with a DEB. VSAM DEBs can be identified by a x01 in the AMTYP field of the formatted DEB (DEBAMTYP, DEB - x3).
   (a) Location by counting DEBs. DEBs are listed on the dump in the reverse order of open (the DEB for the first data set opened is listed last). There will be one DEB for each open non-VSAM (QSAM, BDAM, BPAM, etc.) data set. There will be two DEBS for each open ESDS or RRDS cluster. There will be three DEBs for each open KSDS cluster. If alternate indexes are in use, there will be two additional DEBs for each alternate index cluster belonging to an upgrade set. Each alternate index has a data and index component. If NOUPGRADE or NOUPDATE was specified when the alternate index was defined, it will not be present (i.e., no DEB will have been created).

If the order of open and type of data sets are known, simply count backward from the last DEB listed. Use the DDname check to verify that the DEB located is for the cluster of interest.

(b) Location by checking DDname. The first DEB for a VSAM cluster points to an ACB (access control block). The ACB contains the TIOT offset, as does the DCB, which will yield the cluster's DDname when applied to the TIOT. The first DEB of a VSAM cluster can be identified by the absence of the line beginning with 'DEBAVT" from the formatted DEB listing. The first line of this DEB's listing will begin with "PREFIX." Check each such DEB until the DEB for the cluster of interest is located. An approximation of the counting technique may decrease the number of DEBs to check. The pointers are as follows:

- The address in the 3 low-order bytes of the DEB field labeled DCBADR points to the ACB (DEB + x19, DEBDCBB).
- The 2-byte TIOT offset is at x28 into this ACB (the ACB will be found in the main storage portion of the dump).
- The DDname of this cluster is found in the TIOT at the offset from the ACB.

The DCBADR field of subsequent DEBs for the cluster points to an AMB. The TIOT offset is also located at x28 into the AMB. The DDname of the cluster is found in the TIOT at this offset, in the same way that of an ACB is. Most control blocks chained off the DEB will point back to the TIOT. However, it is necessary to find the DEB pointing to the ACB to know where the DEB group for a cluster begins.

2. Follow the chain of VSAM control blocks for this cluster to locate the current data record.

(a) The second DEB for the cluster (listed immediately after the DEB pointing to the ACB) is the starting place for this chain. This is the DEB for the data component.

- The address in the 3 low-order bytes of the DEB field labeled DCBADR points to the AMB (access method block) for the data component of the cluster (DEB + x19, DEBDCBB).
- At the AMB + xC is the address of the PLH (placeholder) for this cluster (AMBPH).
- At PLH + x24 is the address of the RPL (request parameter list) for this cluster. PLH + x3C may point to the current record.
- At RPL + x20 is the address of the first byte of the current data record. This address will point to either a work area or within a VSAM buffer.

The AMB, PLH, and RPL are not formatted. They wil be found in the main storage portion of the dump.

(b) Data records preceding or following the current record may be found in VSAM buffers. Buffers are described by a chain of BUFC control blocks. The PLH points to the BUFC for the current buffer. There are separate buffers for the data and index components of a cluster. The number of buffers is given in the ACB.

- ACB + x10 Number of data component buffers (halfword)
- ACB + x12 Number of index component buffers (halfword)

Buffers may be located as follows:

- Locate the PLH as described above.
  - At PLH + x34 is the address of the BUFC for the current data buffer.
  - At PLH + xBC is the address of the BUFC for the current index buffer.
- At BUFC + x14 is the address of the buffer described by the BUFC. Other BUFC fields of interest are:
  - + 4 Address of associated AMB or PLH.
  - + 8 RBA for input data set. Not valid unless first BUFC flag byte (+0) is xFF (BUFCAVL).
  - + xC RBA for output data set. Not valid unless high-order bit of the second BUFC flag is on (xF) (BUFCMW). RBA of zero is valid. Both RBA fields refer to current RBA, if present.
  - + x38 Address of next BUFC.
  - + x3C Address of previous BUFC.

VSAM Control Block Structure and Function

VSAM control blocks facilitate the management and interface of two main functions: logical record processing and physical record I/O. VSAM uses many unique control blocks and some common to other access methods. A VSAM cluster is associated with a task by several DEBs which are placed on the TCB/DEB chain when a VSAM open is requested. Catalog-related control blocks are created if necessary. Main storage is allocated for additional control blocks and buffers. Pointers, flags, and other fields are initialized. I/O processing is initiated by requests from the problem program to put or get data. The requests are passed to VSAM's physical I/O handler via control blocks. VSAM logic attempts to optimize performance by trading off actual I/O and data buffering. As a result, physical reads and writes do not usually correspond to logical reads and writes. VSAM control blocks provide the data necessary to synchronize this activity.

Figures 3-4 and 3-5 depict the overall structure of VSAM control blocks. Control blocks related to logical record processing are shown separate from those related to physical record processing, for the sake of simplicity.

The SHOWCB macro can be used in assembly programs to move fields of VSAM control blocks to work areas. These fields can then be displayed for diagnostic purposes. For further information, see *VSAM Programmer's Guide*.

There are at least two DEBs for a VSAM cluster. The first is a "dummy" DEB. This DEB points to the cluster's ACB. It is used by task termination to close the cluster if an abend occurs. The second DEB describes the data component. If the cluster is a KSDS, a third DEB will be created to describe the index component. If alternate indexes are defined, two additional DEBs will be created for each alternate index: one for the data portion of the index, a second for the key portion. All VSAM data sets are DASD resident. With the exception of the dummy DEB, the usage and format of DASD data

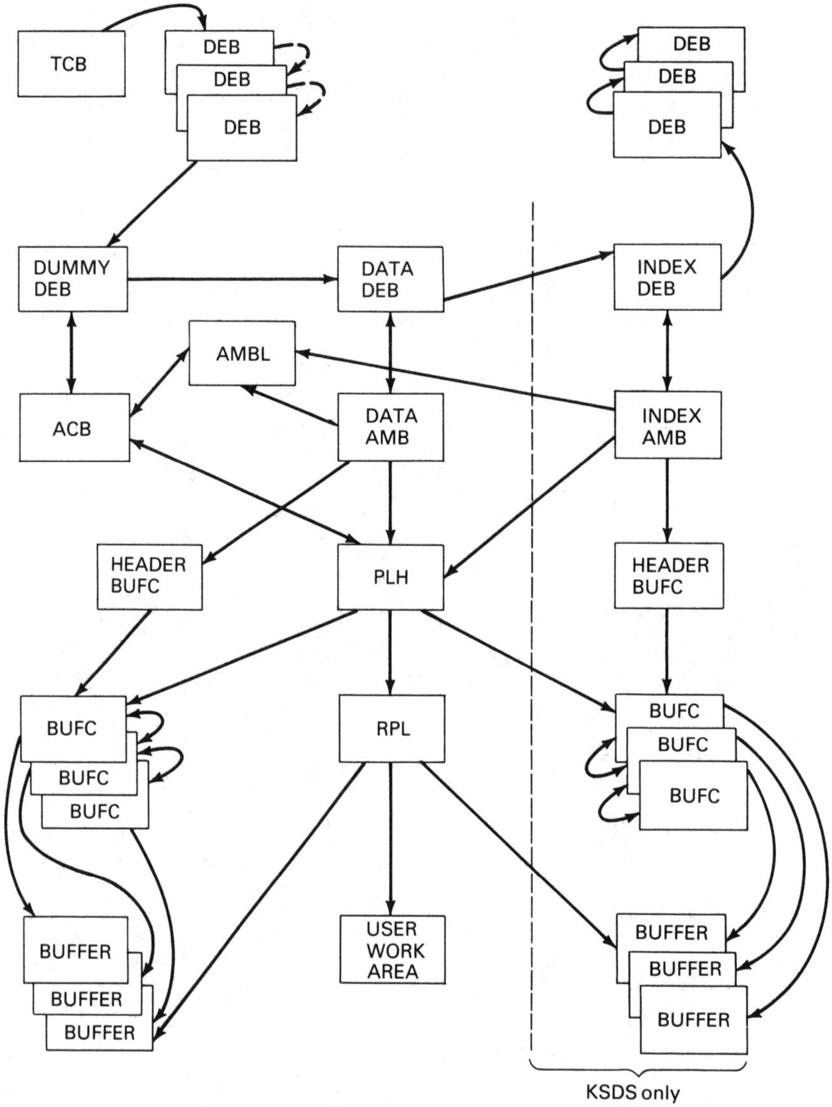

FIGURE 3-4 VSAM Control Blocks: Logical Functions

extent descriptor fields is the same in VSAM DEBs as it is for other access methods. DEB extent fields are described under the Data Extent Block in 4.2, Dump Components. The data and index DEBs point to an AMB.

The function of remaining control blocks is as follows. Relevant fields are noted. The actual contents of these fields depend on how VSAM is used by the problem program. Data or an address may not always be present.

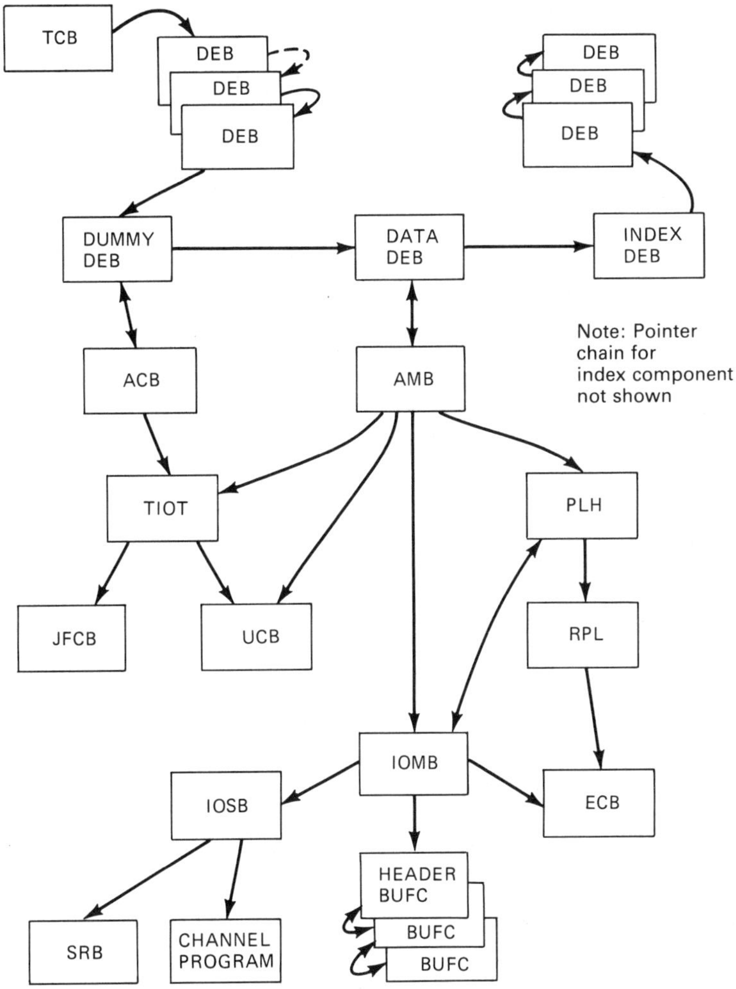

FIGURE 3-5 VSAM Control Blocks: Physical Functions

- *ACB (access control block)*. Pointed to from a "dummy" DEB (DEBDCBB, DEB + x19). The ACB associates a cluster with the TIOT and JFCB. The ACB address plus:
  - (a) 4 ACBAMBL: address of the AMBL
  - (b) x10 ACBBUFND: number of data buffers (halfword)
  - (c) x12 ACBBUFNI: number of index buffers (halfword)
  - (d) x28 ACBTIOT: TIOT offset (halfword)
  - (e) x2D ACBDEB: address of the "dummy" DEB for this ACB and its cluster
  - (f) x31 ACBERFLG: 1-byte error flag (see "VSAM Logic" for interpretation)

(g) x34 ACBUJFCB: address of the JFCB (DD statement parameters) for this cluster
(h) x3C ACBBLKSZ: halfword block size
(i) x3E ACBLRECL: halfword logical record length

- *AMB (access method block)*. Pointed to from the index and data DEBS (DEBDCBB, DEB + x19). The AMB points to or from most other VSAM control blocks, providing a base control block. The AMB address plus:

  (a) 8 AMBBUFC: address of the header BUFC
  (b) xC AMBPH: placeholder address
  (c) x1C AMBIOBAD: IOB address
  (d) x28 AMBTIOT: TIOT offset (halfword)

- *AMBL (access method block list)*. Pointed to from the ACB and AMB(s). Used to control sharing of clusters between tasks. The AMBL address plus:

  (a) x8 AMBLACB: ACB address
  (b) x34 AMBLDTA: data AMB address
  (c) x38 AMBLIX: index AMB address

- *PLH (placeholder)*. Pointed to from the AMB. Contains pointers to current buffers and user request list. Facilitates translation of logical and physical data positions. The PLH address plus:

  (a) x14 PLHCRPL: address of the current RPL
  (b) x34 PLHDBUFC: address of the current data BUFC
  (c) x3C May contain the address of the current or next logical record
  (d) x4C PLHDIOB: address of the cluster's IOMB
  (e) xBC PLHIBUFC: address of the current index BUFC
  (f) xC8 PLHIXSPL: address of the 32-byte index search parameter list
  (g) xF8 PLHKEYPT: may point to the current key or relative record number

- *RPL (request parameter list)*. Describes the current request made for I/O. Points to the current data record. The RPL address plus:

  (a) 2 RPLREQ: 1-byte request type
  (b) 4 RPLPLHPT: address of the PLH
  (c) 8 RPLECB: address of the ECB or the ECB itself
  (d) xD RPLERREG: 1-byte status code returned upon completion of a request;

      x00 Normal completion
      x08 Logical error
      x0C Physical I/O error

  (e) xE RPLCMPON: 1-byte status code which is meaningful when alternate indexes are present. Indicates which component was active if an error has occurred (RPLERREG not equal zero) and the result of any upgrades that were in progress:

      x00 Base cluster upgrade successful

x01 Possible error in base cluster upgrade
x02 Alternate index upgrade successful
x03 Possible error in alternate index upgrade
x04 Upgrade set upgrade successful
x05 Possible error in upgrade set upgrade

(f) xF RPLERRCD: 1-byte status code further indicating the nature of an error (RPLERREG not equal zero) (see *VSAM Logic* for interpretation)
(g) x18 RPLDACB: address of the ACB
(h) x20 RPLAREA: address of the work area for the current record or the address of the current record in the buffer
(i) x24 RPLARG: address of the current search argument
(j) x40 RPLDDDD: RBA of last completed I/O operation

- *BUFC (buffer control block)*. Pointed to from the PLH. The BUFC describes a data or index buffer and serves as the interface between the VSAM I/O and buffer management routines. The BUFCs for a component of a cluster are chained together. Each chain originates in a "header" BUFC which is pointed to from the AMB. The header BUFC points to the first BUFC in the chain. The PLH points to the BUFC that points to the buffer containing the current physical record. Each BUFC points forward and backward on the chain.

  The contents of the buffer pointed to vary depending on the kind of I/O that is being done. For sequential input, VSAM reads ahead of the requested record to the extent of available buffers. On output, the synchronization of logical and physical I/O is more complex since VSAM tries to optimize buffer space and physical I/O. Maintenance of index integrity also affects physical/logical synchronization.

  Relevant BUFC fields are at the BUFC address plus:

  (a) 4 BUFCPLH or BUFCAMB: address of the PLH or the AMB
  (b) 8 BUFCDDDD: RBA for an input cluster; valid only if first BUFC byte is xFF (BUFCAVL)
  (c) xC BUFCORBA: RBA for an output cluster; valid only if the high-order bit of the second BUFC status byte is on (x08)
  (d) x14 BUFCBAD: address of the buffer described by this BUFC
  (e) x38 BUFCUCUP: address of the next BUFC
  (f) x3C BUFCUCDN: address of the previous BUFC

- *IOMB, IOSB, and SRB*. These control blocks serve the same function as the IOB does for non-VSAM access methods. They facilitate the transfer of data to and from main storage, channels, and DASD storage. These control blocks rarely provide data useful for application debugging. The IOSB contains the same CSW and sense bytes found in the IOB. Their contents are relevant if VSAM internal logic errors occur. See *MVS Diagnostic Techniques* for a further discussion.
- *VGTT, PSB, and JSCB*. These VSAM-related control blocks are used primarily for allocation of main storage to VSAM routines. They do not provide any significant application debugging information.

3.6 SYSTEM COMPLETION CODE CROSS-REFERENCE

The SCC cross-reference provides some direction for debugging abend SCCs which are not explicitly covered in this book. For example, suppose that you get a 101 SCC. A 101 abend is not covered. By checking the cross-reference you see that information given about a 301 abend may apply. For unusual abends, there is no directly related information.

Table 3-4
SCC Cross-Reference

SCC Group	*MVS Function*	*Macro Name*	*Related SCC Diagnostics*
00x	Data management	CHECK, PUT, GET	001, 002
01x	Data management	OPEN, CLOSE	x13, x14
03x	Data management/ ISAM	OPEN, CLOSE	03x
08x	Virtual storage management		x04, x0A
0Cx	Program interrupt handler		0Cx, 0Cx diagnostics
x00	Data management	EXCP	400
x01		WAIT	301
x02		POST	102
x03	Task termination	EXIT	C03
x04	Virtual storage management	GETMAIN	x04, x0A
x05	Virtual storage management	FREEMAIN	x04, x0A
x06	Program management	LINK, LOAD, ATTACH, DELETE, XCTL	x06
x0A	Virtual storage management	GETMAIN (R TYPE)	x0A, x04
x0E	Interrupt handler	SPIE	0Cx diagnostics
x12	Data management	BLDL/FIND	x06, B14
x13	Data management	OPEN	x13, x14, x37
x14	Data management	CLOSE	x14, x13, x37
x15	Data management	CLOSE (T TYPE)	214, 714, B14
x22	Task management	MGCR/QEDIT	x22
x37	Data management	EOV	x37, x14, x13
x40	Data management	RDJFCB	x37, x14, x13
x44	Data management	SYNADAF	001, x37
x6B		MODESET	Fxx
x78	Virtual storage management	GETMAIN/ FREEMAIN	x04, x0A
x79	I/O supervisor		See *Locating VSAM Data Records* for SCC 279
x7D	Task management		102, 301
xFC	Supervisor		Fxx

TABLE 3-5
SCC Diagnostics by SCC Group

Group	*SCC Diagnostics*
00x	001, 002
03x	031, 03B, 03D
0Cx	0C1, 0C2, 0C3, 0C4, 0C5, 0C6, 0C7, 0C8, 0C9, 0CA, 0CB, 0CC, 0CD, 0CE, 0CF
x00	400
x01	301
x02	102
x03	C03
x04	604, 804
x06	106, 406, 506, 706, 806
x0A	80A
x13	013, 113, 213, 413, 513, 613, 713, 813, 913, A13, C13
x14	214, 714, B14
x22	122, 222, 322, 522
x37	137, 237, 637, 737, B37, D37, E37
Fxx	Fxx

However, 1.3, General Debugging Procedure, and 5.2, Basic Techniques, apply to any abend. Table 3-4 is organized by SCC group, and indicates which SCCs are covered in a group. Thus x00 refers to any SCC ending in 00 and beginning with a hex digit (100, 200, C00). Table 3-5 shows by SCC group which specific SCCs are covered in the SCC diagnostic section. All System Completion Codes are documented in *System Codes* and Volume 1 of *Debugging Handbook*.

3.7 DEBUGGING ABENDS UNDER TSO

The TSO facility of MVS allows users to execute programs in an online mode. TSO commands are similar in many respects to JCL statements. The main difference is in the syntax used to specify the problem program's environment. MVS handles a TSO session much as it handles a batch job. Each major TSO command or CALL is treated like a job step. When an abend occurs under TSO, system messages and the system completion code are displayed on the TSO user's terminal instead of being printed by JES.

To debug abends in programs run via TSO, follow the standard debugging procedure. When reviewing JCL related causes under the SCC diagnostic, substitute the TSO command operands used for the JCL parameters listed. The keywords for TSO and JCL are identical in many cases and very similar when not. The ALLOCATE and ATTRIBUTE TSO commands have the same function as the DD statement. The CALL command is the equivalent of the EXEC statement with a STEPLIB DD. Other TSO commands function like batch utility programs, since the same program is often invoked. LINK uses the familiar HEWL program, PROTECT functions like IEHPROGM; DELETE, LIST-

CAT, and LISTDS function like IDCAMS; and so on. For example, suppose that a B37 abend has occurred in a program invoked by the TSO CALL command. Look up B37 in 2.2, SCC Diagnostics. Under the JCL related causes, you note that errors on the DD statement SPACE parameter can cause a B37 abend. The SPACE operand of the TSO ALLOCATE command is its equivalent. Further inspection of the ALLOCATE command operands for errors suggested by the B37 JCL diagnostics may yield a solution.

An ABEND dump may be obtained under TSO by specifying an ALLOCATE command similar to the SYSUDUMP or SYSABEND DD statement in a job step. The dump may be directed to a JES SYSOUT data set for immediate printing or written to a TSO data set for later use. To get a dump on SYSOUT, use the TSO command:

```
ALLOCATE DD(SYSUDUMP) SYSOUT(A)
```

To direct the dump to a TSO data set, for example, DUMP.LIST, use the TSO command:

```
ALLOCATE DD(SYSUDUMP) DSN(DUMP.LIST) SPACE(10 1) TRA
```

The actual space requirement will vary. SYSABEND could also be specified in either command. SYSMDUMP cannot be directed to SYSOUT, so if a SYSMDUMP is needed, the second form with DCB information would be required.

3.8 DUMPING AND PRINTING DATA

It is often useful for debugging to print the contents of a data set, its label, or other associated information. This section describes several IBM utility programs that provide this service. These utilities are not the only means available for dumping and printing. Non-IBM utility programs are on the market and many installations have or can write their own. However, IBM utilities are the only ones immediately available to all MVS users.

The dumping and listing functions are summarized by utility. A functional description with a JCL example follows. The utility programs may also be executed via TSO, provided that the equivalent TSO command is given. See *OS/VS2 TSO Command Language Reference,* for further information.

The JCL examples are intended to generally show job step statements, DD parameters, and the minimum utility control statements needed to create the dump or listing described. You will need to provide a JOB statement and appropriate DD parameters for the data set of interest. VOLUME and UNIT are not given for the input data sets, unless required. Uncataloged data sets will always require VOLUME and UNIT. DISP=SHR is usually given. This will allow other tasks to read or update while you are listing the data set. DISP=OLD may be specified to ensure that no updates are done while your print is in progress. STEPCAT or JOBCAT DD statements may be used to point to a user catalog. Several user catalogs can be concatenated in single STEPCAT or JOBCAT.

Spacing and continuation of statements are used to make the examples as readable as possible. Readability is always desirable, but any syntactically correct equivalent will produce the same results. Control statements for the utilities described here require that column 1 is blank. The first character of the control statement begins in column 2.

The utilities described also perform many other functions, and usually have several output format options. The relevant IBM publication is cited for each utility. Refer to the publication for a full description of the utility's functions and requirements.

The utility programs and their dumping and printing functions are as follows:

- AMBLIST
  - (a) Prints load module data:
    - * Date and time created.
    - * CSECT identification (IDR) records.
    - * External symbol dictionary.
    - * Cross-reference.
  - (b) Prints hex dump of load module.
  - (c) May select a member, members, or an entire load library.
- IDCAMS
  - (a) Prints a VSAM cluster:
    - * By key.
    - * By RBA.
    - * By record number.
    - * Starting or ending at a specific record.
    - * Character or hex dump format.
  - (b) Prints non-VSAM data sets:
    - * Sequential (physical sequential and direct).
    - * ISAM.
    - * Character or hex dump format.
  - (c) Lists user or system catalog entries.
- IEBISAM
  - (a) Prints an ISAM data set:
    - * In key sequence.
    - * In character or hex dump format.
- IEBPTPCH
  - (a) Prints tape labels:
    - * Standard or nonstandard.
    - * Character or hex dump format.
  - (b) Prints partitioned data sets:
    - * Member.
    - * Directory.

- IEHDASDR
  (a) Prints hex dump of DASD tracks starting and ending at user-specified track.
- IEHLIST
  (a) Formats and prints:
    * DASD data set labels (DSCB).
    * PDS directory entries.
    * Volume table of contents (VTOC).

Printing Sequential and Direct Data Sets

The IDCAMS utility may be used to print sequential and direct data sets. The data sets are printed in physical record sequence—any implicit key in a direct data set cannot be interpreted by IDCAMS to sequence output records. DCB parameters DSORG, RECFM, BLKSIZE, and LRECL must be supplied. The example shows how to obtain a horizontal dump of a direct data set. The JCL for a sequential data set would require the same parameters and control statements.

```
//DUMPDIR   EXEC PGM=IDCAMS
//SYSPRINT DD SYSOUT=A
//BDAMDD    DD
//  DSN=BDAMDSN,
//  DCB=(DSORG=PS,
//          RECFM=FB,
//          BLKSIZE=12000,
//          LRECL=250),
//  DISP=SHR
//SYSIN     DD *
  PRINT INFILE(BDAMDD)
/*
```

Tape resident data sets may be printed by IDCAMS as well as disk resident sequential data sets. For more information on IDCAMS, see *Access Method Services*.

Printing Partitioned Data Set Members

The IEBPTPCH utility will print or dump members of a partitioned data set. The first example shows how to obtain a hex dump of the member CNTLCARD from a card-image PDS named MYLIB.

```
//DUMPMBR   EXEC PGM = IEBPTPCH
//SYSPRINT DD SYSOUT = A
//SYSUT1    DD
//  DSN = MYLIB,
//  DISP = SHR
//SYSUT2    DD  SYSOUT = A
//SYSIN     DD *
  PRINT TYPORG = PO,MAXNAME = 1,MAXFLDS = 1
  MEMBER NAME = CNTLCARD
  RECORD FIELD = (80,1,XE,1)
/*
```

If the MEMBER control statement is omitted, all members in the PDS specified by SYSUT1 will be printed.

Printing Partitioned Data Set Directories

A PDS directory functions as the data set label for a PDS. A directory is composed of at least one 256-byte directory block. A directory block contains from 3 to 21 variable-length entries, each describing a member of the PDS. An entry contains:

- The 8-byte member name.
- TTR address of the first record.
- A flag byte.
- Up to 62 bytes of user-defined data.

For a detailed explanation of these fields, see *Data Management Services*. Either IEBPTPCH or IEHLIST will access a PDS directory. IEBPTPCH may be used to dump addresses, flags, and user-defined fields. IEHLIST will print member names.

To dump the directory of a PDS, DCB parameters RECFM=U and BLKSIZE=256 and the control parameter TYPORG=PS must be specified.

```
//DUMPDIR  EXEC PGM=IEBPTPCH
//SYSPRINT DD SYSOUT=A
//SYSUT1   DD
//  DSN=MYLIB,
//  DCB=(RECFM=U,
//        BLKSIZE=256),
//  DISP=SHR
//SYSUT2   DD SYSOUT=A
//SYSIN    DD *
  PRINT TYPORG=PS,MAXFLDS=1
  RECORD FIELD=(256,1,XE,1)
/*
```

For more information about IEBPTPCH, see *MVS Utilities*.

The next example shows how to use IEHLIST to obtain a formatted listing of three PDS directories, which all reside on the same volume. From 1 to 10 directories may be listed in a single step.

```
//PRINTDIR EXEC PGM=IEHLIST
//SYSPRINT DD SYSOUT=A
//PDSDD    DD
//  UNIT=SYSDA,
//  VOL=SER=234567,
//  DISP=SHR
//SYSIN    DD *
  LISTPDS DSNAME=(MYLIB,PRIVATE.LINKLIB,X.DATA),  *
          VOL=SYSDA=234567,                       *
          FORMAT
/*
```

For more information about IEHLIST, see *MVS Utilities*. Note that continuation characters for the control statements (asterisk) are required in column 71.

Printing ISAM Data Sets

The IEBISAM utility may be used to print an ISAM data set in key sequence. A character or hex dump format may be selected.

```
//DUMPISAM EXEC PGM=IEBISAM,
//  PARM='PRINTL'
//SYSPRINT DD SYSOUT=A
//SYSUT1    DD
//  DSN=ISAMDSN,
//  DCB=DSORG=IS,
//  DISP=SHR
//SYSUT2    DD SYSOUT=A
/*
```

The PARM specification on the EXEC statement controls the output format. PARM='PRINTL' specifies a hex dump output format. PARM='PRINTL,N' specifies a character output format. For more information about IEBISAM, see *MVS Utilities*.

ISAM data sets may also be printed by IDCAMS. DCB parameters DSORG, RECFM, BLKSIZE, and LRECL must be specified. The data set will be printed in key sequence.

```
//DUMPISAM EXEC PGM=IDCAMS
//SYSPRINT DD SYSOUT=A
//ISAMDD    DD
//  DSN=ISAMDSN,
//  DCB=(DSORG=IS,
//          RECFM=FB,
//          BLKSIZE=13000,
//          LRECL=100),
//  DISP=SHR
//SYSIN     DD *
     PRINT INFILE(ISAMDD)
/*
```

For more information about IDCAMS, see *Access Method Services*.

Printing VSAM Components

The IDCAMS utility program can be used to obtain a hex dump or print of VSAM cluster components. Specifying the cluster name will list records in key sequence. Specifying the data or index components will list control intervals in ascending RBA sequence. The starting and ending key, RBA, or record number may be specified. Output may be formatted in one of three ways: character, where either the EBCDIC character or a space is printed for each byte; hex, where the two-digit hexadecimal value of each byte is printed; dump, where a format similar to the ABEND dump of main storage (hexadecimal and character) is output. Dump is the default format. The example shows how to obtain a horizontal hex dump of a cluster: first by key, then by RBA for the data component and by RBA for the index component.

```
//VSAMDUMP EXEC PGM=IDCAMS
//CLUSTRDD DD
//   DSN=CLUSTER.NAME,
//   DISP=SHR
//DATADD    DD
//   DSN=DATA.NAME,
//   DISP=SHR
//INDEXDD   DD
//   DSN=INDEX.NAME,
//   DISP=SHR
//SYSPRINT DD SYSOUT=A
//SYSIN     DD *
 PRINT INFILE(CLUSTRDD)
 PRINT INFILE(DATADD)
 PRINT INFILE(INDEXDD)
/*
```

For more information about IDCAMS and VSAM, see *Access Method Services*.

Listing Load Module Data

The AMBLIST utility may be used to print the following data about any load module:

- Date of translation (compile or assemble)
- Version of translator
- Date of link-edit
- Version of linkage editor
- Link-edit attribute settings (e.g., only loadable)
- Cross-reference
- External symbol dictionary (ESD)
- CSECT identification records (IDRs)

The JCL and AMBLIST control statements that follow will print all the items listed above for all the members in the PDS specified by the SYSLIB DD statement.

```
//PRINTOBJ EXEC PGM=AMBLIST
//SYSPRINT DD SYSOUT=A
//SYSLIB    DD
//  DSN=PRIVATE.LINKLIB,
//  DISP=SHR
//SYSIN     DD *
    LISTIDR   TITLE=('IDR OF PRIVATE.LINKLIB')
    LISTLOAD TITLE=('XREF AND ESD MAP OF PRIVATE.LINKLIB')
/*
```

The control statements given allow all AMBLIST defaults to be taken. The TITLE operand causes a page title to be printed on every new page. Additionally, a history of SPZAP mods, a hex dump of the object code, and other output may be obtained. This utility is useful for verification of load library contents and for creating a link map if the original map is not available or cannot be recreated. For more information about AMBLIST, see *Service Aids*.

Listing Catalog Entries

IDCAMS may be used to list system catalog entries. Catalog entries contain "groups" of data about the data sets they represent. The data contained vary considerably depending on the type of data set represented. The groups are:

- Allocation
- Associations
- Attributes
- Data space
- Generation data group (GDG)
- Non-VSAM
- History
- Protection
- Statistics
- Volume
- VSAM volume space

Access Method Services gives a detailed explanation of these groups.

The example shows how to list all the catalog entries in the system catalog with the high-level qualifier of PROJECT.123. If a user catalog is of interest, simply include a JOBCAT or STEPCAT DD statement. The ALL command will cause all catalog data to be printed. If the ALL command is omitted, the default is to list only the data set names from the catalog.

```
//PRINTCAT EXEC PGM=IDCAMS
//SYSPRINT DD SYSOUT=A
//SYSIN    DD *
   LISTCAT ENTRIES(PROJECT.123.*) ALL
/*
```

For more information about IDCAMS, see *Access Method Services*.

Listing DASD Labels

The IEHLIST utility may be used to print DASD data set labels (DSCB—data set control block) contained in a VTOC (volume table of contents). The fields in these labels are formatted and titled by IEHLIST. The example shows how to print the DSCBs for three data sets: A.B.1, A.B.2, and X.Y.DATA.

```
//PRINTLBL EXEC PGM=IEHLIST
//SYSPRINT DD SYSOUT=A
//DASDDD   DD
//  UNIT=3350,
//  VOL=SER=123456,
//  DISP=SHR
//SYSIN    DD *
    LISTVTOC VOL=3350=123456, FORMAT,                          *
          DSNAME=(A.B.1,A.B.2,X.Y.DATA)
/*
```

For more information about IEHLIST, see *MVS Utilities*. Note that a continuation character for the control statements (asterisk) is required in column 71. For more information about DASD labels, see Table 3-3, *Data Management Services,* or the DSCB entry in *Debugging Handbook*.

Listing Tape Labels

The IEBPTPCH utility may be used to print standard or nonstandard tape labels. Standard labels are 80 bytes long and contain printable (EBCDIC) data. Labels are made accessible by specifying BLP (bypass label processing) and data set sequence number on the DD statement.

There are several considerations when using BLP. Under BLP, a tapemark is interpreted as end of file. A tapemark is a special character which is recognized by the tape drive. The presence of a tapemark is indicated to Data Management when an exception bit in the CSW is turned on. Tapemarks are placed after each header label, end-of-volume label, trailer label, and after the last block of a data set. This allows the label to be processed as a data file. BLP must be defined in your installation's cataloged reader procedure. If it is not, BLP will default to NL (no label) processing. NL is similar to BLP. NL checks volume labels, however. If an expired or invalid volume label is found, a new one will be written.

The data set sequence number, *D,* needed to print labels can be calculated from the data set sequence number for the data set associated with the labels of interest. The formulas are

$$D_{\text{hdr}} = (D_{\text{sl}} \times 3) - 2$$
$$D_{\text{eof}} = (D_{\text{sl}} \times 3)$$

where D_{hdr} is the data set sequence number needed to print header labels under BLP, D_{eof} is the data set sequence number needed to print end-of-file labels under BLP, and D_{sl} is the standard label (SL) data set sequence number for the data set of interest.

For example, the sequence number to print the header label of the ninth data set on a reel would be 25: $(9 \times 3) - 2$. The sequence number to print the trailer label of the twelfth data set on a reel would be 36: 12×3. These formulas apply to IBM standard labels. Other labeling conventions may require different calculations.

For IBM standard labels, the type of label is indicated by the first four characters of the label:

VOL1	Volume label
HDR1	Data set header
HDR2	Data set header
EOV1	End of volume
EOF1	End of data set
EOF2	End of data set
UHLn	User header (*n* may be a number from 1 to 8)
UTLn	User trailer (*n* may be a number from 1 to 8)

If the data set is the first on the volume, the volume header will be printed with the data set header. If a data set extends over one reel, the calculation of the label's sequence number must be made relative to the reel that contains the label of interest. The formula for *D* is used in the manner outlined above. You must specify the correct volume number in the SYSUT1 DD statement. There will be an EOV (end of volume) label at the end of each reel in a multireel data set. The EOV label is present only when a data set is continued on a subsequent reel. For more information about tape labels, see Table 3-3 and *OS/VS Tape Labels*.

The sample JCL that follows will print the header label for the ninth data set on the requested reel (see the example above). Only one label group can be printed per step, so one step will be needed for each header or trailer group you wish to print. As given, the control statements will cause the label to be printed as a string of 80 characters. By making use of the FIELD parameter, individual label fields may be separated or printed in hexadecimal. Since BLP is specified, no DSNAME specification is needed (a label does not have a data set name). The DISP specification will cause the reel to be rewound and unloaded. VOLUME must be given since DSNAME is omitted. The UNIT, VOLUME, and data set sequence number depend on the tape of interest and your installation's standards.

```
//LISTTLBL EXEC PGM=IEBPTPCH
//SYSPRINT DD SYSOUT=A
//SYSUT1    DD
//  DCB=(LRECL=80
//          BLKSIZE=80,
//          RECFM=F),
//          DSORG=PS),
//  DISP=(OLD,
//          DELETE,
//          DELETE),
//  VOL=SER=123456,
//  LABEL=(25,
//          BLP),
//  UNIT=TAPE
//SYSUT2    DD SYSOUT=A
//SYSIN     DD *
    PRINT MAXFLDS=1
    RECORD FIELD=(80,1,,1)
/*
```

For more information about IEBPTPCH, see *MVS Utilities*.

Dumping DASD Tracks

In the rare circumstances when the actual physical contents of a track must be known, the IEHDASDR utility may be used. It may be useful to investigate DASD hardware errors. An absolute track address is specified on input, and a hex dump of the track is output. No indication of the usage of the tracks as data sets is given.

The example shows how to dump tracks from a DASD volume 123456. FROMDD specifies the DDname of the DASD volume to be dumped. BEGIN and END specify the first and last tracks to be printed in the format CCCCTTTT, where CCCC is a cylinder and TTTT is a track number within the cylinder.

```
//DUMPDASD EXEC PGM=IEHDASDR
//SYSPRINT DD SYSOUT=A
//INDD      DD
//  UNIT=3350,
//  VOL=SER=123456,
//  DISP=SHR
//SYSIN    DD *
    DUMP FROMDD=INDD, TODD=SYSPRINT,
    BEGIN=00000000, END=00050030
/*
```

For more information about IEHDASDR, see *MVS Utilities*. For more information about DASD devices, see *Data Management Services*. IEHDASDR is not available under MVS/XA. DFDSS (data facility data set services) must be used.

3.9 ABEND DEBUGGING UNDER MVS/XA

MVS/XA is a major revision of MVS which uses 31-bit addressing instead of 24-bit addressing. It has a substantially modified I/O subsystem to speed I/O operations. The use of 31-bit addressing means that up to 2 gigabytes of virtual storage may be addressed, instead of 16 megabytes with 24-bit addressing. MVS/XA is designed to run on IBM's mid-1980s top of the line processors and peripherals. It uses some new instructions not in the basic S/370 instruction set. Even in an industry where an order-of-magnitude increase in compute power is not unusual, MVS/XA and its associated hardware are quite impressive.[2]

From an application debugging point of view, the best news about MVS/XA is that (1) it does not present any substantially new problems, (2) it does not require substantially new debugging techniques, and (3) it provides improved debugging output. However, as with any change in complex software, there will be problems and quirks. As MVS/XA becomes a mature operating system, these bugs and their solutions will become generally known. As of the date of this book's publication, IBM users generally had only started to convert to MVS/XA.

Some significant aspects (for debugging) of MVS/XA are:

- Most control blocks of use in application debugging (e.g., DCB, RB, DEB, ACB) have not changed. They still use 24-bit addressing. This is in large part due to the fact that XA's data management still resides below 16 megabytes of virtual storage.
- The new instructions do not cause program check interrupts.
- The changes to the I/O subsystem are at a level both well removed from the application program interface and rarely of interest in applicaton debugging.
- The use of 31-bit addressing is optional; 24-bit addressing is still fully supported.
- The output of ABEND has been improved. The abending module and the displacement into this load module are automatically calculated and printed. Of course, this displacement still requires further analysis. Several new dumping options are available:
  (a) A 10-line "Symptom Dump" showing the PSW, load module offset, and registers at entry to abend may be obtained automatically.
  (b) A "Summary Dump" version of SYSUDUMP and SYSABEND can be obtained optionally. This format shows control blocks and load module offset but only 1K of storage preceding and following the PSW address.
  (c) SNAP, SYSUDUMP, AND SYSABEND dump indexes list the active load module names alphabetically with their page numbers.

[2] For an overview of XA features and differences from MVS 3.8, see: Ronald L. Bond, "The View from White Plains," *Datamation,* May 1983, pp. 139–152; Robert T. Fertig, "The View from the Trenches," *Datamation,* May 1983, pp. 125–136; and *MVS/XA Conversion Notebook,* GC28-1143, IBM Corporation.

Problems to Anticipate

There are at least three new areas that are likely to produce abends under XA.

The addressing mode used (24- or 31-bit) may be changed as execution progresses. The XA linkage editor has two new attributes: AMODE (addressing mode) and RMODE (residence mode). AMODE controls the use of 24- or 31-bit addressing. RMODE determines if a module may be loaded only below 16 MB, or above or below 16 MB. Main storage protection rules have been altered somewhat. Given these factors, 0C4 and 0C1 abends are the probable result.

The rules for GETMAIN have been changed somewhat. x04 abends (GETMAIN) should be anticipated. In particular, SCC 504 will result under MVS/XA when overlapping addresses are specified to GETMAIN.

The third main new source of abends or incorrect output under MVS/XA will be incorrect interpretation of addresses. Many existing programs and supervisor routines with 24-bit addressing use the high-order byte of address fields for control data (flags, bit switches, counters, etc.). If a 24-bit address with a flag byte is interpreted as a 31-bit address, the correct result will be obtained only if the high-order byte is zero. Conversely, if the high-order byte of a 31-bit address is interpreted as control data, incorrect output or an abend is highly probable.

If an abend occurs under MVS/XA, one of the first diagnostic efforts should be to rule out a 24/31-bit address misinterpretation. This is especially true for programs originally written for 24-bit addressing. The possibility of this kind of error should also be recalled when all other analysis fails to provide a solution.

It is of the highest importance in the art of detection to be able to recognize out of a number of facts which are incidental and which are vital. Otherwise your energy and attention must be dissipated instead of being concentrated.

Arthur Conan Doyle
The Adventures of Sherlock Holmes:
"The Adventure of the Reigate Squire"

4

THE ANATOMY OF A DUMP

4.1 INTRODUCTION

This section explains the contents of an MVS ABEND- or SNAP-generated dump. Each dump component is identified, its function and relation to other components described, and its use in debugging indicated. A general dump format is presented, identifying each component. Finally, a discussion of the options for obtaining dumps is given.

A dump is useful when the SCC reference section, system messages, or inspection of JCL or program source listings fail to provide a clear indication of the abend cause. Dump analysis should be viewed as one of the last steps in the debugging process. Dumps are cumbersome, difficult to work with, consume large quantities of paper, and frequently are maddeningly inconclusive. However, they do provide an extensive quantity of data, down to the bit level, about what was going on when the problem program failed. The contents of program storage, general registers, and usually the object code that caused the abend are printed. Most of the control blocks used to provide supervisor support services are listed as well. The dump gives a snapshot of the problem program and its system environment when the ABEND or SNAP macro was issued.

The system environment for batch job streams is created on a step basis. Batch job streams are composed of steps, and each step is executed sequentially. The problem program load module specified by an EXEC statement, a TSO call, or a program management SVC causes a task or subtask to be created. A task is the basic unit of work in the system. It is often said, "My job blew up." Technically, what happened is that the task created from a job step abended. Jobs do not abend; job step tasks do. Task creation is accomplished by the job scheduling and program management functions of the supervisor. Once a task is active, the task management function controls execution by allocating system resources to the task and facilitating its progress. The task invokes the data management function of the supervisor to perform I/O operations as needed.

The problem program and its associated supervisor services are jointly known as a task. An abend dump provides a snapshot of the contents of main storage used by the task. When the hardware, program, task, or data management services detect an error, control of execution may be passed to the ABEND SVC. ABEND formats and prints the contents of main storage related to the task and terminates execution. In addition to finding, formatting, and printing control blocks, storage, and registers, ABEND "cleans up" the failing task. Cleanup consists of releasing the system resources allocated to the task (I/O devices, main storage, etc.) and resetting supervisor flags and pointers such that task termination does not interfere with the execution of other active tasks or the supervisor itself.

The default abend processing may be overridden by user-specified exits. The SPIE and ESTAE macros, various abend exits, and abend related JCL parameters may be used to fine-tune how and when an ABEND dump is produced. More information about these facilities is given in the section Debugging Tools for each programming language.

The ABEND dump has two main parts: (1) a formatted listing of supervisor control blocks and (2) a semiformatted "dump" of main storage containing the data and instruction areas for each routine in the problem program's load module. Depending on the dumping option selected, main storage is reserved for the supervisor and dynamically allocated main storage blocks (subpools) may also be listed.

All supervisor functions create and use control blocks. A control block is an area of main storage composed of fields containing the data necessary to perform a particular supervisor function. They are defined, created, and updated by the supervisor in the same fashion as an application program would create flags, pointers, or accumulators in the main storage to control and facilitate its own execution. Roughly 200 control blocks are defined in MVS; typically about 20 are formatted and listed on an abend dump. Certain control blocks occur a variable number of times; for example, one DCB (data control block) is created for every non-VSAM data set defined in a job step. The relationship of control blocks within and across functions is often complex. Their existence and composition change constantly as the execution progresses. Figure 4-1 shows a schematic overview of MVS control blocks that appear on an ABEND dump.

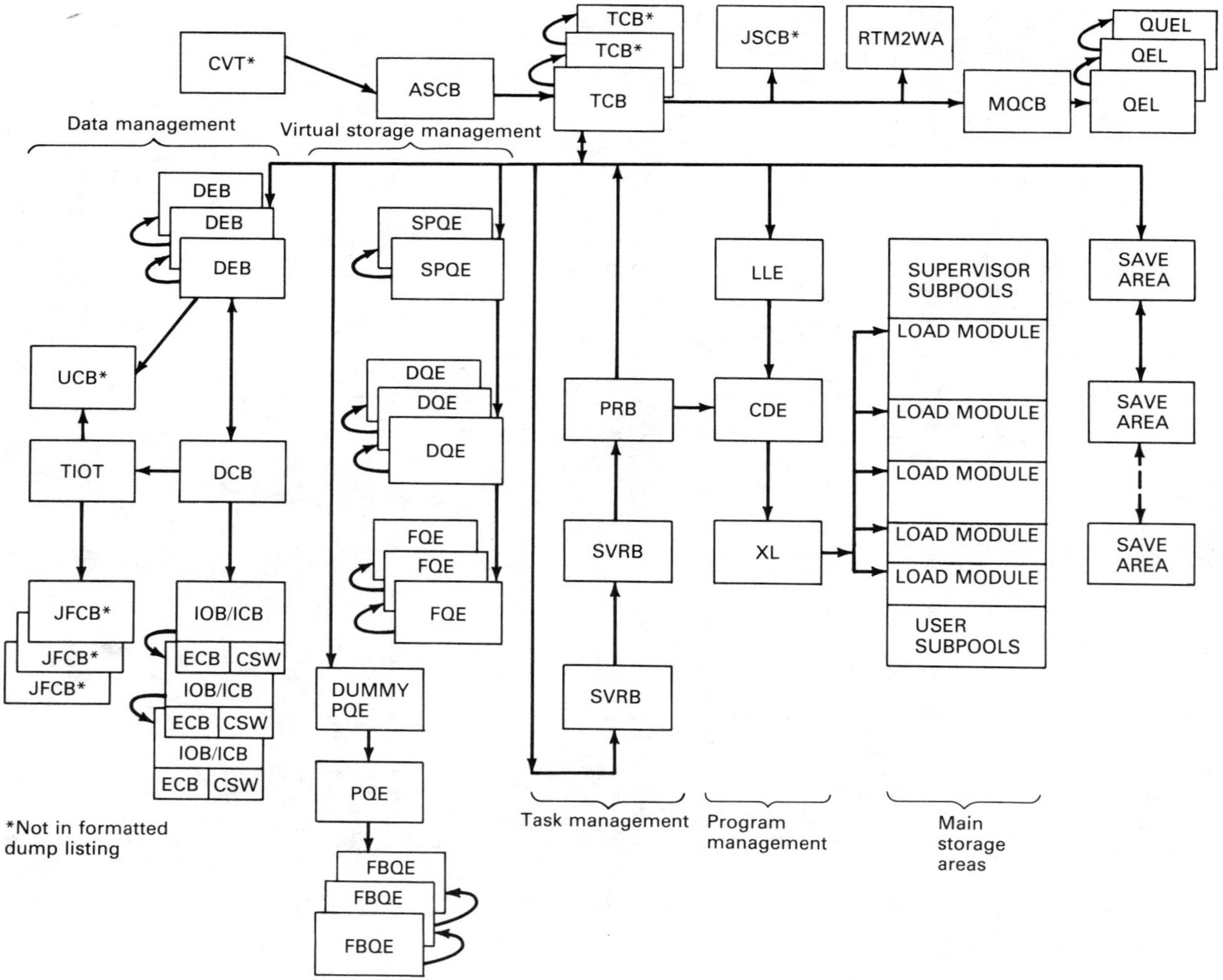

FIGURE 4-1 MVS Control Block Overview

4.2 DUMP COMPONENTS

The content and format of a dump varies from one installation to the next for at least three reasons. First, each installation may select more or less dump output via the SYS1.PARMLIB members that control ABEND processing (see 4.4, Obtaining Dumps). Second, MVS is a constantly evolving system. Successive releases with new control blocks, features, and formats are generally installed on schedules determined by each installation. Third, some installations make their own modifications to MVS components above and beyond what IBM provides. Therefore, the dump components presented here are representative of a typical MVS ABEND dump. No attempt is made to present all possible formats and control blocks.

Diagram Conventions

This section identifies and describes the function and use of the data fields printed on a typical ABEND or SNAP generated dump. A generalized representation of a dump is presented since the content of an actual dump is highly dependent on the composition of the task in question. Nearly all of the fields that can appear on a dump are described. However, some fields which are of little use in application debugging have been truncated or omitted. No attempt is made to describe the numerous messages that can accompany the formatted fields. Most of these are of little use in debugging, self-explanatory, and documented in *Debugging Handbook*. A series of diagrams, each showing one or two control blocks as they would appear on the dump, is given. Relevant portions of the control block listing are labeled. The labels refer to items in a discussion of the diagram. For control blocks with a complex structure, a schematic diagram accompanies the discussion. The schematic shows logical or functional relationships to supplement the explosion diagram and the discussion.

Each diagram contains either a single control block or a group of related fields. The sequence and format of the diagram is the same as it would appear in the actual dump; left to right, start to finish, top to bottom, and relative line positioning has been preserved. Constant fields and titles are spelled out. Fields whose contents vary are shown by symbolic conventions. The conventions used to indicate constant or variable fields in the dump diagrams are as follows:

LABEL	Uppercase print indicates a field identifier or message printed by ABEND.
x	Lowercase x represents 1 hexadecimal digit (4 bits, a nibble, a half byte), usually the contents of storage.
t	Lowercase t represents 1 alphanumeric character, usually part of a message string.
n	Lowercase n represents 1 decimal digit.

Two other conventions have been used in the diagrams. (1) Vertical dots indicate that a formatted line of dump output may be repeated an indefinite number of times in an actual dump. (2) Vertical dashes indicate that the formatted lines of dump output have been expanded for clarity. In the actual dump output, each line will appear without any intervening space.

In the text that follows the diagram, all or some of the following items will appear as appropriate and in the order given:

1. Diagram number. A control block, major field, or message is numbered to tie it to its description. The diagram numbers do not appear on the actual dump. The field label appearing on the dump follows the diagram number.

2. Where appropriate, the following items are enclosed in brackets:

   (a) IBM defined field name
   (b) Field type, indicating the data format as follows:
      * Address: a 3-byte virtual storage address
      * Binary: a binary digit used as a counter, offset index, etc.
      * Bit string: a byte whose individual bits are to be interpreted as switches, flags, or indicators
      * Text: a group of bytes each containing 1-byte EBCDIC character codes
      * Control block: a data structure used for supervisor control purposes
   (c) The offset in bytes of a particular field from the start address of its associated control block or data structure. Offsets are given in decimal and hexadecimal and are always prefixed by a plus (+) or minus (−) sign. The sign indicates the direction of the offset. Offsets are relative to the start address of the control block. An offset of +0 represents the first byte of the control block; +xD, the fourteenth byte; and so on. Where a subfield is repeated a variable number of times and has a structure of its own, the offset is given relative to the beginning of the subfield, not the control block. These offsets are indicated by a "R" subscript (e.g., $+10_R$). Where an offset is not meaningful, the word "variable" appears.
   (d) The length of the field in decimal number of bytes or "variable" where appropriate.

3. Expansion of the field name or its acronym.

4. Description of the contents and their function and relation to other fields.

5. Use in debugging.

Descriptions of the diagrams follow. For more information about the control blocks listed, see *Debugging Handbook*. Publications related to the function a control block supports may also provide additional information.

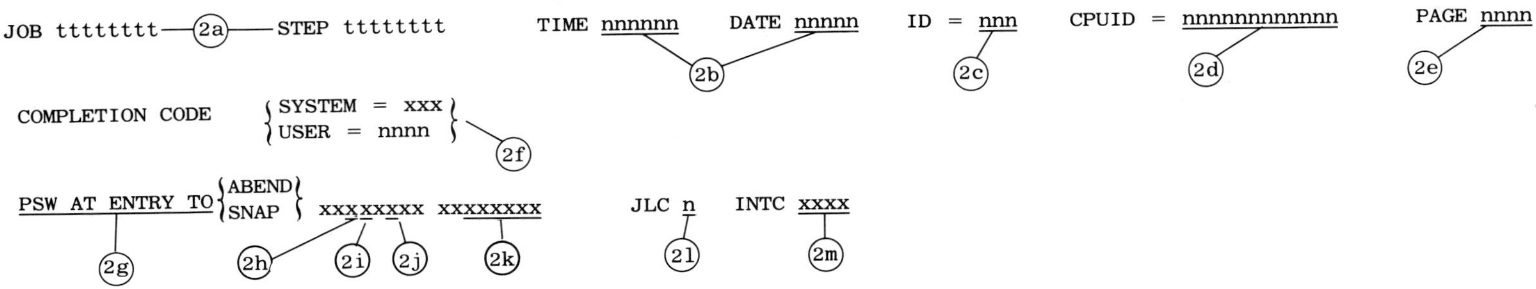

FIGURE 4-2 Dump Header

System Control Blocks

FIGURE 4-2 Dump Header

2. The page header. This line appears at the top of every page in the dump.

2a. The job and step names of the task that abended, as specified on the JOB and EXEC statements.

2b. The time and date that ABEND processing began. This time is given in military format (24-hour day) as hours, minutes, and seconds (two digits each). The date is in Julian format, with two digits for year of the century and three digits for the Julian day of the year.

2c. ID indicates which task caused the ABEND and is represented by this dump: 000—the terminating task, 001—subtask of the terminating task, 002—originating task of the terminating task. Most problem program abends will show 000.

2d. CPUID. This field gives the serial number of the CPU and its model. The model number is the last four characters. For example, nnnnnnnn3081 indicates a model 3081 processor.

2e. PAGE indicates the page number of the dump. This number is referenced in the index on the last dump page.

2f. COMPLETION CODE. This will be either (1) the three-digit hexadecimal System Completion Code (SCC) assigned by the supervisor (e.g., 0C7, B13, etc.) preceded by the word "SYSTEM," or (2) a user-assigned completion code passed in the parameter list to the ABEND or SNAP macro preceded by the word "USER." Interpretation of System Completion Codes is detailed in Section 2.2. The meaning of user completion codes is defined by the programmer.

2g. PSW AT ENTRY TO. The line identified by this label contains the PSW (program status word). It also indicates whether the dump was generated by the SNAP or ABEND macro. The PSW is a doubleword special-purpose register which controls program execution. It contains bit flags and points to the address of the next instruction to be executed—either in the problem program or in a supervisor routine. There are two PSW formats: basic control mode (BC) and extended control mode (EC). See *Principles of Operation* for more information.

2h. Bits 8 through 11 (represented by the third hexadecimal digit) are the PSW storage access key. This nibble either allows or inhibits store or fetch operations to protected addresses in main storage.

2i. Bits 12 through 15 each have specialized functions. The first bit flags the PSW as EC or BC mode. If this hexadecimal digit is between 0 and 7, a BC mode PSW is present; if it is between 8 and F, an EC mode PSW is present. The remaining 3 bits indicate if a machine check has occurred and what state the system is in: wait or execution, problem or supervisor. Most problem program abends will show a PSW in the problem state. PL/I programs, however, frequently are abended in the supervisor state.

2j. Bits 20 through 23, represented by the sixth hexadecimal digit, are the program mask bits. Each of these bits enables or disables a particular program exception interrupt. If set to 1, detection of the corresponding exception causes an interrupt and usually an abend. The exceptions controlled are:

Bit	*Exception*	*Abend SCC*
20	Fixed-point overflow	0C8
21	Decimal overflow	0CA
22	Exponent overflow	0CD
23	Significance	0CE

See 3.2, 0Cx Abend Diagnostics, for further discussion.

2k. The instruction address. The address of the next instruction to be executed. If a supervisor abend has occurred, this address is typically of little use in debugging the problem program. If a user or a program interrupt abend has occurred, this address will help to pinpoint the instruction that caused the abend.

2l. ILC. Instruction length code. The length in bytes of the next instruction. Often the PSW instruction address minus the ILC is the address of the abending instruction.

2m. INTC. Interruption code. This will contain either the program interrupt code or the SVC number that caused the interrupt.

FIGURE 4-3 Address Space Control Block

3a. ASCB. Address space control block and the address of the ASCB for the problem program address space. The ASCB contains data for address space control. It is of limited use in application debugging.

3b. JSTL [ASCBJSTL, binary, +80, +50, 4]. Job step CPU time limit in TOD clock units. May be of use in debugging x22 abends. See SCC 322 for an explanation of its format.

3c. EJST XJST [ASCBEJST, binary, +64, +40, 8]. Elapsed job step time in TOD clock units. This field indicates how long a job step has been running. It may be of use in debugging x22 abends. See SCCs 322 and 522 for further explanation.

3d. SWTL [ASCBSWTL, binary, +196, +C4, 4]. Step wait time limit in TOD clock units. May be of use in debugging x01 and x22 abends. See SCC 322 for an explanation of its format.

3e. SRBT [ASCBSRBT, binary, +200, +C8, 8]. Accumulated SRB (service request block) time in TOD clock units. SRBs are created by the supervisor to dispatch I/O processing. This field may give some indication of an I/O-bound job. See SCC 322 for an explanation of its format.

FIGURE 4-4 Task Control Block

4a. TCB [TCB, control block, 360]. Task control block label and address of this TCB. The TCB contains data associated with the abending task. It is located in the SQA (system queue area) and is constantly updated by the supervisor.

ASCB xxxxxxxx

+0	ASCB	C1E2C3C2	FWDP	xxxxxxxx	BWDP	xxxxxxxx	CMSF	xxxxxxxx	SVRB	xxxxxxxx	SYNC	xxxxxxxx
+18	IOSP	xxxxxxxx	TNEW	xxxxxxxx	CPUS	xxxxxxxx	IDSQ	xxxxxxxx	IODP	xxxxxxxx	RESV	xxxxxxxx
+30	LDA	xxxxxxxx	RSM	xxxxxxxx	CSCB	xxxxxxxx	TSB	xxxxxxxx	EJST	xxxxxxxx	XJST	xxxxxxxx
+48	EWST	xxxxxxxx	XWST	xxxxxxxx	JSTL	xxxxxxxx	ECB	xxxxxxxx	UBET	xxxxxxxx	TLCH	xxxxxxxx
+60	DUMP	xxxxxxxx	FW1	xxxxxxxx	TMCH	xxxxxxxx	ASXB	xxxxxxxx	FW2	xxxxxxxx	SRBS	xxxxxxxx
+78	VSC	xxxxxxxx	RCTP	xxxxxxxx	LOCK	xxxxxxxx	LSQH	xxxxxxxx	QECB	xxxxxxxx	MECB	xxxxxxxx
+90	OUCB	xxxxxxxx	OUXB	xxxxxxxx	FMCT	xxxxxxxx	XMPQ	xxxxxxxx	IQEA	xxxxxxxx	RTMC	xxxxxxxx
+A8	MCC	xxxxxxxx	JBNI	xxxxxxxx	JBNS	xxxxxxxx	SRQ	xxxxxxxx	VGTT	xxxxxxxx	PCTT	xxxxxxxx
+C0	SMCT	xxxxxxxx	SWTL	xxxxxxxx	SRBT	xxxxxxxx	ATME	xxxxxxxx	LSMQ	xxxxxxxx	LSPL	xxxxxxxx
+D8	TCBS	xxxxxxxx	TCBL	xxxxxxxx	WPRB	xxxxxxxx	SRDP	xxxxxxxx	LOCI	xxxxxxxx	CMLH	xxxxxxxx
+F0	CMLC	xxxxxxxx	SSOM	xxxxxxxx	ASTE	xxxxxxxx	LTOV	xxxxxxxx	ATOV	xxxxxxxx	ETC	xxxxxxxx
+108	LXR	xxxxxxxx	STKH	xxxxxxxx	GQEL	xxxxxxxx	LQEL	xxxxxxxx	GSYN	xxxxxxxx	XTCB	xxxxxxxx
+120	FW3	xxxxxxxx	GXL	xxxxxxxx	EATT	xxxxxxxx	EAT1	xxxxxxxx	INTS	xxxxxxxx	INT1	xxxxxxxx
+138	FW4	xxxxxxxx	RCMS	xxxxxxxx	IOSC	xxxxxxxx	PKXC	xxxxxxxx	NSQA	xxxxxxxx	ASM	xxxxxxxx
+150	RESV	xxxxxxxx	TCME	xxxxxxxx								

(3a) (3b) (3c) (3d) (3e)

FIGURE 4-3 Address Space Control Block

4b. RBP [TCBRBP, address, +0, +0, 4]. Address of the currently executing load module's RB. This should point to the last RB listed under ACTIVE RBS.

4c. DEB [TCBDEB, address, +8, +8, 4]. Address of the first DEB associated with this task.

4d. TIO [TCBTIO, address, +12, +C, 4]. Address of the task I/O table for this task.

4e. MSS [TCBMSS, address, +24, +18, 4]. Address of the last SPQE for this task.

4f. PK-FLG [TCBPKF, bit string, +28, +1C, 1]. Storage protection key in the first byte, followed by several other flag bytes. The first nibble (represented by the leftmost hex digit) is the TCBFLAG field. This is the job step storage protection key. The meaning of the key is:

Key	*Storage Usage*
0	Supervisor private
1	Job scheduler and JES
2	VSPC
5	Data management
6	TCAM, VTAM
7	IMS
8	Problem program virtual (V=V)
9-F	Problem program real (V=R)

This value controls access to storage in subpools 0 through 127 (space within a region).

4g. JLB [TCBJLB, address +40, +28, 4]. Address of the JOBLIB or STEPLIB DCB, if specified for this job. May be of use in x06 and 0Cx abends. Zeros if no JOBLIB or STEPLIB DD statement specified.

4h. JPQ [TCBJPQ, address, +44, +2C, 4]. Address of the most recent addition to the CDE list [located in the job pack area (JPA)].

4i. FSA [TCBFSA, address, +112, +70, 4]. Address of the save area established by the problem program—the first save area.

4j. DPQE [TCBPQE, address, +152, +98, 4]. Address of the job step DPQE, less 8 bytes.

4k. JSCB [TCBJSCB, address, +180, +B4, 4]. Address of the JSCB for this step.

4l. RTMWA [TCBRTWA, address, +224, +E0, 4]. Address of the RTM2 work area for this task.

4m. UKY [TCBUKYSP, address, +268, +10C, 4]. Address of the SPQE for subpools 229 and 230—user protectable and private storage areas. The O/C/EOV work area is in subpool 230.

FIGURE 4-5 Program Request Block

5a. ACTIVE RBS. This label precedes a list of the request blocks (RBs) associated with the abending task. An RB is created when the supervisor fetches a nonresident load module and

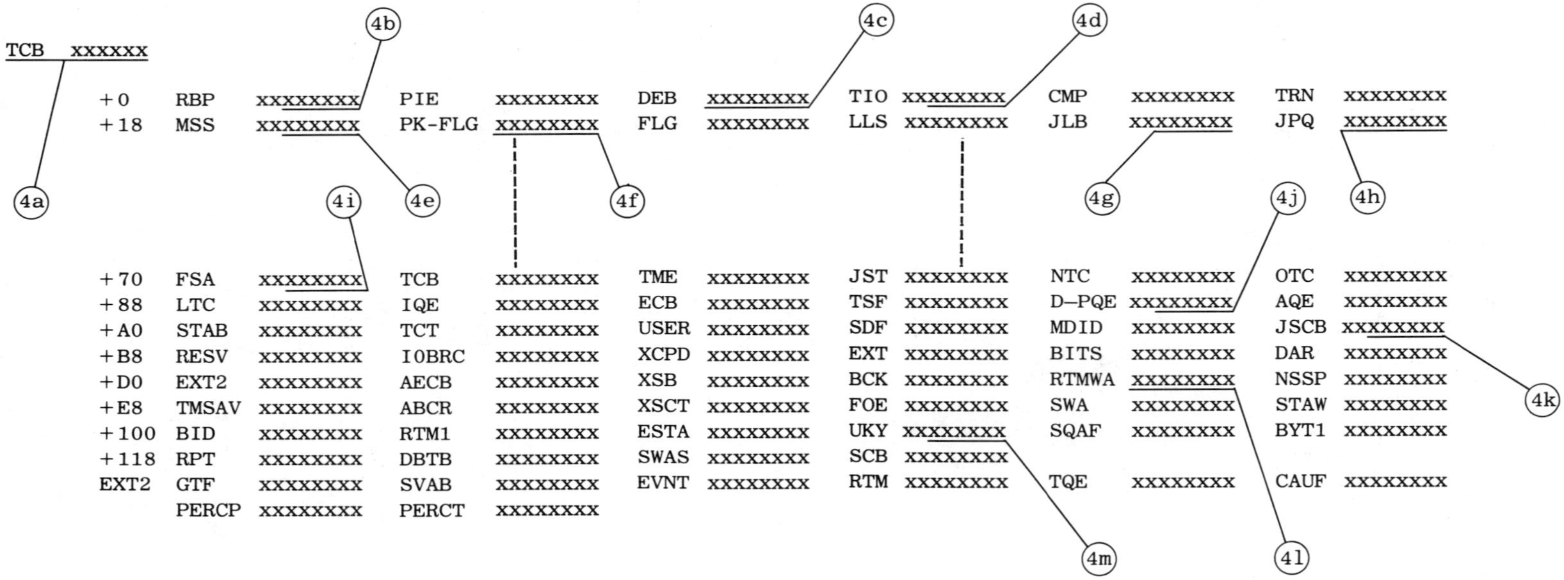

FIGURE 4-4 Task Control Block

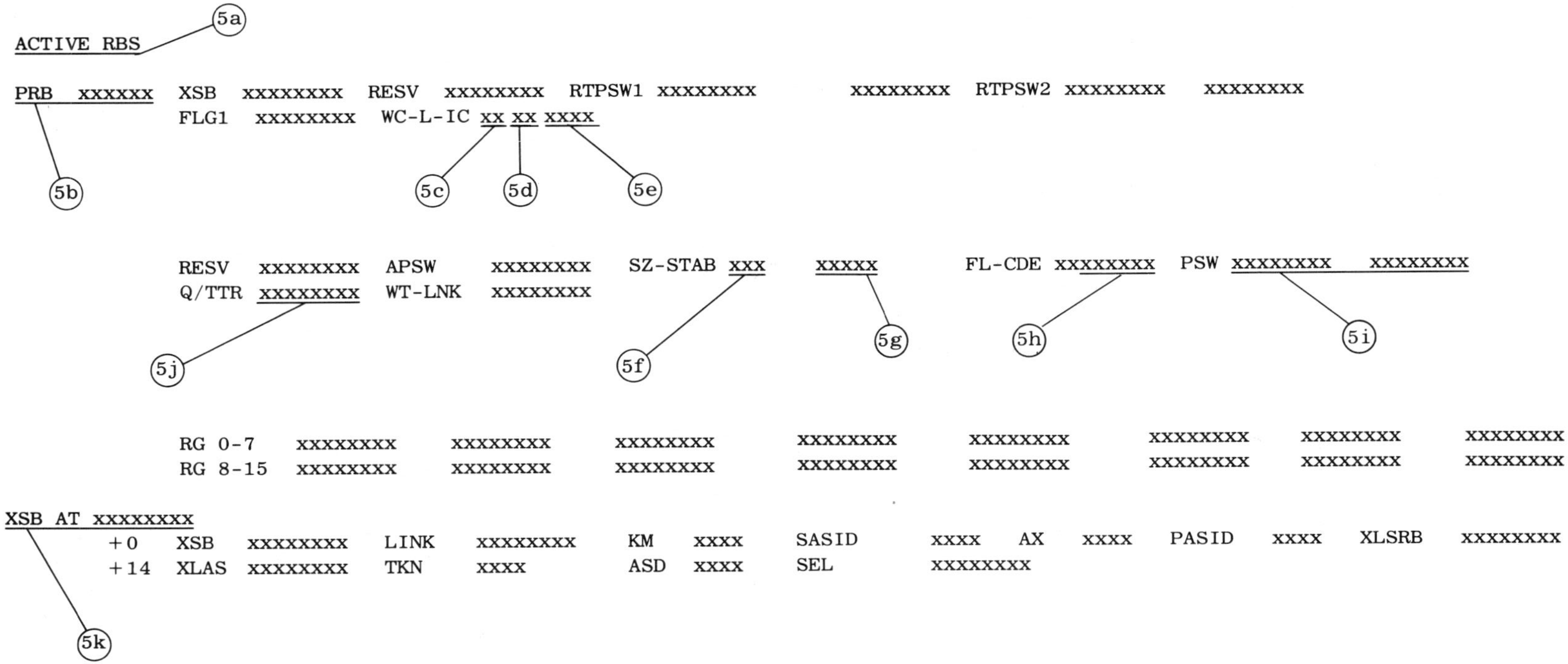

FIGURE 4-5 Program Request Block

for some types of SVC interrupts. Each RB points the next; the RB chain describes the status of all load modules associated with the executing task. There are four types of RBs: PRB (program), SVRB (supervisor), IRB (interruption), and TIRB (task interruption). PRBs and SVRBs are most commonly found on ABEND dumps. RBs are listed in order of creation: the oldest first, the newest last. Since two SVCs are needed to process an ABEND, the last two RBs listed will always be the SVRBs created for the SVCs used to generate the dump and terminate the task. The number and kind of RBs preceding these two will depend on what modules were active when the ABEND occurred. The third RB from the last is usually the one created for the module that issued the ABEND. If it is a PRB, the ABEND was issued from the problem program. If it is an SVRB, the ABEND was issued from a supervisor routine.

All RBs are maintained in the LSQA and contain data and pointers needed for module execution. They are used to store data needed to resume execution if an interrupt occurs.

5b. PRB [PRB, control block, 136]. Program request block. This label indicates that a PRB located at the given address follows. A PRB is created for problem program load modules. A PRB is used to store data if an interrupt occurs.

5c. WC-L-IC [RBWCSA, binary, −4, −4, 1]. Wait count save area. Number of requests waiting for this module when the task was terminated.

5d. WC-L-IC [RBINLNTH, binary, −3, −3, 1]. Instruction length code. Length of the last instruction executed.

5e. WC-L-IC [RBINTCOD, binary, −2, −2, 2]. Interrupt code. The last two hexadecimal digits will contain either (1) the hardware interruption code (e.g., 07 for an 0C7 abend) or (2) the SVC number (in hex) of the supervisor or data management routine that issued the abend [e.g., 37 (SVC 55) for an B37 SCC]. In the second case, this field is particularly useful to gain a first clue to the type of processing that failed. For example, if the field contained x37 in a 001 abend, it means that SVC 55 (end of volume) issued the ABEND because a problem occurred at end of volume.

5f. SZ-STAB [RBSIZE, binary, +8, +8, 2]. Size of this RB in double words.

5g. SZ-STAB [RBSTAB, bit string, +10, +A, 2]. Status byte 1.

5h. FL-CDE [RBCDE1, address, +13, +D, 3]. Address of the CDE entry that corresponds to this PRB. By finding this address in the left-hand column of the CDE (see 8a. below), the name and address of the load module and other data may be found.

5i. PSW [RBOPSW, bit string and address, +16, +10, 8]. User's old resume-PSW. May be useful for determining next problem program instruction with supervisor abends.

5j. Q/TTR [RBPGMQ1, address, +25, +19, 3]. Program queue. Indicates a request for the same serially reusable program by both an SVRB and an PRB. The track address of the load module.

5k. XSB AT. This label precedes a formatted XSB (extended status block) at the address given. There is one XSB for each RB. The XSB is used for cross-memory-task dispatching. It does not provide any data useful for application debugging.

FIGURE 4-6 Supervisor Request Block

6a. SVRB [SVRB, control block, 224]. Supervisor request block. This label indicates that an SVRB at the given address follows. An SVRB is created for most types of SVC requests.

FIGURE 4-6 Supervisor Request Block

As with a PRB, an SVRB is used to store data if an interrupt occurs. All the fields up to EXTSA are the same as the PRB.

6b. WC-L-IC [RBINTCOD, binary, −2, −2, 2]. Interrupt code. For an SVRB, this field will contain the hexadecimal SVC number for the SVC associated with this SVRB. For example, x0D for SVC 13, the ABEND SVC.

6c. RG 0-7 RG 8-15 [RBGRSAVE, binary, +32, +20, 64]. General register save area. The contents of general registers 0 through 15 when the SVC associated with this SVRB was entered. Lists the register contents of the program that called or invoked the SVC associated with this SVRB. The SVRB that immediately follows the RB for the abended module contains the register contents when ABEND was issued; these should be the same as the REGS AT ENTRY TO ABEND. R14 in this area may point to the next problem program instruction.

6d. EXTSA [RBEXSAVE, binary, +96, +60, 48]. Request block extended save area. Used by program management SVCs (LINK, LOAD, XCTL, ATTACH, DELETE) as a work area. May contain module name or pointer to BLDL list. See SCC 806.

FIGURE 4-7 Load List

7a. LOAD LIST. This label precedes a list of all modules for this task brought into main storage by the LOAD macro. The list is composed of control blocks called LLEs (load list elements). Two columns are used to list the entries.

7b. NE [LLECHN, address, +0, +0, 4]. LLE chain. The address of the next element on the load list.

7c. RSP-CDE [LLECDPT, address, +4, +4, 4]. LLE CDE pointer. Address of the CDE for this module.

7d. CNT [LLECOUNT, binary, +8, +8, 2]. Responsibility count. For each load request for this module, this count is incremented by one. For each DELETE request, this count is decremented by one. If the count reaches zero, the copy is removed from storage.

FIGURE 4-8 Contents Directory Entry

8a. CDE [CDE, control block, variable]. This label precedes a list of contents directory entry control blocks. A CDE is created for each load module associated with the task. Unlike the LLE, modules may be placed in the CDE by any program management SVC. Each CDE is used to control the usage of a particular module. Except for certain supervisor functions, the most recent addition is at the address pointed to from the TCBJPQ field.

8b. Address of this CDE.

8c. NCDE [CDCHAIN, address, +0, +0, 4]. Address of next entry in the CDE list.

8d. RBP [CDRRBP, address, +4, +4, 4]. Request block pointer. For reentrant modules, the address of the last RB to control this module. For serially reusable modules (most problem programs), the address of the RB next scheduled to use this module. For LOADed modules, this field will contain zeros.

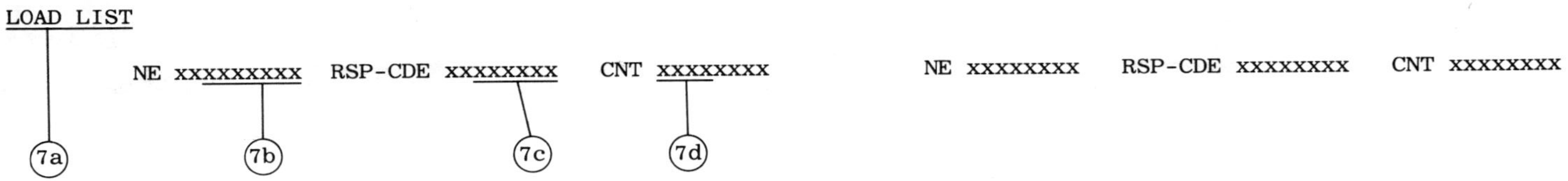

FIGURE 4-7 Load List

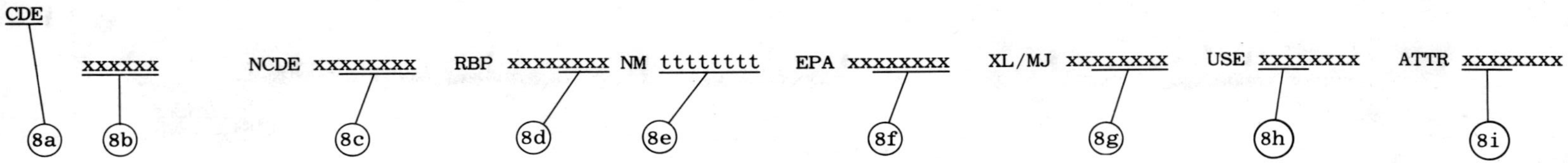

FIGURE 4-8 Contents Directory Entry

8e. NM [CDNAME, text, +8, +8, 8]. Name of the module, the alias, or entry point represented by this CDE.

8f. EPA [CDENTPT, address, +16, +10, 4]. The relocated virtual entry point address of this module. This address and the PSW are frequently useful in determining the displacement into the load module of the abending instruction. This address is not necessarily the module load point address. See 5.2, Basic Techniques.

8g. XL/MJ [CDXLMJP, address, +20, +14, 4]. Pointer to the start of the extent list for this module. For a minor CDE, specifies the start address of major CDE. A minor CDE is created when an alias is present or the IDENTIFY macro has been used to name a module.

8h. USE [CDUSE, binary, +24, +18, 2]. Count of total module use.

8i. ATTR [CDATTR, bit string, +28, +1C, 2]. Attribute flags one and two. Indicates usage characteristics for this module.

FIGURE 4-9 Extent List

9a. XL [XTLST, control block, 16]. This label precedes the extent list. There is one extent list for every major CDE. There may be multiple entries within an extent list if the load module it represents contains multiple CSECTs, with a pair of LN and ADDR fields for each CSECT.

9b. Address of this extent list entry. This address is also given in XL/MJ field of the CDE. By finding the CDE XL/MJ with this address, the name of the module can be found.

9c. SZ [XTLLNTH, binary, +0, +0, 4]. Length of this extent list entry. An extent list that describes a single CSECT is always 16 bytes long. Additional CSECTs require an additional 8 bytes.

9d. NO [XTLNRFAC, binary, +4, +4, 4]. Number of relocation factors for this load module. If the load module represented here was loaded as a single block, this field will be 1. If several CSECT blocks have been scattered throughout the module as a result of specifying the SCTR parameter to the linkage editor, this value will indicate how many relocatable blocks there are.

9e. LN [XTLMSBLN, binary, +9, +9, 3]. CSECT block length in bytes for this extent. The first byte of this field is always x80.

9f. ADR [XTLMSBAD, address, +13, +D, 3]. The virtual address of the load module CSECT described by this extent list. This address is the same as the EPA field of the CDE if the entry point is at word zero of the load module. If it is not, the module has multiple entry points or its entry point begins at some offset from the start of the CSECT. This field is used for calculating load module displacement.

9g. LN and ADR pairs are repeated, from left to right and then down, for each additional CSECT in the load module.

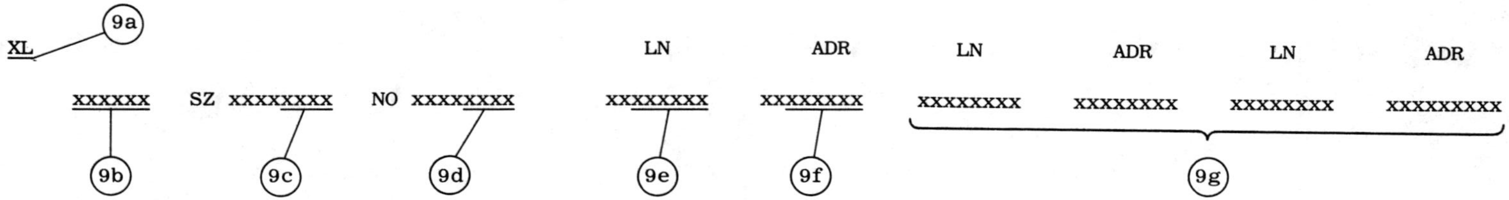

FIGURE 4-9 Extent List

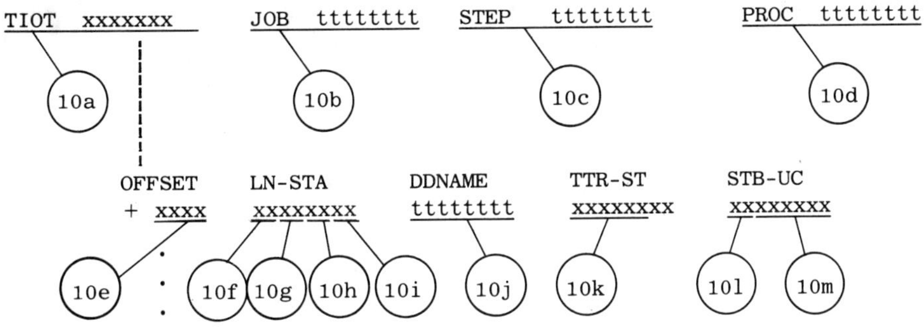

FIGURE 4-10 Task I/O Table

FIGURE 4-10 Task I/O Table

10a. TIOT [TIOT, control block, variable]. Task input-output table. The TIOT provides the data management routines (e.g., OPEN, CLOSE, EOV) with pointers to the JFCBs (data set parameters specified in the DD statements), DCBs (data set parameters specified by the problem program) and UCBs (control block for the data set's device). The TIOT is composed of a 24-byte "header" containing the job name, step or procedure step name, and the length of remaining fields. The header is followed by a variable number of DD entries. For non-concatenated data sets, there will be one TIOT entry for every DD statement specified for the step. There will be one TIOT entry for every data set specified in a concatenated list, but only the first entry will contain the DDname. The TIOT is useful in determining which data set is represented by a DCB or an ACB.

10b. JOB [TIOCNJOB, text, +0, +0, 8]. The job name under which this task was running.

10c. STEP [TIOCSTEP, text, +8, +8, 16]. The step name this task was running under.

10d. PROC [TIOCSTEP, text, +8, +8, 16]. The procedure step name this task was running under. If this field appears (it is suppressed if the job step was not a procedure step), then TIOCSTEP (10c) gives the job step name that invoked the procedure.

10e. OFFSET. The hexadecimal byte displacement of this entry from the start of the TIOT. The offset for the first entry is always x18, the length of the "header." Subsequent offsets increment by x14. These offsets are also given in the DCB and the ACB. By matching the offset from a DCB or an ACB to a TIOT entry, the DDname can be determined.

10f. LN-STA [TIOELNGH, binary, $+0_R$, $+0_R$, 1]. The byte length of this entry (typically x14).

10g. LN-STA [TIOESTTA, bit string, $+1_R$, $+1_R$, 1]. Status byte A. Contains bit switches related to tape and DASD processing.

10h. LN-STA [TIOEWTCH, binary, $+2_R$, $+2_R$, 1]. Number of devices requested for this data set.

10i. LN-STA [TIOELINK, bit string, $+3_R$, $+3_R$, 1]. Flag byte. Contains bit switches indicating various output options.

10j. DDNAME [TIOEDDNM, character string, $+4_R$, $+4_R$, 8]. The DDname specified for this data set by a DD statement.

10k. TTR-ST [TIOEJFCB, address, $+12_R$, $+C_R$, 3]. The track address (TTR) of the JFCB for this data set.

10l. STB-UC [TIOESTTB, bit string, $+16_R$, $+10_R$, 1]. Status byte B. Indicates device-dependent processing for this data set.

10m, STB-UC [TIOEFSRT, address, $+17_R$, $+10_R$, 3]. Address of the device UCB allocated to this data set.

FIGURE 4-11 Allocated Virtual Storage

11a. VSM. This label precedes a list of the virtual storage management control blocks. This set of control blocks describes how virtual storage has been allocated to the task. There are two main groups: (1) control blocks that describe the storage available in the task's private area, and (2) control blocks that describe, by subpool, the storage allocated to the task from the private area. A subpool is a numbered block of storage of variable size. Certain subpools are restricted to supervisor use and have specialized functions. Subpools 0 through 127 are reserved for problem program usage. Subpools are acquired and released through the use of GETMAIN (SVC 4), FREEMAIN (SVC 5), and program management macros. VSM control blocks are infrequently used in debugging. With virtual storage operating systems and massive quantities of real storage, many storage problems are simply resolved by increasing storage allocation. Under MVS, the virtual maximum storage available to a user (batch job, TSO user, etc.) is the same. The REGION parameter of the JOB statement only places an upper limit on how much storage may be obtained by a GETMAIN. However, for jobs that run in fixed real storage, the JCL REGION parameter determines the upper limit of physical storage.

Both groups of VSM control blocks originate in the TCB. Figure 4-12 gives an overview of VSM control blocks. The chains that describe virtual storage available in the tasks private area are: DPQE (dummy partition queue element), PQE (partition queue element), and the FBQE (free block queue element) chain. The TCB points to the DPQE, which points to the PQE. The PQE defines the virtual storage allocated to the job's private area. One PQE is established for an address space. The PQE allocation is determined by installation defaults or by a JOB statement REGION parameter. The PQE points to a chain of FBQEs. Each FBQE describes a contiguous block of virtual storage available in the private area. If the available storage is fragmented, there will be multiple FBQEs. As storage is assigned to subpools, FBQEs are updated to reflect the assignment.

The storage assigned to subpools (available for use by the problem programs), is described by the following chain: the SPQE (subpool queue element), DQE chain (descriptor queue element) and the FQE (free queue element) chain. The number of SPQEs depend on the number of subpools allocated to the task. Each 4K block of storage assigned to a subpool is represented by a DQE. Storage may be assigned out of a 4K block in units as small as 8 bytes. The FQE describes the available continuous blocks of storage within the block identified by the DQE.

The PQE defines the total virtual storage allocated to the user private area. The storage remaining out of this initial allocation is given by the FBQE. The SPQE-DQE-FQE chain describes the storage that has been assigned to the task. The FQE control blocks indicate the actual start and end addresses of this allocation.

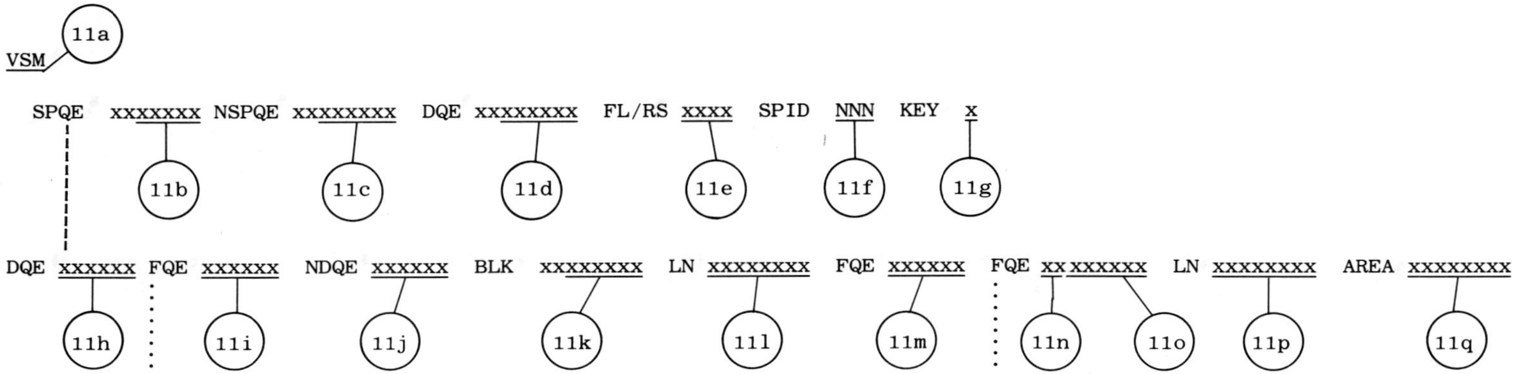

FIGURE 4-11 Allocated Virtual Storage

The amount of virtual storage available to the task is equal to the sum of the fullword SZ (13o) fields to the right of the FBQE (13l) fields under the DPQE (13a).

The amount of virtual storage allocated to the task is equal to the sum of the second LN (11p) fields [between the FQE (11n) and AREA (11q)] following each DQE (11h).

11b. SPQE [SPQESECT, control block, 16]. Address of a subpool queue element containing the description of the storage within a subpool.

11c. NSPQE [SPQEAD, address, +0, +0, 4]. Address of next oldest SPQE.

11d. DQE [SPDQEPTR, address, +4, +4, 4]. Address of first DQE for this subpool.

11e. FL/RS [SPQEFLGS, bit string, +8, +8, 1] SPQE flags. Indicates various attributes of the SPQE and the subpool.

11f. SPID [SPQEID, binary, +10, +A, 1]. Number of the subpool described by this SPQE.

11g. KEY [SPQEKEY, +11, +B, 1]. Storage key of the task owning this subpool.

11h. DQE [DQESECT, control block, 16]. Address of a descriptor queue element containing a description of 4K of contiguous space held by a subpool.

11i. FQE [DQFQEPTR, address, +0, +0, 4]. Address of the first FQE for this block.

11j. NDQE [DQEPTR, address, +4, +4, 4]. Address of the next DQE associated within this subpool.

11k. BLK [DQEBLKAD, address, +8, +8, 4]. Address of the first 4K block described by this DQE.

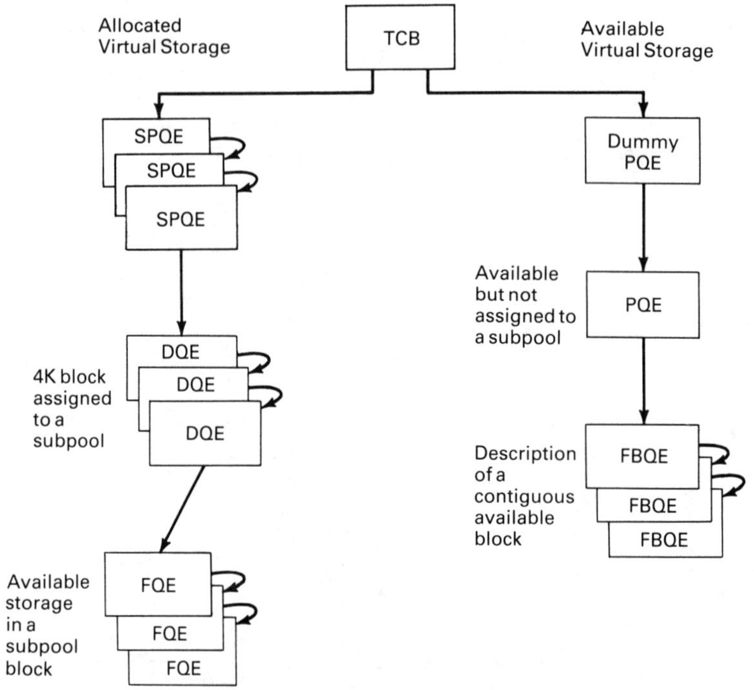

FIGURE 4-12 Virtual Storage Control Blocks

11l. LN [DQELNTH, binary, +12, +C, 4]. Length of the area described by this DQE.

11m. FQE [FQESECT, control block, 16]. Address of a free queue element control block which describes contiguous blocks of storage allocated from the subpool described by the DQE to the left.

11n. FQE [FQTYPE, bit string, +0, +0, 1]. Flag byte for the FQE. x80 indicates intra–region storage. x40 indicates storage crosses a page boundary.

11o. FQE [FQEPTR, address, +1, +1, 3]. Pointer to next lower-address free area.

11p. LN [FQELNTH, binary, +4, +4, 4]. Number of bytes represented by this FQE.

11q. AREA [FQAREA, address, +8, +8, 4]. Address of the last byte represented by this FQE.

FIGURE 4-13 Available Virtual Storage

13a. D-PQE. Address of the dummy partition queue element. The DPQE is an intermediate pointer between the TCB and the FQE.

13b. FIRST. Address of the first PQE contained in the DPQE.

13c. PQE [PQESECT, control block, 32]. Address of a partition queue element which defines the storage allocated to private area of this task.

13d. FFB [PQEFFBQE, address, +0, +0, 4]. Address of the first FBQE associated with this PQE. If no FBQE exists, this points back to the PQE.

13e. LFB [PQEBFBQE, address, +4, +4, 4]. Address of the last FBQE associated with this PQE. If no FBQE exists, this points back to the PQE.

13f. NPQ [PQEFPQE, address, +8, +8, 4]. Address of the next PQE or zero if none exists.

13g. PPQ [PQEBPQE, address, +12, +C, 4]. Address of the previous PQE or zero if none exists.

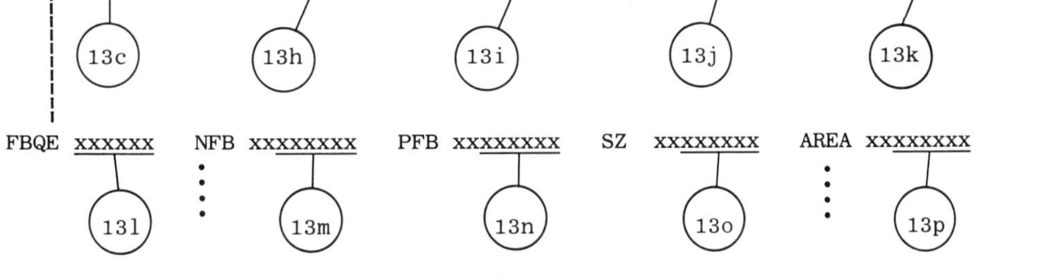

FIGURE 4-13 Available Virtual Storage

13h. TCB [PQETCB, address, +16, +10, 4]. Address of the TCB for this job step. The TCB that "owns" the storage described by this VSM chain.

13i. RSI [PQESIZE, binary, +20, +14, 4]. Size of the private area described by this PQE in bytes.

13j. RAD [PQEREGN, address, +24, +18, 4]. The virtual address of the first byte in the private area described by this PQE.

13k. FLG [PQERFLGS, PQEHRID, VMMFLGS, bit string, +28, +1C, 3]. Flag bytes. x0 in the third byte indicates that this PQE represents a virtual storage; x1 indicates real storage.

13l. FBQE [FBQESECT, control block, 16]. Free block queue element. Address of an FBQE that defines the available storage in the private area described by the PQE.

13m. NFB [FWDPTR, address, +0, +0, 4]. Address of the next FBQE, or if none exists, the address of the PQE.

13n. PFB [BCKPTR, address, +4, +4, 4]. Address of the previous FBQE. If none exists, the address of the PQE.

13o. SZ [SIZE, binary, +8, +8, 4]. Number of bytes available in the block described by this FBQE.

13p. AREA [FBQAREA, address, +12, +C, 4]. The virtual address of the first byte in the private area described by this FBQE.

FIGURE 4-14 TCB Summary

14a. TCB SUMMARY. The data following this header come from the TCB chain for the abended task. The supervisor must create several TCBs prior to creating the problem program TCB. The TCB SUMMARY lists the address and some status data for each TCB associated with the problem program. There are three basic TCB chains, depending on how the task was started.

* Batch jobs (submitted via an initiator) have:
  - Region control task TCB
  - Dump TCB
  - Started task control TCB
  - Initiator TCB
  - Job step TCB (problem program)
  - Subtask TCBs (created by the problem program, if any)
* TSO user:
  - Region control task TCB
  - Dump TCB
  - Started task control TCB
  - TSO LOGON TCB
  - Terminal monitor program TCB
  - Additional TCBs for TSO initiated subtasks (commands, CLISTS, problem programs executed via CALL command)
* Operator-started job:

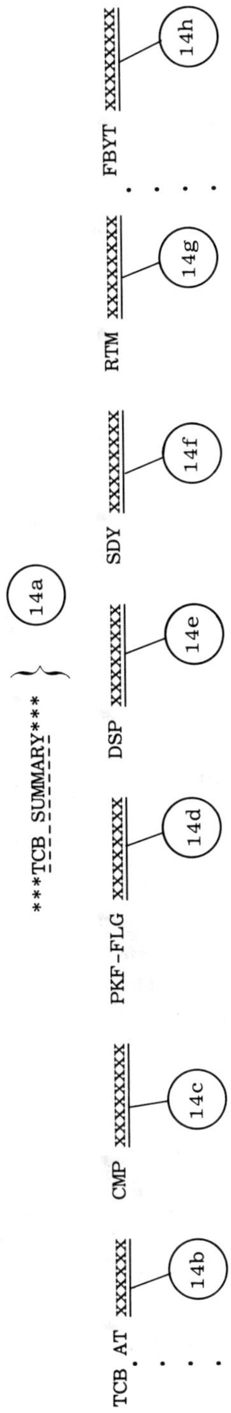

FIGURE 4-14 TCB Summary

- Region control task TCB
- Dump TCB
- Started task control TCB
- Started job TCB

14b. TCB AT. Address of the TCB for the following line of data.

14c. CMP [TCBCMP, binary, +16, +10, 4]. Task Completion Code and status indicators. The System Completion Code is in the third, fourth, and fifth hex digits.

14d. PKF-FLG [TCBPKF, bit string, +28, 1C, 4]. Storage protection key in first byte, followed by several other flags.

14e. DSP [TCBFLGS, bit string, +29, +1D, 4]. Dispatching flags. There are 4 flag bytes in this field.

14f. SDY [TCBSCNDY, bit string, +172, +AC, 4]. Secondary nondispatchability flags. If any bit is on, the task is nondispatchable.

14g. RTM [TCBRTWA, address, +224, +E0, 4]. Address of the RTM2 work area of this TCB.

14h. FBYT [TCBFBYT, bit string, +276, +114, 2]. This field contains two flag bytes, TCBFBYT1 and TCBFBYT2. The last 2 bytes are not used.

FIGURE 4-15 Local Queue Control Block Print

15a. LOCAL QUEUE CONTROL BLOCK PRINT. This label indicates that the following section is composed of control blocks used to coordinate system-wide usage of resources available to more than one user or task. A single system resource (e.g., a disk data set) could be requested by more than one task or user; some management of this conflict must be provided. System resources include devices, data sets, and main storage. For data sets, this control is most often indirectly invoked via the DISP parameter of the DD statement. Simultaneous attempts to write to the same data set are either prevented entirely (DISP=OLD) or allowed to "take turns" (DISP=SHR). Resources that cannot be shared used are serially reusable. Controlling access to such resources is called serialization.

The supervisor maintains a system-wide set of control blocks to manage resource concurrency. They are the major queue control block (QCB), the minor queue control block (QCB), and the queue element list (QEL). The assembly language programmer may control resource usage with the ENQ and DEQ macros. However, almost all of the necessary control is provided by the supervisor, and indirectly by DISP parameters.

The major QCB identifies a generic class of resources, for example, data sets. A minor QCB is always associated with a major QCB and identifies a specific resource within the class—for example, a particular data set. The QEL is associated with the minor QCB and identifies the task issuing the request and whether the request is for shared or exclusive usage.

15b. MAJOR NAME [MAJNAME, text, QCB + 16, +10, 8]. Name of a major QCB. SYSDSN is a typical name for system data sets.

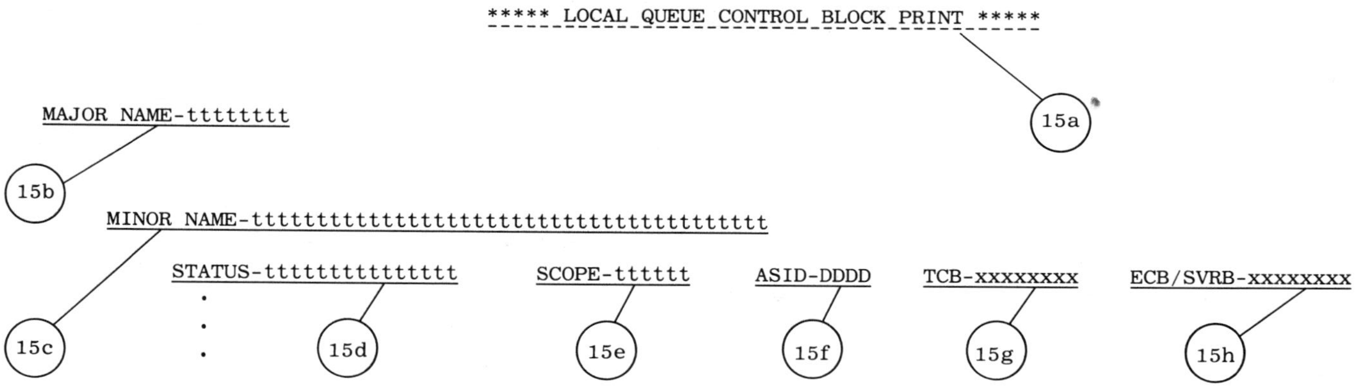

FIGURE 4-15 Local Queue Control Block Print

15c. MINOR NAME [MINNAME, text, QCB + 20, +16, variable]. Name of resource enqueued (e.g., a data set name).

15d. STATUS [QELQFLGS, bit string, QEL + 12, +C, 1]. Indicates the relation of the enqueing task to the resource.

15e. SCOPE [MINFLGS, bit string, QCB + 17, +11, 1]. Indicates the extent of serialization.

15f. ASID [MINASID, binary, QCB + 18, 12, 2]. The address space of the owner task.

15g. TCB [QELTCB, address, QEL + 8, 8, 4]. Address of the TCB for the task issuing the ENQUE.

15h. ECB/SVRB [QELSVRB, address, QEL + 16, 10, 4]. Address of the SVRB issuing the ENQUE or its ECB.

FIGURE 4-16 Data Extent Block

16a. DEB [DEB, control block, variable]. Address of a data extent block, followed by a partially formatted dump of a DEB. The DEB contains data about the physical characteristics of the data set which are typically available only after it has been opened. All DEBs are chained together. The first DEB is pointed to from the TCB and subsequent DEBs point to the next DEB. The DEB is most often of use for OPEN/CLOSE/EOV and DASD I/O related abends.

DEBs are listed on the dump in reverse order of open (the DEB for the first data set opened is listed last). Typically, the first DEB listed is for the dump data set (e.g., SYSUDUMP). There will be one DEB for each non-VSAM data set that has been opened. There will be two DEBs for each open ESDS or RRDS VSAM cluster; three DEBs for each KSDS VSAM cluster; and two additional DEBs for each alternate index associated with a base cluster (one for the data component, one for the index). See 3.5, Locating VSAM Data Records, for further explanation of the role the DEB plays in VSAM processing. The AMTYPE field (see paragraph 16c below) indicates which access method is used with a particular DEB.

The DEB is composed of many fields. Their location and order are dependent on the type of data set associated with the DEB. The prefix section contains certain device-dependent data and describes the structure of the DEB. The basic section is the start of the DEB proper and is pointed to from the TCB or previous DEB. The basic section describes the usage of the data set, points to related control blocks, and defines the structure of the device- and access method-dependent sections.

Immediately following the basic section, a device-dependent section will be present. For unit record (e.g., card reader, printer), magnetic tape, or telecommunications devices, a device description will be found. For the 3525 card punch/reader, a special extension is created. For telecommunication devices, the UCB address is repeated for each line assigned. For non-ISAM DASD data sets, there will be a variable number of 16-byte extent descriptors, one for every extent in the data set. (An extent is a contiguous block of tracks allocated to the data set.) Each extent descriptor contains start and stop addresses for both the cylinders and tracks comprising the extent and the total number of tracks in each extent. For ISAM data sets, the extent descriptors are preceded by one 16-byte ISAM dependent section which describes the prime, index, and overflow extents for the data set. The ISAM dependent section also points to the access method descriptor for the data set. The ISAM dependent section is followed by a variable number of 16-byte extent descriptors which are identical to the non-ISAM extent descriptors. See SCCs 001 and B37 under 2.2, SCC Diagnostics, for a discussion of extent descriptor fields.

After the device dependent section, the access method dependent section is found. This section varies considerably with the access method in use. The field labeled AMTYPE in the DEB prefix indicates which access method is in use (see paragraph 16c below).

The last two sections of the DEB are the subroutine name section and the DEB extension. The subroutine name section contains the 2 low-order bytes of the supervisor module names used by OPEN to process this DEB. The extension consists of pointers and flags. These two sections are rarely of use in problem program debugging.

16b. Appendage vector table. Pointed to by DEBAPPAD (+ 29 in the DEB basic section). Contains entry point addresses for user-defined I/O processing routines for the data set associated with the DEB. Appendages are typically used with EXCP processing. See *Data Management Macros* for more information.

16c. DEB prefix table. Contains the address of the I/O support work area, the DSCB address (for DASD data sets), the address of the DEB extension, and the length of the DEB. The field labeled AMTYP [DEBAMTYP, bit string, −3, −3, 1] indicates the access method in use for the data set associated with the DEB. The AMTYP access method codes are:

x00	None: No access method specified
x01	VSAM: Virtual storage
x02	EXCP: Execute channel program
x04	TCAM: Telecommunications
x08	GAM: Generalized
x10	TAM: Basic telecommunications
x20	BPAM: Basic partitioned
x20	SAM: Sequential
x40	QSAM: Queued sequential
x40	BDAM: Basic direct
x80	ISAM: Indexed sequential
x81	SUBSYS: JES spooled
x84	TCAMAP: TCAM application

16d. DEB basic section. Defines some relationships between the task and the physical characteristics of the data set. Indicates the structure of the device- and access method-dependent sections.

16e. TCBADR [DEBNMSUB, binary +0, +0, 1]. Number of subroutines loaded in order to open this data set. Corresponds to the number of entries in the subroutine section.

16f. TCBADR [DEBTCBB, address, +1, +1, 3]. Address of the TCB for this DEB's task.

16g. NEXTDEB [DEBAMLNG, binary, +4, +4, 1]. The byte length of the access method dependent section. For BDAM, this is a word count, not a byte count.

16h. NEXTDEB [DEBDEBB, address, +5, +5, 3]. Address of the next DEB in the chain.

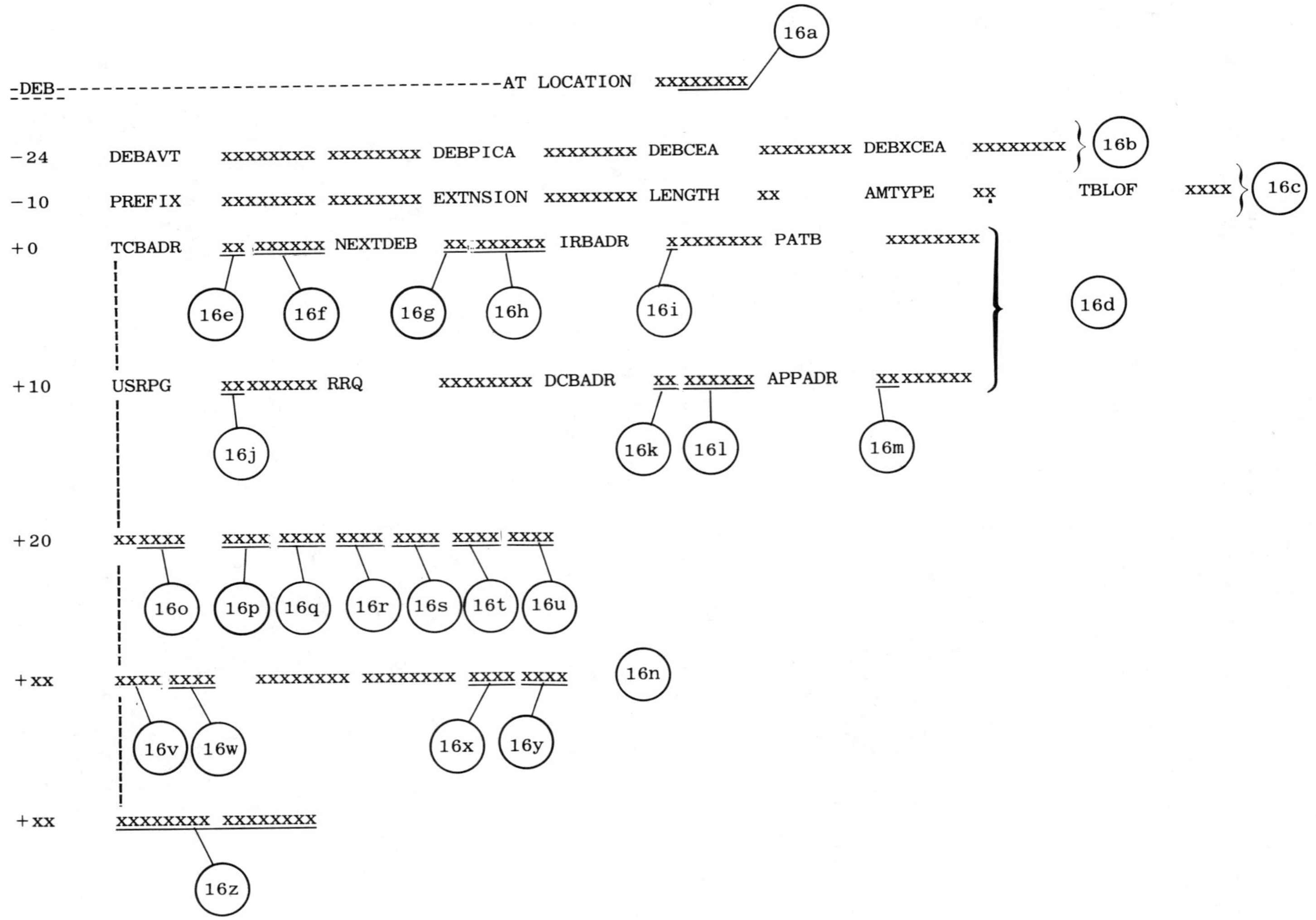

FIGURE 4-16 Data Extent Block

16i. IRBADR [DEBOFLGS, bit string, +8, +8, 1]. Data set status flags. The first 2 bits of this flag indicate the data set status disposition (the first subparameter of the DISP parameter of the DD statement). Since these bits and the adjacent 2 lower-order bits are represented by a single hexadecimal digit, the interpretation of that digit is as follows:

Digit	*High-Order Bits*	*Data Set Disposition*
4-7	01	OLD
8-A	10	MOD
C-F	11	NEW

16j. USRPG [DEBNMEXT, binary, +16, +10, 1]. Number of extents contained in the device dependent section of this DEB. For non-DASD data sets, this is always one; for non-ISAM DASD data sets, the number of extents specified by the DSCB; for ISAM data sets, the number of extents plus one since the ISAM dependent section is counted as well.

16k. DCBADR [DEBPROTG, bit string, +24, +18, 1]. Task storage protection key. The high-order nibble (first hexadecimal digit) contains the task protection key. The low-order nibble is a constant x'F', which identifies the control block as a DEB.

16l. DCBADR [DEBDCBB, address, +25, +19, 3] DCB address. The address of the DCB (ACB or AMB for VSAM data sets) associated with this DEB.

16m. APPADR [DEBEXSCL, binary, +28, +1C, 1]. DEB extent scale. Indicates the type of device dependent data beginning at location +32. x02 indicates that the device dependent section contains unit record, magnetic tape, or telecommunications data. x04 indicates that DASD (either ISAM or non-ISAM) data are contained in the device dependent section.

16n. Device dependent section, access method section, and subroutine section. The remainder of the DEB contains the device, access method, and subroutine sections. These sections will vary in length and content depending on the data set in question. A DEB representing a DASD data set accessed under QSAM would have one extent descriptor for each physical extent, and a QSAM access method section followed by a subroutine section. The format of components in the device and access method section will be different if another device or access method is in use.

16o. [DEBUCBA, address, $+1_R$, $+1_R$, 3]. Address of the UCB for this extent. The UCB defines the physical characteristics of the device associated with this DEB's data set.

16p. [DEBBINUM, binary, $+4_R$, $+4_R$, 2]. BIN number for this extent if a data cell is in use. Zeros otherwise.

16q. [DEBSTRCC, binary, $+6_R$, $+6_R$, 2]. Starting cylinder address for this extent.

16r. [DEBSTRHH, binary, $+8_R$, $+8_R$, 2]. Starting track address for this extent.

16s. [DEBENDCC, binary, $+10_R$, $+A_R$, 2]. Ending cylinder address for this extent.

16t. [DEBENDHH, binary, $+12_R$, $+C_R$, 2]. Ending track address for this extent.

16u. [DEBNMTRK, binary, $+14_R$, $+E_R$, 2]. Number of tracks allocated to this extent.

Items 16v, 16w, 16x, 16y refer to the QSAM, EXCP, BSAM access method dependent section only.

16v. [DEBVLSEQ, binary, $+1_R$, $+1_R$, 1]. Multivolume data set volume sequence number. For tape data sets this is the number of the volume being processed, relative to the previous number of volumes processed. If this current volume was the first mounted for this data set, this value would be 1 even if the volume was not the first of the data set. For DASD data sets, this represents the actual (not relative) ordinal volume number of the data set.

16w. [DEBVOLNM, binary, $+2_R$, $+2_R$, 2]. Total count of volumes in a multivolume data set.

16x. [DEBBLKSI, binary, $+12_R$, $+C_R$, 2]. Maximum block byte length for this data set.

16y. [DEBLRECL, binary, $+14_R$, $+E_R$, 2]. Maximum logical record byte length for this data set.

16z. [DEBSUBID, text, $+0_R$, $+0_R$, variable]. The low-order 2 bytes of the name of each supervisor subroutine that was used to open this data set. A variable number of routines will be called depending on the data set characteristics, so this string will vary in length. For example, if this string contained xD1F0C7F8, system routines IGG019J0 and IGG019G8 were used to open the data set. Only the 2 low-order bytes are needed since data management routines begin with IGG019xx by convention.

FIGURE 4-17 Data Control Block

17a. DCB [DCB, control block, variable]. Data control block. One DCB is created for each non-VSAM data set to be accessed by the problem program (concatenated data sets share a single DCB). The DCB's function is to describe the current status of a data set. For example, current volume, logical record buffer address, and some device status information are maintained in the DCB. The current content and format of the DCB changes as a data set is opened, accessed, and closed. There are six basic DCB formats. The format used depends on the access method selected for the data set. Although there is much similarity between the structure and component function in each of the six basic formats, usage and field content within each format varies considerably.

The DCB has a three-stage life cycle. First, the skeleton DCB created at translation time is "completed" by OPEN. Second, as I/O is performed, fields relating to the current status of the data set are updated. Third, most fields are restored to a preopen state by CLOSE to allow the task to terminate normally. (OPEN and CLOSE perform many other functions as well.)

The completion process begins with the DCB as initialized by the source language translator. DCB parameters supplied via the source code are translated into the object code constants. When an OPEN is issued for a data set, additional parameters are obtained from the JFCB, which contains all DD statement parameters, and from the data set label, if it exists. These additional parameters are moved into the DCB. DCB completion is a process of filling in blanks. Once defined, a parameter cannot be overridden. For example, if block size is given via source code, it cannot be changed later by the DD statement or data set label. The order of completion determines the precedence of the sources: problem program over DD statement and label, DD statement over label. Conflicts or omissions in supplying DCB parameters frequently result in x13 (OPEN) abends.

Once successfully opened, the DCB's main use is to point to other control blocks or

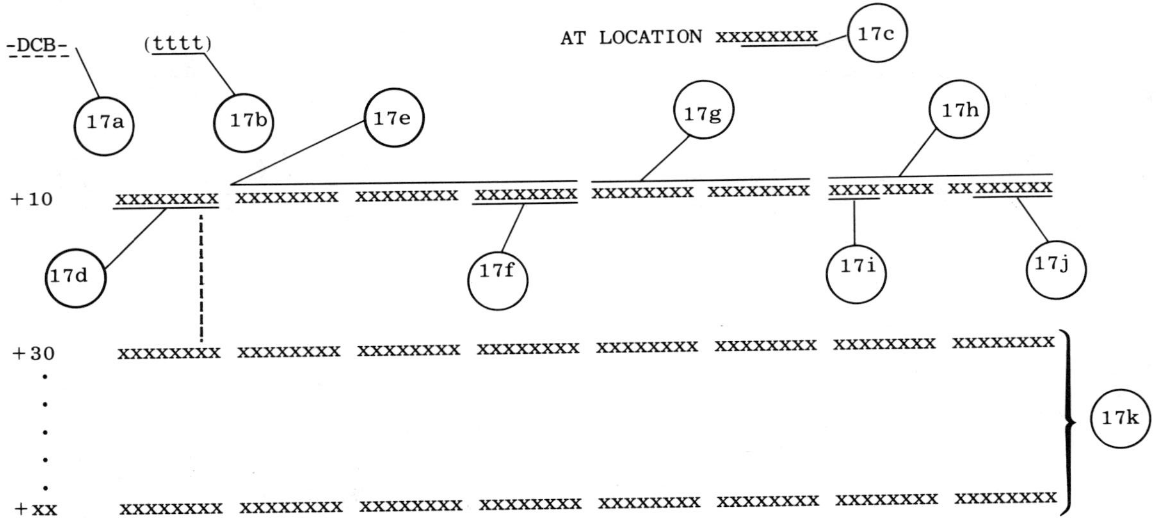

FIGURE 4-17 Data Control Block

buffers that contain data needed to facilitate record I/O. It is also used to handle end-of-volume (EOV) processing.

When a DCB is closed, certain fields are updated to indicate successful completion of I/O operations. The DCB is then restored to its preopen state so that it may be reopened or removed by task termination. If a DCB field has been erroneously or inadvertently modified while the DCB was open, an x14 (CLOSE) abend often results.

The DCB is useful in analyzing most data management abends and for finding current data records when needed. The DCB shown in Figure 4-17 does not represent a particular format. The format of the DCB varies considerably depending on the access method used. For more information about the six DCB layouts, see *Debugging Handbook*. Paragraph 17b indicates which DCB format is present. Fields that are used frequently are labeled. The listing of the DCB always begins at +x10 from its start address (17c).

17b. Access method. This label indicates the type of access method used (see also DEB AMTYP in paragraph 16c). The DCB format present can be determined from this label.

Label	*DCB Format*	*Access Method*	*Device Types*
QSAM	DCB1	EXCP, SAM, BPAM	DASD, tape, card, OCR, paper tape, MICR
ISAM	DCB2	BISAM, QISAM	DASD
BDAM	DCB3	BDAM	DASD
BTAM	DCB4	BTAM	Terminal, DC controller
TCAM	DCB5	TCAM	Terminal, DC controller
GAM	DCB6	GAM	Graphic

17c. AT LOCATION. This label precedes the address of the DCB. This address is also given in the associated DEB (see paragraph 16l above). This address is also frequently found in R1 or R2 of various register save areas when a data management abend occurs. When looking for the offending DCB by using a register address, this is the field to scan.

17d. End of the device dependent section. Format varies with device in use.

17e. Access method common interface section. Same for all access methods.

17f. [DCBIOBAD, address, +28, +1C, 4]. IOB address if chained scheduling is in use.

17g. Foundation block extension.

17h. Foundation section. The contents of this area change when the DCB is opened. Before OPEN and after CLOSE, the DDname specified by the problem program is placed here. While open, see paragraphs 17i and 17j.

17i. [DCBTIOT, binary, +40, +28, 2]. The offset into the TIOT for this DCB's DDname. By scanning the TIOT for this number, the DDname for this DCB can be found. If the DCB is not open, see paragraph 17h. All six DCB formats share this field.

17j. [DCBDEBAD, address, +44, +2C]. Address of the DEB associated with this DCB, while this DCB is open.

17k. The remainder of the DCB is formatted to service a particular access method.

FIGURE 4-18 Input Output Block

18. IOB [IOB, control block, variable]. Input output block. The IOB is created when a data set is opened. It serves as a common work area for data management routines handling logical record transfers and channel programs handling physical record transfers. The contents of the IOB are updated after each transfer. The IOB's main use in debugging is to provide data about hardware errors that occur during physical I/O.

18a. The message in this area will indicate which access method is in use and whether chained scheduling is active. Chained scheduling allows multiple I/O requests from different tasks to the same device to be processed simultaneously, improving throughput. If chained scheduling is active, DCBIND2 (DCB + x3D) will be set to x04.

18b. AT LOCATION. Address of this IOB. This address may be contained in the DCBIOBAD (see paragraph 17f above) if chained scheduling is not active.

18c. [IOBPREFX, section, variable]. The size of the IOB prefix section depends on whether chained scheduling was used or not. If not, this field begins at −8 from the IOB start address. Contains various flags and pointers, depending on the access method in use.

18d. FLAG [IOBFLAG1, bit string, +0, +0, 1]. First IOB flag byte. If set to x04, a permanent I/O error has occurred.

18e. FLAG [IOBFLAG2, bit string, +1, +1, 1]. Second IOB flag byte.

18f. SENS [IOBSENS, bit string, +2, +2, 2] The I/O supervisor will place the unit sense bytes into this field if a unit check (device I/O error) occurs. Sense-byte bit settings are device dependent. If this field is set to x10FE, sense bytes could not be obtained from the failing device. For a detailed list of sense bytes, see *Debugging Handbook*.

18g. ECBPT [IOBECBCC, bit string, +4, +4, 1]. The channel program completion code, also the first byte of the event control block for this IOB. The meaning of ECB completion codes for non–telecommunications devices are:

x00	No I/O operations issued yet.
x41	Permanent error, usually a wrong-length record. Check CSW.
x42	Violation of DASD extent address. Attempt to seek beyond a valid extent address. Compare IOBSEEK with DEB extent descriptors. CSW not useful.
x44	I/O was intercepted because of previous error. Nonpermanent.
x49	Attempt to read past end of file. CSW not useful.
x4B	Error occurred while attempting to retry an I/O for a tape device. Either a CSW of zero was loaded in the IOB or an unexpected load point was found on a tape.
x4F	While attempting to recover from a DASD I/O error, the home address or record 0 became unreadable.
x7F	Successful completion of requested I/O operation.

18h. ECBPT [IOBECBPB, address, +5, +5, 3]. The address of the ECB that is to be POSTed upon completion of an I/O event.

18i. CSW [IOBCSW, +9, +9, 7]. The last CSW (channel status word) for the I/O requested. The CSW points to CCW for this request and indicates the device status and the result of the last I/O operation.

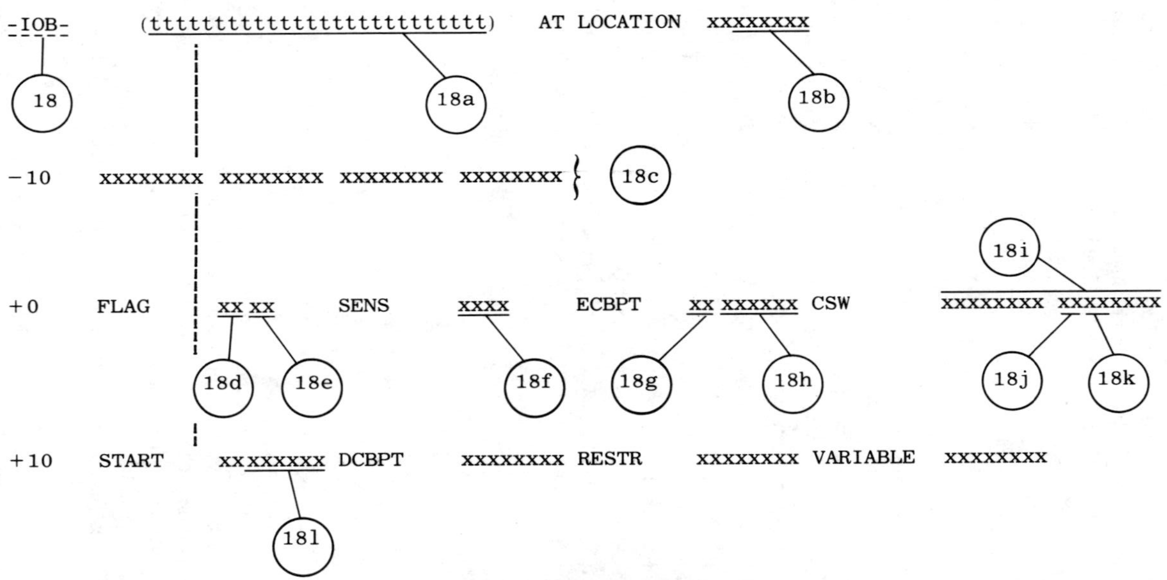

FIGURE 4-18 Input Output Block

18j. CSW unit status byte. The bits set here are generated by an I/O device or control unit. The bits (relative to the start of the CSW) indicating an error are:

36 (x08)	Channel end: set on to indicate that channel is available. Indicates successful I/O operation.
37 (x04)	Device end: set on to indicate that device available. Indicates successful I/O operation.
38 (x02)	Unit check: set on when sense data are available. May indicate a normal condition. Raised when an invalid CCW is present.
39 (x01)	Unit exception: raised when an unusual condition is detected by the device or controller. Depending on the device, may signal a normal state.

18k. CSW channel status byte. The bits set here are generated by the channel associated with a device or controller. The bits (relative to the start of the CSW) indicating an error are:

41 (x80)	Incorrect block length: too many or too few bytes were transferred to or from the device.
42 (x20)	Program check: invalid CCW, CAW, or IDAW.
44 (x08)	Channel data check: parity error in data.
45 (x07)	Channel control check: hardware malfunction in the channel.
46 (x02)	Interface control check: channel has detected a malfunction in the I/O device.

18l. DCBPT [IOBDCBPT, address, +20, +14, 4]. Address of the DCB associated with this data set.

FIGURE 4-19 Interrupt Control Block

19. ICB [ICB, control block, variable]. Interrupt control block. The ICB is used only to support

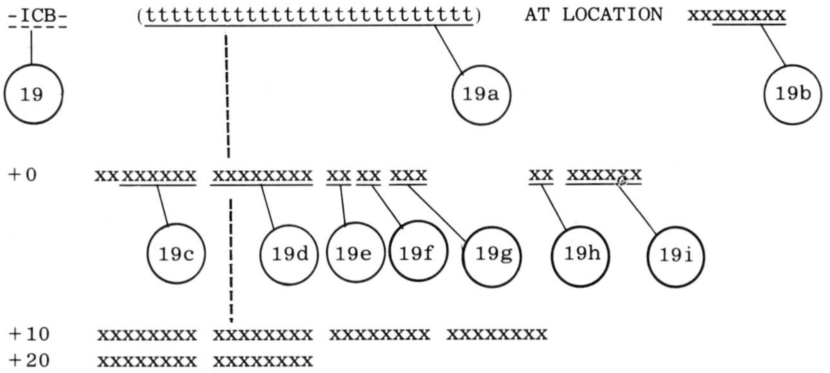

FIGURE 4-19 Interrupt Control Block

chained scheduling of sequential access (SAM) data sets. The ICB functions like an IOB—it is a common work area for routines handling logical record transfers and channel programs handling physical record transfers. The IOB and ICB have many identical fields. There is one ICB for each QSAM buffer. The current ICB is pointed to from DCBIOBA (DCB + x44). ICBs are chained together. The first ICB is pointed to from IOBCICB (IOB − 3) in the IOB prefix.

19a. The message in this area will indicate the access method type.

19b. AT LOCATION. Address of this ICB.

19c. [ICBNICBA, address, +0, +0, 4]. Pointer to the next ICB.

19d. [ICBNECB, bit string, +4, +4, 4]. Event control block for this ICB.

19e. [ECBFLAG1, bit string, +8, +8, 1]. First ICB flag byte. If set to x04, a permanent I/O error has occurred.

19f. [ICBFLAG2, bit string, +9, +9, 1]. Second ICB flag byte.

19g. [ICBSENS, bit string, +10, +A, 2]. ICB sense bytes. See paragraph 18f above.

19h. [ICBECBCC, bit string, +12, +C, 1]. ICB ECB completion code. See paragraph 18g above.

19i. [ICBECBPB, address, +13, +D, 3]. ICB ECB address. See paragraph 18h above.

FIGURE 4-20 RTM2 Work Area

20. RTM2WA [control block, 972]. Recovery termination manager work area. The contents of a storage block used by the RTM (recovery termination manager) are listed following this label. There is little information here of use in debugging problem program abends. RTM is a supervisor routine called from the ABEND macro (SVC 13). It terminates the abending task in a "graceful" fashion by performing necessary housekeeping on active control blocks, freeing various allocated resources and formatting the ABEND dump. The RTM function is unique to MVS. Its purpose is to quarantine the failing task to prevent failure of nonrelated tasks. Most of the occasionally significant data in the RTM2WA is formatted in the following section, the RTM2WA SUMMARY.

```
-RTMRWA-----------------------------------AT LOCATION  xxxxxxxx
   |
  (20)

+0       xxxxxxxx xxxxxxxx xxxxxxxx xxxxxxxx xxxxxxxx xxxxxxxx xxxxxxxx xxxxxxxx
  .
  .
  .
  .
  .
+3A8     xxxxxxxx xxxxxxxx xxxxxxxx xxxxxxxx xxxxxxxx xxxxxxxx xxxxxxxx xxxxxxxx
+3C8     xxxxxxxx
```

FIGURE 4-20 RTM2 Work Area

FIGURE 4-21 RTM2 Summary

21. RTM2WA SUMMARY. This label precedes a list of selected fields formatted from the RTM2WA.

21a. COMPLETION CODE [RTM2CC, binary, +29, +x1D, 3]. The three-digit hexadecimal system completion code. This is the same as the completion code listed on the first page of the dump.

21b. ABENDING PROGRAM NAME/ADDRESS. Under certain rare conditions these fields will contain the name and entry point address of the abending module. However, they do not provide this information for most problem program abends.

21c. REGS AT TIME OF ERROR [RTM2EREG, binary, +60, +x3C, 64]. A copy of general registers 0 through 15 at entry to abend. These are the same as the registers at entry to abend listed with the main storage dump.

21d. EC PSW AT TIME OF ERROR [RTM2EPSW, binary, address, +124, +x7C, 16]. The extended control format PSW at entry to abend. This is the same as the PSW formatted on the top of the first page of the dump.

21e. RTM2WA BIT FLAG SUMMARY. The messages that follow this label are interpretations of some flag bytes contained in the RTM2WA.

FIGURE 4-22 STAE Summary

22a. STAE CONTROL BLOCK AT LOCATION [SCB, control block, 20]. Specify task abnormal exit (STAE) control block. This label indicates that a formatted listing of an SCB at the indicated address follows. An SCB is created to service a STAE or ESTAE (extended STAE) SVC request. These macros establish an exit to be used when either a system or user ABEND occurs. Optionally, a retry routine may be invoked and task or subtask termination can be controlled. The SCB is not often useful for problem program debugging. See *Supervisor Services* for more information about STAE/ESTAE.

22b. NEXTSCB [SCBCHAIN, address, +0, +0, 4]. Next SCB address. Multiple SCBs for a task are allowed. When they exist, each points to the next. This field gives the address of the next SCB.

22c. USEREXIT [SCBEXIT, address, +4, +4, 4]. Entry point address of a user error routine specified to the ESTAE/STAE macro. Control is passed to this routine under certain error conditions.

22d. PARMLIST [SCBFLGS1, bit string, +8, +8, 1]. First SCB flag byte. Indicates type of ESTAE/STAE request and disposition of I/O processing upon entry into ABEND. See paragraph 22h.

22e. PARMLIST [SCBPARMA, address, +9, +9, 3]. Address of the parameter list passed to the ESTAE/STAE to create this SCB.

22f. TCB/RB [SCBFLAGS2, bit string, +12, +xC, 1]. Second SCB flag byte. Indicates user state at entry to ABEND (key 0, supervisor mode). See paragraph 22i.

22g. TCB/RB [SCBOWNRA, address, +13, +xD, 3]. Address of the "owner" of this SCB. The owner will be either a TCB or an RB (task or subtask).

```
(21)---RTM2WA SUMMARY

+1C     COMPLETION CODE            xxxxxxxx   (21a)

+8C     ABENDING PROGRAM NAME      tttttttt   (21b)

+94     ABENDING PROGRAM ADDRESS   xxxxxxxx   (21b)

+3C     REGS AT TIME OF ERROR      xxxxxxxx xxxxxxxx xxxxxxxx xxxxxxxx xxxxxxxx xxxxxxxx xxxxxxxx xxxxxxxx  (0-7)
                                   xxxxxxxx xxxxxxxx xxxxxxxx xxxxxxxx xxxxxxxx xxxxxxxx xxxxxxxx xxxxxxxx  (8-F)
                                                                    (21c)
+7C     EC PSW AT TIME OF ERROR    xxxxxxxx xxxxxxxx xxxxxxxx xxxxxxxx
   .                                                    (21d)
   .
   .
   .
   .
   .
   .                      RTM2WA BIT FLAG SUMMARY
   .
+2C8    tttttttttttttttttttttttttt
        tttttttttttttttttttttttttt

+B4     tttttttttttttttttttttttttt    (21e)

+B5     tttttttttttttttttttttttttt

+B7     tttttttttttttttttttttttttt
```

FIGURE 4-21 RTM2 Summary

```
-STAE CONTROL BLOCK-----------------------AT LOCATION xxxxxxxx
                                                         (22a)

+0      NEXTSCB xxxxxxxx USEREXIT xxxxxxxx PARMLIST xxxxxxxx TCB/RB xxxxxxxx SCBDATA xxxxxxxx
                  (22b)            (22c)          (22d) (22e)        (22f) (22g)

                          SCB BIT FLAG SUMMARY

+8      tttttttttttttttttttttttttt }
        tttttttttttttttttttttttttt }  (22h)
        .
        .
        .
+C      tttttttttttttttttttttttttt }
        tttttttttttttttttttttttttt }  (22i)
        .
        .
```

FIGURE 4-22 STAE Summary

22h. The bit flags contained in SCBFLAGS1 (22d) are interpreted here.

22i. The bit flags contained in SCBFLAGS2 (22f) are interpreted here.

FIGURE 4-23 Save Area Trace

23. SAVE AREA TRACE. This heading precedes a list of register save areas that point to each other. The SAVE AREA TRACE is not a trace of all subroutine calls made, nor does it indicate directly which module was in control when the abend occurred. A save area is created once a module is brought into execution. The register contents of the calling module and pointers to previous and next save areas are contained in a save area. A save area allows the register contents of a calling module to be restored when control is returned. A save area is established at a given location once and reused each time control is passed. Upon entry into a called module, creation of the save area is typically the first thing done (Assembly language programmers must write the code to do this; for higher-level languages it is compiler generated). Save area creation and usage is part of the standard linkage convention. It is not mandatory, however. Just before a branch or call is made, the calling program loads four addresses into the following registers:

R1 Address of a parameter list passed to and from the subroutine (see Locating Parameter Lists, Chapter 5, Source Code Debugging, for the language in use)

R13 Address of a save area, established by the calling program, for the subroutine to use

R14 Address of the next instruction to be executed in the calling program—the return address

R15 Address of the subroutine entry point

The contents of R2 through R12 depend on the calling program. The "call" is made by branching to the address in R15. Upon entry into the subroutine, a save area is created as soon as the subroutine's base address is established.

The save area is created by storing the contents of R14, R15, and R0 through R12 at the address pointed to by R13. The save area chain is created next. The subroutine moves the address established for its save area to the LSA field of the save area just created. The calling program's save area address (R13) is moved to the HSA of subroutine's save area. These two moves establish the bidirectional save area chain, which is followed to print the SAVE AREA TRACE.

Just before returning to the calling program, the contents of the save area are moved back into the registers. The return to the calling program is made by branching to the address in R14. When execution resumes at this address (i.e., the calling program is back in control), the registers are as they were when the call was made, allowing the calling program to continue. Any altered data are transferred via the parameter list, or R0 in some cases. R15 may also be altered, since the entry address is assumed to be unnecessary and recreateable after control is returned. If R15 is altered, it typically contains a return code indicating the result of the call. By convention, a return code of zero indicates a successful call and return. Figure 4-24 shows the general flow of save area creation and usage.

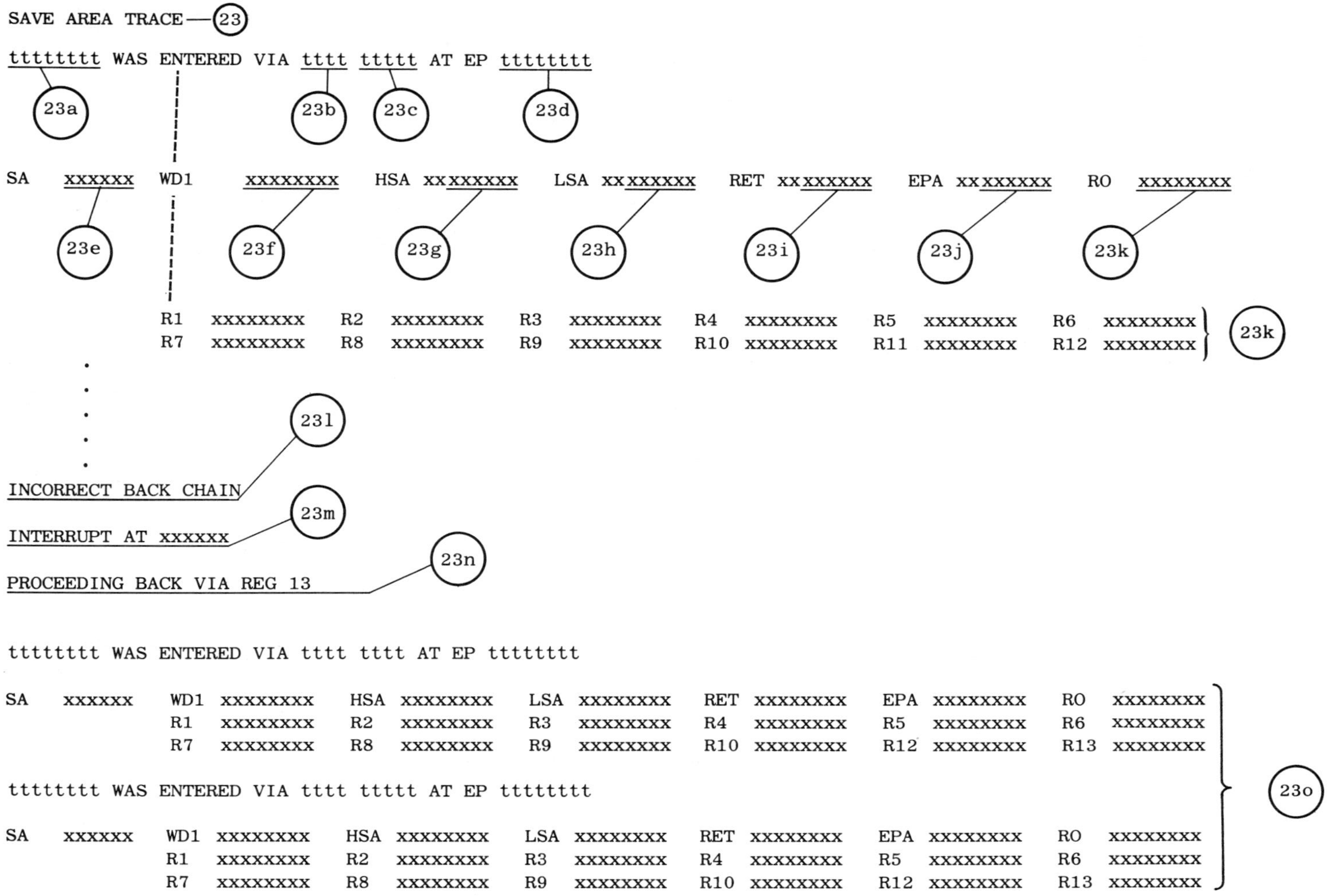

FIGURE 4-23 Save Area Trace

Register 14 contains the return address in the calling module—the next instruction to be executed when control is returned. This field is labeled RET and it is the single most useful part of the save area trace.

The save area trace has two parts, the forward trace and the backward trace. The forward trace consists of the save areas listed between the headings SAVE AREA TRACE and INTERRUPT AT. The first save area listed is created by the supervisor and is pointed to by the TCBFSA field of the TCB. Subsequent SAs are created as other modules are called or linked into. SAs are chained together by the LSA and HSA fields. The last SA printed is the most recently created. The backward trace follows the heading PROCEEDING BACK VIA REGISTER 13. R13 of REGS AT ENTRY TO ABEND will point to the current abending module's save area if it has been established as such and has not been altered. If a call has been made from the abending module, this save area will be initialized. Register 13 must be nonzero and point to a fullword (multiple of 4) storage address or the backward trace will not be printed.

23a. WAS ENTERED. The module name that was called is given here.

23b. VIA. The name of the program management macro (e.g., CALL, LINK, LOAD) that obtained the module.

23c. If the ID operand was specified to the program management macro, it will be listed here.

23d. AT EP. The entry point name of the module, if specified, will be given here. If the ID operand was specified to the SAVE macro, its contents will follow the entry point name. If the IDENTIFY statement was supplied at link-edit time, its contents will be listed here.

23e. SA. The save area address followed by its formatted contents.

23f. WD1. First word of the save area. Used by PL/I to maintain its environment when calls to non-PL/I modules are made, or to contain flags for PL/I dynamic storage allocation.

23g. HSA. Second word of the save area. HSA points to the previously established save area, which contains the register environment of the program that called the program establishing the save area pointed to by HSA. The HSA points back one save area, which is the same as two levels of context. The HSA of the first save area will be zeros.

23h. LSA. Third word of the save area. LSA points to the next save area. The LSA of the last save area will be zeros in most cases. If R13 does not point to a save area, the assumed LSA will be garbage.

23i. RET. Fourth word of the save area. Contents of register 14 when the called module was entered. The return address in the calling module. The next instruction to be executed, as specified by the calling module.

23j. EPA. Fifth word of the save area. Contents of register 15 when the called module was entered. The entry point address of the called module, as specified by the calling module or supplied by the program management macro used to invoke the called module.

23k. R0 . . . R12. The contents of general-purpose registers 0 through 12 when the called module was entered. These registers reflect the calling module's most recent environment. They may be useful to determine what the calling module was doing prior to issuing the CALL, LINK, and so on. For example, R2 of this area may point to the DCB for a data set accessed prior to the call that created the save area.

23l. INCORRECT BACK CHAIN. This message is printed if the HSA field of the next SA does not point to the previous SA. Serves as a warning that the storage area formatted and listed as an SA may not be an actual SA, since the backward pointer is invalid.

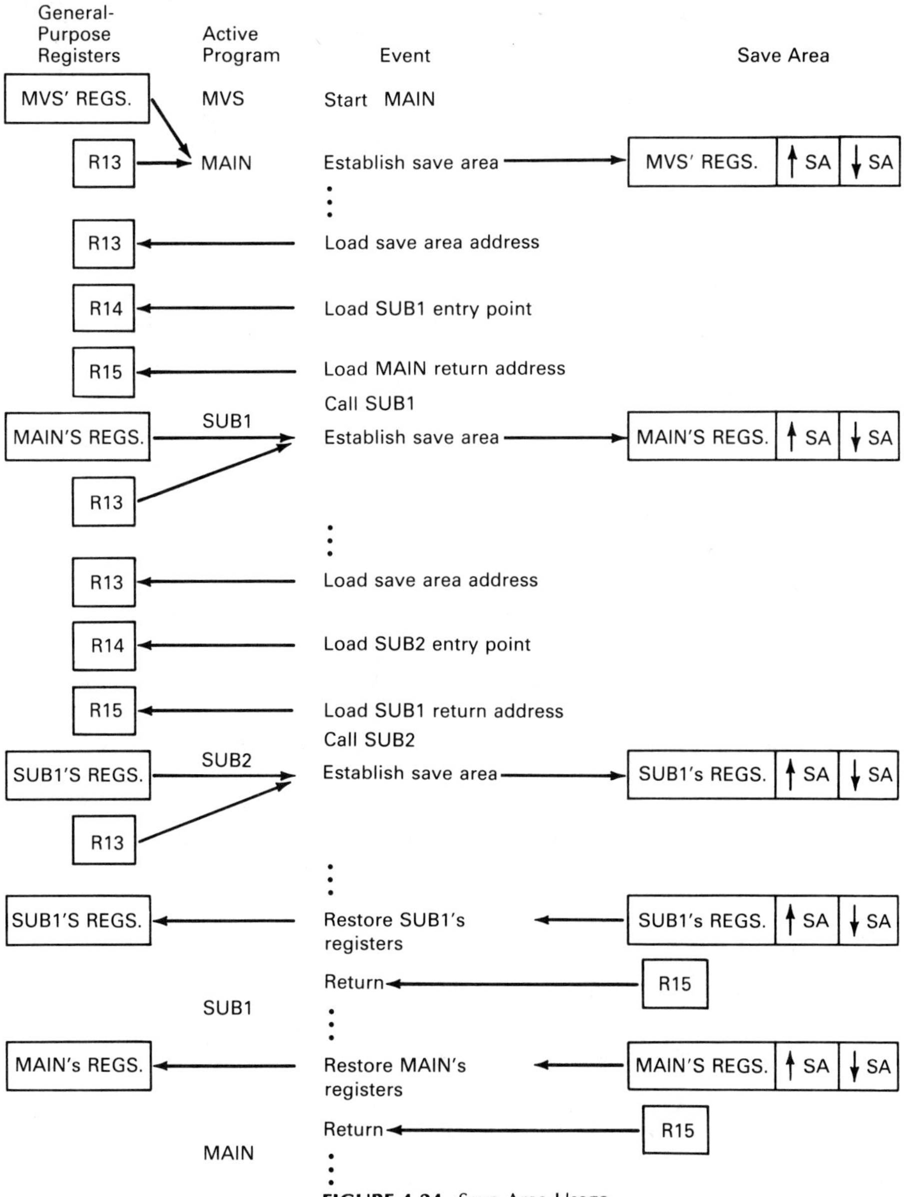

FIGURE 4-24 Save Area Usage

23m. INTERRUPT AT. This message ends the forward save area trace. The instruction address from the resume PSW of the last PRB in the RB queue is listed here (RBOPSW). This address is usually not the address of the abended instruction in either the problem program or a supervisor routine.

23n. PROCEEDING BACK VIA REG 13. This message precedes the backward save area trace. Register 13 at entry to abend is assumed to point to a save area. If register 13 points to a fullword in storage and is nonzero, the assumption is considered valid by the dump formatting program. This storage area is formatted and listed as a save area. In turn, this block is then assumed to point to a second save area, which is also formatted and listed. In most cases these assumptions are true.

23o. The two save areas found by the backward chain are listed in standard format.

Main Storage Areas

The second part of an ABEND dump is a semiformatted listing of the main storage area associated with a task and the address space in which it was executing. In MVS, main storage is divided into areas by usage. Several areas are for the exclusive use of MVS; some may be shared between tasks (address spaces) and some are for the exclusive use of a task. These relationships and the names given to the various areas are diagrammed in Figure 4-25. An ABEND dump may list or exclude any of these areas. The dumping parameters established for your installation determine which areas are printed.

Three other items appear in the dump main storage section: the registers at entry to ABEND, formatted trace table entries, and a dump index. These items and main storage areas are described in the order in which they are printed.

The printed format of each main storage area is the same. The dump shows 32 bytes of main storage per line. The far left-hand column gives the virtual address of the first byte in the line, followed by a hexadecimal representation of 32 successive bytes of storage. One hexadecimal digit represents a nibble (4 bits); 2 digits, a byte; 8 digits, a word. The right-hand column shows the same 32 bytes as characters. If the byte's bit pattern corresponds to an EBCDIC code for characters blank (x40), A–Z or 0–9, the character is printed. If not, a period is printed. If two or more successive 32-byte sections of storage are identical, only the first section will be printed. Printing resumes with the next unequal 32-byte section.

FIGURE 4-26 Supervisor Storage Areas

Typically, Supervisor Storage Areas are only listed on a SYSABEND dump. Each installation may select the storage areas to be listed. Usually, a subset is selected.

26a. PSA. Prefixed save area. The first 4K of storage. Functionally part of the nucleus area. Contains data used by MVS task management function. Rarely of interest for application debugging.

26b. NUCLEUS. MVS nucleus area. The remaining storage of the system area. The system area (PSA and nucleus) occupies at least the first 64K addresses of real (and virtual) storage. Its contents are established by IPL (initial program load) and NIP (nucleus initialization program). It is nonpageable and nonswapable. The nucleus contains the CVT (communications vector table). The CVT is the interface between the MVS functions which are permanently resident in the nucleus and pageable functions (e.g., data management). It contains the addresses of the control blocks used by MVS functions. The CVT is a "root" control block.

The nucleus contains the UCB associated with each I/O device. The nucleus is rarely of interest for application debugging.

26c. ALLOCATED LSQA. The portion of the local system queue area allocated for this address space. Contains control blocks and lists that are unique to the address space, page and segment tables, and control blocks used by the region control task (RCT). The RCT handles swap-in and swap-out for an address space.

26d. SP 229, SP 230. Dump of subpools 229 and 230. Contains many control blocks used by data management. The DEB chain is found here as well as the O/C/EOV work area for each open data set.

26e. ALLOCATED SQA. Dump of the allocated portions of the system queue area (SQA). SQA contains control blocks and lists describing general system resources or processes. For

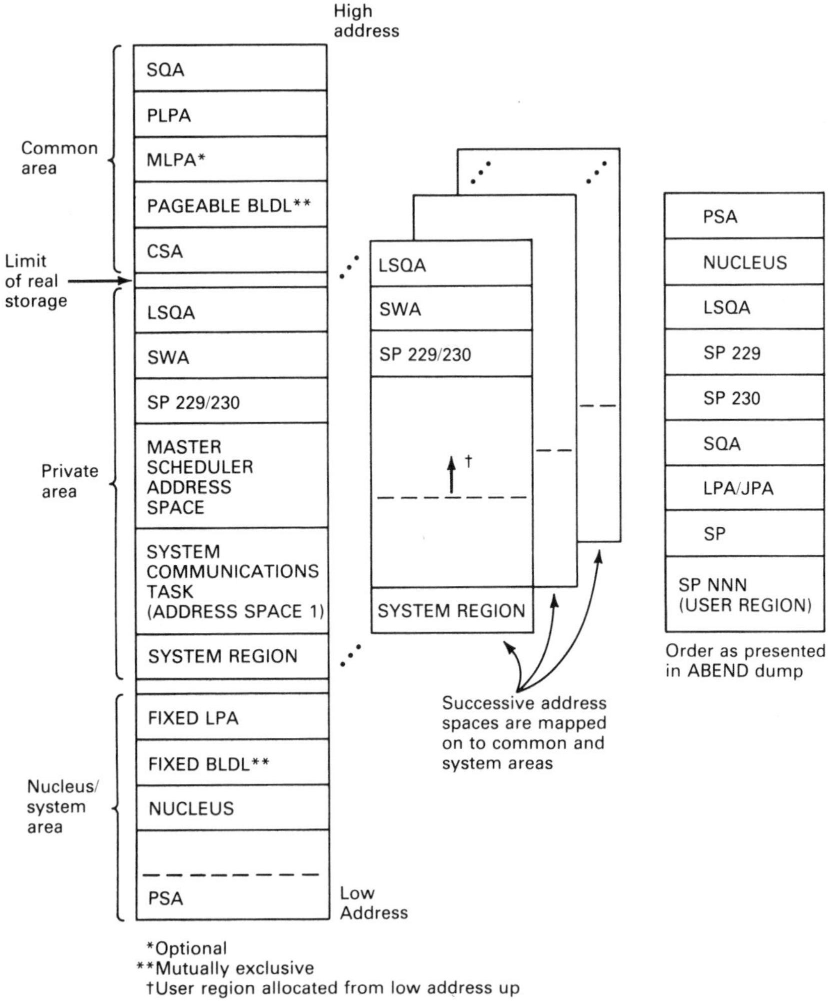

FIGURE 4-25 MVS Main Storage Areas

```
PSA (26a)
xxxxxx   xxxxxxxx xxxxxxxx xxxxxxxx xxxxxxxx xxxxxxxx xxxxxxxx xxxxxxxx xxxxxxxx  *................................*
NUCLEUS (26b)
xxxxxx   xxxxxxxx xxxxxxxx xxxxxxxx xxxxxxxx xxxxxxxx xxxxxxxx xxxxxxxx xxxxxxxx  *................................*
ALLOCATED LSQA (26c)
xxxxxx   xxxxxxxx xxxxxxxx xxxxxxxx xxxxxxxx xxxxxxxx xxxxxxxx xxxxxxxx xxxxxxxx  *................................*
SP 229 (26d)
xxxxxx   xxxxxxxx xxxxxxxx xxxxxxxx xxxxxxxx xxxxxxxx xxxxxxxx xxxxxxxx xxxxxxxx  *................................*
SP 230 (26d)
xxxxxx   xxxxxxxx xxxxxxxx xxxxxxxx xxxxxxxx xxxxxxxx xxxxxxxx xxxxxxxx xxxxxxxx  *................................*
ALLOCATED SQA (26e)
xxxxxx   xxxxxxxx xxxxxxxx xxxxxxxx xxxxxxxx xxxxxxxx xxxxxxxx xxxxxxxx xxxxxxxx  *................................*
SP 236 (26f)
xxxxxx   xxxxxxxx xxxxxxxx xxxxxxxx xxxxxxxx xxxxxxxx xxxxxxxx xxxxxxxx xxxxxxxx  *................................*
SP 237 (26f)
xxxxxx   xxxxxxxx xxxxxxxx xxxxxxxx xxxxxxxx xxxxxxxx xxxxxxxx xxxxxxxx xxxxxxxx  *................................*
```

FIGURE 4-26 Supervisor Storage Areas

example, the CDE is contained here. SQA is nonswappable and nonpageable. SQA storage is allocated from subpool 245.

26f. SP 236, SP 237. Dump of subpools 236 and 237. These two subpools contain the scheduler work area (SWA). The SWA is created by job step initiation and contains control blocks that are active for the duration of the task. The TIOT, JFCB, and JFCBX are contained in the SWA.

FIGURE 4-27 Registers and Problem Program Storage

27a. REGS AT ENTRY TO ABEND. This title indicates that contents of the general registers at the time the ABEND macro was entered follow.

27b. FLTR 0-6. The four doubleword floating-point registers, 0, 2, 4, and 6, are listed here in hexadecimal.

27c. REGS 0-7, REGS 8-15. The 16 general fullword registers are listed here in hexadecimal. The register contents are frequently useful in data management abends for locating control blocks, and in 0Cx abends for calculating the address referenced by the abending instruction. Less frequently, the registers can provide information about call/return sequences, invalid branches, and runaway loops.

27d. ACTIVE LOAD MODULES. This header precedes a dump of the load modules present on the load list (see LOAD LIST, paragraph 7a). A load module consists of instructions, data structures, and constants requiring main storage. The load module for the problem program, those called dynamically and active supervisor routines, will be listed.

27e. LPA/JPA MODULE. This header precedes the dump of a load module. The module's name is given. The module was found in the LPA (link pack area) or the JPA (job pack area). The LPA contains system routines loaded at IPL time. The JPA contains modules loaded for the current task. See 5.2, Basic Techniques, for a description of the structure of the load modules produced by the various language translators.

27f. SVC MODULE. This header precedes a dump of an SVC module which was active when the ABEND was issued. An active SVC is indicated by the presence of an SVRB on the RB chain when ABEND was entered. The name of the SVC module will be printed.

27g. SP nnn. Dump of user subpools 001 through 127. Various access methods obtain virtual storage from these subpools for buffers and tables. The usage of these areas varies considerably by application.

FIGURE 4-28 Formatted Trace Table

28a. TRACE TABLE. This header precedes a formatted listing of the TTEs (trace table entries). A TTE is created when a system interrupt is processed and GTF is not active. If not listed under this heading, the unformatted trace table is contained in the SQA (SP 230). Each entry is x20 bytes long and begins with x07 or x04. Scan the SQA dump for a series of lines beginning with x07 or x04.

28b. TTE TYPE. Indicates the type of interrupt that this entry represents:

DSP	Task dispatch: make this task ready for continued execution
EXT	External interrupt: special service required—system clock, hardware error, or emergency signal

```
REGS AT ENTRY TO ttttt  (27a)

    FLTR 0-6      xxxxxxxxxxxxxxxx    xxxxxxxxxxxxxxxx        xxxxxxxxxxxxxxxx    xxxxxxxxxxxxxxxx }  (27b)

    REGS 0-7      xxxxxxxx  xxxxxxxx  xxxxxxxx  xxxxxxxx      xxxxxxxx  xxxxxxxx xxxxxxxx  xxxxxxxx }  (27c)
    REGS 8-15     xxxxxxxx  xxxxxxxx  xxxxxxxx  xxxxxxxx      xxxxxxxx  xxxxxxxx xxxxxxxx  xxxxxxxx }

ACTIVE LOAD MODULES  (27d)

LPA/JPA MODULE     tttttttt  (27e)

xxxxxx   xxxxxxxx xxxxxxxx xxxxxxxx xxxxxxxx   xxxxxxxx xxxxxxxx xxxxxxxx xxxxxxxx   *................................*
  |
  |
SVC MODULE     tttttttt  (27f)

xxxxxx   xxxxxxxx xxxxxxxx xxxxxxxx xxxxxxxx   xxxxxxxx xxxxxxxx xxxxxxxx xxxxxxxx   *................................*
  |
  |
SP nnn  (27g)
xxxxxx   xxxxxxxx xxxxxxxx xxxxxxxx xxxxxxxx   xxxxxxxx xxxxxxxx xxxxxxxx xxxxxxxx   *................................*
  .
  .
  .
  .
```

FIGURE 4-27 Registers and Problem Program Storage

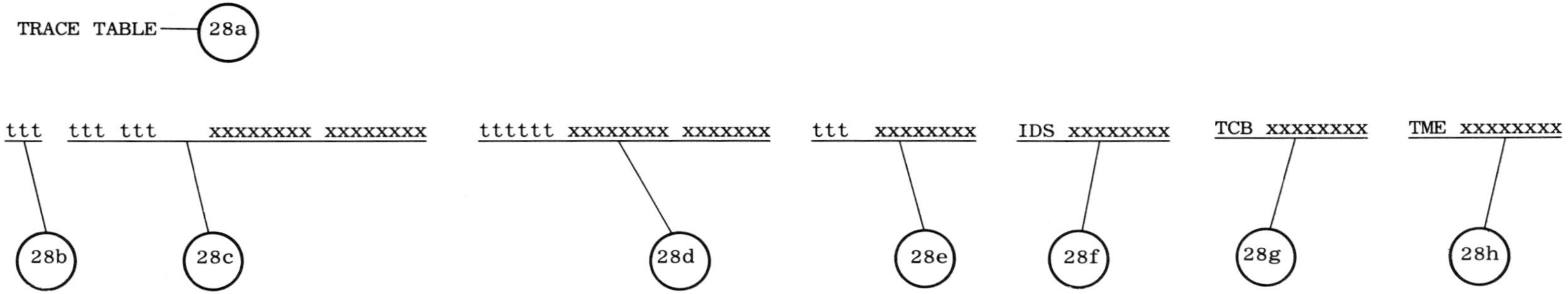

FIGURE 4-28 Formatted Trace Table

I/O	I/O interrupt: channel that has completed an I/O operation requires service
ISD	Initial SRB dispatch: request to process an SRB
PGM	Program interrupt: result of page faults, event monitor request, or program error (0Cx interrupt)
SIO	Start I/O: request to begin execution of a channel program
SRR	Suspend SRB redispatch: see ISD
SVC	Supervisor call interrupt: supervisor routine was requested via the SVC instruction

28c. PSW or CAW. This entry lists the contents of the indicated field, at the time of the interrupt.

28d. R15/R0 or CSW. This entry lists the contents of R15 and R0 at the time the interrupt occurred. R15 may contain a branch address.

28e. R1, ISB or RES. The contents of R1 (possible parameter list address) or IOSB address.

28f. IDS. CPU and address space IDs (2 bytes each).

28g. TCB. Address of the TCB associated with this interrupt.

28h. TME. The middle 4 bytes of the doubleword TOD (time of day) clock field. May be useful in diagnosing waits or swapped-out tasks.

An index to the major sections of the dump is printed on the last page. This index will point you to the first page of a group or control blocks or a main storage area.

4.3 FINDING AN ADDRESS

To find an address, try to determine which main storage area contains the address. Problem program instructions and data will be under an LPA/JPA header, buffers will probably be in SP 001, the O/C/EOV work area in SP 230, and so on. The last page of the dump gives an index of the page numbers for main storage areas. Begin looking for an address at the first page for its area. If you are not sure which area contains the address, you must look through each area. Areas are not listed in ascending address order. Within an area, addresses are in ascending order.

Once you have located the area, scan the left-hand column of addresses until you find an address greater than or equal to the one of interest. The preceding line should contain the address you are looking for. If you cannot find the address, it is probably in a main storage area not printed in your dump. There are generally two reasons for this. First, your installation's dump parameters do not select this area. Second, the control block or area has been deallocated from your task. In any case, double-check your search. Reading dumps is hard. It is easy to misread or overlook an address. Also, if you have computed the address by base plus displacement hexadecimal arithmetic, recheck your calculation. Even with a hexadecimal calculator, this arithmetic is prone to error. We mortals are encumbered with a mere xA digits, not x10.

Once you have located your address, you will probably want to find another address at some hex displacement plus or minus your current address. Calculate the next address

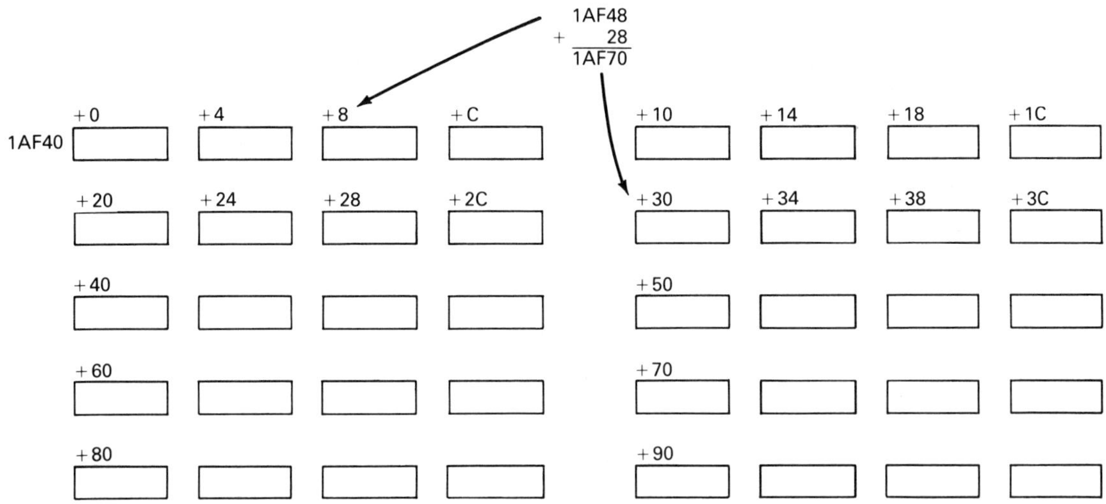

FIGURE 4-29 Finding Addresses by Rows and Columns

and repeat the search described above as needed. Addresses that are nearby (the same printed page, for example) may be located by inspection.

Figure 4-29 shows a visual technique for locating addresses. Note that each column contains a fullword—4 bytes. One line contains 32 bytes—8 fullwords. This means that the address of the first byte of each successive line is x20 more than the preceding line. Committing this relationship between lines and columns to memory will enable you to

Table 4-1
Row/Column Address Equivalents

Hex Displacement[a]	*Column/ Row Equivalent*
4	1 column
8	2 columns
C	3 columns
10	4 columns
14	5 columns
18	6 columns
1C	7 columns
20	8 columns/1 row
40	2 rows
60	3 rows
80	4 rows
100	5 rows
300	20 rows

[a]Positive displacements move right and down, negative displacements left and up.

find a particular address more rapidly. For example, the address of a DCB is x1AF48 and you want to locate the TIOT offset, which is x28 from this address (x1AF70). x20 equates to one row down, x8 to two columns right. So, by dropping down one row and looking right two columns from the base address, you have found the offset. Table 4-1 lists the row and column equivalents of some hexadecimal displacements.

4.4 OBTAINING DUMPS

The portions of main storage and the control blocks listed on an ABEND dump are determined by the SYS1.PARMLIB members:

IEAABD00 SYSABEND format
IEADMP00 SYSUDUMP format
IEADMR00 SYSMDUMP format

See *Service Aids* for more information about abend parms. The contents of a SNAP dump are determined in the SNAP macro call. See *Supervisor Services* for more information about SNAP. A SYSABEND dump will generally list the supervisor storage areas described above. In the interest of paper conservation, standard practice is to use SYSUDUMP unless SYSABEND is needed for a specific reason (e.g., to list the O/C/EOV work area).

A DD statement is required for a formatted dump. The minimum DD statement is:

```
//SYSUDUMP DD SYSOUT=A
```

for a SYSUDUMP, or

```
//SYSABEND DD SYSOUT=A
```

for a SYSABEND dump. Parameters may be added to control the print format. If the 3800 printing subsystem (high-speed laser printer) is part of your installation, a higher-density dump may be printed. CHARS = DUMP will give a dump with 204 characters per line, twice the normal amount.

Dumps are often printed at 12 lines per inch. In addition to any special FCBs your installation has defined, FCB = STD3 will print 8 lines per inch, which is somewhat easier to read. Dumps may be output to DASD or tape and listed at a later time.

For information about obtaining dumps under TSO, see 3.7, Debugging Abends under TSO. For information about obtaining on demand dumps via source program statements, see four sections called Program-Initiated Dumps, for the source language of interest, in Chapter 5, Source Code Debugging.

A third option exists. Abend dumps may be written to a data set defined by a SYSMDUMP DD statement. The parameters for this DD statement must agree with the requirements of the utility program to be used to display or print the dump. A SYSMDUMP may be printed by the AMDPRDMP utility or may be displayed under TSO using the IPCS facility. Both programs provide a number of formatting and selection options. For more information about AMDPRDMP, see *Service Aids*. For more information about IPCS, see *OS/VS2 MVS Interactive Problem Control System (IPCS) User's Guide and Reference*.

Debugging is possibly the most important aspect of programming. Few programmers, especially those involved in control program modification, ever produce a perfect solution in one run; abnormal termination is inevitable and must be prepared for.

OS/VS1 Debugging Guide

The difficult way to analyze a dump is to look at each address space and task individually, looking at its request blocks and resume-PSWs to determine what it was doing (or waiting for) at the time of the dump.

OS/VS2 Debugging Handbook

A disciplined approach is important; resist the tendency to go off on tangents upon finding the first unexplainable condition. After gathering all the facts, try to resolve the "cause and effect" situations you are bound to uncover. Generally, at this point you will have isolated the error and can start a detailed component/process analysis.

MVS Diagnostic Techniques

5

SOURCE CODE DEBUGGING

5.1 INTRODUCTION

The initial task of abend debugging is to determine which component caused the error. If the abend is not due to error in the interface with the supervisor (JCL, link-edit, etc.), an examination of the problem program source and object code listings is usually necessary.

Source program statements generally consist of operations on fields in main storage or invoke supervisor services. Language translators convert source statements into relocatable object code. The linkage editor resolves external references (subroutine calls) and creates a load module. Finally, the loader places load modules in main storage and binds relocatable base addresses to virtual addresses. Although the general function of the language translators is similar, their mechanics differ considerably. They all must produce executable object code in a format acceptable to the linkage editor. The translation process, however, is unique to each language. Except for assembly language, there is not a direct correspondence between source statements and object code. The differences in object code generated by each language translator can be understood if each translator is viewed as a programmer; each with its own style of coding, favorite tricks, maddening idiosyncrasies, and occasional moments of lucidity. This chapter explains how to work from the object code and task management control blocks in the dump back to the program source statement that was involved in the abend. There are four main parts: 5.2, Basic Techniques, which explains how to get from an SCC and an abend PSW to an object module address; 5.3, Object Code Analysis, which shows how to interpret the abending instruction and calculate the effective address of its operands; 5.4, Data Storage Formats, which explains all the main storage formats operands will reference; and fourth, the sections on source code analysis, which explain how to find the source program statement that corresponds to the abending object module address and any source program data field. Debugging aids available in each language are identified.

5.2 BASIC TECHNIQUES

Figure 5-1 shows the data gathering process typically required for abend debugging. The procedural steps outlined under 1.3, General Debugging Procedure, are complementary. Taken together, they provide a comprehensive analytical approach for debugging problem program abends. Each box in Figure 5-1 represents a basic step in the process. Although the diagram flows left to right, the steps actually needed are determined by the abend at hand. The diagram follows data flow diagram conventions. Sources of data are indicated by base lines. Flows of data are indicated by arrows in or out of a box. Boxes represent a transformation (your analysis) of an input into an output.

Classify the SCC

Abends fall into two main groups: program check (SCCs 0C1 through 0CF) and supervisor (all other SCCs). Supervisor abends can be subdivided into program related and environmental. Program-related supervisor abends are generally a result of incorrect usage of a supervisor service, such as OPEN or CLOSE, as invoked by the program. Environmental supervisor abends are generally the result of a failure to establish the required execution environment for the problem program—insufficient resources allocated via JCL, errors in utility program parameters, or incorrect usage of execution-time supervisor services. The distinction is useful in that environmental supervisor abends are usually correctable by supplying new JCL or utility parameters and reexecuting. No detailed program or dump analysis is required.

Program-related supervisor abends often require examination of formatted or unformatted control blocks from the dump. This analysis usually provides information about conflicting, incorrect, or missing supervisor service parameters.

Program check abends usually require an inspection of the object code related to and including the abending instruction.

Classifying program check abends is simple. SCCs 0C1 through 0CF are program

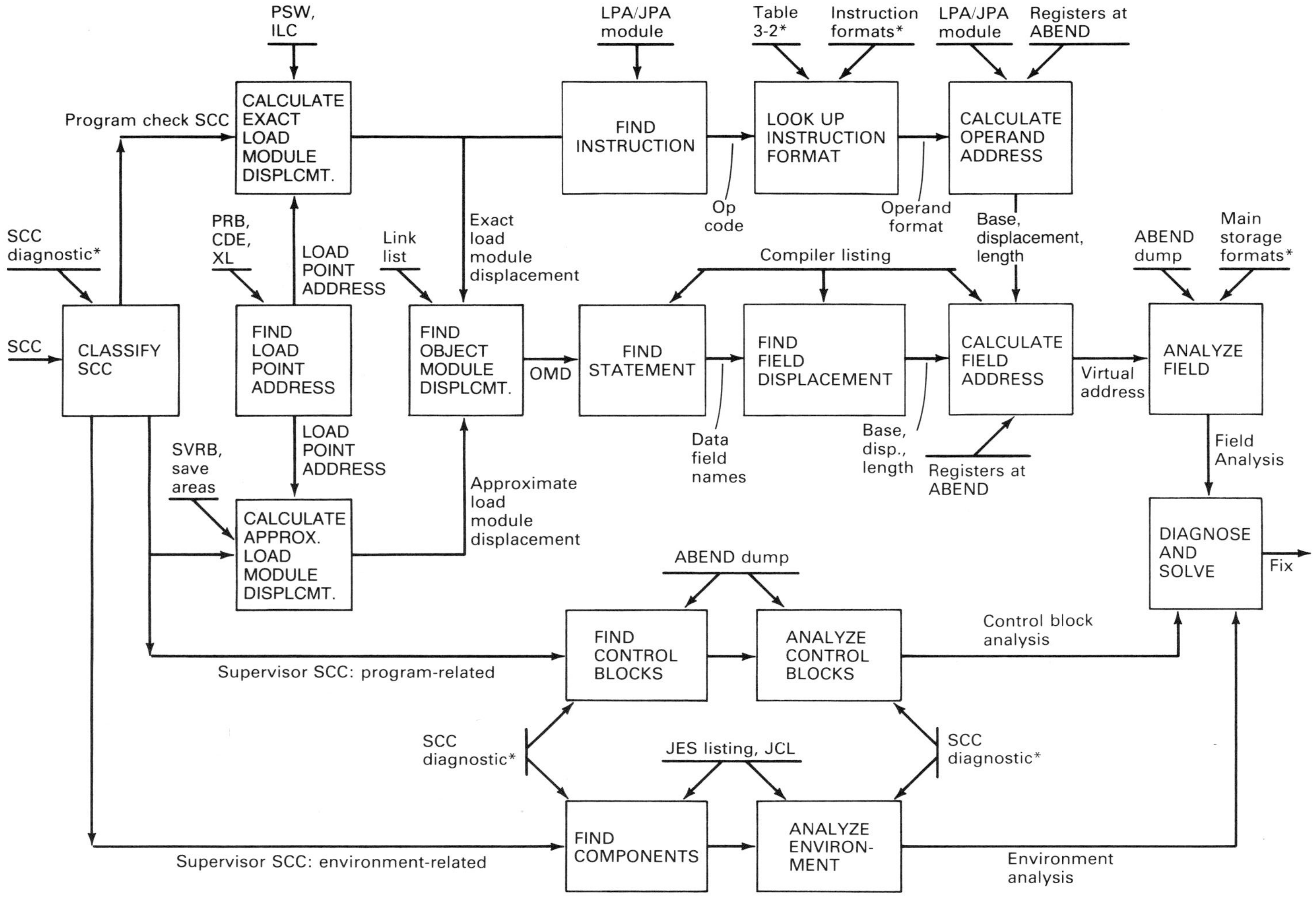

* Topic in this book

FIGURE 5-1 The Debugging Process

check abends. Distinguishing between environmental and program-related supervisor abends is not as easy. The possible causes in the SCC diagnostics are designed to aid in this. An SCC may result from either environmental or program causes, or both (e.g., SCC 001).

The steps that follow once the classification has been made are:

- For program check abends:
  - (a) Find the load module entry point address for the abending module.
  - (b) Calculate the load module displacement at abend.
  - (c) Find the abending object module.
  - (d) Find and analyze the abending source statement.
  - (e) Diagnose the problem and implement a solution.
- For program-related supervisor abends:
  - (a) Analyze the save area trace or RB chain to find the load point address of the problem program.
  - (b) Calculate the load module displacement of the next instruction.
  - (c) Find the abending object module.
  - (d) Find and analyze the abending statement.
  - (e) Find and analyze the related control blocks.
  - (f) Diagnose the problem and implement a solution.
- For environment-related supervisor abends:
  - (a) Determine which component was related to the abend (JCL, linkage-editor, catalog management, etc.).
  - (b) Analyze the specification or interface error.
  - (c) Diagnose the problem and implement a solution.

In some cases, all three procedures or a subset from each group may be needed.

Find the Problem Program Load Point Address

The load point address of the problem program is the virtual storage address where the problem program load module begins. The load point address is found by an analysis of task management control blocks, starting with the RB (request block) chain printed in the dump under ACTIVE RBS. The first PRB listed will probably be for the problem program. In most cases, there is only one PRB, followed by two or three SVRBs.

The third RB from the bottom of the RB chain is associated with the load module that invoked ABEND. This RB can be either a PRB or an SVRB. For supervisor abends, the SVRB immediately following the last PRB will be for the supervisor routine (SVC) that issued the ABEND. For both program check and supervisor abends, at least two more SVRBs will follow—one for SNAP and one for SYNCH. These two SVCs are issued to format and print the dump. A typical sequence of RBs in a program check abend dump is

```
ACTIVE RBS
      •
      •
      •
   PRB             ← Problem program RB
      •
      •
      •
  SVRB             ← SNAP RB
      •
      •
      •
  SVRB             ← SYNCH RB
```

A typical sequence of RBs in a supervisor abend dump is

```
ACTIVE RBS
      •
      •
      •
   PRB             ← Problem program RB
      •
      •
      •
  SVRB             ← RB for SVC that issued the abend
      •
      •
      •
  SVRB             ← SNAP RB
      •
      •
      •
  SVRB             ← SYNCH RB
```

The SVC that issued the ABEND may be identified from the last byte of the SVRB field labeled WC-L-IC when the third-from-last RB is an SVRB. This byte contains the SVC number in hex.

The RB for the load module that issued the ABEND should contain the same PSW as the PSW AT ENTRY TO ABEND. The abending PRB's FL-CDE field points to an entry in the CDE. This entry will describe the problem program, in most cases. The CDE entry usually gives the name of the abending load module in NM and its load point address in EPA. EPA is not a valid load point address in all cases. The XL/MJ field of the CDE points to an entry in the XL (extent list). The address of this XL entry in the column titled ADR gives the true load point address of the module named in NM. Use the XL address if it differs from the CDE EPA as the load point address. Under certain circumstances with PL/I programs, the CDE pointed from the PRB will not be the problem program CDE. See 5.8, PL/I Analysis, Finding the Abending Statement, for further information.

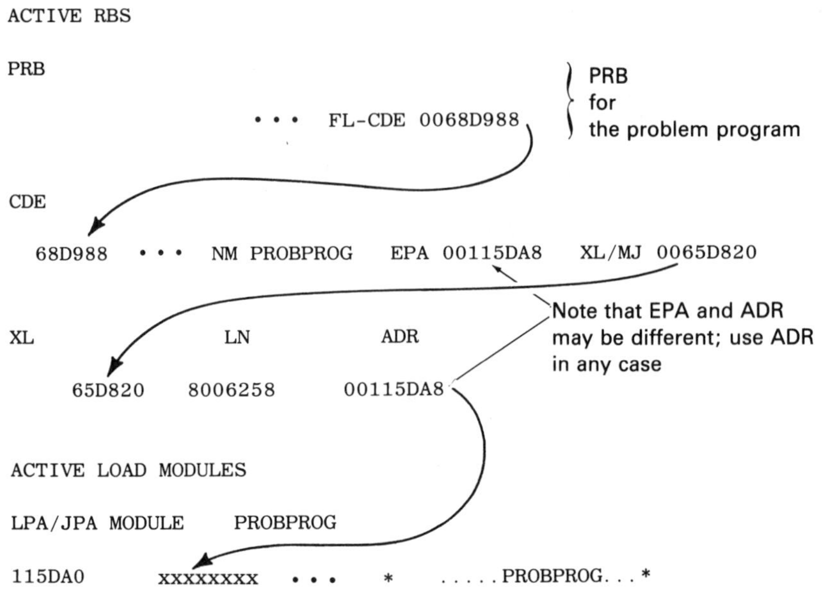

FIGURE 5-2 Locating the Problem Program Load Point Address

As a final check on the load point address determined from the XL ADR or CDE EPA, turn to the ACTIVE LOAD MODULES section of the dump. The load point address calculated above should point to the first byte of storage listed under an LPA/JPA MODULE. The module name is given in the LPA/JPA title as well. The 8-byte module name may also be found near the start of the module. Figure 5-2 summarizes the relationship of the RB chain, the CDE, and the XL.

Determine the Load Module Displacement

The load module displacement is the address of the abending instruction relative to the start of the load module. This is the address of the abending instruction before the load module was relocated and bound to a base virtual address. It is used to determine which object module contains the abending instruction (load modules may be composed from many different object modules). Depending on the type of abend, you may determine an exact or approximate load module displacement. Program check abends will yield an exact displacement; supervisor abends will yield an approximate load module displacement.

Calculating an Exact Load Module Displacement

The PSW AT ENTRY TO ABEND usually contains the address of the next instruction to be executed. Check the section Relevant Dump Items under the SCC diagnostic. Some program interrupts result in the current instruction address in the PSW. The ILC contains the length of the current instruction. The virtual address of the abending instruction is given by subtracting the ILC from the PSW, except as noted in the SCC diagnostic.

The load module displacement is given by subtracting the load point address (as found above) from the address of the abending instruction. There are two situations in which this technique will not give the address within the problem program load module:

- The abend occurred in a supervisor routine. In this case, see the following section regarding approximate displacement.
- The next address has been incorrectly loaded (see SCC 0C1). In this case, see 3.2, 0Cx Abend Diagnostics, Diagnosing an Invalid Branch.

Calculating An Approximate Load Module Displacement

For supervisor abends, the PSW will point to an address within a supervisor module. This address is rarely of use for problem program debugging. There are several possible means to find the next address to be executed in the problem program. They are based on the fact that this next address must be stored, so that execution may continue after the supervisor module returns control. The next instruction address may be in:

- The PRB's PSW (second word of RBOPSW, RB + x10)
- R14 of abending SVRB's register save area (listed in the SVRB)
- RET under the last SA in SAVE AREA TRACE

Check each address to see if it falls within the problem program load module. Usually, at least one of the three will. The approximate load module displacement is then calculated by subtracting the load point address from this next instruction address. A return address should be immediately preceded by an instruction to transfer control out of the problem program load module. Thus, a good test of a return address is to check the code immediately preceding it. This instruction will usually be an SVC (0Axx) or a BALR (05xx), because these instructions are commonly used to transfer control out of the problem program load module. If none of these addresses yield a meaningful displacement, an analysis of main storage fields, buffers, tables, or variables may indicate what portion of code was active when the SVC was issued. Execution-time traces may be required to pinpoint the statement that required the supervisor service. Fortunately, many supervisor abends may be debugged without knowing the exact instruction or statement at fault.

The SAVE AREA TRACE can provide useful information when supervisor modules are invoked by standard linkage conventions (call and return). For example, the data management macros READ, WRITE, GET, and PUT are called. However, supervisor modules such as OPEN, CLOSE, EOV, GETMAIN, and LINK are invoked by an SVC (supervisor call) instruction. The SVC instruction causes a hardware interrupt. An interrupt is functionally similar to a call, but is implemented differently. The standard call and return linkage conventions are not followed, so there is no save area in the trace for an SVC module. A save area is established in the SVRB for the SVC. The usage of an SVC save area is functionally similar to a standard linkage save area. The "return address" of a supervisor call is created by storing the double word PSW immediately prior to the SVC interrupt. It is stored at fixed real storage location 32, which is part of the PSA (Prefixed storage area). The PSA is listed on a SYSABEND dump if the SDATA=NUC dumping option is in effect.

When invoked by call, the standard save area conventions are followed. Each save area contains the return address in the calling program. This address is the next instruction to be executed upon completion of the called program. The return address usually points to the instruction in the calling program immediately following the one that invoked the supervisor service that abended. However, there are several cases where the return address will not point to this instruction. This will happen if the return address was:

- Not set (no return intended)
- Purposely set to some other address (implicit branch upon return—a poor coding practice) by either the calling or called module
- Overlaid or set incorrectly

The format and use of the save area are discussed in 4.2, Dump Components, Save Area Trace.

Find the Object Module Displacement

Load modules are typically composed of several object modules. Figure 5-3 shows how a hypothetical load module, PROBPROG, would be composed of object modules PROB-PROG, B, C, X, and Y. Module B has two additional entry points, B1 and B2. When a load module is created by the linkage editor and either the MAP or XREF option is specified, a listing giving the displacements of each object module in the load module is created. This listing is essential for debugging. If a link map was not generated or not available, see 3.8, Dumping and Printing Data, Listing Load Module Data. Relinking the abending load module is not a desirable means to create a link map. If the linkage editor parameters, control statements, or the component object modules are different from those used to create the abending load module, the addresses given in the link map will probably not correspond to those in the dump. This may result in an inconclusive or incorrect diagnosis and, in turn, an inappropriate solution. This situation may be avoided if MAP or XREF is always specified to the linkage editor.

Figure 5-4 shows a link map example for load module PROBPROG. Each entry under the CONTROL SECTION NAME column corresponds to an object module created from a source code module. If additional entry points were coded, their name and length are listed to the right under the ENTRY NAME heading. The example shows three such entry points.

With the link map and the previously calculated load module displacement, you can (1) identify which object module was involved in the abend, and (2) calculate the displacement in the abending object module. This second displacement will yield the source code statement that was involved with the abend.

To identify the object module involved in the abend, scan down the ORIGIN column

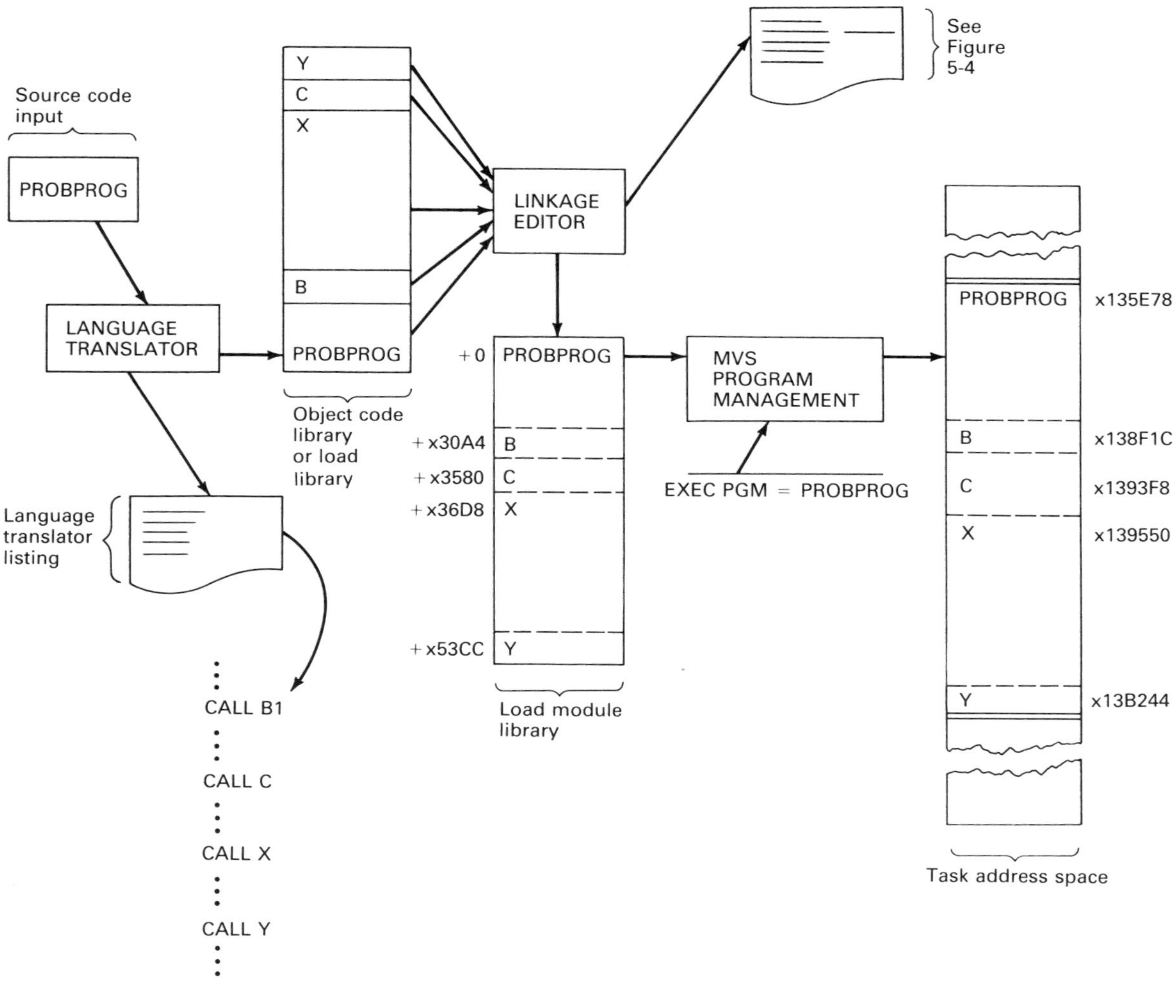

FIGURE 5-3 Load Module Structure

CONTROL SECTION			ENTRY					
NAME	ORIGIN	LENGTH	NAME	LOCATION	NAME	LOCATION	NAME	LOCATION
PROBPROG	00	30A2						
B	30A4	4DC	B1	31A4	B2	3208	B3	3358
C	3580	158						
X	36D8	1CF4						
Y	53CC	DFC						

ENTRY ADDRESS 00

TOTAL LENGTH 61C8

****PROBPROG DOES NOT EXIST BUT HAS BEEN ADDED TO DATA SET

FIGURE 5-4 Link Map Example

in the link map until you find an address greater than your load module displacement. The module named on the previous line contains the displacement, and therefore was involved with the abend. If the last origin address listed is less than your load module displacement, the last object module probably contains the displacement. Verify that it does by adding the ORIGIN and the LENGTH for the last module. The load module displacement should be less than this sum. If the displacement is still not within the last module, you may have:

- Calculated the load module displacement incorrectly
- Obtained an incorrect or out-of-date link map

Once the abending object module has been identified, the next step is to calculate the displacement from the start of the abending object module. The object module displacement is calculated by subtracting the origin address of the abending object module from the load module displacement. The object module displacement is then used in conjunction with the language translator listing to locate the source statement involved in the abend.

The following examples show how load and object module displacements would be calculated for some common abends. Examples use the displacements given for the hypothetical load module PROBPROG, as shown in Figure 5-4. Let

PSW	=	PSW instruction address (3 rightmost bytes), obtained from the dump PSW AT ENTRY TO ABEND
ILC	=	instruction length code, obtained from the dump
LPA	=	load point address, obtained from task management control blocks, as described above
NEXT	=	next instruction address, obtained from the PRB PSW, SVRB R14, or RET, as described above
LMD_a	=	load module displacement (approximate)
LMD_e	=	load module displacement (exact)
OMD	=	object module displacement
SCC	=	system completion code

All addresses and calculations are given in hexadecimal. The origin address used in the examples is taken from the sample linkage editor listing depicted in Figure 5-4.

Example 1

Program check in a mainline:
Given

SCC = 0C7
PSW = 136424
ILC = 6
LPA = 135E78

Then

$$LMD_e = PSW - LPA - ILC$$
$$LMD_e = 136424 - 135E78 - 6$$
$$LMD_e = 5A6$$

Scanning the link map, displacement x5A6 is found in module PROBPROG. Then

$$OMD = LMD - ORIGIN\ address$$
$$OMD = 5A6 - 00$$
$$OMD = 5A6$$

The abending instruction is located at x5A6 into module PROBPROG.

Example 2

Program check in a subroutine:
Given

$$SCC = 0CB$$
$$PSW = 142EFC$$
$$ILC = 4$$
$$LPA = 13E6EC$$

Then

$$LMD_e = PSW - LPA - ILC$$
$$LMD_e = 142EFC - 13E6EC - 4$$
$$LMD_e = 480C$$

Scanning the link map, displacement x480C is within module X. Then

$$OMD = LMD - ORIGIN\ address$$
$$OMD = 480C - 36D8$$
$$OMD = 1134$$

Thus the abending instruction is at x1134 into object module X.

Example 3

Program check in module with multiple entry points:
Given

$$SCC = 0C6$$
$$PSW = 116580$$
$$ILC = 4$$
$$LPA = 113288$$

Then

$$LMD_e = PSW - LPA - ILC$$
$$LMD_e = 116580 - 113288 - 4$$
$$LMD_e = 32F4$$

Scanning the link map, displacement x32F4 is found within module B. Then

$$OMD = LMD - ORIGIN\ address$$
$$OMD = 32F4 - 30A4$$
$$OMD = 250$$

Since module B has several entry points, we also note that a displacement of x250 falls between entry point B2 and B3.

Example 4

Program-related supervisor abend:
Given

$$SCC = 001$$
$$PSW = DA9366$$
$$ILC = 4$$
$$LPA = 143FB0$$
$$NEXT = 1494BA$$

Then

$$LMD_a = NEXT - LPA$$
$$LMD_a = 1494BA - 143FB0$$
$$LMD_a = 550A$$

Notice that x550A is an approximate displacement. In this example, NEXT was obtained from R14 of the first SVRB's save area. Note that the PSW address and the ILC are *not* used to calculate the load module displacement. It should be the next instruction to be executed after the supervisor service was invoked. Scanning the link map, displacement x550A is found within module Y. Then

$$OMD = LMD - ORIGIN\ address$$
$$OMD = 550A - 53CC$$
$$OMD = 13E$$

Thus the next instruction to be executed after the call that resulted in the abend is at x13E into module Y. This is usually the instruction immediately following the call. The specific steps to locate the source statement from the object module displacement are given under each language.

5.3 OBJECT CODE ANALYSIS

It is useful to know machine code instruction formats for at least two reasons. First, machine code addressing conventions must be understood to locate the registers or main storage fields used by an instruction. Second, some familiarity with instruction formats is needed to make use of the optional object code listings generated by language translators (COBOL PMAP, FORTRAN LIST, and PL/I LIST). To examine the particular instruction that abended: (1) find the instruction and determine its type from the operation code, (2) calculate the effective address of the operands and analyze their contents, and (3) analyze the context of the instruction. An example from an 0C4 abend follows. The PSW points to 13CFAA and the ILC is 6. The abending instruction is 6 bytes long and is at location 13CFA4. The 6 bytes at this address are

```
D2 03 E0 00 60 20
```

Looking up the op code D2 in Table 3-2, we find that the instruction is an MVC, a SS type. An MVC instruction uses a single length field. By applying the SS format to the object code operands, we are able to determine the operand fields.

D2	03	E	000	6	020
Op code	L1	B1	D1	B2	D2

Thus the base register for operand 1 (B1) is register E (14). Operand 1 is located at a displacement of x000 from the address in register 14. The base register for operand two is register 6 and operand two is located at a displacement of x020 from the address in register 6. The abending instruction was attempting to move 4 bytes starting at the effective address R6 + x20 to the effective address at R14 + x0. An addressing exception occurred when this was attempted. To determine what the invalid address was, the contents of the two base registers must be examined from REGS AT ENTRY TO ABEND. R6 = x0013CC10, R14 = x00000000. The effective address of operand 1 was 00000000; of operand 2, 0013CC30. Clearly, operand 1 was incorrect. No base address was loaded in register 14. In this particular case, a LINKAGE SECTION header had been incorrectly coded in a COBOL program. The data item referenced was under the incorrect header. No code was generated to load its base register. The 0C4 resulted.

Other instruction formats and data storage formats may be analyzed by following these steps. The following two sections on instructions and data describe the formats used in S/370.

Basic Instruction Formats

This section presents the five basic instruction formats and describes how to locate the registers or main storage their operands reference. There are some 200 basic instructions in the S/370 instruction set. An instruction is composed of an operation code and one or two operands. The operation code specifies the action to be performed on the operands. For example,

```
AR  R1,R2
```

is the symbolic instruction to add the contents of register 2 into register 1. AR is the mnemonic for the operation code x1A. R1 and R2 are the operands that designate the sending and receiving registers. The general form of S/370 instructions is an operation code followed by the address specification for one or two operands. When shown as language translator output, the mnemonic for the operation code is printed as well as operand address specifications. The actual operation code, register number, byte displacement, and length in object code format are listed in the main storage dump.

Operands are specified in one of three ways: as a register number, as an effective virtual storage address, or as an immediate value where the operand is contained within the instruction. An effective address is derived from a base register, an index register, and a displacement. The base register contains an address such as the program entry point or a page boundary. The start address of a field (its first byte), relative to this base, is given by the displacement. Multiple occurrences of fields from this displacement are specified by the index register. Finally, for variable-length fields, a length field gives the length. The more complex the address specification, the longer the instruction length. Variation in address specification accounts for the different instruction lengths. Finally, operand addresses may be given in explicit or implicit form. In the implicit form, the programmer codes symbolic data names in operand fields. The assembler converts these to base, index, displacement, and length specifications as needed. In the explicit form, the programmer or language translator supplies the base, index, displacement, and length operand specifications without an intervening symbolic field name.

The six basic instruction formats are discussed below as well as variations of operand address specification. The format of a particular instruction may be determined from Table 3-2 or *System 370 Reference Summary*. Look up the operation code or the mnemonic and read the instruction type. IBM conventions for the fields in the operand specifications have been followed. They are:

Op code	Operation code
R1	Operand one register
R2	Operand two register
X2	Operand two index register

I2 Operand two immediate value
B1 Operand one base register
B2 Operand two base register
D1 Operand one displacement
D2 Operand two displacement
L1 Operand one length
L2 Operand two length

There are several important conventions about instruction format and length. Object code fields come in standard sizes with a few exceptions. Operation code (op code) is 1 byte except for RRE, S, and SSE formats; these are 2 bytes. Register specifications (B1, B2, R1, R2, X1, X2) are always 1 nibble. Displacements (D1, D2) are always 3 nibbles. Lengths may be 1 or 2 nibbles. Lengths and displacements are always relative to zero. Thus an object code operand whose length field is 7 and displacement field is xC specifies an operand 8 bytes long located at the thirteenth byte from its base address. Implicit or explicit symbolic instructions never use hexadecimal digits, unless coded as an immediate operand. Registers, displacements, and lengths are always given in decimal.

Table 3-2 gives a partial list of S/370 instructions, by op code. See *System/370 Reference Summary, Principles of Operation,* and *Assembly Language Reference* for more information. The instructions listed in Table 3-2 can result in program check abends. The table does not list instructions that do not cause program check abends.

RR Instruction Format

The RR (register to register) type instruction acts on two registers. The instruction is 2 bytes long, formatted as follows:

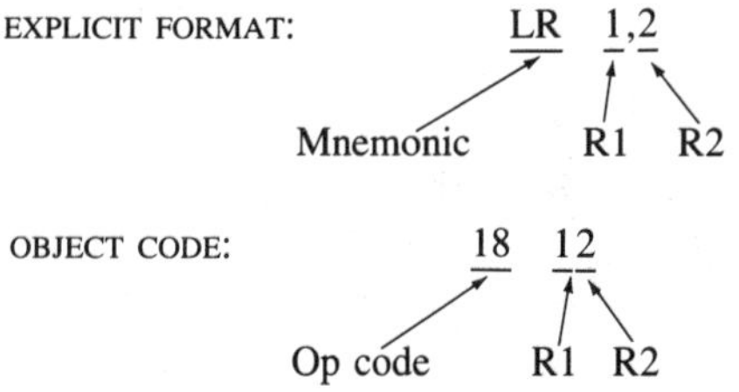

The register addresses are 0 through F, requiring 4 bits each. The example shows how the contents of register 2 could be copied into register 1 using the LR (load register) instruction. The BCR, SPM, and SVC instructions have slightly different formats.

RX Instruction Format

The RX (register to indexed storage) type instruction acts on a register and a fixed-length virtual storage field. The register operand may be either a sending or a receiving field. The storage operand is specified via a base, index, and displacement. The BC instruction has a slightly different format.

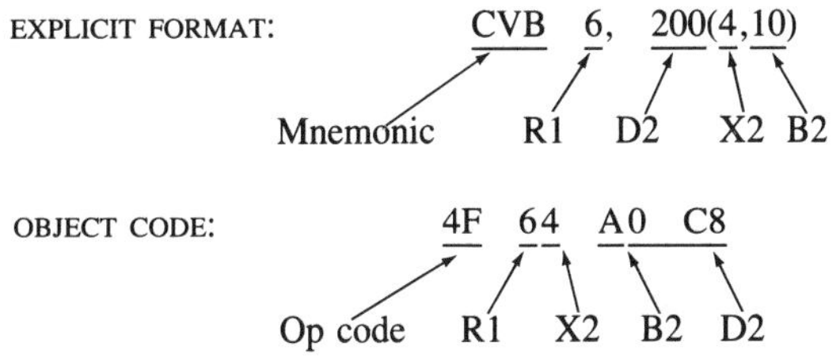

The example shows how the CVB (convert to binary) instruction could be used to convert an 8-byte internal decimal field in storage at the address equal to base register 10 plus index register 4 plus a displacement of xC8. The fullword binary equivalent of this field would be placed in register 6. By convention, if 0 is specified for the index register, the effective address of operand 2 is simply the base register address plus the displacement.

RS Instruction Format

The RS (register to storage) type of instruction is used when one operand in storage is to act on an operand in one or more registers. A range of registers may be specifed as either the sending or receiving field. RS instructions are 4 bytes long. For the ICM, STCM, and CLM instructions, the second register specification may be replaced with a bit mask controlling the type positions of the sending or receiving fields.

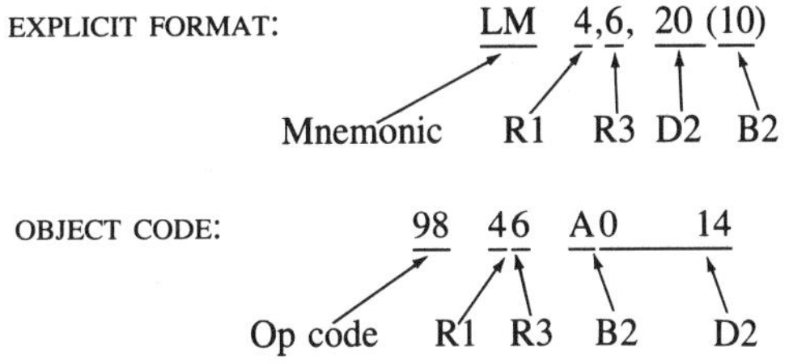

The example shows the LM (load multiple) instruction. 12 bytes of main storage beginning at the address specified by the second operand would be transferred into registers 4, 5, and 6. Note that the length is determined by the number of registers specified.

SI Instruction Format

The SI (storage/immediate) instruction type acts on the second operand, a virtual storage address specified by base and displacement. The first operand is a constant, contained within the instruction. The LPSW, SSM, TIO, and TS instructions do not use the first operand.

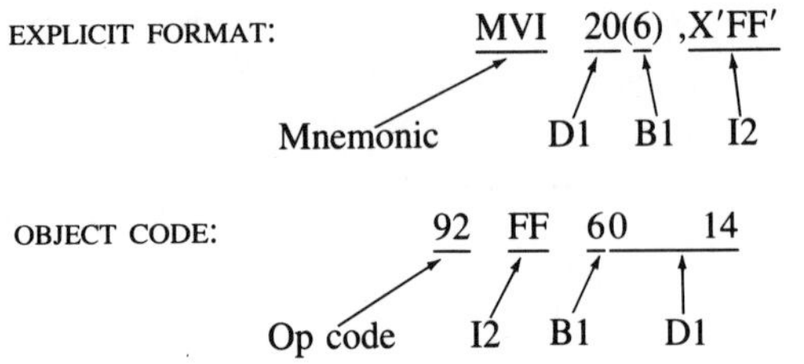

In the example above, the MVI (move immediate) instruction would cause value xFF to be moved into the byte at the address specified by the base address in register 6 plus a displacement of x14.

S Instruction Format

The S type of instruction is used to initiate I/O transfers and to perform various supervisor-level housekeeping functions. Nearly all S type of instructions are privileged—they cannot be executed in the problem state. The S type of instruction's op code is 2 bytes long.

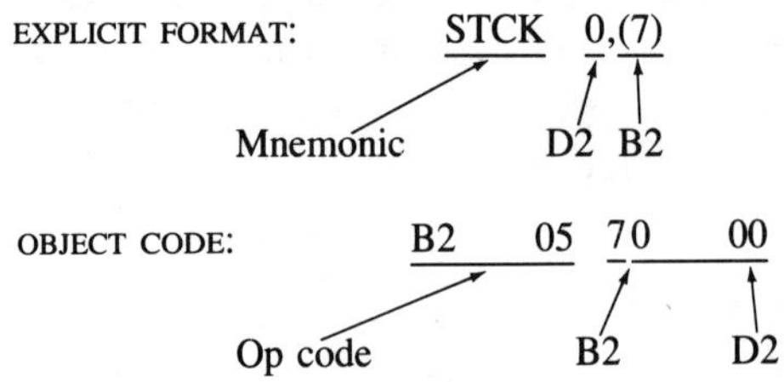

The STCK (store clock) instruction in the example above would transfer the 8-byte TOD clock field to the address specified by the base register and displacement.

SS Instruction Format

The SS (storage to storage) type of instruction is used to transfer data from one storage location to another. The sending and receiving addresses may be the same. The length of the sending and receiving fields is variable. The length operand is relative. A length of zero causes a transfer of 1 byte. There are two subformats of the SS type of instruction, which differ in the length specification. The first format allows a single length specification, 1 byte long. The second allows two length specifications, for the sending and receiving fields, 1 nibble each. Examples of both types follow.

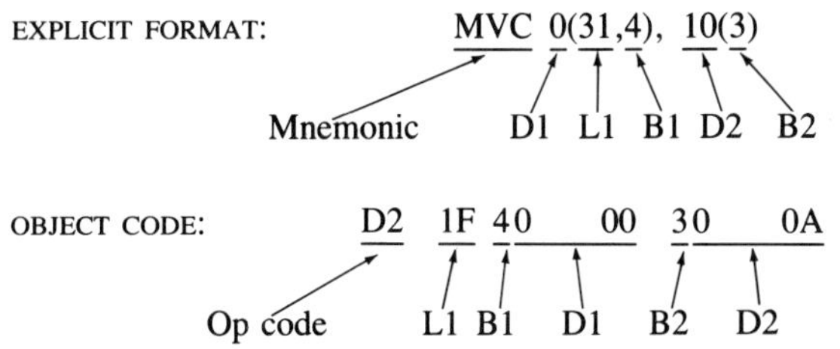

The MVC (move characters) instruction is an example of the single-length SS format. In this example, 32 bytes would be transferred, starting from the address given by register 4 to the address given by register 3 plus xA.

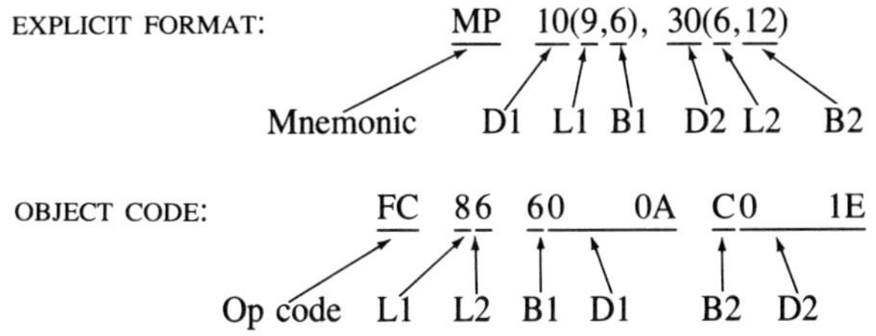

The MP (multiply packed) instruction is an example of the dual-length SS format. In this example, operand 1 is both the product and a multiplicand. The length of operand 1 (the receiving field) is 8 bytes. The multiplier field is 6 bytes long.

The SRP instruction allows an additional immediate operand, 1 nibble long.

5.4 DATA STORAGE FORMATS

The S/370 instruction set operates on four basic data formats: (1) variable-length alphanumeric byte strings, often encoded by EBCDIC or ASCII conventions; (2) binary integer digits 16 or 32 bits long, signed or unsigned; (3) floating-point hexadecimal fractions 32, 64, or 128 bits long; and (4) internal (packed) decimal fields from 1 to 8 bytes long. Language translators make use of these formats under varying names and with varying rules. See Appendix C for a list of language-specific implementations of the basic storage formats.

The format of the data plays a large part in determining how it will be addressed. For example, alphanumeric data and internal decimal fields are byte addressable. Floating-point and binary fields must be aligned on a halfword or fullword address. These constraints are reflected in the format of the instructions used to manipulate the various data types.

The formatting rules and a discussion of the general usage of each type follows. An example showing how to interpret each format's hexadecimal representation (as it would be found in a dump) is also given.

Variable-Length Alphanumeric

This format is frequently used to store data to be manipulated as text, or to be displayed or printed. Each byte is encoded by EBCDIC rules (less frequently by ASCII or other rules). *System/370 Reference Summary,* gives a complete list of EBCDIC and ASCII encoding. The number of bytes a field may contain is, in theory, limited only by available main storage. As a practical matter, a number of factors—buffer size, compiler limitations, device capacity, instruction limits, and so on—constrain the size of a field. A subset of EBCDIC data, external decimal, follows some encoding rules worth noting. External decimal allows a sign (plus or minus) to be encoded in a numeric field, without adding a separate sign byte to the field. The rightmost digit of the field is given an "overpunch." The term reflects the fact that when punched cards were the dominant input medium, a sign on a numeric field was indicated by an additional punch in the rightmost digit column. This additional punch was made in row 11 or 12 and was called an overpunch. Translated in EBCDIC, an external decimal (zoned) digit with a sign will have the same encoding as the characters { through I (positive) or } through J (negative). Table 5-1 shows this relationship. For example, the external decimal field 1234C represents +12343 (a positive number); 1234Q represents −12348 (a negative number).

Data communications protocols such as BSC and SDLC use byte-based variable-length data. Nonprinting characters have special meaning in these protocols. Typically, they delimit a message field or convey transmission-related data. For example, x02 (STX) indicates "start of text," x2E (ACK) indicates "message acknowledged," x61 (NAK) indicates "negative message acknowledgment."

Table 5-1
External Decimal Sign Conventions

Unsigned			*Negative*			*Positive*		
Value	*Hex*	*As Printed*	*Value*	*Hex*	*As Printed*	*Value*	*Hex*	*As Printed*
0	F0	0	−0	D0	}	+0	C0	{
1	F1	1	−1	D1	J	+1	C1	A
2	F2	2	−2	D2	K	+2	C2	B
3	F3	3	−3	D3	L	+3	C3	C
4	F4	4	−4	D4	M	+4	C4	D
5	F5	5	−5	D5	N	+5	C5	E
6	F6	6	−6	D6	O	+6	C6	F
7	F7	7	−7	D7	P	+7	C7	G
8	F8	8	−8	D8	Q	+8	C8	H
9	F9	9	−9	D9	R	+9	C9	I
				(11 punch)			(12 punch)	

Table 5-2

Binary Integer Formats

Decimal Value	*Signed Format* Binary				Hex	*Unsigned Format* Binary				Hex
+65,535	(interpreted as −1)				—	1111	1111	1111	1111	FFFF
+32,767	0111	1111	1111	1111	7FFF	0111	1111	1111	1111	7FFF
+ 256	0000	0001	0000	0000	0100	0000	0001	0000	0000	0100
+ 10	0000	0000	0000	0000	000A	0000	0000	0000	0110	000A
0	0000	0000	0000	0000	0000	0000	0000	0000	0000	0000
− 10	1111	1111	1111	0110	FFF6[a]	(interpreted as +65,526)				
− 512	1111	1110	0000	0000	FE00	(interpreted as +65,024)				
−32,767	1000	0000	0000	0001	8001	(interpreted as +32,769)				

[a]Note that this form is equivalent to one's complement plus 1. One's complement is also defined as the diminished radix complement. Two's complement is the radix complement. One's complement plus 1 is equal to two's complement. These operations are defined as follows: Let I be a binary integer of N bits. The two's complement of I is $2^N - I$. Similarly, the one's complement of I is $(2^N - I) - 1$.

Binary Integer

Binary integer fields are either 16 bits (a halfword) or 32 bits (a fullword) long. They may be signed or unsigned. If signed, the leftmost bit is used for a sign. S/370 instructions do not support radix point scaling of binary fields. However, the problem program may impose its own.

For signed operations, positive numbers are represented as true binary numbers. Negative numbers are represented in two's complement. Two's complement is obtained by inverting the bit pattern of the digit's absolute value (sign bit included) and adding 1. Table 5-2 shows examples of signed and unsigned binary fields. The maximum and minimum values that can be represented in the various binary integer formats are given in Table 5-3.

Table 5-3

Binary Integer Ranges

	Halfword (16 Bits) Minimum	*Halfword (16 Bits)* Maximum	*Fullword (32 Bits)* Minimum	*Fullword (32 Bits)* Maximum
Signed	−32,767	+32,767	−2,147,483,647	+2,147,483,647
Unsigned	0	+65,535	0	+4,294,967,295

Converting Binary to Decimal

Conversion from binary to decimal numbers is straightforward for positive unsigned values. Appendix B gives conversion tables. For signed binary fields, additional steps are needed. The presence of a signed field must be determined from its context—the raw data are not conclusive. If a field is processed as a signed field, the leftmost bit is used to indicate the sign. When on (equal to 1), a negative value is indicated. The first byte of a negative value will be printed as x80 through xFF.

Once identified, conversion of a negative signed binary digit is straightforward. Subtract the absolute value of the number to be converted from xFFFF (for halfword fields) or xFFFFFFFF (for fullword fields), then add 1 to the result and reverse the sign. This yields the same result as inverting the bit pattern by taking two's complement. Several examples follow (examples show decimal arithmetic equivalent). This method is valid only for negative numbers. For positive numbers, use the standard conversion table in Appendix B or an equivalent.

Example 5

Convert negative-valued signed halfword field xFFF6:

1. Subtract from xFFFF	FFFF	65,535
	− FFF6	− 65,526
	9	9
2. Add 1	+ 1	+ 1
3. Reverse sign	− A	− 10

xFFF6 = −10

Example 6

Convert xFE00:

FFFF	65,535
− FE00	− 65,024
1FF	511
+ 1	+ 1
− 200	− 512

xFE00 = −512

Example 7

Convert x8001:

	FFFF		65,535
−	8001	−	32,769
	7FFE		32,766
+	1	+	1
−	7FFF	−	32,767

x8001 = −32,767

Example 8

Convert negative-value signed fullword field xFFA31BC2:

	FFFF FFFF		4,294,967,295
−	FFA3 1BC2	−	4,288,879,554
	5C E43D		6,087,741
+	1	+	1
−	5C E43E	−	6,087,742

xFFA31BC2 = −6,087,742

Internal Decimal

Internal decimal is so named because it is derived from the zoned, external decimal format by "packing." This transformation removes the "zones" from external decimal digit codes. Figure 5-5 shows this transformation. There are no instructions for arithmetic with external decimal fields. External decimal must be converted to binary, floating-point, or internal decimal format before any arithmetic operations can be done.

Internal decimal fields vary in length from 1 to 8 bytes. Values in the range $\pm 10^{16} - 1$ may be represented. No radix scaling is performed at an instruction level. COBOL and PL/I provide software facilities that allow up to 15 digits of fractional precision. Table 2-1 compares several internal decimal definitions and values. Internal decimal is not used in FORTRAN. An internal decimal field consists of a 1 nibble sign in the rightmost nibble, and at least 1 and up to 15 digit nibbles, in 2-nibble increments, after the first. The hexadecimal value of each digit nibble exactly corresponds to its decimal value. Thus an internal decimal field x123F represents decimal 123. Table 5-4 lists the valid nibble bit patterns for internal decimal fields. The sign nibble is typically set to xC, xD, or xF (positive, negative, or absolute value).

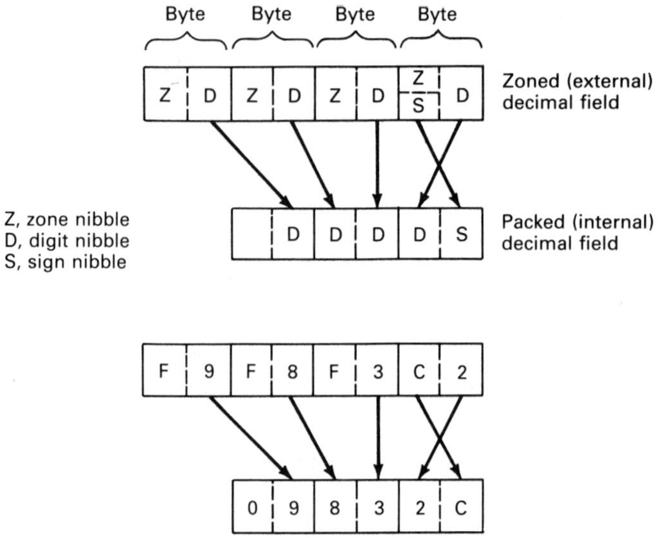

FIGURE 5-5 Packing External to Internal Decimal

Table 5-4
Internal Decimal Digit Format

Nibble Content		*Interpretation*	
Binary	*Hex*	*Digit Position*	*Sign Position*
0000	0	0	Invalid
0001	1	1	Invalid
0010	2	2	Invalid
0011	3	3	Invalid
0100	4	4	Invalid
0101	5	5	Invalid
0110	6	6	Invalid
0111	7	7	Invalid
1000	8	8	Invalid
1001	9	9	Invalid
1010	A	Invalid	Plus sign
1011	B	Invalid	Minus sign
1100	C	Invalid	Plus sign[a]
1101	D	Invalid	Minus sign[a]
1110	E	Invalid	Plus sign
1111	F	Invalid	Absolute value[a]

[a]Most commonly used value.

Converting Internal Decimal to Decimal

Conversion of internal decimal fields is a simple matter. The hexadecimal representation is equivalent to the decimal value. The rightmost nibble contains the sign, which is interpreted according to Table 5-4. Decimal point scaling must be inferred from the context in which the field is used.

Floating Point

The floating-point data format uses a convention similar to scientific notation. It facilitates calculation with very large integers or very small fractions. Radix point scaling is performed automatically. Floating-point numbers are always signed, and come in three sizes: short, long, and extended. The range in magnitude is the same for each size. The number of significant digits (precision) varies. Table 5-5 summarizes the lengths and precision available. For example, the constant π would be represented in short format as 3.141593 and in long format as 3.141592653589793. Figure 5-6 shows the three sizes.

Conceptually, a floating-point field is a hexadecimal number of the form

$$\pm 16^N \times \left(\frac{X_1}{16^1} + \frac{X_2}{16^2} + \cdots + \frac{X_M}{16^M} \right)$$

where

$$-64 \leqslant N \leqslant 63$$

$$M = \begin{cases} 6 & \text{short format} \\ 14 & \text{long format} \\ 28 & \text{extended format} \end{cases}$$

$$X_i = \text{single hexadecimal digit, } i = 1, M$$

Table 5-5
Floating-Point Field Length and Precision

Type	*Length*	*Smallest*[a]	*Largest*[a]	*Number of Significant Digits*
Short	32 bits	5.4×10^{-79}	7.2×10^{75}	7
Long	64 bits	5.4×10^{-79}	7.2×10^{75}	16
Extended	128 bits	5.4×10^{-79}	7.2×10^{75}	33

[a]Approximate, absolute value.

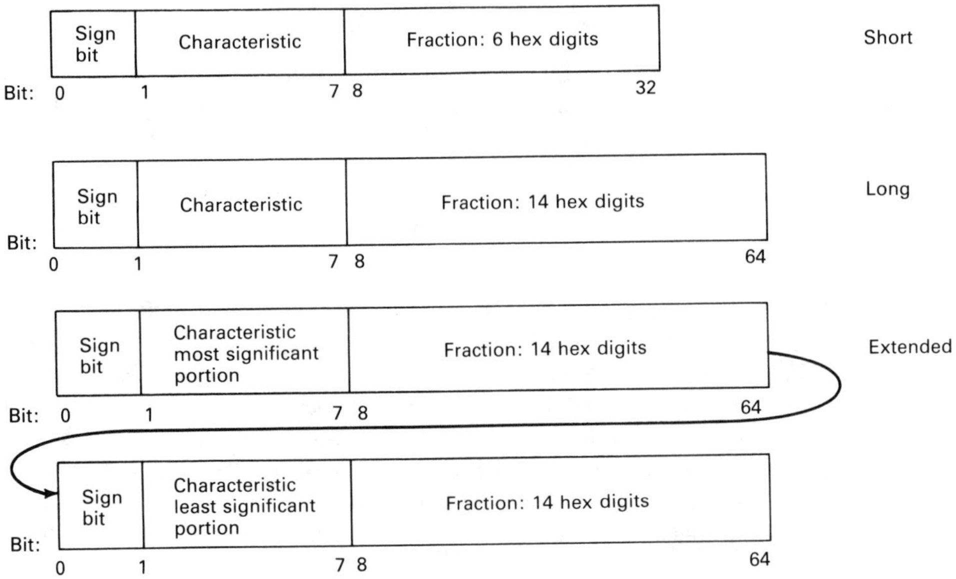

FIGURE 5-6 Floating-point Field Sizes

(Representations are in decimal.) This concept is implemented by defining three subfields: the sign, the characteristic (exponent), and the fraction. The sign and characteristic are of fixed size.[1]

The fraction varies for the short, long, and extended formats. The sign field is 1 bit long. Zero indicates a positive number, 1 indicates a negative number. The quantity zero is represented as a positive number. The characteristic follows the sign and is 7 bits long. It contains the exponent, N, interpreted as a power of 16 in what is called excess-64 format. A characteristic value of 0 (binary 000 0000) represents 16^{-64}; a value of 127 (binary 111 1111) represents 16^{63}. The exponent value is derived by subtracting 64 (x40) from the characteristic. Calculations that would result in an exponent outside this range cause an 0CC or 0CD abend. The fraction field contains either 6, 14, or 28 hexadecimal digits, 1 nibble each. The radix point precedes the leftmost digit when the fraction is "normalized." There are full instruction subsets for both normalized and unnormalized arithmetic. Typically, fractions are normalized—any leading hexadecimal zeros are removed by shifting the digits left and adjusting the exponent accordingly.

For example, the decimal scientific notation number 0.001234×10^5 is in unnor-

[1]A detailed discussion of floating-point computational properties, error due to rounding or truncation, and calculation of sufficiently accurate solutions is given by: William S. Dorn and Daniel D. McCracken, *Numerical Methods with FORTRAN IV Case Studies* (New York: John Wiley & Sons, Inc., 1972), Chapters 2 and 3; and by Brian W. Kernighan and P. J. Plauger, *The Elements of Programming Style* (New York: McGraw-Hill Book Company, 1974). The latter note that "Floating point numbers are like sandpiles: every time you move one, you lose a little sand and pick up a little dirt" (p. 92).

malized form, since two leading zeros are present in the fraction. Normalization results in 0.123400×10^3, which is arithmetically equivalent. The normalized form is preferred since it is easier to use and allows greater precision.

The format of floating-point fields is the same for the sign and characteristic regardless of length. The format of the fraction varies depending on the length. Short and long formats are similar. Extended format uses two long format fields as a single field. This concatenation of fields is analogous to using two scientific notation numbers to represent a single number: $0.12 \times 10^4 + 0.34 \times 10^2$ is the same as 0.1234×10^4. The second component contains the least significant portion of the fraction. Although the number of digits involved is much larger, the same principle is used in extended format floating point. Figure 5-6 compares these three floating-point formats. Internal floating point is not to be confused with external floating point. External floating point is a data entry convention that allows data to be specified in a form similar to scientific notation. It is typically used for input and output of floating-point data.

Converting Floating Point to Decimal

To convert a hexadecimal floating-point field to its decimal equivalent, four steps are needed.

1. *Determine the sign.* If the first hex digit is less than 8 (0 through 7), a positive number is present. If it is greater than 7 (8 through F), a negative number is present.
2. *Determine the value of the characteristic.* This is done by ignoring the sign bit and subtracting 64 from the first byte. Bits 1 through 7 are used for the characteristic (bit 0 is used for the sign). The first hex digit contains the sign bit and the 3 high-order bits of the characteristic. The second hex digit contains the 4 low-order bits of the characteristic. If the first hex digit is greater than 7 (8 through F), subtract x80 from the first byte to obtain the characteristic. If the first hex digit is less than 8 (0 through 7), the first byte may be interpreted as the characteristic, without any subtraction. For example, suppose that the first byte is x6A. The value of the characteristic is x6A or 106. If the first byte were xB0, then xB0 − x80 = x3C. The value of the characteristic is x3C or 60.

   The raw characteristic value is then interpreted according to the excess-64 convention. This is done by subtracting 64 (x40) from the raw characteristic value. The result is an exponent of 16. The fraction field is multiplied by 16 raised to this exponent. For example, a characteristic of x6A (106) indicates that the fractional field is multiplied by 16^{42} ($106 - 64 = 42$). A characteristic of x30 (48) indicates that the fractional field is multiplied by 16^{-16} ($48 - 64 = -16$). Characteristic values greater than 64 (x40) indicate numbers whose absolute value is greater than or equal 1.0. Characteristic values less than 64 (x40) indicate fractional numbers whose absolute value is less than 1.0.
3. *Convert the hexadecimal fraction.* Appendix B gives conversions for hexadecimal fractions. If the fraction is not in the table, it may be converted as follows:

(a) View the fraction as a hexadecimal integer and convert it to a decimal integer.
(b) Divide this result by 16,777,216 (16^6) for short format, or by 72,057,594,037,927,936 (16^{14}) for long format.

The result of this division is the decimal fraction equivalent of the hexadecimal fraction. The short format will produce up to 7 significant decimal digits, the long format up to 16 significant decimal digits. Digits of lower significance are spurious and should be ignored. If an extended number is to be converted, the component long format numbers must be converted separately and then concatenated to obtain the answer.

4. *Evaluate the component fields*. Once the sign, characteristic, and fraction have been found, the value of the floating-point field can be calculated. The sign will indicate that it is positive or negative; the characteristic, the power of 16 to multiply by; and the fraction, the specific quantity represented.

Example 9

Converting a short floating-point number, xC73F20CA, to decimal:

```
      C7     3F 20 CA
      --     --------
       ↑         ↖
Sign and       Fraction
characteristic
```

1. Determine sign:

xC > x7 negative

2. Evaluate characteristic:

C7	to strip sign bit
−80	subtract x80
47	to find true exponent
−40	subtract x40
7	exponent is +7

3. Convert hexadecimal fraction to decimal fraction:

x3F20CA = 4 137 162 convert to equivalent decimal integer

$$\frac{4\ 137\ 162}{16\ 777\ 216} = 0.2465941 \qquad \text{divide by } 16^6$$

4. Evaluate result:

$$C73F20CA = -16^7 \times 0.2465941 = -66{,}194{,}599.68$$

Converting Decimal to Floating Point

There are seven steps needed to determine the equivalent internal hexadecimal floating-point format of a decimal value. An example follows the description of these steps.

1. *Scale the decimal number to be converted to the maximum number of digits representable.* This is a maximum of 7 decimal digits for short floating point, or 15 decimal digits for long floating point. Round to the nearest least significant digit. Note the magnitude of the original number in a power of 10. The magnitude will be used in step 6. For example, 1,234,567,890.0 becomes $1{,}234{,}568.0 \times 10^3$ and 0.030 089 432 217 becomes 3.00894×10^{-2}, for conversion to short floating point.
2. *Convert the integer portion of the decimal to a hexadecimal integer.* If the maximum number of hexadecimal digits is present in the integer, skip to step 4.
3. *Convert the fractional portion of the decimal to a hexadecimal fraction.* If an exact equivalent is not found in Appendix B, use the following iterative method. Multiply the fractional part of the decimal number by 16. Convert the integer portion of the result to hexadecimal and append this digit to converted integer portions of previous multiplications. Multiply again, but ignore the integer portion of the previous result. Continue this process until the fraction result is zero, or one more than the allowed number of hexadecimal digits has been obtained (either 7 or 15). The number of integer digits obtained in step 2 must be included in this comparison. For example, if three digits were obtained from step 1, four more fractional digits could be placed into a short format number. Therefore, four fractional digits should be converted. If the integer exceeds the allowed size, it should be rounded to fit.
4. *Round the resulting hexadecimal string to 6 or 14 hexadecimal digits.* If the last digit is less than 8, it is dropped. If it is greater than or equal to 8, add one to the next most significant digit and drop the last digit.
5. *Concatenate the integer and the fraction, then normalize the result.* If the result digit string contains leading zeros, shift the radix point to the right until there are no leading zeros. For example, x0.000AF2 becomes x0.AF2000, for a shift right of three positions. If the result digit string contains leading integer digits, shift the radix point to the left of the most significant digit. For example, x2F.BA46 becomes x0.2FBA46, for a shift left of two positions. If the radix was shifted, the value of the exponent must change. If the shift was to the left, the exponent is more positive. If the shift was to the right, the exponent is more negative. Thus a right shift of three positions will increase the exponent by 3; a left shift of two positions will decrease the exponent by 2.

6. *Calculate the value of the normalized exponent.* If no scaling was performed (see step 1), the exponent is as derived in step 5. Simply add or subtract this value from 64 to convert to excess 64 notation. For example,

$$64 + (+3) = 67 = \text{x43} \quad \text{or} \quad 64 + (-2) = 62 = \text{x3E}$$

However, if scaling was performed in step 1, additional calculation must be done. The power of 10 extracted must be converted to hexadecimal and multiplied by the partially converted number (the result of step 5). The product must then be truncated, rounded, and normalized. Following the example in step 1, by scaling we have

$$1{,}234{,}568 \times 10^3 = \text{x12D688} \times \text{x3E8} = \text{x49960340}$$

Truncating to six most significant digits gives us

$$\text{x49960340} \simeq \text{x499603} \times 16^2$$

Normalizing yields

$$\text{x499603} \times 16^2 = \text{x0.499603} \times 16^8$$

The exponent is +8. Therefore, the excess-64 exponent is

$$64 + 8 = 72 = \text{x48}$$

The final short-form floating-point value is x48499603.

7. *Append the sign bit.* If the number to be converted is positive, the exponent value may be used as is. If the number to be converted is negative, add x80 to the exponent.

A note of caution. There are decimal fractions that cannot be accurately converted to hexadecimal. For example $^1/_{10}$ (0.1) in decimal results in a nonterminating hexadecimal fraction of x0.1999999 . . . , just as $^1/_3$ results in a nonterminating decimal fraction of 0.33333 . . . .

Example 10

Converting decimal number −638.53016 to floating-point format:

1. Integer to hex integer: 638 = ×27E
2. Fraction to hex fraction (need 4 digits):

```
      .53016
   ×     16
8 <[8].48256
```

```
      .48256
    ×     16
7 ⟨ 7.72096
      .72096
    ×     16
B ⟨ 11.53536
      .53536
    ×     16
8 ⟨ 8.56576
```

∴ .53016 ≃ .87B8

3. Round: 27E.87B8

   ```
   27E.87B8
   +      8
   --------
   27E.87C
   ```

4. Normalize: .27E87C — shift radix left by 3 — Exponent is +3

5. Convert exponent to excess 64:
   64 + 3 = 67 = x43

6. Append sign bit: since negative, add x80

   ```
     x43
   + x80
   -----
     xC3
   =====
   ```

Final result as short-format floating point:

$$-638.53016 = \text{C327E87C}$$

5.5 ASSEMBLY LANGUAGE ANALYSIS

> Q. Anyone know what the KISS rule is?
> A. Sure, "Keep It Simple, Stupid."
> A. Isn't it, "Keep It Stupid, Simple"?
>
> *Anon.*

Finding the Abending Statement

Locating an assembly language statement once the object module displacement has been calculated is straightforward. Simply scan down the assembler listing of CSECTs under the column titled LOC. The hexadecimal displacement of each instruction relative to the start of the object module (CSECT) is printed in this column. When the address under LOC matches the object module displacement, stop—you have found the statement involved with the abend.

Finding the Abending Data Fields

Once the abending instruction has been located in the assembler listing, the operands may be analyzed. If implicit format addressing was coded, the explicit format addresses are given under the column titled OBJECT CODE. The cross-reference generated by the assembler is useful to trace a particular field's usage and locate its definition. The section Object Code Analysis explains how to find operands in the main storage dump using the explicit address format.

There are no intervening conventions that complicate finding data in data structures in assembly language programs. The logic of the program at hand may require complex data structures (multilevel tables, storage overlays, dynamically allocated storage, etc.). However, only basic addressing conventions may be used. Since any such data structures are application dependent, not language dependent, they cannot be described here. Their usage and structure must be inferred from the actual code and available documentation.

There is a simple programming technique to aid location of program storage fields in a dump. Define a text field in the source code with an appropriate message as the first and last storage definition statements. Fields, buffers, tables, and so on, can be labeled in a similar fashion. When the load module is printed in the dump, these messages are readily found by scanning the right-hand text column of the dump. The start and extent of a program's storage may be found at a glance. Figure 5-7 shows how such labels would appear. These program storage delimiters could be coded as

```
DC CL32 'PROBPROG STORAGE STARTS HERE'
   •
   •
   •
DC CL32 'PROBPROG STORAGE ENDS HERE'
```

Finding Parameter Lists

Because of the flexibility of assembly language, the interface conventions for user-written subroutines are program dependent. However, interfaces with supervisor modules and called programs written in other languages must follow standard linkage convention (with the exception of PL/I). Most assembly language programs follow these conventions as well.

The standard linkage convention requires register 1 to point to a list of fullword addresses, each address pointing to a unique item in the parameter list. The high-order byte of the last item in the list is set to x80 (the high-order byte of preceding items is x00). Register 1 of REGS AT ENTRY TO ABEND or of a recent SA (save area) may point to a parameter list of interest. See Save Area Trace under Dump Components for more information about linkage conventions and save area usage.

If data are passed into the program via the PARM parameter of the EXEC statement, register 1 at entry to the main program will point to the data given in PARM. The first SA will show this address in R1. The address in R1 points to a 2-byte length field, which

```
124420 D7D9D6C2 D7D9D6C7 40E2E3D6 D9C1C7C5   40E2E3C1 D9E3E240 C8C5D9C5 40404040   *PROBPROG STORAGE STARTS HERE     *
124440 00000000 00000001 00000002 00000003   00000001 00000002 00000003 00000004   *................................*
124460 00000000 00000000 00000000 00000000   00000000 00000000 00000000 00000000   *................................*
     LINES 124480-1247E0 SAME AS ABOVE
124800 00000001 00000002 00000000 00000000   00000012 00007FFF 00000000 00000000   *................................*
124820 00000000 00000000 00000000 00000000   00000000 FFFFFFFF 00000000 00000000   *................................*
124840 D7D9D6C2 D7D9D6C7 40E2E3D6 D9C1C7C5   40C5D5C4 40C8C5D9 C5404040 40404040   *PROBPROG STORAGE ENDS HERE       *
```

FIGURE 5-7 Program Storage Labels

gives the length of the parameter string in binary. The actual parameter string, up to 100 bytes, immediately follows the halfword length field.

Debugging Tools

Execution Traces

There are no predefined facilities in IBM assembly language to trace execution logic and print the contents of selected fields as execution progresses. However, given the inherent flexibility of assembly language, programming such traces is simple if somewhat tedious.

The simplest means to effect a trace is to issue a WTO (write to operator) macro (SVC 35) with ROUTCDE = 11. This will direct the WTO message to a predefined JES data set (e.g., SYSOUT = A). The destination data set for this ROUTCDE (programmer information) is defined at system generation. The advantages of a WTO trace are:

- No DCB, OPEN, or CLOSE macros needed
- No additional JCL
- Easy to insert for debugging
- Easy to remove when no longer required

The first 8 bytes of a WTO message are usually a message code. Depending on your installation's standards, you may want to use a message code or your module name. For example,

```
WTO 'PROBPROG START MAIN LOOP',ROUTCDE=11
```

For more information about WTO, see *Supervisor Services*.

For programs that are run under TSO, the TPUT/TGET macro (SVC 93) allows for line-by-line input and output to the TSO user's terminal. The TPUT/TGET macro is functionally similar to the COBOL ACCEPT and DISPLAY verbs. The macro could be used to output trace messages and to accept input for further debugging logic. For more information about TPUT/TGET, see *OS/VS2 TCAM Logic*.

If additional flexibility in tracing is desired, the programmer can construct a DCB for SYSOUT data set, OPEN the DCB, and then format and write trace records as needed. The format and write logic would be inserted at points of interest in the program. This process may be simplified by coding a subroutine that will perform tracing functions. At each trace point in the calling program, a trace parameter list would be built and a call to the trace utility executed. A thumbnail specification for such a utility follows. The parameter list and output format are intended to suggest how such a utility might function. The address of the variable-length parameter list would be placed in R1. The list would contain the following:

Byte	*Field/Usage*
0	Flag byte, used to pass control information: x00 Print data in this list. x01 Issue SNAP dump macro. x02 Close output data set. x03 Output date and time. x04 Output to SYSOUT. x05 Output to disk.
1, 3	Message text address. The address of a message to output with the trace, relevant to the particular trace point.
4, 7	Last instruction address in the calling module.
8, 11	CSECT start address.
12, 15	Address of a print list. List of data fields to print. The list would contain a variable number of entries, one for each field to print: 0–7 Field name. x80 in first byte indicates end of data field list. 8–11 Field start address. 12–13 Field length (bytes). 14 Print format flag: x00 Hex x01 Character

This data structure could be produced by a user-written macro. The parameter list fields would be processed as follows:

- *Flag byte:* Could be used to invoke related trace or dump facilities, such as SNAP.
- *Message text address:* The message terminator could be the last two consecutive blanks (x4040), found scanning backward from the end of the field.
- *Last instruction address and CSECT start address:* Used to calculate displacement into the object module issuing the trace. Also allows the CSECT module name (CSECT address plus xC) to be displayed.
- *Data field list:* For each item on the list, the following processing would take place:
  (a) The field name would be printed.
  (b) The contents of main storage starting at the field address and continuing for the number of bytes in field length would be printed as indicated by the print format flag. Hex and character are two common formats. Other options depending on the field format may be useful.

The output of the routine might appear as shown in Figure 5-8. Using indentation in the message text which corresponds to logical nesting in the program is often useful for trace analysis.

```
 •
 •
 •
>MAIN LOOP  PROBPROG  003AF0  083124  13:30:75  27483
 FIELDA  F0F0F0F0F0F0  FIELDB  4040404040CA3B90
 >TABLE LOOKUP  PROBPROG  004CD8
     >READ TABLE  PROBPROG  004DE0
       >READ FILE A  PROBPROG  004FBA
          AKEYVAL  F1F2F3F4
          AKEYVAL  F2F1F9F0
          AKEYVAL  F3F0F4F2
       >READ FILE B  PROBPROG  0050BC
          BKEYVAL  C0C1C2C3  F3F0F4F2
       >MERGE LOGIC  MERGESUB  0003A0
       ...TAKING NEVER CAN HAPPEN BRANCH
       ...ISSUING SNAP MERGESUB  000BF8
     >READ TABLE  PROBPROG  004DE0
 •
 •
 •
```

FIGURE 5-8 Assembly Language Trace Output Example

Online Debugging

The TEST command of TSO allows:

- Step-through execution of a program
- Dynamic alteration of registers, data, or instructions
- Display of certain supervisor control blocks

TEST is oriented toward assembly language programs. Familiarity with assembly language addressing is needed to make use of many TEST subcommands. For more information about TEST, see *OS/VS2 TSO Command Language Reference*.

Program-Initiated Dumps

Dumps are easily produced by an assembly language program. To produce a dump without causing termination of execution, issue the SNAP macro. The SNAP macro requires an open DCB and a DD statement. The DDname for the SNAP output can be any name except SYSUDUMP, SYSABEND, or SYSMDUMP. The content of a SNAP dump is not controlled by the system parameters that control ABEND dumps. The control blocks and portions of main storage dumped are selected by parameters specified in the SNAP macro instruction.

The ABEND macro may also be issued. It causes task termination to be invoked, a standard dump (using system dump parameters) to be printed, and optionally, gives a user completion code. An ABEND may be forced by purposely causing a program check interrupt. For example, x00 may be moved to the next instruction's operation code, resulting in an 0C1. An instruction can be altered to an execute (x44) which specifies itself as the object instruction, resulting in an 0C3. For more information about SNAP and ABEND, see *Supervisor Services*.

Controlling Abends

Two macro instructions are available which allow the assembly language programmer to modify the abnormal termination environment. ESTAE (extended STAE—specify task abnormal exit) and SPIE (specify program interruption exit) provide a means to intercept impending ABENDs. The flow chart in Figure 5-9 shows the general relationship of these macros. Both are used to provide the address of a user recovery routine to be

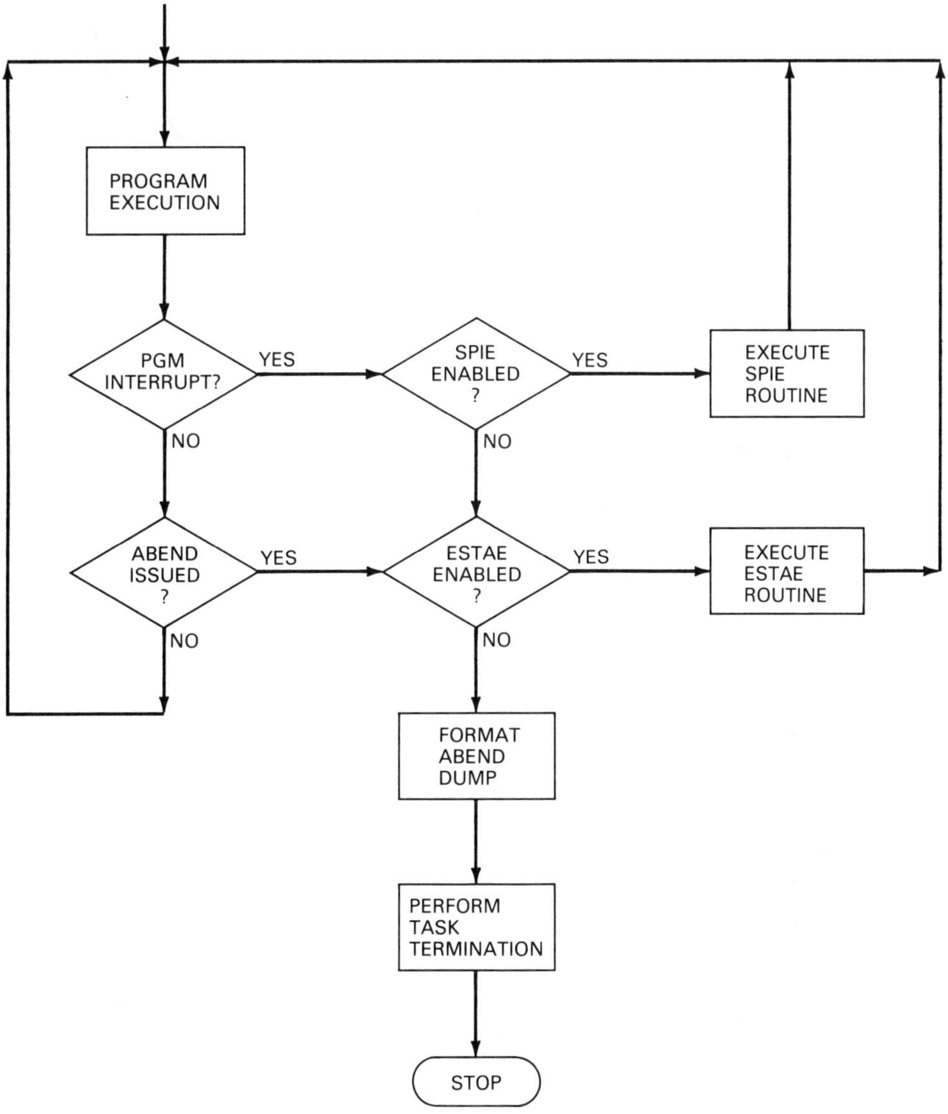

FIGURE 5-9 SPIE/ESTAE Logic

executed when an ABEND is issued. The ESTAI parameter of the ATTACH macro provides the same function for subtasks created by ATTACH. The PSW bits that enable program check interrupts may also be controlled by the assembly language programmer. See 3.2, 0Cx Abend Diagnostics, Controlling Interrupts. For more information about ESTAE, SPIE, and ATTACH, see *Supervisor Services*.

Assembler Options for Debugging

The following assembler options are suggested to provide useful debugging information.

ALIGN	Check all data for correct alignment. Create error message if improper boundary found. Default option.
ESD	Create external symbol dictionary. Default option.
MLOGIC	Expand and number all macro definitions.
RLD	Create relocation dictionary. Default option.
XREF(full)	Create a cross-reference listing of all symbols used in the assembly, including those defined but not referenced.

5.6 COBOL ANALYSIS

> Just don't get too complicated, Eddie. When a guy gets complicated he's unhappy, and when he's unhappy—his luck runs out. . . .
>
> *Raymond Chandler*
> *The Blue Dahlia*

Finding the Abending Statement

Locate the object module displacement as described under 5.2, Basic Techniques. The statement that corresponds to this address is found by examining the compiler output generated by the CLIST or PMAP option. CLIST (condensed listing) gives the statement number and object module displacement of every COBOL verb in the program. PMAP (program map) results in listing very similar to the output of the Assembler. It shows how each verb was translated into object code. The verb and its statement number are followed by object code explicit form instructions. For most debugging purposes the CLIST format is sufficient. In the CLIST format, the source statement number of a verb (e.g., MOVE, ADD, etc.) is followed by a hexadecimal displacement. This displacement is the address of the first instruction that was generated from this verb, since one verb results in many instructions. Scan the CLIST for a pair of verbs whose object code addresses immediately precede and follow the object module displacement.

The first verb of this pair is the verb associated with the abend. For example, suppose that the object module displacement was x2A28 and a portion of the CLIST showed

```
906 IF 002A24     907  MOVE 002A40
```

The IF statement on line 906 is associated with the abend since the object displacement is greater than the IFs and less than the MOVEs. COBOL allows more than one verb per statement, so make sure that the correct verb is analyzed.

If a PMAP has been generated and the CLIST is not present, a similar analysis is performed. In the PMAP, scan down the column of object code addresses, third from the left, until you find an address that matches the object module displacement calculated previously. The statement number and verb corresponding to this address will be printed immediately above or on this line and to the left.

If the object module displacement does not fall within the program at hand, or does not match to a particular PMAP displacement, check all calculations, beginning with the load module displacement. Make sure that the listings are current.

The STATE compiler option in conjunction with a SYSDBOUT DD statement will automatically print the abending statement number. See Debugging Tools and Compiler Options below.

Finding the Abending Data Fields

Depending on the particular problem an abend presents, the specific contents of data fields may provide useful debugging information. The data fields of interest may or may not be associated with the abending statement. For example, suppose that an 0C7 abend has occurred and you have determined that statement 906 was at fault. Further suppose that statement 906 was

```
IF A EQUAL B
```

You would want to examine the actual contents of fields A and B to see if either contained invalid data. Upon inspection, suppose you found that A contained invalid data. Just prior to statement 906 was

```
MOVE TABLE (IX) TO A.
```

You may want to examine the contents of TABLE (IX). To do so, you would need to find the current value of IX and determine the offset into TABLE it represents. You may need to examine other fields as well. In any case, the first step is to determine the data name(s) of interest. Once they have been identified, there are two ways to find data fields in the dump: first, by locating the data name in the DMAP section of the compiler listing and using the base and displacement information given there to calculate its effective address; and second, by using the internal name from the PMAP to look up the data name and its base and displacement in the DMAP.

With the first method, scan the third column of the DMAP, titled "SOURCE NAME" for the field of interest. Fields in the DMAP are listed in order of definition. For large programs you may be able to save time by first locating the data name in the cross reference and then estimating its relative position in WORKING-STORAGE.

With the second method (using the internal name) the scan is simplified since the DMAP is listed in internal name order.

Once the field of interest has been located, the entries in the DMAP columns titled BASE and DISPL are the next items to analyze. BASE indicates how COBOL has assigned a base register to the field. DISPL gives the displacement from the base register to the first byte of the field. The entry under BASE requires further analysis.

There are three main types of entries in the BASE column:

1. Entries for control block associated with an FD: for example DCB = nn, FIB = nn. There is one BL assigned to each FD. The 01 level data name which immediately follows this entry points to the buffer for that data set.
2. Entries for data defined within the program's WORKING-STORAGE, for example, BL =1.
3. Entries for data defined outside of the program's WORKING-STORAGE and identified in the LINKAGE SECTION: for example, BLL =3.

The technique used to obtain the base address for a data item with a BL or BLL entry is straightforward. BL and BLL addresses are initialized by a COBOL library subroutine before user-written code begins execution. Separate work areas for BLs and BLLs are established. The first fullword of the work area is the base address for BL1; the second fullword, for BL2; the third, for BL3; and so on. The same convention applies to BLL base addresses.

The displacement of the first BL or BLL "cell" is found under the TGT (task global table) section of the compiler listing. The hexadecimal displacement given on the line BL CELLS is the displacement from the start of the module to the first BL cell. Similarly, the displacement given for BLL CELLS points to the first BLL cell.

A BL or BLL base address is found as follows:

1. Find the BL or BLL displacement in the TGT.
2. Add the displacement to the load module start address. This is the effective address of the BL or BLL work area.
3. The first 4 bytes of this area are for BL1 or BLL1. Count over as many fullwords (4 bytes) as needed to find the BL or BLL of interest. For example, BL4 is at the fourth fullword, BLL3 is at the third fullword from the BL or BLL start address.

A second technique may be used to locate the base address of a data item from a BL. Following the MEMORY MAP, LITERAL POOL, and PGT sections, a short section titled REGISTER ASSIGNMENT is printed. This section indicates which general register is associated with a BL (base locator). The entry

```
REG6    BL =3
```

means that general register 6 is the base register for any data item with a BL =3 entry under BASE.

There is a third method to determine the address of the first BL or BLL cell. Three items are needed: (1) the BL or BLL TGT offset as described above, (2) the SA TGT offset, and (3) the contents of register 13. Register 13 usually points to the problem program's save area. The save area is the first item in the TGT and its offset is given by the TGT SA entry. The first BL or BLL address is calculated as follows:

Register 13 address
− SA offset
+ BL(L) offset

= First BL(L) cell address

In programs with large WORKING-STORAGE sections, several BLs may be associated with the same register. During execution, base addresses are loaded into these registers as needed. Therefore, the contents of the register associated with a BL may not be the base address of a given data item at the time the dump was taken. The effective address of a data item is then calculated as follows:

Base address (from BL CELL, BLL CELL, or register assigned)
+ Displacement (from DMAP or PMAP)
= Effective address

The length and type of the data item are given in the DMAP as well. Items addressed by a BL base will be found in the main storage dump of the load module that defines them. Items addressed by a BLL base will be found in the main storage dump of calling program—not in the dump of the load module that defines them in a LINKAGE SECTION. BLL-based addressing is also used for SD (sort division) items and items passed to or from an internal SORT.

There is a simple programming technique to aid location of program storage fields in a dump. Define a text field in the source code with an appropriate message as the first and last storage definition statements. Fields, buffers, tables, and so on, can be labeled in a similar fashion. When the load module is printed in the dump, these messages are readily found by scanning the right-hand text column of the dump. The start and extent of a program's storage may be found at a glance. Figure 5-7 shows how such labels would appear. These program storage delimiters could be coded as

```
01 FILLER PIC X(32) VALUE   'PROBPROG STORAGE STARTS HERE'
      •
      •
      •
01 FILLER PIC X(32) VALUE   'PROBPROG STORAGE ENDS HERE'
```

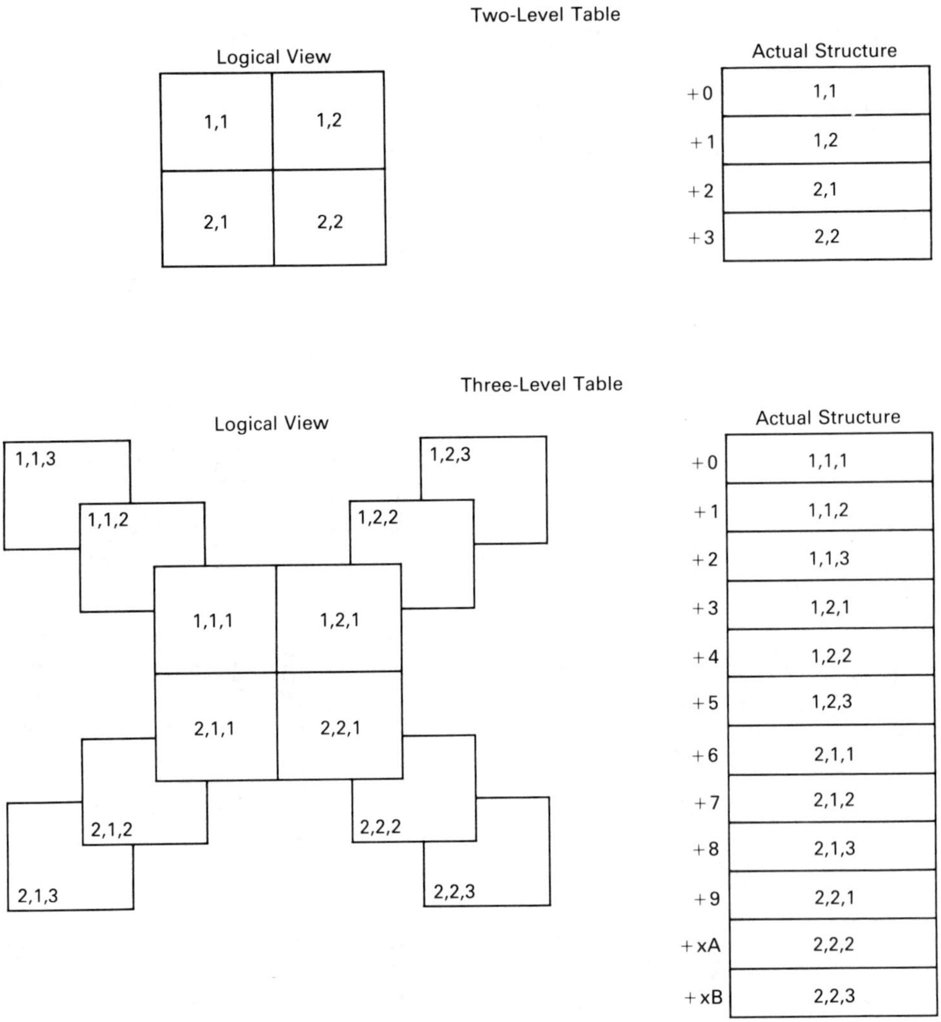

FIGURE 5-10 COBOL Table Structure

Finding Table Entries

COBOL tables are stored in row-major order. This means that a table entry is assigned an actual storage location by varying the rightmost occurs value first. Figure 5-10 illustrates this relationship for a two- and a three-level table, each consisting of 1-byte entries.

The effective address calculation outlined above is insufficient for finding entries in table data structures where there are multiple occurrences of an entry. The additional steps required to find the entry pointed to by current indexes or subscripts are:

1. If indexing is used, locate the index cells associated with the table. This will provide a physical displacement.
2. If subscripting is used, locate the subscript fields using the BL or BLL analysis given above. Convert the relative occurrence number into a physical displacement.
3. Sum the physical displacements to find the current entry.

If indexing is in use (the table definition specifies the INDEXED BY clause) the indexes are stored in a work area. This work area is initialized and updated by COBOL generated code. There is one fullword in the index cell area for every index name defined by the program. The cells are assigned as indexes are defined; the first statement that defines an index is assigned the first fullword index cell; the second definition, the second cell; and so on.

The address of the first index cell is found under the TGT section of the compiler listing. The hexadecimal displacement given on the line INDEX CELLS is the displacement from the start of the module to the first index cell. The index cells contain a displacement in bytes which is equivalent to the current logical index value. Indexes are base relative—an index of 0 points the first entry. For example, if the twentieth entry of a table of 10 byte entries was the current item, its associated index cell would contain x000000BE (decimal 190) since $(20 - 1) \times 10 = 190$. The current displacement into an indexed table is derived by summing the contents of all index cells associated with the table. The inverse of this calculation, determining the logical (occurs) value of a physical displacement, is given by

$$I = \frac{D}{L} + 1$$

where

I = logical (occurrence) value of an index
D = current physical displacement (from an index cell)
L = length in bytes of a single occurrence of this level and all subordinate levels

In the example above,

$$\begin{aligned} I &= \frac{\text{xBE}}{10} + 1 \\ &= \frac{190}{10} + 1 \\ &= 20 \end{aligned}$$

If subscripting is in use, working storage fields are defined to hold subscripts. Subscripts are logical (occurrence) values, not physical displacements as indexes are.

The subscripts in use with a table must be determined from context. COBOL does not provide any special processing for subscripts. To determine the physical displacement represented by a set of subscripts, first locate the subscript fields and determine their content. The physical displacement they represent is given by the formula

$$D = \sum_{i=1}^{N} L_i(S_i - 1)$$

where

D = current physical displacement from start of the table
N = number of levels subscripted; $1 \leq N \leq 3$
L_i = length in bytes of a single occurrence of level i and all subordinate levels
S_i = current value of the subscript associated with ith level
i = the number, reading left to right, of an occurs level. Thus C is the third occurs level (i = 3) of TABLE(A,B,C).

For example, assume a three-level table defined as follows:

```
01  TABLE.
    05  LEVEL-1 OCCURS 3.
        10  LEVEL-2 OCCURS 4.
            15  LEVEL-3 OCCURS 100.
                20  FLD-A PIC X(5).
                20  FLD-B PIC 9(5).
01  TABLE-SUBS COMP.
    05 SUB-1 PIC 9(2).
    05 SUB-2 PIC 9(2).
    05 SUB-3 PIC 9(3).
```

Assume that

SUB-1 = x0003
SUB-2 = x0001
SUB-3 = x005F

and that SUB-1 is used for LEVEL-1; SUB-2 for LEVEL-2; and SUB-3 for LEVEL-3. The lengths of each level are

$$\begin{aligned} L_1 &= 4 \times 100 \times 10 \\ &= 4000 \\ L_2 &= 100 \times 10 \\ &= 1000 \\ L_3 &= 10 \end{aligned}$$

Then

$$D = \sum_{i=1}^{N} L_i(S_i - 1)$$

$$= 4000(3 - 1) + 1000(1 - 1) + 10(95 - 1)$$

$$= 8940 \text{ or x22EC}$$

With the physical displacement derived from either index or subscript analysis, the current displacement and its effective address can be calculated as follows:

Base address of the table (BL, BLL, or register)
\+ Displacement from base (DMAP)
\+ <u>*D* (displacement of current entry)</u>
= Effective address of current entry

Finding Parameter Lists

Data passed to and from called subroutines by the CALL 'SUB' USING PARM-LIST construct may be found in main storage in a different manner than that used in the DMAP/BL/BLL analysis. COBOL calling/called interfaces follow standard IBM linkage conventions. This means that register 1 is used to point to a list of fullword addresses. Each address in the list points to a unique item in the parameter list. The high-order byte of the last item in the list is set to x80 (the high-order byte of preceding items is x00) to indicate the end of the list. For example, the statement

```
CALL 'SUBPROG' USING FIELD-1
                     FIELD-2
                     FIELD-3.
```

would result in the parameter list shown in Figure 5-11. Note that one address is present for each entry in the USING list. This address is the effective address of the start of the field—elementary or group item. These items could also be found by the DMAP/BL analysis. On the called program side, the corresponding items in the LINKAGE SECTION could be found by looking up their names in the DMAP and using the BLL analysis. However, the BLL CELLs of the called program are not initialized until the program is actually called.

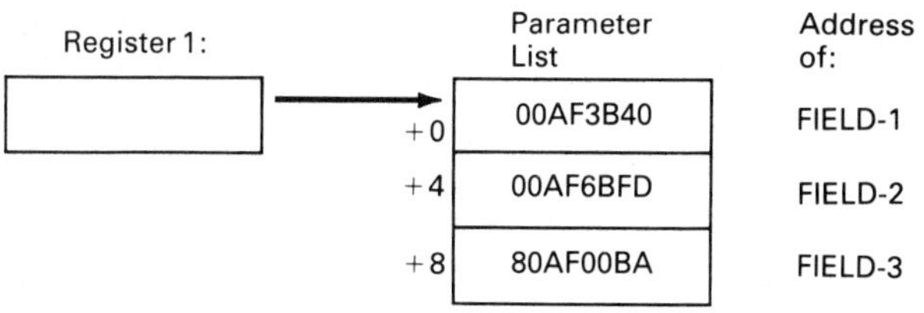

FIGURE 5-11 COBOL Parameter Lists

Occasionally, the parameter list BL or BLL cells are inadvertently overlaid. Comparing addresses for consistency may indicate the cause of an abend. Register 1 of REGS AT ENTRY TO ABEND or of a recent SA (save area) may point to a parameter list of interest. See 4.2, Dump Components, Save Area Trace, for more information about linkage conventions and save area usage.

If data are passed into the program via the PARM parameter of the EXEC statement, register 1 at entry to the main program will point to the data given in PARM. The first SA will show this address in R1. The address in R1 points to a 2-byte length field, which gives the length of the parameter string in binary. The actual parameter string, up to 100 bytes, immediately follows the halfword length field.

Debugging Tools

Execution Traces

The COBOL verbs DISPLAY, EXHIBIT, TRACE, and ON provide useful execution-time traces. No OPEN or CLOSE, FD, or SELECT statements are required. However, compiler-generated OPEN and CLOSE processing is done for each execution of these statements. Their convenience incurs greater processing time.

- DISPLAY writes a variable number of text messages and data items on any sequential output device. SYSOUT is commonly used. DISPLAY may be used at any point in the program.
- EXHIBIT provides similar capabilities to DISPLAY. In addition, logic can be generated by COBOL to output data fields when their content is changed. The COBOL data name may also be automatically output with the field contents.
- TRACE causes a paragraph or section name to be printed each time it is entered. This facility may be switched on and off during program execution by the READY or RESET qualifiers.
- An ON verb is similar to an IF statement, but performs automatic counting.

There are three additional COBOL features that facilitate selective execution of traces and debugging logic: the WITH DEBUGGING MODE statement, USE FOR DEBUGGING declaratives, and DEBUG packets.

- The SOURCE COMPUTER WITH DEBUGGING MODE statement acts as an inline compiler switch. When present, any source statement with a D in column seven is compiled. When not present, source statements with a D in column 7 are treated as comments.
- USE FOR DEBUGGING declaratives specify code to be executed whenever a specified procedure, file, or working storage item is referenced. When executed, current program-related data are made available to the declarative. These data include the name, statement number, and contents of the file, working storage item, or procedure whose reference resulted in the execution of the declarative. Com-

pilation of USE FOR DEBUGGING declaratives is controlled by the DEBUG compiler option.

- DEBUG "packets." The execution of any paragraph can be superseded by coding a DEBUG replacement for it. The key word DEBUG is coded in column 1, followed by the paragraph name to be overridden in column 8.

Additional trace facilities are available through compiler options. COBOL will print the source statement number involved with an abend if:

- The STATE option is specified at compile time.
- A SYSDBOUT DD statement is placed in the job step.

A trace of the paragraph names executed prior to the abend can also be obtained if:

- The FLOW option is specified at compile time.
- A SYSDBOUT DD statement is placed in job step.

Both trace facilities also print the PROGRAM-ID, the system or user completion code, and the last PSW. The compiler debug options and trace statements are not allowed under certain of IBM's application environments (e.g., CICS). In any case, they should not be used in production programs, due to their relatively high execution overhead. For more information about COBOL execution tracing facilities, see *COBOL Programmer's Guide*.

Online Debugging

COBOL programs may be executed under the TEST command of TSO (see 9.9, Assembly Language Analysis, Online Debugging). However, TEST is not well suited to the needs of most COBOL programmers. An IBM program product called TESTCOB provides an excellent online debugging facility for COBOL. However, it is an IBM-licensed program and is not available in all installations. TESTCOB runs under TSO and provides:

- Easily set break points. Execution may be stopped at any point in the program to be resumed on command or upon a prespecified condition.
- Ability to list any portion of storage or data buffers using data names instead of addresses.
- Execution traces similar to the TRACE verb.
- Commands to display source code statements.
- Commands to modify the value of any working storage item.

Symbolic debugging output required for TESTCOB is written to a data set defined by the SYSUT5 DD statement in the compile step. This output will not be created if USE FOR DEBUGGING or WITH DEBUGGING MODE statements are present. For more information about TESTCOB, see *IBM OS COBOL Interactive Debug Terminal User's Guide and Reference*.

Program-Initiated Dumps

Two kinds of dumps may be obtained from COBOL programs. A "symbolic dump" showing COBOL-generated work areas and user-defined working storage may be obtained when:

- An abend occurs.
- A particular program is called.
- A particular paragraph or verb is executed.

The symbolic dump shows:

- The current record associated with an FD, SD, or RD
- The current or abending statement number
- A formatted dump of TGT (task global table) fields
- A formatted dump of working storage, showing individual table entries

To obtain a symbolic dump, the program is compiled with the SYMDMP option. Symbolic debugging output is written to a data set defined by a SYSUT5 DD statement in the compile step. This output will not be created if USE FOR DEBUGGING or WITH DEBUGGING MODE statements are present. The creation of the dump is specified by control statements read in under a SYSDBG DD statement included in the problem program's job step. The control statements determine when the dump will be produced and what portions of the load module will be dumped. For more information about the COBOL symbolic dump, see *COBOL Programmer's Guide*.

An ABEND dump may be obtained, and the step terminated, with a user return code by calling a COBOL library subroutine ILBOABN0 that invokes ABEND. The call is coded as

```
01 USER-COMPLETION-CODE      PIC S9(3) COMP.
                 .
                 .
                 .
   MOVE 123 TO USER-COMPLETION-CODE.
   CALL "ILBOABN0" USING USER-COMPLETION-CODE.
```

An ABEND dump produced will be formatted according to installation dump parameters.

Controlling Abends

There are no COBOL facilities that facilitate execution-time alteration of the abnormal terminal environment.

Compiler Options for Debugging

The following compiler options are suggested to provide useful debugging information.

CLIST	Produces verb/statement/displacement list necessary to locate abending statement.
COUNT	Causes the number of times each verb within a procedure is executed to be counted. The counts are printed when execution ends. Both the SYSDBOUT and SYSCOUNT DD statements are required. May be useful for diagnosing loops, incorrect logic, or inadequate testing.
DEBUG	Controls compilation of USE FOR DEBUGGING declaratives. DEBUG activates these declaratives, NODEBUG deactivates them.
DMAP	Produces base and displacement list necessary to locate abending or other data fields.
FLOW=nn	Causes list of last nn paragraph names to be printed in the event of an abend.
PMAP	Produces an object code listing that is formatted like output from the assembler.
STATE	Causes the statement number of an abending statement to be printed out when a SYSDBOUT DD statement is specified.
SXREF	Produces cross-reference and procedure names of data names sorted by name.
SYMDMP	Allows for dynamic list of symbolic dump.
TEST	Required if program is to be executed under TESTCOB (IBM OS COBOL interactive debug). Overrides FLOW, STATE, and SYMDMP.
XREF	Produces a two-part cross-reference of data names and procedure names. The list is printed in source order (first defined, first printed).

5.7 FORTRAN ANALYSIS

Non sunt multiplicanda entia praeter neccesitatum.
Do not complicate things more than necessary.

"Occam's Razor"
Occam, c. 1300

Finding the Abending Statement

Identify the object module and locate the object module displacement as outlined in 5.2, Basic Techniques. The steps needed to find the statement from the object module displacement depend on which FORTRAN compiler was used—G or H.

FORTRAN G

The object code listing generated by the compiler option LIST provides instruction offsets, statement numbers, and generated code in explicit form. The leftmost column of the LIST output is titled LOCATION and contains the displacement into the object module for each instruction. Scan down this column until an address equal to the object module displacement is found.

The instruction on this line was generated from the statement involved in the abend. Scan up from this line in the second column from the left, titled STA NUM (statement number). The first entry in the STA NUM column, preceding the instruction just located, is the number of the source statement involved in the abend.

If the MAP option was specified without LIST, a condensed listing of displacements and statement numbers is generated. This output is called the STATEMENT LABEL MAP. The statement number of each noncontinued line is preceded by a hexadecimal displacement. This displacement is the address of the first instruction that was generated from this statement. Since one statement results in many instructions, scan the MAP for a pair of statements whose LOCATION addresses precede and follow the object module displacement. The first statement of this pair is the statement associated with the abend. For example, suppose that the object module displacement was x0340 and a portion of the MAP showed

```
LOCATION STA NUM LABEL LOCATION STA NUM LABEL
00031A      350           00038F      352    128
```

The statement on line 350 is associated with the abend since the object module displacement is greater than 350's and less than 352's.

If the object module displacement does not fall within the program at hand, or does not match a particular LOCATION, check all calculations, beginning with the load module displacement. Make sure that the listings are current.

FORTRAN H

The object code listing generated by the LIST compiler option provides instruction offsets, program labels, object code, explicit form instructions, and variable names. There is no convenient mapping of instructions to source statement numbers, as in the G compiler.

Locating the statement involved with the abend is a two-step process. First, find the instruction in the LIST object code that corresponds to the object module displacement. Second, determine the statement associated with the abending instruction. Several techniques for locating this statement follow.

To locate the instruction corresponding to the object module displacement, scan down the leftmost column of the object code listing. This column contains a six-digit hexadecimal displacement for each instruction generated. When an address that matches the object module displacement is found, stop. The instruction on this line is the one involved with the abend. The second column from the left contains the object code for this instruction. The third column from the left contains the statement label associated with an instruction, if any. A label number is printed for the first instruction generated from a labeled statement. If a label number is not printed, the instruction was either generated by statement without a label or is not the first instruction generated from a labeled statement.

There are several ways to determine which statement is associated with the abending instruction, ranging from quick and dirty to slow and certain. The simplest and quickest is to approximate the statement by comparing source and object code. The most accurate and time consuming is to code debugging labels on every source program statement in the vicinity of the abending instruction, then recompile, link, and execute to recreate the abend. The specific methods follow.

* *Identification by consecutive labeled statements.* The abending instruction may be in a labeled statement immediately followed by another labeled statement. If so, the first statement is the one involved with the abend. Consecutive labeled statements are identified by finding the first label preceding the abending instruction, then checking the source code to see if a labeled statement immediately follows. Figure 5-12 shows how consecutive labels appear in the object code and source listings. Suppose that the object module displacement was xDBA. The label immediately preceding this displacement is 2020. By examining the source listing, it is determined that label 2020 is immediately followed by label 2025. Therefore, any instruction between displacement xDA4 and xDBC has been generated from the statement with label 2020.

* *Approximation by inspection of variable names.* The variable names referenced by each instruction are printed on the far right-hand side of the object code listing. Generally, variables are compiled in source code order. Expressions with complex par-

```
                      •
                      •
000DA4     58         •  70 D 060     2020     L   7,  96(0,13)          I
000DA8     58            60 7 024              L   6,  36(0, 7)

                      •
                      •
                      •
000DBC     50            10 7 02C              ST  1,  44(0, 7)      MAXVAL
000DC0     58            70 D 060     2025     L   7,  96(0,13)
000DC4     58         •  00 7 02C              L   0,  44(0, 7)      MAXVAL
                      •
                      •

                      •
                      •
                      •
       2020         MAXVAL = VECT01(I) * VECT02(J)
       2025         IF(MAXVAL.LE.CURVAL) GOTO 3000
                      •
                      •
                      •
```

FIGURE 5-12 Finding Consecutive Labels

enthetical nesting may cause different orderings. By comparing the pattern of variable names on the right-hand side of the listing to their sequence in the source statements, the statement associated with the abending instruction may be approximated. Typically, the last instruction generated from an assignment type statement, ⟨result⟩ = ⟨expression⟩, is to store the result. The pattern of variable name references in the object code generated for an assignment type statement is by hierarchy of evaluation (lowest to highest), ended by storing the result into its variable.

* *Location with debugging labels.* The general vicinity of the abending statement may be established by approximation (see above) or by looking for the nearest labels immediately preceding and following the object module displacement. Since labels are the only sure way to associate an object module displacement with a source statement in FORTRAN H, if no existing labels bracket the abending statement, debugging labels must be coded. These temporary debugging labels will allow you to locate the abending statement directly. They should be removed when the debugging process is complete. Code debugging labels on every statement in the vicinity of the abending instruction. To avoid confusion, try to resist the temptation to make other program changes. Select debugging label numbers which are easily distinguished from existing label numbers. This eases later removal and minimizes the chance of branching to or deleting the wrong label. Compile the relabeled program. Before attempting to recreate the abend, check the new compiler LIST output. Verify that the suspect object code has been bracketed by the new debugging label numbers.

Link and execute the program with the debugging labels. Although a compile is sufficient to bracket object code within the new debugging labels, there is no guarantee that the new code will be meaningful for interpretation of the old abend. Recreating the abend with the new code is the surest method for an accurate analysis.

Once the abend has been recreated, use the analysis of consecutive labeled statements described above to locate the abending statement. If the debugging labels have not bracketed the abending instruction, reevaluate the vicinity of the source statement associated with the abend, and code more debugging labels. Recompile, link, and execute.

Finding FORTRAN Variables

FORTRAN variables are addressed by the conventional base register and displacement scheme. Neither the G or the H compiler explicitly lists the base register assignments or program variable displacements. The object code listing generated by the LIST option of either compiler provides base register assignments and displacements in the instructions referencing the variable. The technique for finding the base register and displacement is slightly different for the G and H FORTRANs. Both methods yield the starting byte address of a variable.

There is a simple programming technique to aid location of program storage fields in a dump. Define a text field in the source code with an appropriate message as the first and last storage definition statements. Fields, buffers, tables, and so on, can be labeled in a similar fashion. When the load module is printed in the dump, these messages are readily found by scanning the right-hand text column of the dump. The start and extent of a program's storage may be found at a glance. Figure 5-7 shows how such labels would appear. These program storage delimiters could be coded as

```
DIMENSION LBL1(8)
DATA LBL1/'PROBPROG STORAGE STARTS HERE'/
     •
     •
     •
  other data-defining statements
     •
     •
     •
DIMENSION LBL2(8)
DATA LBL2/'PROBPROG STORAGE ENDS HERE'/
```

FORTRAN G

To find the base and displacement for a FORTRAN G variable, scan down the far right-hand column of the object code listing titled BCD OPERAND until the variable name of interest is found. Note that this reference does not have to be associated with the abending statement or instruction. Any reference to the variable of interest will supply the base register and displacement. An explicit form of the instruction referencing this variable is given to left of the variable name. This instruction will contain the base register assigned to the variable and the displacement from this base register. See 5.3, Object Code Analysis, for a detailed description of how to interpret the instruction format. The type and length of the variable can be determined from the source code definition. For example, suppose that a variable DELTA was of interest. A line referencing DELTA might look like this:

```
00103A  1004  2025     L      0,104(0,10)      DELTA
```

The instruction that this line represents is at x103A from the start of the object module, and was generated from source statement 1004, which had the program label 2025. By analyzing this instruction (Load, RX format), the base register is found to be 10 and the displacement is 104 (x68). Therefore, DELTA will be found at R10 + x68. Since an index register of 0 is specified, the index is not used in calculating the effective address.

FORTRAN H

To find the base and displacement for a FORTRAN H variable, scan down the right-hand side of the object code listing. There is no column header on the H listing. Look for the name of the variable of interest. Note that this reference does not have to be associated with the abending statement or instruction. Any reference to the variable of interest will supply the base register and displacement. When found, an explicit form of the instruction referencing this variable is given to the left of the variable name. This instruction will contain the base register assigned to the variable and the displacement from this base register. See 5.3, Object Code Analysis, for a detailed description of how to interpret the instruction format. The type and length of the variable can be determined from the source code definition. For example, suppose that a variable BETA was of interest. A line referencing BETA might look like this:

```
000DA6   50 10 7 92C      ST      1, 44( 0, 7)  BETA
```

The instruction this line represents is at xDA6 from the start of the object module. The object code (as it would appear in the dump) is x5010792C. No program label is present (if this instruction was the first generated from a labeled statement, the label number would be printed between the instruction address and the object code). The explicit form of the instruction, ST 1, 44(0,7), is followed by the variable name referenced—BETA in this example. By analyzing this instruction (STORE, RX format), the base register is found to be 7 and the displacement is 44 (x2C). Therefore, BETA will be found at R7 + x2C. FORTRAN H gives the hexadecimal object code in addition to the explicit form of the instruction. The first two digits are the operation code (x50 in the example above).

Finding Elements in FORTRAN Arrays

FORTRAN arrays (both G and H) are stored in column-major order. This means that an array element is assigned an actual storage location by varying the leftmost subscript first. Figure 5-13 illustrates this relationship for a two- and a three-dimensional array, each consisting of 1-byte entries.

The address of the first byte of a FORTRAN array is determined by the analysis given above. To calculate the address of an element within the array:

1. Determine the address of the array (the variable name used to identify the array will yield this address).
2. Determine the value of all subscripts used with the array. This is done by finding each subscript's effective main storage address. The content of the field at this address is the current value of the subscript (determine the field length from the source definition).
3. Calculate the displacement represented by the current values of the subscripts. The calculation is as follows:

$$N = \sum_{i=2}^{P} \left[(S_i - 1) \prod_{j=1}^{i-1} M_j \right] + S_1 - 1$$

where

S_i = current value of the ith subscript; $2 \leq P \leq 7$, numbering subscripts from left to right; for array X(I,J), J is the second subscript (S_2)
M_j = dimension of the jth vector of the array; for X(100,6), $M_2 = 6$

N = occurrence number, relative to the start of the array, of the element pointed to by all S_i; $i = 1, P$

The formula for N above may be used for any constant-size-element, column-major array of any dimension. However, the following is offered as a computational shortcut for arrays of one, two, and three dimensions. Variables are as defined above.

$$N(1) = S_1 - 1$$
$$N(2) = (S_1 - 1) + (S_2 - 1)M_1$$
$$N(3) = (S_1 - 1) + (S_2 - 1)M_1 + (S_3 - 1)M_1M_2$$

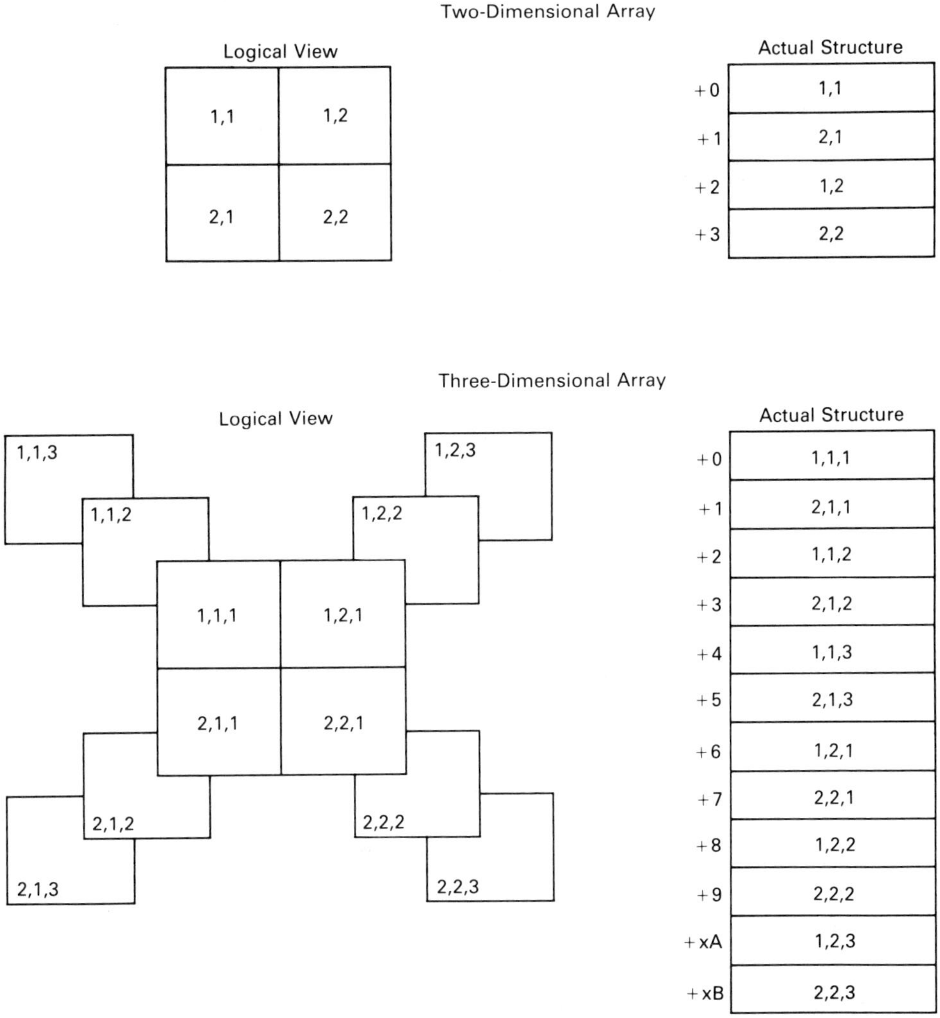

FIGURE 5-13 FORTRAN Array Structure

The effective address of the *N*th element is given by

$$E = B + D + (N - 1)L$$

where

E = effective address of the *N*th element
B = base address of the array (obtained from a register)
D = displacement to the array from the base address
N = as above
L = length (in bytes) of each array element—depends on type

Finding Argument Lists

Data passed to and from called subroutines by the CALL SUBRTN(A,B,C) construct may be found in main storage in a different manner than that used for LIST/variable name analysis. FORTRAN G and H calling/called interfaces follow standard IBM linkage conventions. Register 1 points to a list of fullword addresses, each address pointing to a unique item in the argument list. The high-order byte of the last item in the list is set to x80 to indicate the end of the list. The high-order byte of the preceding items is x00. For example, the statement

```
CALL NEWTON(COEF,NCOEF,EPSIL,ROOTS,NROOTS)
```

would result in the argument list shown in Figure 5-14. One address is present for each entry in the list. This address is the effective address of the start of the variable or array. They may be found by the LIST/variable name analysis in either the calling or called program. However, the base registers in the called program are not initialized until the program is actually called. Occasionally, an argument list or base register is inadvertently modified. Comparing addresses for consistency may indicate the cause of an abend. Register 1 of REGS AT ENTRY TO ABEND or of a recent SA (save area) may point to an argument list of interest. See 4.2, Dump Components, Save Area Trace, for more information about linkage conventions and save area usage.

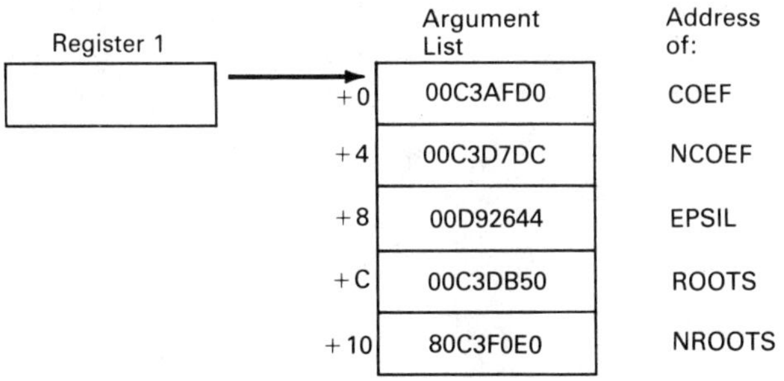

FIGURE 5-14 FORTRAN Argument Lists

FORTRAN makes special use of register 0 and register 2 for function subroutines. The result calculated is returned in register 0 if the function is an integer type. For single-precision floating-point type, the value is returned in floating-point register 0; for extended-precision and complex types, in floating-point registers 0 and 2.

If data are passed into the program via the PARM parameter of the EXEC statement, register 1 at entry to the main program will point to the data given in PARM. The first SA will show this address in R1. The address in R1 points to a 2-byte length field, which gives the length of the parameter string in binary. The actual parameter string, up to 100 bytes, immediately follows the halfword length field.

Debugging Tools

Execution Traces

FORTRAN provides several statements that facilitate execution traces. The statements are:

UNIT	Defines on which unit to write trace output. Default is SYSOUT.
TRACE	Causes statement and label numbers to be printed as they are executed. May be turned ON and OFF by the program.
SUBTRACE	Causes the name and value assigned to a variable or array specified in the INIT statement to be printed every time it is changed.
SUBCHK	If a subscript is outside the bounds of an array, this statement will cause the array name and the subscript to be printed.

Online Debugging

FORTRAN programs may be executed under the TEST command of TSO (see 5.5, Assembly Language Analysis, Online Debugging). However, TEST is not well suited to the needs of most FORTRAN programmers. An IBM program product called TESTFORT provides an excellent online debugging facility for FORTRAN G. However, it is an IBM-licensed program and is not available in all installations. TESTFORT runs under TSO and provides:

- Easily set break points. Execution may be stopped at any point in the program to be resumed on command or at a prespecified address.
- The ability to list portions of storage or data buffers.
- Execution traces.
- Commands to display source code statements.
- Commands to modify the contents of program variables when execution is interrupted.

For more information about TESTFORT, see *IBM FORTRAN Interactive Debug for OS (TSO) and VM/370 (CMS) Terminal User's Guide.*

Program-Initiated Dumps

The DUMP and PDUMP library subroutines provide a facility for selectively dumping portions of main storage during execution. DUMP terminates the program after printing the requested data; PDUMP returns to the calling program. The call allows a variable number of argument triplets. Each triplet is composed of a starting variable, ending variable, and an output format flag. The call

```
CALL PDUMP (X1,X1,0)
```

would list the contents of X1 in hexadecimal. For simple variables, the start and end are the same. Subscripted array elements may also be given as start and end addresses. By using EQUIVALENCE definitions, as much or little of a contiguous portion of main storage as desired may be output.

The subroutines associated with the extended error handling facility provide some additional flexibility in obtaining traces. The number of times a particular type of error may occur before termination is determined by this facility. Each time an error occurs, a message followed by an abbreviated register or PSW dump is output. By adjusting the termination limit, few or many occurrences of an error may be monitored. The output provides sufficient data to calculate the object module displacement when an error occurs. The trace output contains a brief descriptive message, contents of registers 14, 15, 0, and 1, and an entry point address. This trace message may be generated as needed by calling the ERRTRA subroutine. The other subroutines and the error table used in the extended error handling facility are well documented in the FORTRAN G and H Programmer's Guides.

Controlling Abends

There are no FORTRAN facilities that allow execution time alteration of the abnormal termination environment.

Compiler Options for Debugging

The following compiler options are suggested to provide useful debugging information.

DUMP	(H only) causes an ABEND dump to be printed when an ABEND error is detected (dump DD statement required).
FORMAT	(H only) causes a "Structured Source Module Listing" to be printed. This listing shows the span of control for loops.
LIST	(G and H) causes a formatted object code listing to be printed. This listing gives the explicit form of the generated instructions. It is essential for abend debugging.
MAP	(G) produces a list of variables, formats, and subroutines. An address is listed, but it has no use in calculating the actual effective address.

If MAP is specified without LIST, a condensed list of statement numbers and offsets is produced. This table is useful for locating an abending statement.

MAP (H) produces a list of variables showing their name, usage, and type. An address is listed, but it has no use in calculating the actual effective address.

XREF (H only) produces a cross-reference list, showing where variables and labels are defined and referenced, by statement number.

5.8 PL/I ANALYSIS

Daddy Warbucks: . . . Ye Gods! How stupid can a man be?
Punjab: Who can say, Sahib? Man's capabilites are infinite.

Leonard Hall
Annie

Finding the Abending Statement

Locate the object module displacement as described under Basic Techniques. In some cases, finding the load point address is not straightforward. The third PRB may point to a PL/I library module in the CDE—not to the problem program. This may result because PL/I loads and unloads its own library modules to handle initialization and errors. These modules pass control to compiled code. The third-from-last RB is associated with the last module loaded before ABEND was invoked. If this RB is a PRB whose FL-CDE points to a PL/I library module, assume that the abend occurred in a compiled code load module—not in the library module. PL/I library modules may be identified by their prefix—"IBM": for example, "IBMBERRB." Scan the CDE NM field for the load module name of the problem program. When found, follow the XL/MJ pointer to the XL as described above to find the load point address. The PSW should point to an instruction within this load module. If it does not, find a load module that does contain the PSW address.

Having found an object module displacement, there are two techniques for locating the PL/I statement associated with it: (1) by scanning the object module listing created by the compiler LIST option, or (2) by analysis of the table of offsets and statement numbers and storage requirements. These listings are generated by the compiler options OFFSET and STORAGE, respectively.

In the first method, scan down the address column of the object code listing (the columns are printed "two-up" on a page). When an address that matches the object module displacement is found, stop. The statement number immediately preceding is the statement involved in the abend. The name of the variable associated with the abending instruction may be listed, possibly preceded by a compiler-generated prefix. The prefix is terminated by two periods. For example:

```
000FAE 78 40 D 0AC          LE 4, FACTOR
000FB2 7C 47 D 0B4          ME 4, VO..DATA(7)
000FB6 D5 00 D 1E2 B 361 CLC BIG.BUCKET, C..0534
```

The first instruction loads a short floating-point variable FACTOR into register 4. Register 4 is multiplied by a long floating-point variable in an array DATA (7). The third instruction compares BIG.BUCKET to a temporary compiler-generated variable.

The second method is more complex. First, the storage requirements listing must be analyzed to determine the offset of each procedure block into the object module. Second, the procedure block that contains the object module displacement must be identified. The displacement relative to this procedure block is then calculated. Third, the Table of Offsets and Statement Numbers is analyzed to find the statement that corresponds to the procedure block offset.

The storage requirements listing is best analyzed by making a table of procedure block offsets. The first procedure block is usually the third item listed, after PROGRAM CSECT and STATIC CSECT. Figure 5-15 shows how to construct a table of procedure block offsets. Each procedure block must begin on a fullword address (an address evenly divisible by 4). Thus, if a procedure block has a length that does not end in x0, x4, x8, or xC, it must be rounded up to the nearest fullword length. For example, xFE2 becomes xFE4, x4A6 becomes x4A8, x103A becomes x103C, x93E becomes x940. However, no adjustment would be needed for xDC0, x2034, xB8, or x1FC. The offset for each successive procedure block is found by rounding up to the nearest fullword size, if necessary. As a final check on this calculation, the total for all adjusted procedure block lengths should equal the PROGRAM CSECT length given in the storage requirements and the link-edit map.

Once the table is constructed, scan down the start address column looking for an offset that is greater than the object module displacement. When found, the procedure block immediately preceding this larger offset contains the object module displacement. Calculate the procedure block displacement by subtracting the offset for the procedure block from the object module displacement. The result is the procedure block displacement. Figure 5-15 shows an example of the procedure block calculation.

There is a shortcut to locating the abending procedure. Each PL/I procedure name is compiled into the object code just before the actual instructions for that procedure. The name is in EBCDIC format. To locate the abending procedure name, find the abending instruction address in the dump. Starting at this address, scan backward (upward, to lower addresses) through the right-hand character format column. When a procedure name is found, stop. This procedure name is the one containing the abending instruction.

Finally, turn to the tables of offsets and statement numbers section of the compiler listing. Find the offset/statement lines for the procedure block identified as containing the object module displacement. Scan right until an offset greater than the procedure block displacement is found. The offset/statement pair immediately prior to the larger offset corresponds to the statement that generated the abending instruction or supervisor call.

STORAGE REQUIREMENTS

BLOCK, SECTION OR STATEMENT	TYPE	LENGTH	(HEX)	DSA SIZE	(HEX)
PROBPROG1	PROGRAM CSECT	2580	A14		
PROBPROG2	STATIC CSECT	936	3A6		
PROBPROG	PROCEDURE BLOCK	538	21A	4304	10D0
START-JOB	PROCEDURE BLOCK	124	76	332	14C
GET-TRANSACTION	PROCEDURE BLOCK	106	6A	64	40
CHECK-FIELDS	PROCEDURE BLOCK	1428	594	5072	13D0
MAIN-TRANSFORM	PROCEDURE BLOCK	834	342	1256	4E8
MAKE-OUTPUT	PROCEDURE BLOCK	210	D2	118	76

PROCEDURE	NOMINAL LENGTH	ACTUAL LENGTH	START ADDRESS
PROBPROG	21A	21C	0
START-JOB	76	78	21C
GET-TRANSACTION	6A	6C	294
CHECK-FIELDS	594	594	300
MAIN-TRANSFORM	342	344	894
MAKE-OUTPUT	D2	D4	BD8

OMD = x 9AE,

MAIN-TRANSFORM IS OFFENDING BLOCK

SINCE x 894 < x 9AE < x BD8.

x 9AE	OBJECT MODULE DISPLACEMENT
− x 894	− START ADDRESS OF OFFENDING BLOCK
= x 11A	= OFFSET INTO OFFENDING BLOCK

FIGURE 5-15 Procedure Block Displacement Circulation

Finding the Abending Data Fields

PL/I uses a rather convoluted internal data management scheme to accomplish its vaunted flexibility. There are five ways in which main storage is defined and accessed:

STATIC	Static fields conform to conventional base plus displacement addressing. The displacement is fixed at compile time.
AUTOMATIC	Automatic fields are contained in variable-length work areas called DSAs (dynamic storage areas). At least one DSA is created for each procedure block. DSAs are chained together. DSAs are allocated when their defining procedure is executed. Once allocated, base register plus displacement addressing is used for fields within the DSA.
CONTROLLED	Controlled variables are addressed via a work area called the pseudo-register vector (PRV). The PRV contains one fullword base address for each controlled variable. The PRV starts at the address in register 12 + x4 (the PRV is within another work area, the TCA—task communication area).
BASED	Based variables are addressed by pointer, not directly. The pointer itself may be a static, automatic, controlled, or based variable.
AREA	Area storage definitions are used to free and allocate storage for based variables. The area itself may be defined as static, automatic, or controlled. To locate an area variable, follow the technique for the storage class of the area.

The basic procedure for finding a PL/I data field in a dump is:

1. Determine the explicit or implicit storage type from the attribute and cross-reference table.
2. Find the displacement, if any, in the variable storage map.
3. Calculate the address and find the data, according to the steps for each storage type. These steps are detailed below.
4. If needed, find the locator/descriptor and apply its offsets to locate the field of interest.

For more information about PL/I internal formats and logic, see *OS PL/I Optimizing Compiler: Execution Logic*.

Locating Static Data

All static fields use register 3 as a base register. Add the field's displacement from the variable storage map to the contents of register 3 at entry to abend to find its effective address.

Locating Automatic Data

Automatic data fields are contained within the DSA for the procedure block that declares the field. Register 13 at entry to abend points to the DSA for the procedure block that was active when the abend occurred. If the field of interest is declared in the currently active procedure block, the DSA pointed to from register 13 will contain this field. Register 13 may be used as a base register. Add the field's displacement from the variable storage map to the contents of register 13 to find its effective address.

If the automatic data field of interest is not defined in the active procedure block, the DSA chain may be followed to locate it.

- R13 points to current DSA.
- DSA + x4C points to next DSA (NAB, next available byte, pointer). If the next address is prefixed by a xFF, it is the last DSA on the chain. If the next address is not prefixed by x00 or xFF, the chain is invalid.

There are several types of DSAs. The DSA containing data fields is a procedure DSA. Procedure DSAs are identified by a x0 in the second nibble of the first DSA byte. The name of the procedure block associated with a DSA may be found by the following pointer chain.

The DSA for the automatic storage of the MAIN procedure is pointed to from the "dummy" DSA. The dummy DSA is indicated by x82 in the first byte. The dummy DSA may be found by following the DSA forward chain (DSA + x4C points to next DSA) or from the TCA (task communications area):

- R12 points to the TCA.
- TCA + x28 points to the TCA appendage.
- TCA appendage + x24 points to the dummy DSA.
- Dummy DSA + x4C points to MAIN's DSA.
- DSA + x4 points to preceding DSA.
- Preceding DSA + x10 may point to the entry point of procedure block associated with original DSA. Procedure block DSAs are identified by a x0 in the second nibble.
- If an actual entry point to a procedure is pointed to, the byte preceding the entry point will contain the number of characters in this procedure block's name (as an 8-bit binary integer).
- The procedure block name is contained in the storage preceding the count byte, for the negative length of the count byte.

DSAs for PL/I library routines will be found on the DSA chain as well as DSAs for source code procedures. Continue to follow the chain until you locate the DSA for the procedure block containing the variable of interest. Figure 5-16 shows the DSA/

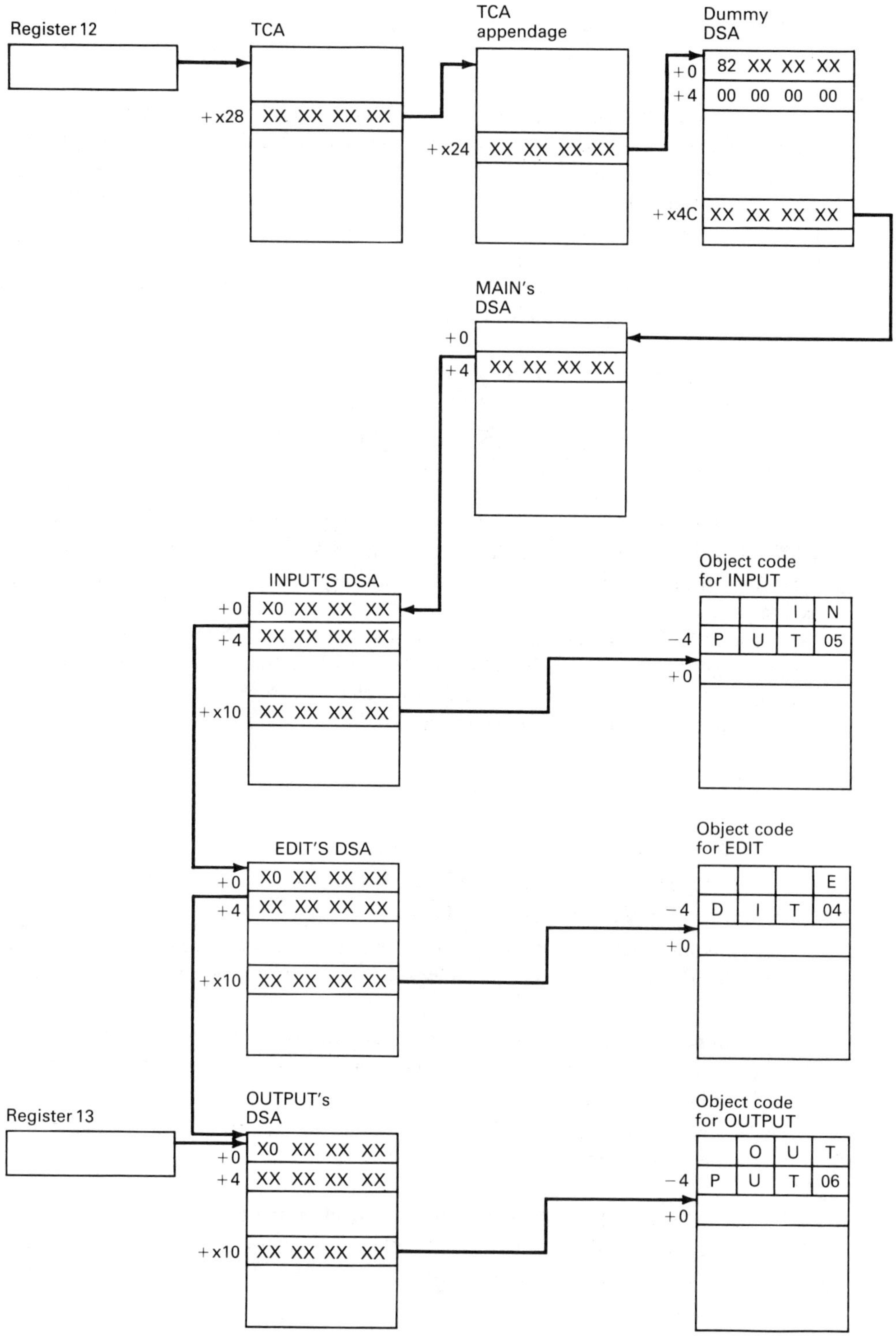

FIGURE 5-16 Procedure Blocks and DSA Chains

procedure block relationship for a program consisting of procedures MAIN, INPUT, EDIT, and OUTPUT. Suppose that OUTPUT was the active procedure when the abend occurred. Register 13 at entry to abend will point to OUTPUT's DSA, but you want to find an automatic variable declared in the EDIT procedure. You would follow the DSA chain, originating in R12, checking each procedure DSA's corresponding name until you found the DSA for EDIT. You would use the address of this DSA as a base address instead of R13 to calculate the effective address of the automatic variables in EDIT.

Locating Controlled Data

Variables or arrays defined as controlled storage are not allocated until used. All controlled storage and FCBs (file control blocks) are addressed from a work area called the pseudo-register vector (PRV). There is one fullword entry in the PRV for each controlled field and file declaration. PRV words are assigned to fields and files in source code sequence. The first declaration uses the first PRV word; the second declaration, the second PRV word; and so on. Each PRV word is initialized to the address of a dummy FCB. The address of the control field or FCB actually used is placed in the PRV when the item is accessed for the first time. Since controlled fields may be "pushed" or "popped" in a stack, the PRV points to the current controlled field. Each controlled field is preceded by a controlled variable block (CVB).

The CVB is structured as follows:

CVB + x0	PRVOFF, 4. Offset into PRV for this field.
CVB + x4	LENGTH, 4. Total length of this field (data portion + CVB size).
CVB + x8	Previous CVB, 4. Address of the fifth word of the last controlled area used (push-pop list), if any.
CVB + xC	Usage count, 4.
CVB + x10	Start of a locator and/or descriptor block for the data portion of this controlled field. The PRV points to this address. The following formats have description blocks: Strings: locator/descriptor Areas: locator/descriptor Structures: locator Arrays: locator Structure or array with adjustable extent: locator/descriptor All other formats do not have a description block.

The PRV is pointed to from the TCA, which is pointed to from register 12. The pointer chain for a controlled variable is then:

- R12 points to the TCA.
- TCA + x4 points to the PRV.
- Let *K* equal the lexical sequence of the controlled field of interest, relative to all controlled fields and files in the program.

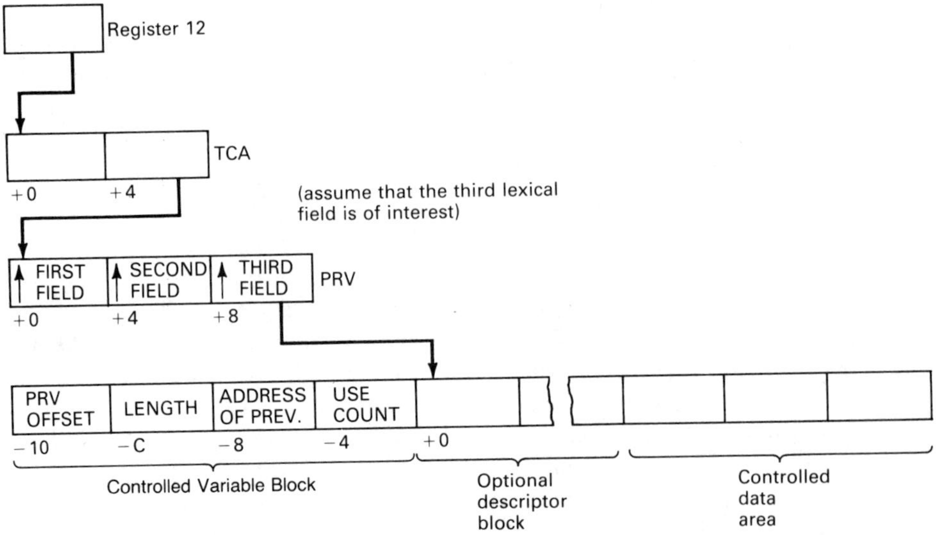

FIGURE 5-17 Locating Controlled Fields

- Let $N = (K - 1) \times 4$, the offset into the PRV for the Kth field (thus fullword 1 would point to the first field and would be found at PRV + 0).
- The address at PRV + N points to the start of controlled data field or a variable-length data descriptor block.
- The address pointed to from the PRV is preceded by the CVB, for 16 bytes.

Figure 5-17 shows these relationships graphically.

Locating Based Data

All based data are accessed by pointer. The pointer itself may be static, automatic, controlled, or based. The pointer contains the virtual address of the based item. To locate the address of a based item, locate the pointer. It will contain the address of the based field. The steps to locate a static, controlled, or automatic field given above may be used. If the pointer itself is based, the originating pointer must be found first.

Locators and Descriptors

In addition to addressing, allocating, and formatting storage classes, PL/I also provides control blocks that describe data items. They are used primarily for data with variable fields and items passed from between procedures. These control blocks are called locators and descriptors. They reside in static internal storage. They are created for:

- Arrays, area, strings, or structures which are:
  - (a) Variable length or adjustable
  - (b) Passed between procedures
- All controlled variables
- All items passed to conversion routines
- All stream I/O items

They are not created for simple numeric fields (e.g., FIXED BINARY, FLOAT DECIMAL) or fixed-length strings [e.g., CHAR (80)].

Generally, descriptors hold data about the variable portions of the field they represent. Locators point to the data and the descriptors. These control blocks are initialized at compile time with available data about a field. As execution progresses, addresses are resolved and changed as needed, and lengths and pointers are updated.

To find descriptors and locators, the static internal storage map is required. This listing is generated by the compiler when both the MAP and LIST options are specified. The variable name associated with the locator or descriptor is printed with its offset. For example,

```
0000F8 0000000000060000 LOCATOR..XDATA
```

indicates that the locator for the variable XDATA is at the static CSECT + xF8. The first word is initialized to zero, the second to x00060000.

Locators and descriptors are addressed relative to the static CSECT. The offset of the static CSECT may be calculated by analyzing the link-edit map. Obtain the name of the static CSECT from the storage requirements compiler listing. Turn to the link-edit cross-reference listing. Scan down the control section name column for the static CSECT name. The hexadecimal offset for the static CSECT is given in the "origin" column. The effective address is

	Load module displacement
+	Static CSECT origin
=	Static CSECT effective address

Adding the locator or descriptor offsets to this address will yield their main storage addresses. The contents may then be examined in the dump. For the layout and usage of various locators and descriptors, see *OS PL/I Optimizing Compiler: Execution Logic*.

Finding Array Elements

PL/I arrays are stored in row-major order. This means that an array element is assigned an actual storage location by varying the rightmost subscript first. Figure 5-18 illustrates this relationship for a two- and a three-dimension array, each consisting of 1-byte elements.

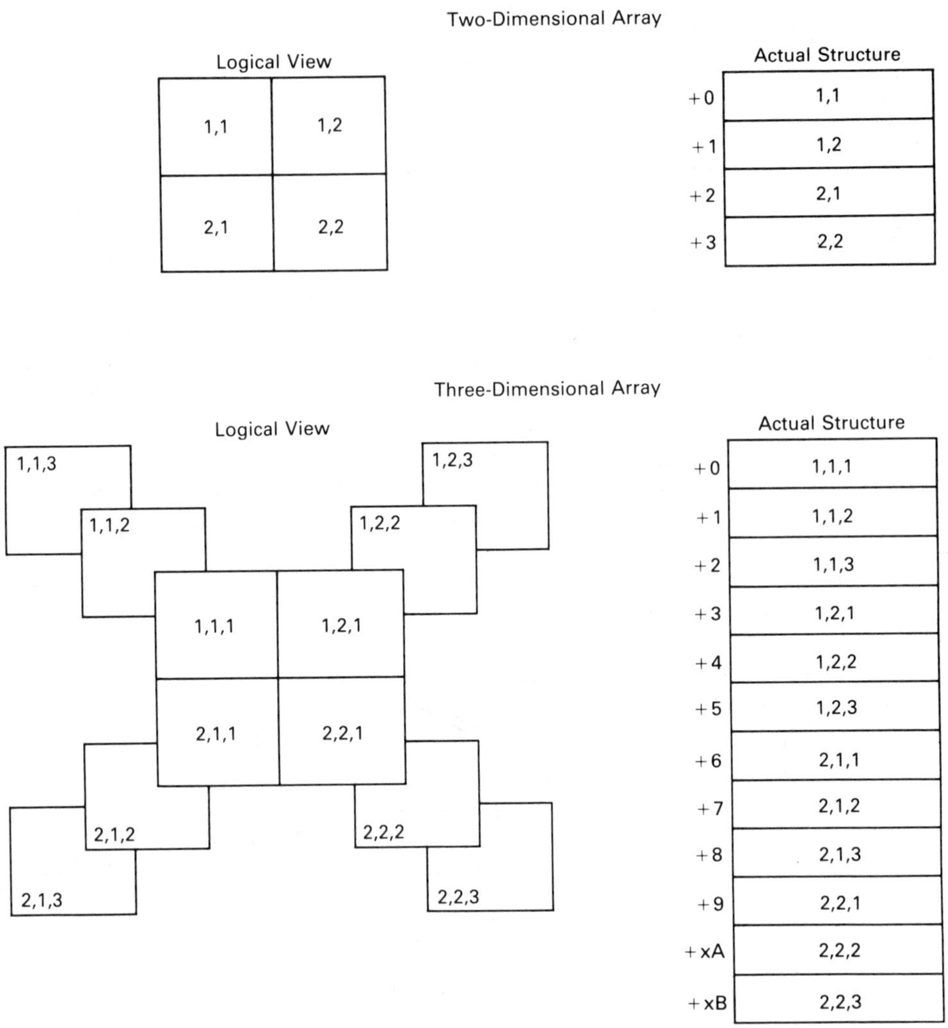

FIGURE 5-18 PL/I Array Structure

PL/I also provides for constructs called arrays of structures and structure of arrays. These constructs allow arrays to have elements that have a structure, or for structures to be composed of arrays. Figure 5-18 illustrates how these items are actually stored. Both constructs also follow the basic row-major storage convention.

For arrays accessed by base-type pointers, the base variable contains the actual address of the last reference. An analysis of subscripts may not be necessary in this case.

To determine the element of an array pointed to by the current set of subscripts, the subscripts must be located and their contents determined. If a different item, pointed to by some other set of subscripts, is of interest, this set of values may be used as well.

In either case, the physical displacement corresponding to the set of subscripts is given by the formula

$$D = \sum_{i=1}^{N} L_i(S_i - 1)$$

where D = current physical displacement from the start of an array
N = number of dimensions; $1 \leqslant N \leqslant 15$
L_i = length in bytes of a single occurrence of dimension i and all subordinate dimensions
S_i = current value of the subscript associated with the ith dimension
i = the number, reading left to right, of a dimension. Thus K is the third dimension of A(I, J, K).

For example, assume a two-dimension array defined as follows:

```
DCL A(12,4) CHAR(4);
```

Assume I and J subscripts,

$$I = 7, \qquad J = 3$$

The lengths of each level are

$$L_1 = 4 \times 4$$
$$L_2 = 4$$

Then

$$D = \sum_{i=1}^{N} L_i(S_i - 1)$$
$$= 16(7 - 1) + 4(3 - 1)$$
$$= 104 \text{ or } x68$$

Thus the element A(7,3) is located at +x68 from the actual origin of the array. The actual origin of the array depends on its storage type, as described above.

Elements within arrays of structures are found in the same manner. For example, assume a structure

```
DCL 1  A(3),
      2  B(4),
      3  C(100),
         X1 CHAR(5),
         X2 CHAR(4);
```

and the current subscripts (for A, B, and C) 3, 1, and 95. The length of each level is

$$\begin{aligned} L_1 &= 4 \times 100 \times 10 \\ &= 4000 \\ L_2 &= 100 \times 10 \\ &= 1000 \\ L_3 &= 10 \end{aligned}$$

Then

$$\begin{aligned} D &= \sum_{i=1}^{N} L_i(S_i - 1) \\ &= 4000(3 - 1) + 1000(1 - 1) + 10(95 - 1) \\ &= 8940 \text{ or x22EC} \end{aligned}$$

Thus the element A(3, 1, 95) is located at +x22EC from the actual origin of the structure. As noted above, this origin address depends on the structure's data type.

Finding Items in a Parameter List

The interface between calling and called modules in PL/I is more complex than the standard linkage convention. PL/I's requirement to maintain its environment—the pointers to various storage areas and current procedure—results in additional data to support a context swap. See *PL/I Programmer's Guide* and *OS PL/I Optimizing Compiler Logic: Execution Logic* for a full description of PL/I linkage conventions. The parameters passed between PL/I procedures follow another set of rules.

Items in procedure to procedure parameter lists are passed following standard register 1 conventions. The DSA for the calling procedure will contain register 1 in its save area (DSA + x18). See the explanation of the DSA chain under Locating Automatic Data, to locate this DSA. Parameter lists are always composed of a series of fullword addresses. The last address in the list contains x80 in the high-order byte (the high-order byte of preceding items is x00). In PL/I, the addresses in this list are usually not the addresses of data items in the symbolic parameter list. For most data items, the address of the locator associated with the data item is placed in the parameter list. See the section Locators and Descriptors above. Simple numeric items and fixed-length strings are passed as actual data addresses.

By declaring an entry point with the ASSEMBLER attribute, PL/I will construct parameter lists that follow the standard linkage conventions. No items on the argument list are optional and the address of the item itself is passed.

Finding I/O Control Blocks

The FCB (file control block) contains some basic data management parameters and points to a DCB or an ACB. The same steps used to locate a controlled field may be used to locate an FCB. The FCB is pointed to from the PRV, at a fullword offset into the PRV which corresponds to the lexical position of the file DECLARE, relative to all other files and controlled variables in the program. Fields of interest in the FCB are:

FCB + x10	Pointer to declare control block (DCLCB); DCLCB + x16 – PL/I file-name
FCB + x14	Address of the ACB or DCB for this data set
FCB + x30	2-byte block size
FCB + x32	2-byte key length
FCB + x34	4-byte record length

Debugging Tools

PL/I has the most extensive set of predefined tracing, debugging, and dumping aids of the four languages presented here. The use of these facilities is well described in *OS PL/I Checkout and Optimizing Compilers: Language Reference Manual,* and *PL/I Programmer's Guide*.

The basic debugging tool is the ON-UNIT statement. Almost any error condition may be intercepted via an ON-UNIT and corrective action may be attempted from the source program. Other debugging features include:

- The GOSTMT and FLOW compiler options (see the compiler options for debugging).
- Conditional execution, based on ON-CODEs for an ON-UNIT.
- The PLIDUMP dynamic dump facility.
- Prefix options to trap errors such as SIZE, STRING RANGE, and SUBSCRIPT RANGE.
- The PUT DATA statement. When executed, the specified variable name and its current value are listed.

Program-Initiated Dumps

The PLIDUMP is invoked by the statement

```
CALL PLIDUMP ('TFCH','PAGE TITLE');
```

A DD statement for the dump output is needed as well, for example:

```
//PLIDUMP DD SYSOUT=A,DISP=MOD
```

The first argument (the options-list) is a string of one- or two-character commands. In the example above, T requests a trace of active procedures, F requests a list of active files and their attributes and buffers, C means to continue (i.e., to return control after the dump is printed), and H gives a hex dump of the program's main storage. Other options are available. See *PL/I Programmer's Guide* for further information.

When run under the TSO, the checkout compiler provides online debugging facilities similar to TEST and TESTCOB. Data may be displayed or changed, specific break points may be set in the code, and various control blocks may be examined.

Controlling Abends

The PL/I routines to intercept program check and supervisor abends are invoked by the SPIE and STAE compiler options or may be specified by the program itself. Typically, these traps are disabled to improve execution response time or throughput. However, they do provide useful debugging information. Using these options also typically prevents ABEND termination (but does not prevent the bug). The following statement would enable the SPIE and STAE traps:

```
DCL PLIXOPT STATIC EXTERNAL CHAR (25) INIT ('SPIE,STAE');
```

A SYSPRINT DD statement is required to receive the execution time diagnostics generated by these options; for example:

```
//SYSPRINT DD SYSOUT=A
```

NOSPIE and NOSTAE disables these PL/I abend traps. When disabled, the normal system abend procedures are invoked in the event of an abend condition. SPIE and STAE should be disabled in any environment in which PL/I is not the major task (e.g., IMS/DC and CICS). This is not just because the SPIE and STAE environment may have to be repeatedly reestablished, but because the exit specified may trap an abend. PL/I may not pass control back to the major task, causing an update made to a recoverable resource to be committed erroneously. This is especially applicable to STAE.[2]

Compiler Options for Debugging

The following compiler options are suggested to provide useful debugging information.

AGGREGATE	Gives length of all major data structures.
ATTRIBUTES	Causes explicit and implicit attributes to be listed.
FLOW(n,m)	Causes compiler-generated code to print a list of the last *n* branches and *m* procedure calls. This printing is initiated by execution of

[2]This rationale for disabling SPIE and STAE was provided by Dave Loveluck.

	the FLOW statement in the problem program. The COUNT option is also required. STMT is suggested as the line-numbering convention.
LIST	Prints object code listing—eases finding object module displacement. See MAP.
MAP	Causes list of static and automatic field displacements to be printed. Both MAP and LIST are required to generate the STATIC INTERNAL STORAGE MAP. This listing is necessary for locator/descriptor analysis.
NOSPIE	See Debugging Tools. Disables program check interrupt error handling. Allows ABEND termination.
NOSTAE	See Debugging Tools. Disables supervisor error handling. Allows ABEND termination.
OFFSET	Prints table of offsets of statements. Required to find abending statement number if LIST not specified.
STORAGE	Prints allocation of major sections of storage. Required to find abending statement number if LIST not specified.
XREF(FULL)	Shows data fields are defined and accessed. Output of ATTRIBUTES is merged when both are specified.

APPENDICES

debugging *n.* Removing a BUG, either by tinkering with the program or by amending the program specification so that the side effect of the bug is published as a desirable feature. *See also* KLUDGE; ONE-LINE PATCH; STEPWISE REFINEMENT.

♦ Fixing one's own errors is such a hazardous and humilitating process that programmers are well advised to observe the Kelly-Bootle Rule: "Avoid debugging! Get it right the first time!" Correcting the work of others, though, has its lighter moments, for it is difficult to suppress the occasional wry chuckle (pronounced *Yahooo!*) as your colleague's blatant howlers are methodically exposed and neatly patched. *See* YOUR PROGRAM.

Stan Kelly-Bootle
The Devil's DP Dictionary

A

Acronyms and Abbreviations

Terms used which may not be readily understood from context are defined here. In general, instruction mnemonics, control block fields, macro names, parameter values, and source language keywords are not included.

ABEND	Abnormal end (macro)
ACB	Access method control block (VSAM control block)
AMB	Access method block (VSAM control block)
AMP	Access method parameter (JCL DD parameter)
AMTYPE	Access method type (DEB field)
ASCB	Address space control block
ASCII	American National Standard Code for Information Interchange
BC	Basic control (PSW mode)
BDAM	Basic direct access method
BISAM	Basic indexed sequential access method
BL	Base locator (COBOL)

BLDL	Build list (program management work area)
BLL	Base locator for linkage (COBOL)
BLP	Bypass label processing (JCL DD parameter)
BPAM	Basic partitioned access method
BSAM	Basic sequential access method
BSC	Binary synchronous
BTAM	Basic telecommunications access method
BUFC	Buffer control block (VSAM)
BUFL	Buffer length
CCW	Channel command word
CDE	Contents directory entry (control block)
CICS	Customer information control system
CSW	Channel status word
CVB	Convert to binary (instruction)
CVT	Communications vector table
DASD	Direct access storage device
DC	Data communications
DCB	Data control block
DD	Data definition (JCL statement)
DEB	Data extent block (control block)
DEN	Density (JCL DD parameter)
DISP	Disposition (JCL DD parameter)
DMAP	Data map (COBOL)
DPQE	Dummy partition queue element (virtual storage management control block)
DQE	Descriptor queue element (virtual storage management control block)
DSA	Dynamic storage area (PL/I)
DSCB	Data set control block (DASD label)
DSN	Data set name
DSNAME	Data set name
DSORG	Data set organization (JCL DD parameter)
EBCDIC	Extended Binary-Coded Decimal Interchange Code
EC	Extended control (PSW mode)
ECB	Event control block
EOF1	End of file label 1
EOF2	End of file label 2
EOV	End of volume
EP	Entry point
EPA	Entry point address
ESD	External symbol dictionary
ESDS	Entry sequenced data set (VSAM)
ESTAE	Extended STAE—specify task abnormal exit
EXCP	Execute channel program
EXLST	Exit list (DCB field)
EXTSA	Extended save area (SVRB field)
FBQE	Free block queue element (virtual storage management control block)
FCB	File control block (PL/I)
FL-CDE	Flags and CDE address (PRB field)
FQE	Free queue element (virtual storage management control block)

GDG	Generation data group
HDR1	Header label 1
HDR2	Header label 2
HEX	Hexadecimal
HSA	High save area
ICB	Interrupt control block
IDR	Identification record (linkage editor)
ILC	Instruction length code
IMS	Information management system
INTC	Interrupt code
I/O	Input/Output
IOB	Input/Output block
ISAM	Indexed sequential access method
JCL	Job control language
JES	Job entry subsystem (2 or 3)
JFCB	Job file control block
JPA	Job pack area
K	1024 bytes
KEYLEN	Key length (JCL DD parameter)
KSDS	Key sequenced data set (VSAM)
LMD	Load module displacement
LPA	Link pack area
LRECL	Logical record length
LSA	Last save area
LSQA	Local system queue area
MACRF	Macro format (DCB macro operand)
MB	Mega byte (1,000K bytes)
MBBCCHHR	Actual DASD address: extent, bin, cylinder, track, record
MSS	Mass storage system
MVS	Multiple virtual storage: release 2.0 and later releases of OS/VS2
MVS/XA	MVS extended architecture
NCAL	No automatic call (linkage editor parameter)
NM	Name (CDE field)
O/C/EOV	Open/close/end of volume
OMD	Object module displacement
OS/VS2	Operating system/virtual storage 2
PDS	Partitioned data set
PLH	Place holder (VSAM control block)
PMAP	Program MAP (COBOL)
PRB	Program request block
PRV	Pseudo-register vector (PL/I)
PSA	Prefixed storage area
PSW	Program status word
QCB	Queue control block
QISAM	Queued indexed sequential access method
QSAM	Queued sequential access method

R	Register
RACF	Resource access control facility
RB	Request block
RBA	Relative byte address
RDW	Record descriptor word
RECFM	Record format (JCL DD parameter)
REG	Register
REGS	Registers
RET	Return address
RKP	Relative key position
RPL	Request parameter list (VSAM/VTAM control block)
RRDS	Relative record data set (VSAM)
RTM2	Recovery termination manager 2
RTM2WA	Recovery termination manager 2 work area
S/370	System 370
SA	Save area
SAM	Sequential access method
SCB	STAE control block
SCC	System completion code
SDLC	Synchronous data link control (DC protocol)
SER	Serial number (of a tape or DASD volume)
SP	Subpool
SPQE	Subpool queue element
SQA	System queue area
STAE	Specify task abnormal exit
SVC	Supervisor call
SVRB	Supervisor request block
SWA	Scheduler work area (subpools 236 and 237)
SYNAD	Synchronous error routine exit
TCA	Task communication area (PL/I)
TCAM	Telecommunications access method
TCB	Task control block
TGT	Task global table
TIOT	Task I/O table
TOD	Time of day
TRTCH	Track recording technique (JCL DD parameter)
TSO	Time-sharing option
TTE	Trace table entry
TTR	Track record address
TTRZ	Track record zero
UCB	Unit control block
VIO	Virtual I/O
VOLSER	Volume serial number (JCL DD parameter)
VOL1	Volume label 1
VS	Virtual storage
VSAM	Virtual storage access method

VSM	Virtual storage management
VTOC	Volume table of contents
WC-L-IC	Wait count–length–interrupt code (field of RB)
WTO	Write to operator (SVC)
XL	Extent list (control block)

B

Conversion Tables

Hexadecimal Mnemonics

xA	Apple
xB	Baker
xC	Charlie
xD	Dog
xE	Edward
xF	Fox

x13CFD0 is read as "one three charlie fox dog zero."

Hexadecimal-to-Decimal Integer Conversion Table

HALF WORD								*HALF WORD*							
BYTE				*BYTE*				*BYTE*				*BYTE*			
BITS: 0123		*4567*		*0123*		*4567*		*0123*		*4567*		*0123*		*4567*	
Hex	*Decimal*	*Hex*	*Decimal*	*Hex*	*Decimal*	*Hex*	*Decimal*	*Hex*	*Decimal*	*Hex*	*Decimal*	*Hex*	*Decimal*	*Hex*	*Decimal*
0	0	0	0	0	0	0	0	0	0	0	0	0	0	0	0
1	268,435,456	1	16,777,216	1	1,048,576	1	65,536	1	4,096	1	256	1	16	1	1
2	536,870,912	2	33,554,432	2	2,097,152	2	131,072	2	8,192	2	512	2	32	2	2
3	805,306,368	3	50,331,648	3	3,145,728	3	196,608	3	12,288	3	768	3	48	3	3
4	1,073,741,824	4	67,108,864	4	4,194,304	4	262,144	4	16,384	4	1,024	4	64	4	4
5	1,342,177,280	5	83,886,080	5	5,242,880	5	327,680	5	20,480	5	1,280	5	80	5	5
6	1,610,612,736	6	100,663,296	6	6,291,456	6	393,216	6	24,576	6	1,536	6	96	6	6
7	1,879,048,192	7	117,440,512	7	7,340,032	7	458,752	7	28,672	7	1,792	7	112	7	7
8	2,147,483,648	8	134,217,728	8	8,388,608	8	524,288	8	32,768	8	2,048	8	128	8	8
9	2,415,919,104	9	150,994,944	9	9,437,184	9	589,824	9	36,864	9	2,304	9	144	9	9
A	2,684,354,560	A	167,772,160	A	10,485,760	A	655,360	A	40,960	A	2,560	A	160	A	10
B	2,952,790,016	B	184,549,376	B	11,534,336	B	720,896	B	45,056	B	2,816	B	176	B	11
C	3,221,225,472	C	201,326,592	C	12,582,912	C	786,432	C	49,152	C	3,072	C	192	C	12
D	3,489,660,928	D	218,103,808	D	13,631,488	D	851,968	D	53,248	D	3,328	D	208	D	13
E	3,758,096,384	E	234,881,024	E	14,680,064	E	917,504	E	57,344	E	3,584	E	224	E	14
F	4,026,531,840	F	251,658,240	F	15,728,640	F	983,040	F	61,440	F	3,840	F	240	F	15
8		7		6		5		4		3		2		1	

Hexadecimal-to-Decimal Fraction Conversion Table

HALF WORD													
BYTE					*BYTE*								
BITS: 0123		*4567*			*0123*				*4567*				
Hex	*Decimal*	*Hex*	*Decimal*		*Hex*	*Decimal*			*Hex*	*Decimal*			
.0	.0000	.00	.0000	0000	.000	.0000	0000	0000	.0000	.0000	0000	0000	0000
.1	.0625	.01	.0039	0625	.001	.0002	4414	0625	.0001	.0000	1525	8789	0625
.2	.1250	.02	.0078	1250	.002	.0004	8828	1250	.0002	.0000	3051	7578	1250
.3	.1875	.03	.0117	1875	.003	.0007	3242	1875	.0003	.0000	4577	6367	1875
.4	.2500	.04	.0156	2500	.004	.0009	7656	2500	.0004	.0000	6103	5156	2500
.5	.3125	.05	.0195	3125	.005	.0012	2070	3125	.0005	.0000	7629	3945	3125
.6	.3750	.06	.0234	3750	.005	.0014	6484	3750	.0006	.0000	9155	2734	3750
.7	.4375	.07	.0273	4375	.007	.0017	0898	4375	.0007	.0001	0681	1523	4375
.8	.5000	.08	.0312	5000	.008	.0019	5312	5000	.0008	.0001	2207	0312	5000
.9	.5625	.09	.0351	5625	.009	.0021	9726	5625	.0009	.0001	3732	9101	5625
.A	.6250	.0A	.0390	6250	.00A	.0024	4140	6250	.000A	.0001	5258	7890	6250
.B	.6875	.0B	.0429	6875	.00B	.0026	8554	6875	.000B	.0001	6784	6679	6875
.C	.7500	.0C	.0468	7500	.00C	.0029	2968	7500	.000C	.0001	8310	5468	7500
.D	.8125	.0D	.0507	8125	.00D	.0031	7382	8125	.000D	.0001	9836	4257	8125
.E	.8750	.0E	.0546	8750	.00E	.0034	1796	8750	.000E	.0002	1362	3046	8750
.F	.9375	.0F	.0585	9375	.00F	.0036	6210	9375	.000F	.0002	2888	1835	9375
1		2			3				4				

Hexadecimal Addition and Subtraction Table

	1	2	3	4	5	6	7	8	9	A	B	C	D	E	F
1	02	03	04	05	06	07	08	09	0A	0B	0C	0D	0E	0F	10
2	03	04	05	06	07	08	09	0A	0B	0C	0D	0E	0F	10	11
3	04	05	06	07	08	09	0A	0B	0C	0D	0E	0F	10	11	12
4	05	06	07	08	09	0A	0B	0C	0D	0E	0F	10	11	12	13
5	06	07	08	09	0A	0B	0C	0D	0E	0F	10	11	12	13	14
6	07	08	09	0A	0B	0C	0D	0E	0F	10	11	12	13	14	15
7	08	09	0A	0B	0C	0D	0E	0F	10	11	12	13	14	15	16
8	09	0A	0B	0C	0D	0E	0F	10	11	12	13	14	15	16	17
9	0A	0B	0C	0D	0E	0F	10	11	12	13	14	15	16	17	18
A	0B	0C	0D	0E	0F	10	11	12	13	14	15	16	17	18	19
B	0C	0D	0E	0F	10	11	12	13	14	15	16	17	18	19	1A
C	0D	0E	0F	10	11	12	13	14	15	16	17	18	19	1A	1B
D	0E	0F	10	11	12	13	14	15	16	17	18	19	1A	1B	1C
E	0F	10	11	12	13	14	15	16	17	18	19	1A	1B	1C	1D
F	10	11	12	13	14	15	16	17	18	19	1A	1B	1C	1D	1E

Hexadecimal Multiplication Table

	1	2	3	4	5	6	7	8	9	A	B	C	D	E	F
1	01	02	03	04	05	06	07	08	09	0A	0B	0C	0D	0E	0F
2	02	04	06	08	0A	0C	0E	10	12	14	16	18	1A	1C	1E
3	03	06	09	0C	0F	12	15	18	1B	1E	21	24	27	2A	2D
4	04	08	0C	10	14	18	1C	20	24	28	2C	30	34	38	3C
5	05	0A	0F	14	19	1E	23	28	2D	32	37	3C	41	46	4B
6	06	0C	12	18	1E	24	2A	30	36	3C	42	48	4E	54	5A
7	07	0E	15	1C	23	2A	31	38	3F	46	4D	54	5B	62	69
8	08	10	18	20	28	30	38	40	48	50	58	60	68	70	78
9	09	12	1B	24	2D	36	3F	48	51	5A	63	6C	75	7E	87
A	0A	14	1E	28	32	3C	46	50	5A	64	6E	78	82	8C	96
B	0B	16	21	2C	37	42	4D	58	63	6E	79	84	8F	9A	A5
C	0C	18	24	30	3C	48	54	60	6C	78	84	90	9C	A8	B4
D	0D	1A	27	34	41	4E	5B	68	75	82	8F	9C	A9	B6	C3
E	0E	1C	2A	38	46	54	62	70	7E	8C	9A	A8	B6	C4	D2
F	0F	1E	2D	3C	4B	5A	69	78	87	96	A5	B4	C3	D2	E1

Powers of 2 and 16

2^n	n		16^n	n
1	0	$2^0 = 16^0$	1	0
2	1	$2^4 = 16^1$	16	1
4	2	$2^8 = 16^2$	256	2
8	3	$2^{12} = 16^3$	4 096	3
16	4	$2^{16} = 16^4$	65 536	4
32	5	$2^{20} = 16^5$	1 048 576	5
64	6	$2^{24} = 16^6$	16 777 216	6
128	7	$2^{28} = 16^7$	268 435 456	7
256	8	$2^{32} = 16^8$	4 294 967 296	8
512	9	$2^{36} = 16^9$	68 719 476 736	9
1,024	10	$2^{40} = 16^{10}$	1 099 511 627 776	10
2,048	11	$2^{44} = 16^{11}$	17 592 186 044 416	11
4,096	12	$2^{48} = 16^{12}$	281 474 976 710 656	12
8,192	13	$2^{52} = 16^{13}$	4 503 599 627 370 496	13
16,384	14	$2^{56} = 16^{14}$	72 057 594 037 927 936	14
32,768	15	$2^{60} = 16^{15}$	1 152 921 504 606 846 976	15
65,536	16			
131,072	17			
262,144	18			
524,288	19			
1,048,576	20			
2,097,152	21			
4,194,304	22			
8,388,608	23			
16,777,216	24			
33,554,432	25			
67,108,864	26			
134,217,728	27			
268,435,456	28			
536,870,912	29			
1,073,741,824	30			
2,147,483,648	31			
4,294,967,296	32			

C

Assembler, COBOL, PL/I, and FORTRAN Equivalents

This appendix identifies some functionally equivalent source language constructs from assembly language, COBOL, PL/I, and FORTRAN. It is provided to facilitate full use of the diagnostic possible cause lists for programs written in any of these four languages. Two caveats apply. First, the equivalency is at a general, functional level. Second, the list itself is not exhaustive. The examples are suggestive, not definitive. Items on the list have been grouped into five main categories:

- Data set terminology
- Program structure and control
- Main storage definition
- Input–output
- Data transformation

The generic column indicates the supervisor terminology or general type of function performed. This column will correspond roughly to items listed in Section 2.2, under diagnostic general causes. Similarly, terms, program keywords, and syntax listed under assembly language or COBOL will be found in their respective diagnostic sections. The items listed under the PL/I and FORTRAN columns are the functional equivalents of the first three columns.[1]

Generic	*Assembly*	*COBOL*	*PL/I*	*FORTRAN*
		Data Set Terminology		
QSAM	Sequential	Physical sequential	CONSECUTIVE	Sequential
BDAM	Direct	Direct	REGIONAL	Direct access
ISAM	Indexed sequential	Indexed sequential	INDEXED	[a]
BPAM	Partitioned	As sequential	As CONSECUTIVE	As sequential
VSAM ESDS	Entry sequenced	Entry sequenced	Entry sequenced	[a]
VSAM RRDS	Relative record	Relative record	Relative record	[a]
VSAM KSDS	Key sequenced	Key sequenced	Key sequenced	[a]
		Program Structure and Control		
Entry point	CSECT EXTRN	PROCEDURE DIVISION. PROGRAM-ID	PROCEDURE	ENTRY, SUBROUTINE
Comments	Anything right of operands, or * in column 1	* in column 7	/* . . . */	C in column 1
Branching	B	GO TO	GO TO	GO TO
Case branching	[b]	GO TO . . . DEPENDING N	DCL X LABEL, GO TO X(N)	GO TO (. . .), N
Looping/ submodules	BCT, BCTR BAL, BALR	PERFORM	DO, CALL	DO
Conditional branching	BC[b]	IF	IF	IF
Subroutine call	CALL[c]	CALL "SUB" USING A,B	CALL SUB(A,B)	CALL SUB(A,B)
Function subroutine	[a]	[a]	F: PROC(X); RETURN	FUNCTION F(X)
Subroutine return	BR	GOBACK EXIT PROGRAM	RETURN	RETURN
Statement labels:				
column position	1	8	any	1
length	1–8	1–30	1–31	1–5
content	alphanumeric	alphanumeric	alphanumeric	numeric
Statement group	[a]	SECTION . . . EXIT label . . . EXIT	BEGIN . . . END	[a]

[1]For a detailed comparison of FORTRAN and PL/I, see Gary DeWard Brown, *FORTRAN to PL/I Dictionary, PL/I to FORTRAN Dictionary* (New York: John Wiley & Sons Inc., 1975).

Generic	*Assembly*	*COBOL*	*PL/I*	*FORTRAN*
End program	RETURN	GOBACK STOP RUN EXIT PROGRAM	RETURN STOP	RETURN STOP
		Main Storage Definition		
External dummy sections	DSECT	[a]	STATIC EXTERNAL	COMMON BLOCK DATA
Explicit storage definition	DC, DS	PICTURE USAGE	DECLARE with Picture or format specification	Items are self-defining
Implicit storage definition	[a]	[a]	DEFAULT	IMPLICIT
Compile-time initialization	DC	VALUE	INIT	DATA
Multiple definitions	DC, DS	REDEFINES, RENAMES	DEF	EQUIVALENCE
Variable-length alphanumeric data	DC CL(1) DC XL(1)	PIC X(1)	BIT, CHAR, STRING	A or H format, LOGICAL
Zoned decimal	DC ZL(1)	PIC 9(1)	CHAR	A or H format
Binary integer halfword	DC H	PIC 9(2) COMP	FIXED BIN(15)	INTEGER, I format
Binary integer fullword	DC F	PIC 9(9) COMP	FIXED BIN(31)	INTEGER*2, I format
Floating point short	DC E	COMP-1	FLOAT DEC	REAL, F or E format
Floating point long	DC D	COMP-2	FLOAT DEC(16)	REAL*8, D format
Internal (packed) decimal	DC PL(3)	PIC 9(5) COMP-3	FIXED(5)	[a]
Complex	[a]	[a]	COMPLEX FLOAT COMPLEX FLOAT(16)	COMPLEX COMPLEX*16
Bit string	DC B	[a]	BIT	[a]
Hexadecimal	DC X	[a]	[a]	Z format
		Input-Output		
Specify data set	DCB, ACB (VSAM)[c]	SELECT, FD, SD	DCL FILE	DEFINE FILE
Specify record format and structure	DS, DC	FD, SD, RD	DCL, EDIT	FORMAT
Open (a data set)	OPEN[c]	OPEN	OPEN	[d]
Read	READ, GET, EXCP[c]	READ	GET	READ
Write	WRITE, PUT, EXCP[c]	WRITE	PUT	WRITE, PRINT, PUNCH

Generic	*Assembly*	*COBOL*	*PL/I*	*FORTRAN*
Specify end of file logic	DCB, ACB EODAD[c]	AT END	ON ENDFILE	END=
Specify I/O error logic	DCB, ACB SYNAD[c] EXLST	FILE STATUS USE AFTER ERROR INVALID KEY	ON (IO condition)	ERR=
Take checkpoint	CHKPT[c]	RERUN	CALL PLICKPT	[a]
Invoke sort	LINK[c] to sort entry point	SORT	CALL PLISRT	[a]
Format report	[a]	REPORT WRITER	[a]	[a]
Read backwards	BSP[c]	OPEN REVERSED	DECLARE . . . BACKWARDS	BACKSPACE
Close (a data set)	CLOSE[c]	CLOSE	CLOSE	REWIND[d]
		Data transformation		
Data movement	MVC A,B[b]	MOVE A TO B	B = A	B = A
Logical operations	N A,B	[a]	A = A&B	A = A.AND.B
Mathematical functions	[b]	[a]	A = LOG(B)	A = LOG(B)
Arithmetic	[b]	COMPUTE, ADD, SUBTRACT, DIVIDE, MULTIPLY	Assignment type statement	Assignment type statement

[a]Not defined for this language.

[b]No direct equivalent instruction or macro. Code varies considerably, depending on the specific operation and storage types.

[c]Macro instruction or macro operand.

[d]The FORTRAN compiler generates code to open a data set on the first access and to close it when the program terminates. REWIND causes an open data set to be closed. Where subsequent access to this data set starts depends on the data set's organization and DD statement specification.

BIBLIOGRAPHY

GENERAL

Boar, B. H. *Abend Debugging for COBOL Programmers*. New York: John Wiley & Sons, Inc., 1976.

Introduction to abend debugging of COBOL programs under OS/MFT and OS/MVT.

Brown, Gary DeWard. *System 370 Job Control Language*. New York: John Wiley & Sons, Inc., 1977.

Useful reference for JCL problems and guide to OS/VS utilities.

Burian, Barbara J. *A Simplified Approach to S/370 Assembly Language Programming*. Englewood Cliffs, N.J.: Prentice-Hall, Inc.,1977.

Introduction to abend debugging of assembly language programs under DOS, OS/MFT, and OS/MVT.

Chapin, Ned. *360/370 Programming in Assembly Language,* 2nd ed. New York: McGraw-Hill Book Company, 1973.

Discussion of general debugging and program interrupts for assembly language programs.

Clary, Wayne. *OS Debugging for the COBOL Programmer*. Fresno, Calif.: Mike Murach and Associates, Inc., 1981.

Rudimentary introduction to abend debugging of COBOL programs under OS/VS2.

Kernighan, Brian W., and Plauger, P. J. *The Elements of Programming Style*. New York: McGraw-Hill Book Company, 1974.

Good housekeeping discourages bugs. This book is an excellent presentation of specific and general programming practices which will prevent some abends and make others easier to diagnose and fix. Examples are given in FORTRAN and PL/I.

Myers, Glenford J. *The Art of Software Testing*. New York: John Wiley & Sons, Inc., 1979. A comprehensive guide to effective, intelligent, and practical testing and debugging.

Rindfleisch, Daniel H. *Debugging System 360/370 Programs Using OS and VS Storage Dumps*. Englewood Cliffs, N.J.: Prentice-Hall, Inc., 1976.

A basic introduction to abend debugging COBOL, FORTRAN, and PL/I programs under OS/MFT/MVT.

Yourdon, Edward, and Constantine, Larry L. *Structured Design: Fundamentals of a Discipline of Computer Program and Systems Design*. Englewood Cliffs, N.J.: Prentice-Hall, Inc., 1979.

This book is an excellent presentation of general-program design techniques which lead to fewer abends and make those that occur easier to diagnose and fix. If you have ever wondered why some code seems as stable as a house of cards, Yourdon and Constantine provide an answer.

IBM TECHNICAL PUBLICATIONS

A list of technical publications from International Business Machines Corporation (IBM) follows. The titles cited here are either referred to in the text or provide significant debugging information. A date and place of publication are not given. The date and edition are not given since the constant flow of technical newsletters would render them automatically obsolete. Always consult the latest edition and technical newsletters for the publication of interest. IBM maintains a current list of all its technical publications, which should be consulted to determine the current publication title and order number. This list is in *IBM System/370 Bibliography*, GC20-0001. IBM publications are prepared in various locations. The place of preparation does not convey any additional information about the publication. Contact the appropriate IBM office to obtain publications. The abbreviated titles cited in the text refer to the full title and order number.

Access Method Services. See *OS/VS2 Access Method Services*.

Assembler Programmer's Guide. See *OS/VS–VM/370 Assembler Programmer's Guide*.

Assembly Language Reference. See *OS/VS–DOS/VSE–VM/370 Assembler Language*.

COBOL Programmer's Guide. See *OS/VS COBOL Compiler and Library Programmer's Guide*.

Data Management Macros. See *OS/VS2 MVS Data Management Macro Instructions*.

Data Management Services. See *OS/VS2 MVS Data Management Services Guide*.

Data Processing Glossary. GC28-1699.

Debugging Handbook. See *OS/VS2 Systems Programming Library: Debugging Handbook*.

FORTRAN G Programmer's Guide. See *IBM OS Code and GO FORTRAN and FORTRAN IV (G1) Programmer's Guide*.

FORTRAN H Programmer's Guide. See *IBM OS FORTRAN IV (H Extended) Compiler Programmer's Guide*.

IBM FORTRAN Interactive Debug for OS(TSO) and VM/370(CMS) Terminal User's Guide. SC28-6885.

IBM OS COBOL Interactive Debug Terminal User's Guide and Reference. SC28-6465. Also known as the TESTCOB Manual.

IBM OS Code and GO FORTRAN and FORTRAN IV (G1) Programmer's Guide. SC28-6853.

IBM OS FORTRAN IV (H Extended) Compiler Programmer's Guide. SC28-6852.

IBM System 360 and System 370 FORTRAN IV Language. GC28-6515.

IBM System/370 Principles of Operation. GA22-7000.

MVS Diagnostic Techniques. See *OS/VS2 System Programming Library: MVS Diagnostic Techniques*.

MVS JCL. See *OS/VS2 MVS JCL*.

MVS Utilities. See *OS/VS2 MVS Utilities*.

OS PL/I Checkout and Optimizing Compilers: Language Reference Manual. GC33-0009.

OS PL/I Optimizing Compiler: Execution Logic. SC33-0025.

OS PL/I Optimizing Compiler: Programmer's Guide. SC33-0006.

OS/VS Access Method Services. GC26-3841.

OS/VS COBOL Compiler and Library: Programmer's Guide. SC28-6483.

OS/VS–DOS/VSE–VM/370 Assembler Language. GC33-4010.

OS/VS Linkage Editor and Loader. GC26-3813.

OS/VS Message Library: VS2 System Codes. GC38-1008.

OS/VS Message Library: VS2 System Messages. GC38-1002.

OS/VS Tape Labels. GC26-3795.

OS/VS Virtual Storage Access Method (VSAM) Programmer's Guide. GC26-3838.

OS/VS—VM/370 Assembler Programmer's Guide. GC33-4021.

OS/VS2 MVS Utilities. GC26-3902.

OS/VS2 MVS Data Management Macro Instructions. GC26-3873.

OS/VS2 MVS Data Management Services Guide. GC26-3875.

OS/VS2 MVS Interactive Problem Control System (IPCS) User's Guide and Reference. GC34-2006.

OS/VS2 MVS JCL. GC28-0984.

OS/VS2 MVS Overview. GC28-0984.

This publication describes how the components of MVS function and interact in a concise manner.

OS/VS2 Supervisor Services and Macro Instructions. GC28-0683.

OS/VS2 System Programming Library: Data Management. GC26-3830.

OS/VS2 System Programming Library: Debugging Handbook. Volume 1: GC28-1047; Volume 2: GC28-1048; Volume 3: GC28-1049.

OS/VS2 System Programming Library: MVS Diagnostic Techniques. GC28-0725.

Although oriented primarily toward debugging MVS itself, some useful information for application debugging is provided here.

OS/VS2 System Programming Library: Service Aids. GC28-0633.

OS/VS2 TSO Command Language Reference. GC28-0646.

Covers the use of TEST online debugging facility, as well as simpler TSO commands.

OS/VS2 Virtual Storage Access Method (VSAM) Logic. SY26-3825.

PL/I Programmer's Guide. See *OS PL/I Optimizing Compiler: Programmer's Guide*.

Principles of Operation. See *IBM System 370 Principles of Operation*.

Service Aids. See *OS/VS2 System Programming Library: Service Aids*.

Supervisor Services. See *OS/VS2 MVS Supervisor Services and Macro Instructions*.

System Codes. See *OS/VS Message Library: VS2 System Codes*.

System Messages. See *OS/VS Message Library: VS2 System Messages*.

System/370 Reference Summary. GX20-1850.

Once known as the green card, then as the yellow card, and now as the yellow book, this brief set of tables is a highly useful tool.

VSAM Logic. See *OS/VS2 Virtual Storage Access Method (VSAM) Logic*.

VSAM Programmer's Guide. See *OS/VS Virtual Storage Access Method (VSAM) Programmer's Guide*.

INDEX

*n indicates footnote as source of entry.

†Italic page number indicates figure or table as source of entry.

B

E

F

O

P

Q

R

T

0